LOVE OR MONEY

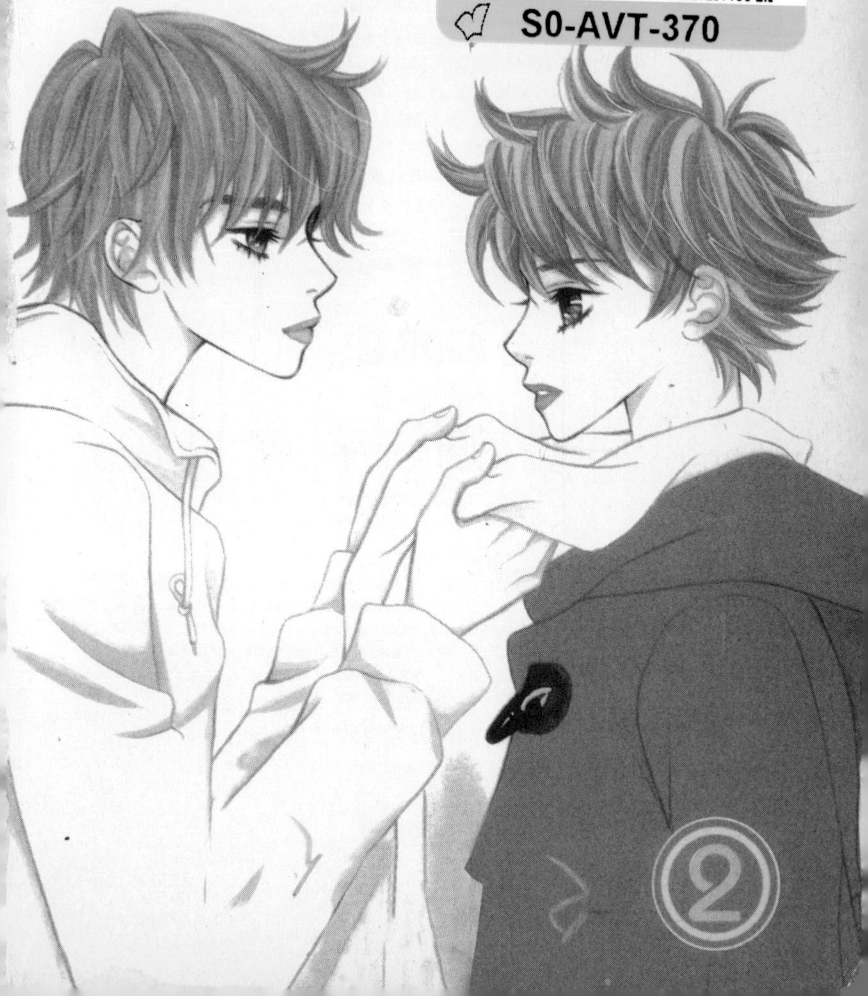
2

Love or Money, Volume 2
created by Sang-Eun Lee

Translation - Grace Min
English Adaptation - Avra Douglas
Retouch and Lettering - Eva Han
Production Artist - Vicente Rivera, Jr.
Cover Design - Anna Kernbaum

Editor - Julie Taylor
Digital Imaging Manager - Chris Buford
Pre-Press Manager - Antonio DePietro
Production Managers - Jennifer Miller and Mutsumi Miyazaki
Art Director - Matt Alford
Managing Editor - Jill Freshney
VP of Production - Ron Klamert
Editor-in-Chief - Mike Kiley
President and C.O.O. - John Parker
Publisher and C.E.O. - Stuart Levy

A  Manga

TOKYOPOP Inc.
5900 Wilshire Blvd. Suite 2000
Los Angeles, CA 90036

E-mail: info@TOKYOPOP.com
Come visit us online at www.TOKYOPOP.com

ISBN: 1-59532-249-3
First TOKYOPOP printing: March 2005
10 9 8 7 6 5 4 3 2 1
Printed in the USA

LOVE OR MONEY

Volume 2

by
Sang-Eun Lee

HAMBURG // LONDON // LOS ANGELES // TOKYO

IN THE LAST

LOVE
OR
MONEY

YENNI IS A CUTE AND FEISTY 15-YEAR-OLD...
AND TOTALLY OBSESSED WITH GETTING
RICH! SHE RUNS A VERY PROFITABLE
BUSINESS--TOO BAD IT'S LOAN-SHARKING
AT SCHOOL. HER WEALTHY GRANDMOTHER
IS SO SHOCKED THAT SHE DECIDES TO
HIT YENNI WHERE IT REALLY HURTS: IN THE
POCKETBOOK! IF YENNI DOESN'T STOP
HER MONEY-GRUBBING WAYS AND MARRY AN
HONEST BOY, SHE'LL BE WRITTEN OUT OF
GRANDMA'S WILL. CAN YENNI GET HER ACT
TOGETHER AND TAKE THE ULTIMATE PAYOFF?
BEFORE SHE CAN FIGURE THIS OUT, HER
GRANDMA DIES...AND SHE FINDS SHE MUST
MARRY JAE-HEE SHIN BY THE TIME SHE'S
TWENTY TO GET HER 15-MILLION-DOLLAR
INHERITANCE. OTHERWISE, ALL THE MONEY
GOES TO HER ENEMY, IN-YOUNG PARK! WHAT
WILL SHE DO?!

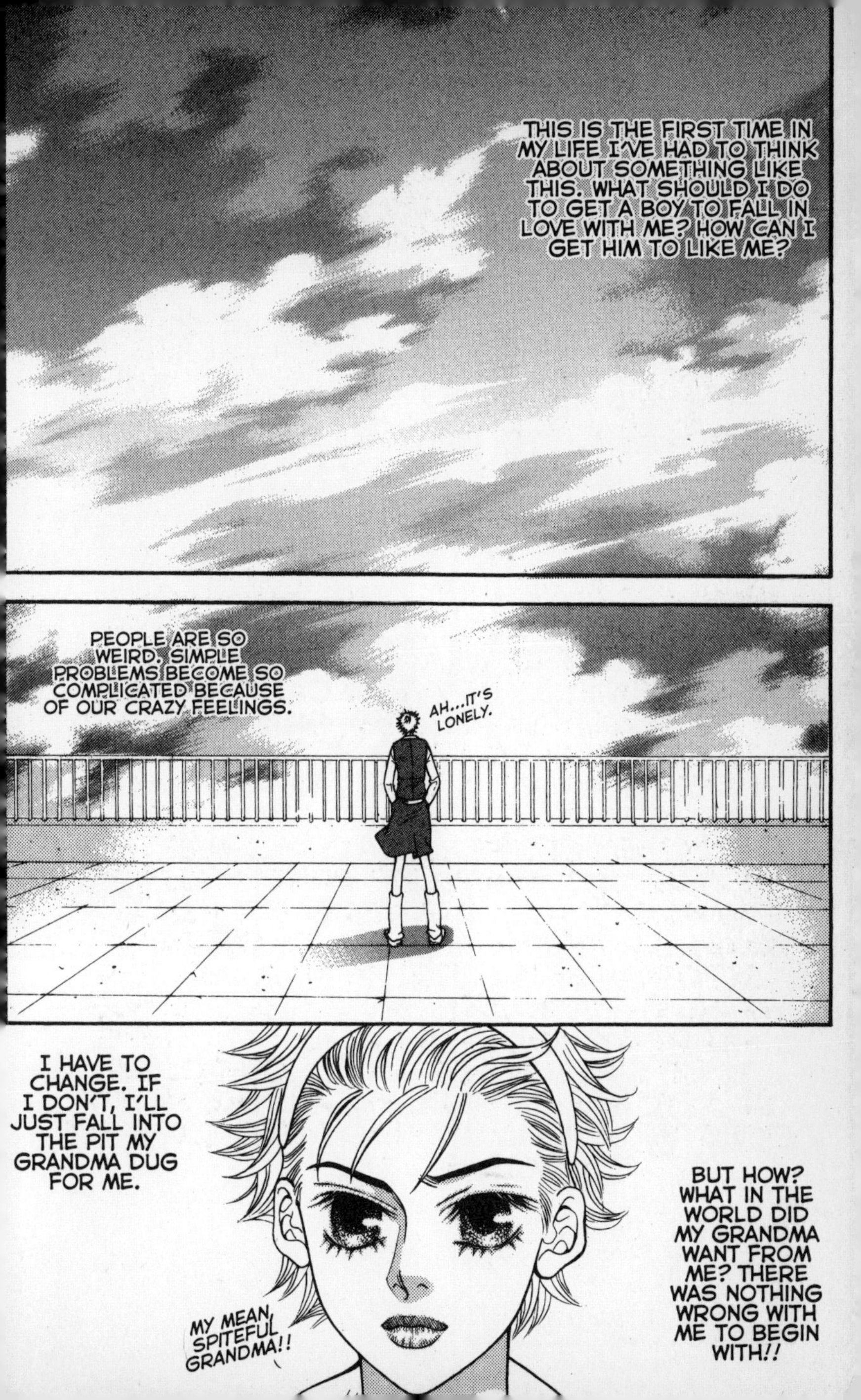
THIS IS THE FIRST TIME IN MY LIFE I'VE HAD TO THINK ABOUT SOMETHING LIKE THIS. WHAT SHOULD I DO TO GET A BOY TO FALL IN LOVE WITH ME? HOW CAN I GET HIM TO LIKE ME?
PEOPLE ARE SO WEIRD. SIMPLE PROBLEMS BECOME SO COMPLICATED BECAUSE OF OUR CRAZY FEELINGS.
AH...IT'S LONELY.
I HAVE TO CHANGE. IF I DON'T, I'LL JUST FALL INTO THE PIT MY GRANDMA DUG FOR ME.
MY MEAN, SPITEFUL GRANDMA!!
BUT HOW? WHAT IN THE WORLD DID MY GRANDMA WANT FROM ME? THERE WAS NOTHING WRONG WITH ME TO BEGIN WITH!!

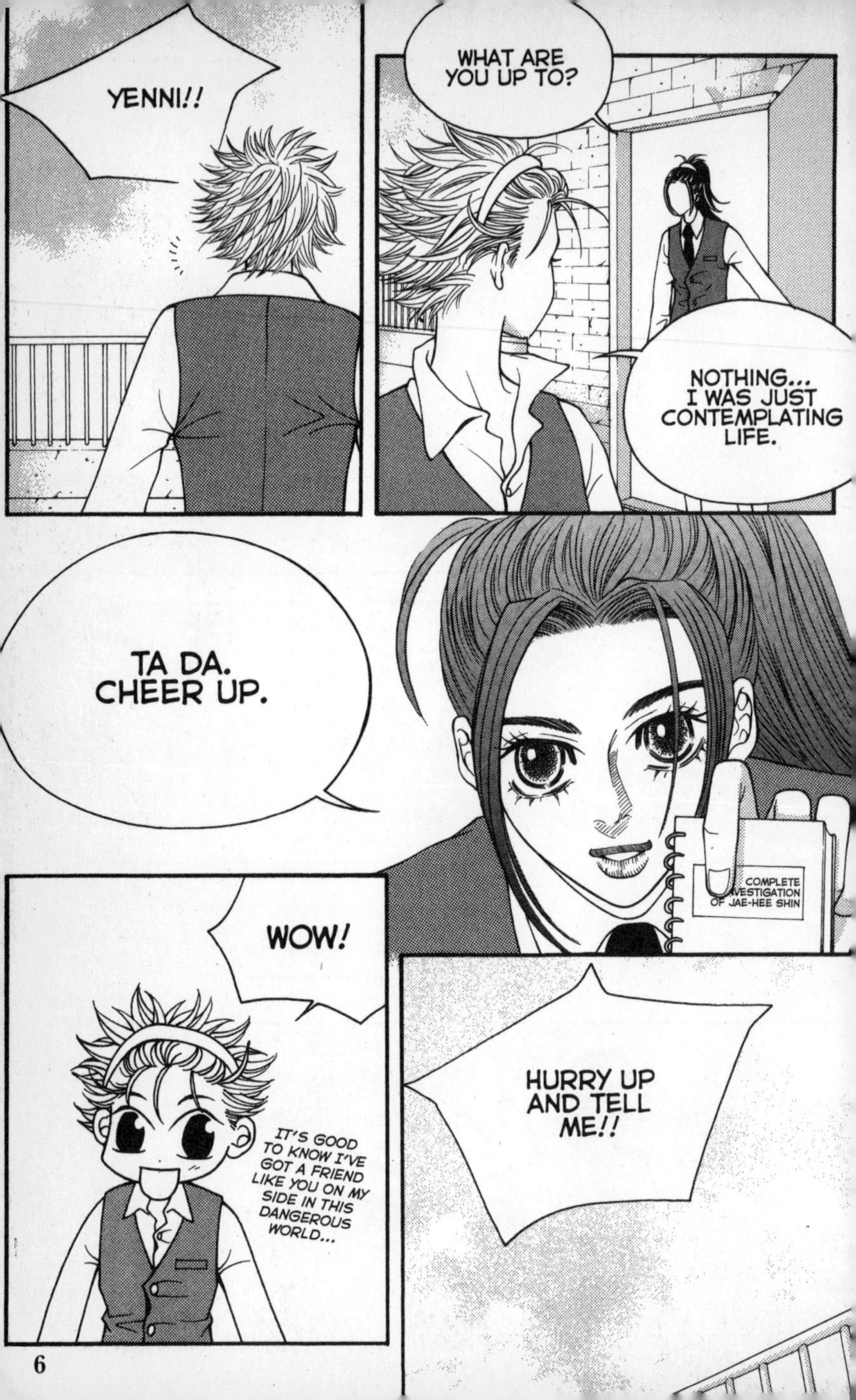
YENNI!!
WHAT ARE YOU UP TO?
NOTHING... I WAS JUST CONTEMPLATING LIFE.
TA DA. CHEER UP.
COMPLETE
VESTIGATION
OF JAE-HEE SHIN
WOW!
IT'S GOOD TO KNOW I'VE GOT A FRIEND LIKE YOU ON MY SIDE IN THIS DANGEROUS WORLD...
HURRY UP AND TELL ME!!

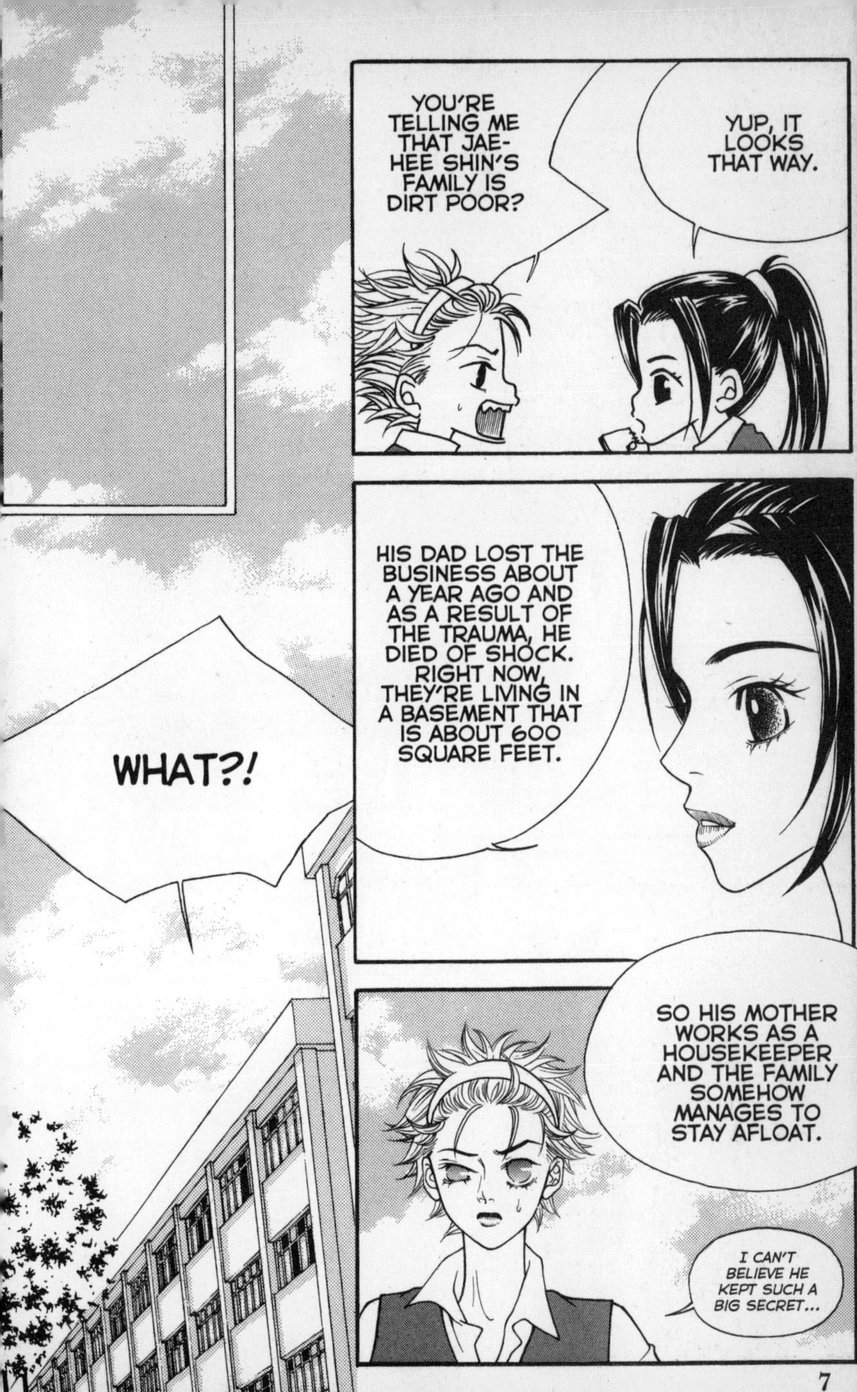
WHAT?!
YOU'RE TELLING ME THAT JAE-HEE SHIN'S FAMILY IS DIRT POOR?
YUP, IT LOOKS THAT WAY.
HIS DAD LOST THE BUSINESS ABOUT A YEAR AGO AND AS A RESULT OF THE TRAUMA, HE DIED OF SHOCK. RIGHT NOW, THEY'RE LIVING IN A BASEMENT THAT IS ABOUT 600 SQUARE FEET.
SO HIS MOTHER WORKS AS A HOUSEKEEPER AND THE FAMILY SOMEHOW MANAGES TO STAY AFLOAT.
I CAN'T BELIEVE HE KEPT SUCH A BIG SECRET...

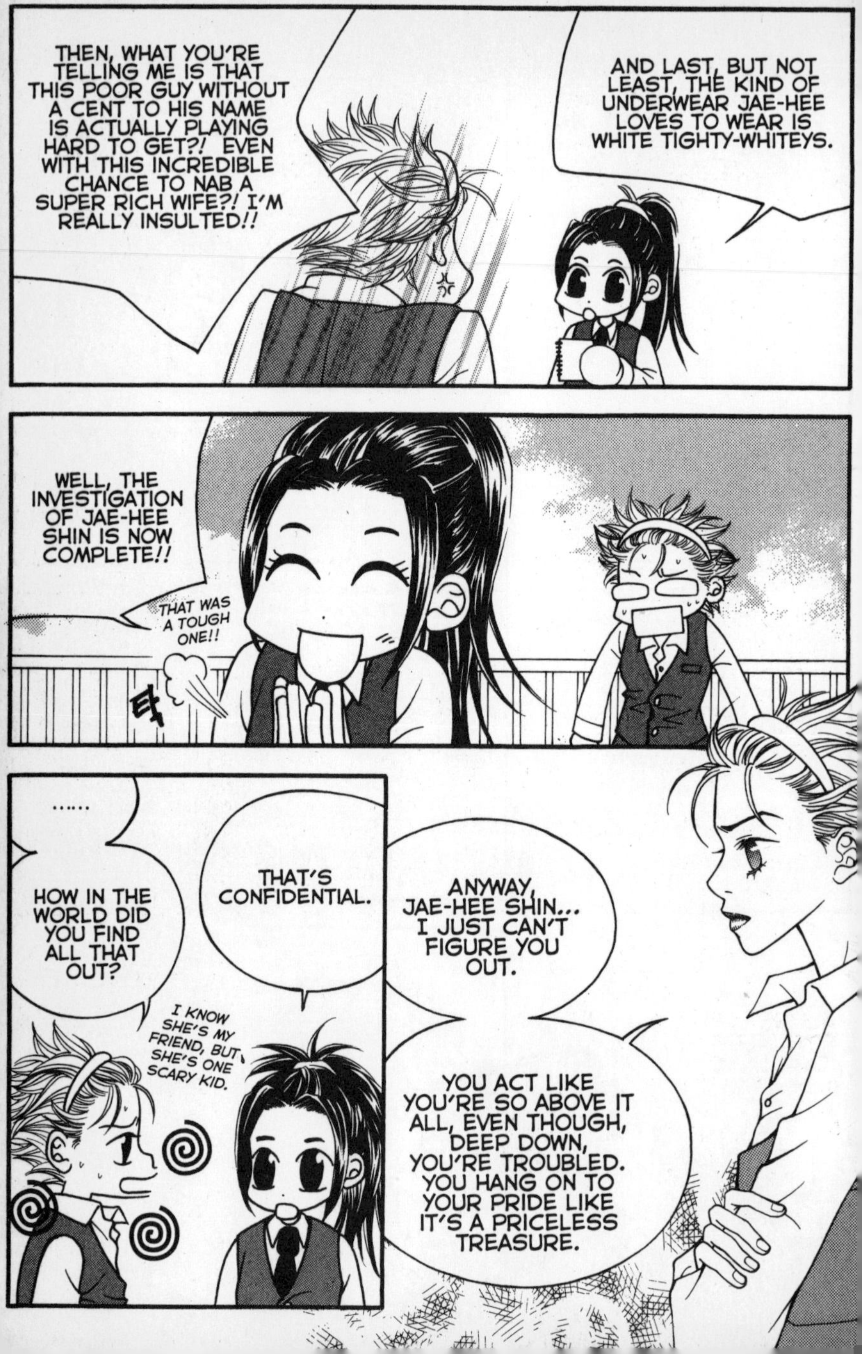
THEN, WHAT YOU'RE TELLING ME IS THAT THIS POOR GUY WITHOUT A CENT TO HIS NAME IS ACTUALLY PLAYING HARD TO GET?! EVEN WITH THIS INCREDIBLE CHANCE TO NAB A SUPER RICH WIFE?! I'M REALLY INSULTED!!
AND LAST, BUT NOT LEAST, THE KIND OF UNDERWEAR JAE-HEE LOVES TO WEAR IS WHITE TIGHTY-WHITEYS.
WELL, THE INVESTIGATION OF JAE-HEE SHIN IS NOW COMPLETE!!
THAT WAS A TOUGH ONE!!
탁
......
HOW IN THE WORLD DID YOU FIND ALL THAT OUT?
THAT'S CONFIDENTIAL.
I KNOW SHE'S MY FRIEND, BUT SHE'S ONE SCARY KID.
ANYWAY, JAE-HEE SHIN... I JUST CAN'T FIGURE YOU OUT.
YOU ACT LIKE YOU'RE SO ABOVE IT ALL, EVEN THOUGH, DEEP DOWN, YOU'RE TROUBLED. YOU HANG ON TO YOUR PRIDE LIKE IT'S A PRICELESS TREASURE.

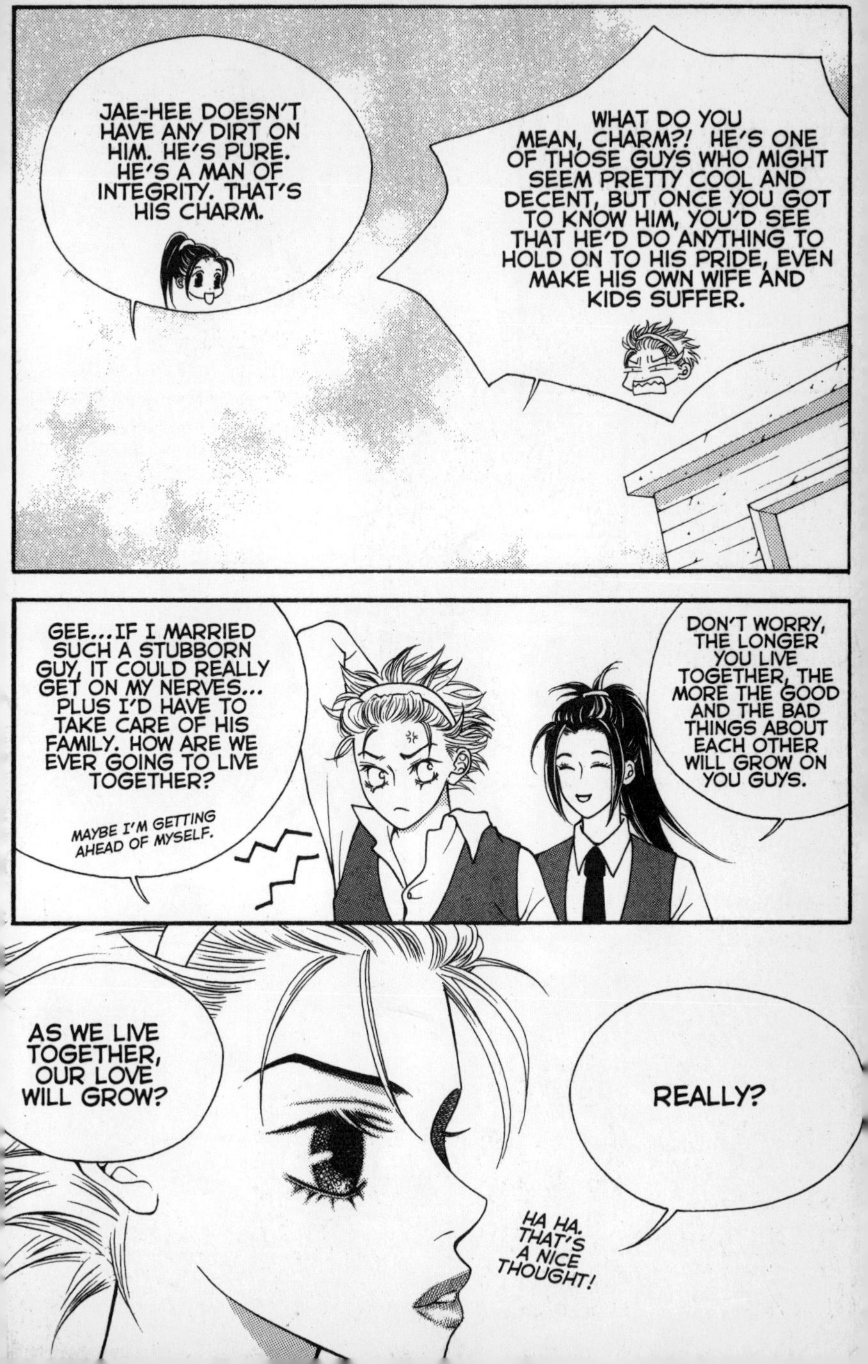

JAE-HEE DOESN'T HAVE ANY DIRT ON HIM. HE'S PURE. HE'S A MAN OF INTEGRITY. THAT'S HIS CHARM.
WHAT DO YOU MEAN, CHARM?! HE'S ONE OF THOSE GUYS WHO MIGHT SEEM PRETTY COOL AND DECENT, BUT ONCE YOU GOT TO KNOW HIM, YOU'D SEE THAT HE'D DO ANYTHING TO HOLD ON TO HIS PRIDE, EVEN MAKE HIS OWN WIFE AND KIDS SUFFER.
GEE...IF I MARRIED SUCH A STUBBORN GUY, IT COULD REALLY GET ON MY NERVES... PLUS I'D HAVE TO TAKE CARE OF HIS FAMILY. HOW ARE WE EVER GOING TO LIVE TOGETHER?
MAYBE I'M GETTING AHEAD OF MYSELF.
DON'T WORRY, THE LONGER YOU LIVE TOGETHER, THE MORE THE GOOD AND THE BAD THINGS ABOUT EACH OTHER WILL GROW ON YOU GUYS.
AS WE LIVE TOGETHER, OUR LOVE WILL GROW?
HA HA. THAT'S A NICE THOUGHT!
REALLY?

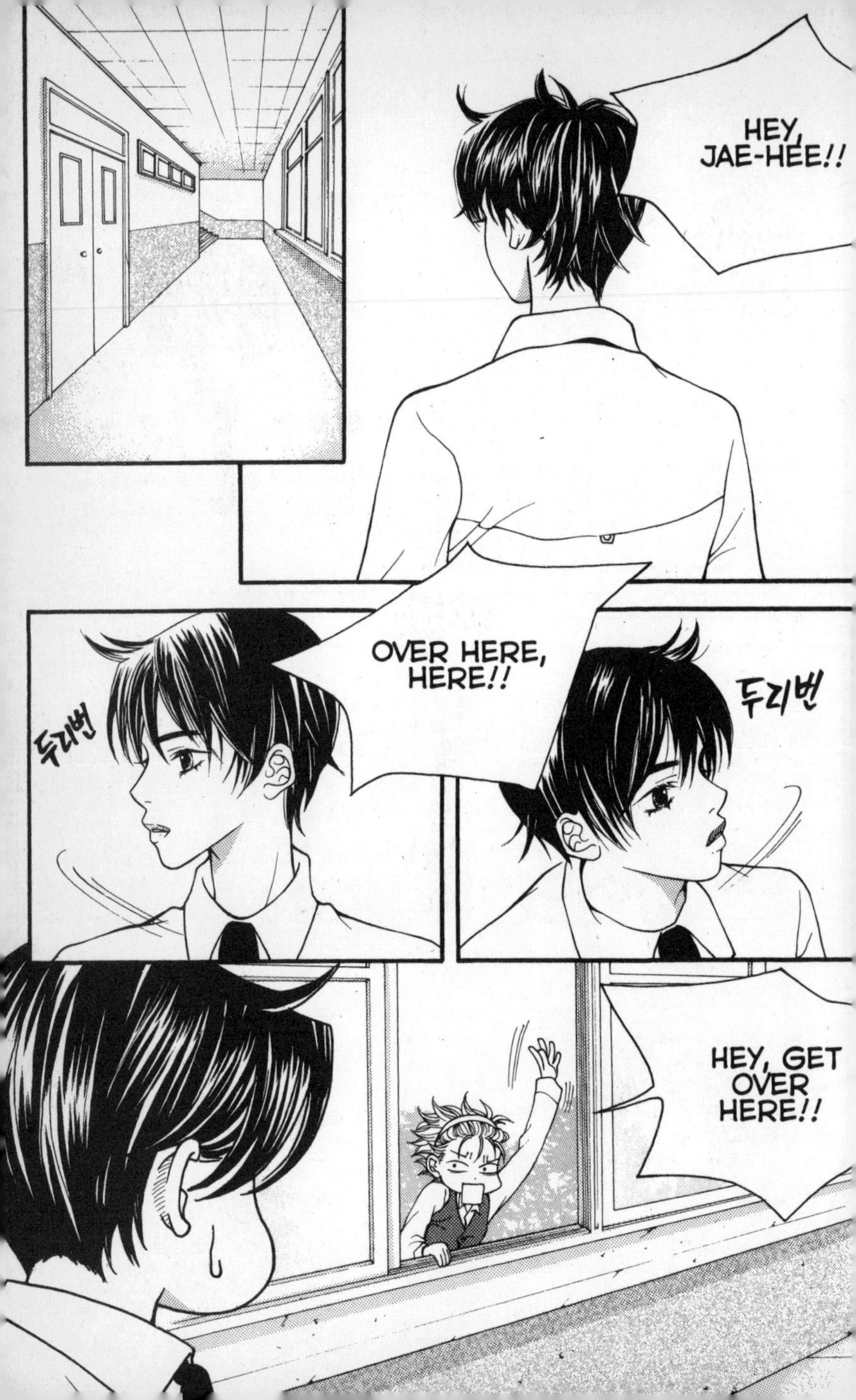
HEY, JAE-HEE!!
두리번
OVER HERE, HERE!!
두리번
HEY, GET OVER HERE!!

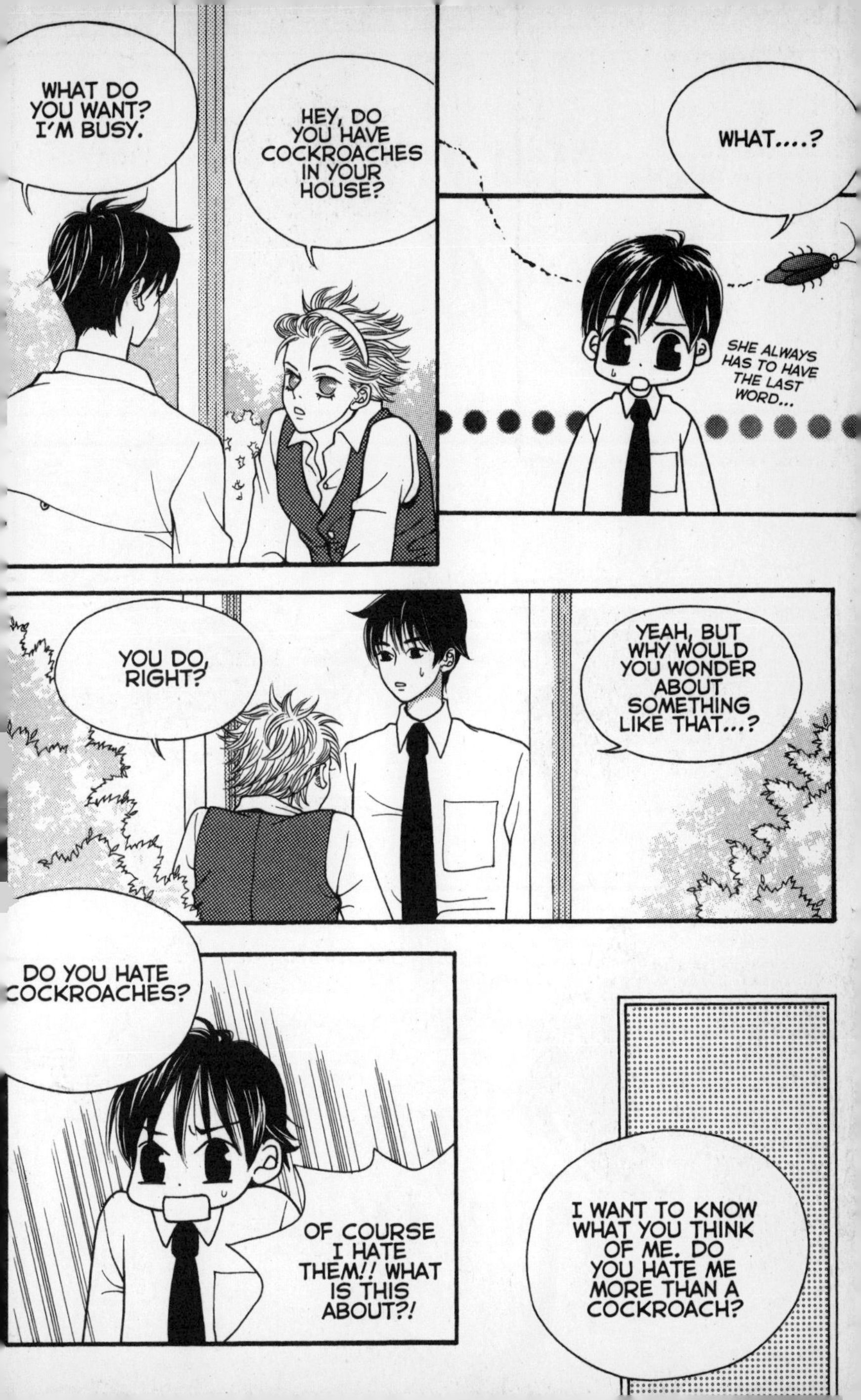
WHAT DO YOU WANT? I'M BUSY.
HEY, DO YOU HAVE COCKROACHES IN YOUR HOUSE?
WHAT....?
SHE ALWAYS HAS TO HAVE THE LAST WORD...
YOU DO, RIGHT?
YEAH, BUT WHY WOULD YOU WONDER ABOUT SOMETHING LIKE THAT...?
DO YOU HATE COCKROACHES?
OF COURSE I HATE THEM!! WHAT IS THIS ABOUT?!
I WANT TO KNOW WHAT YOU THINK OF ME. DO YOU HATE ME MORE THAN A COCKROACH?

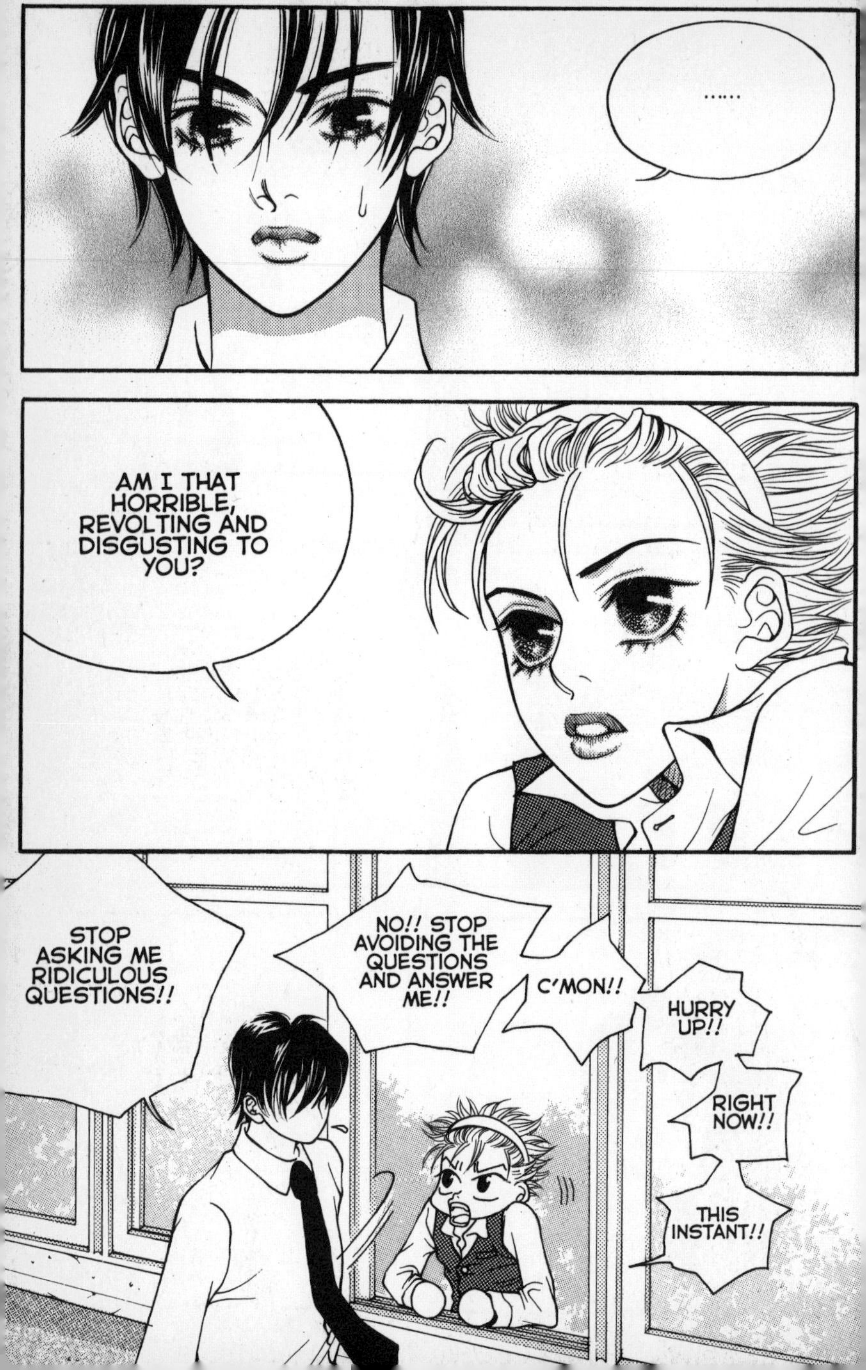
......
AM I THAT HORRIBLE, REVOLTING AND DISGUSTING TO YOU?
STOP ASKING ME RIDICULOUS QUESTIONS!!
NO!! STOP AVOIDING THE QUESTIONS AND ANSWER ME!!
C'MON!!
HURRY UP!!
RIGHT NOW!!
THIS INSTANT!!

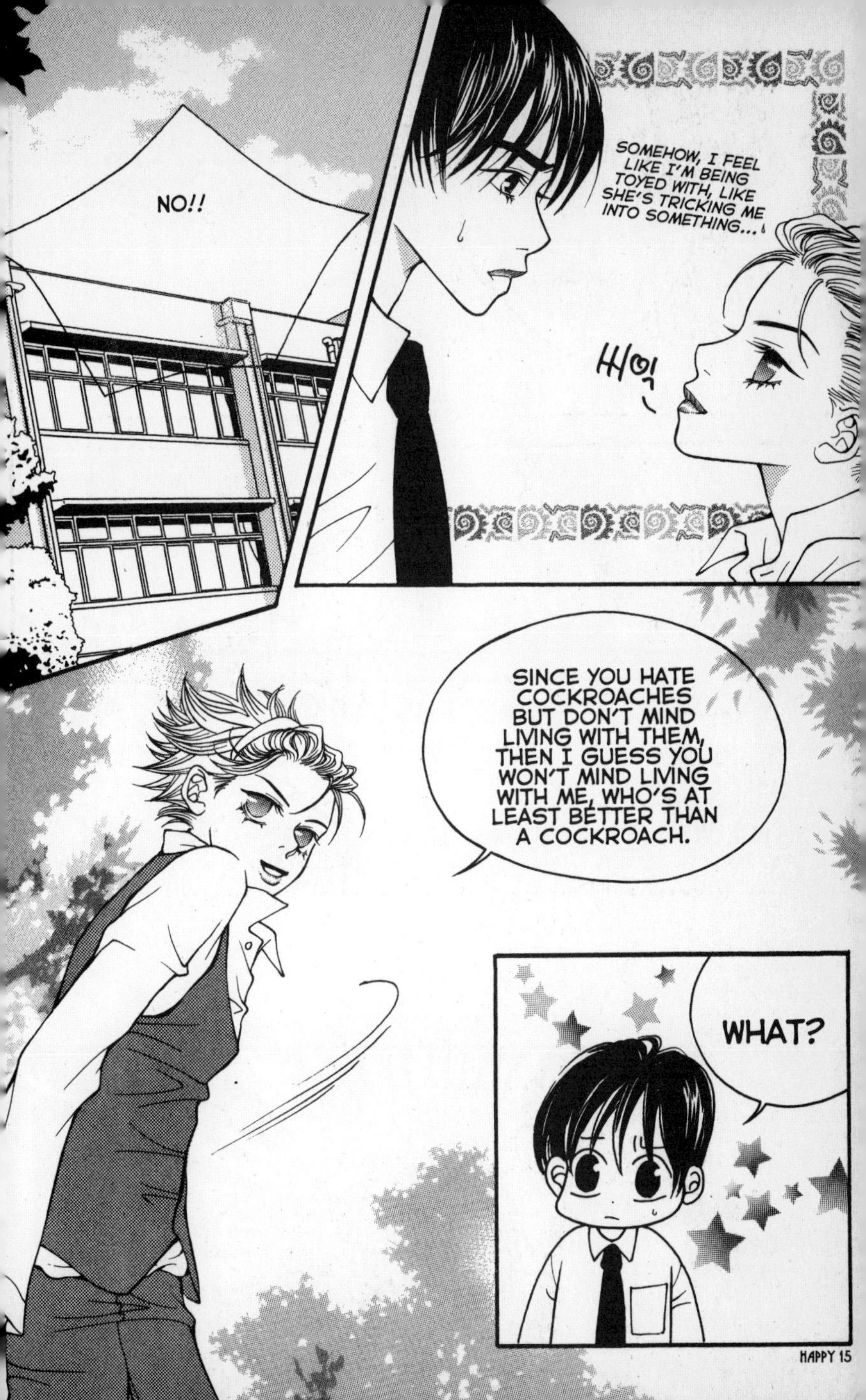
NO!!
SOMEHOW, I FEEL LIKE I'M BEING TOYED WITH, LIKE SHE'S TRICKING ME INTO SOMETHING...
씨익
SINCE YOU HATE COCKROACHES BUT DON'T MIND LIVING WITH THEM, THEN I GUESS YOU WON'T MIND LIVING WITH ME, WHO'S AT LEAST BETTER THAN A COCKROACH.
WHAT?

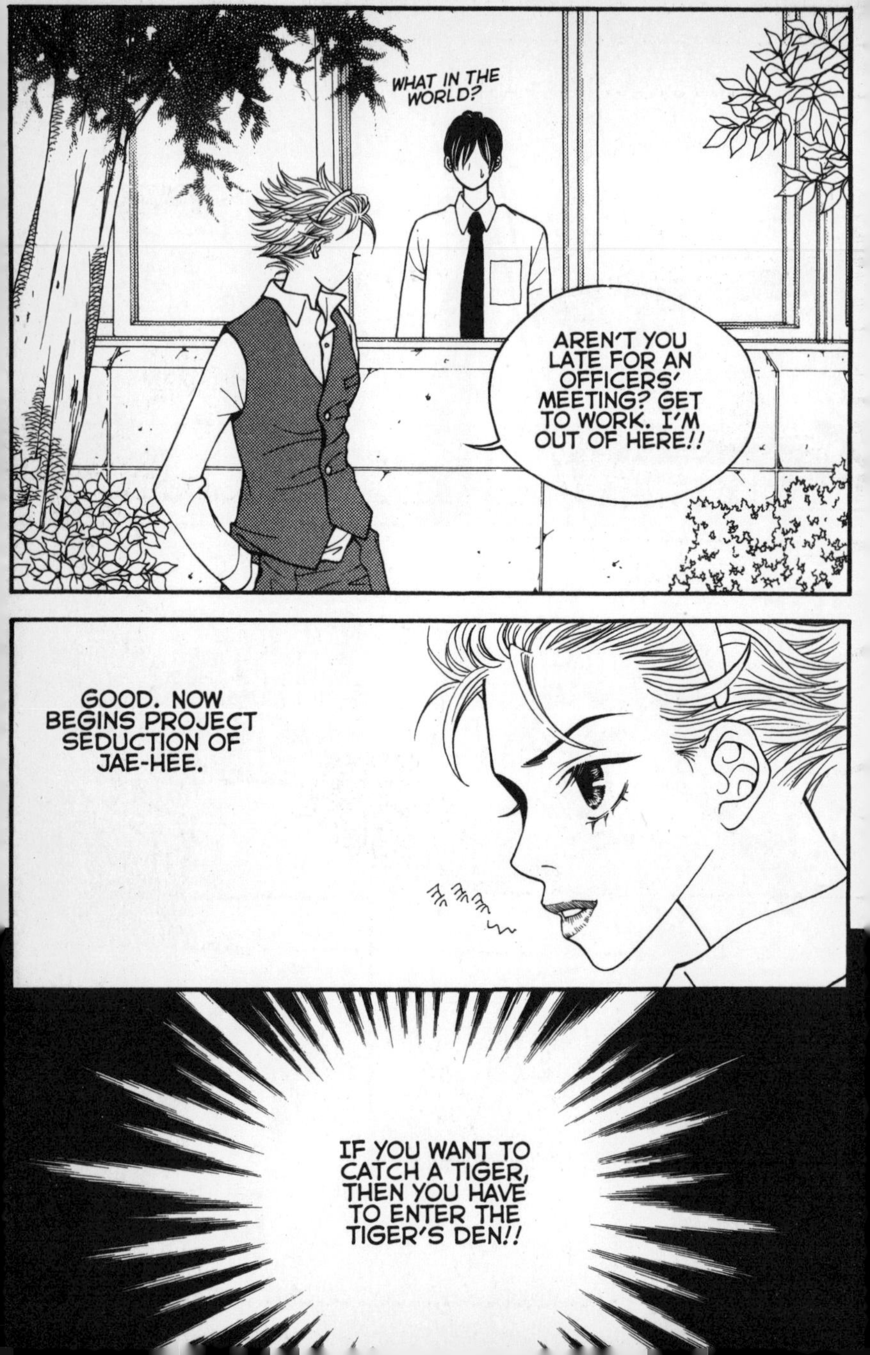
WHAT IN THE WORLD?
AREN'T YOU LATE FOR AN OFFICERS' MEETING? GET TO WORK. I'M OUT OF HERE!!
GOOD. NOW BEGINS PROJECT SEDUCTION OF JAE-HEE.
IF YOU WANT TO CATCH A TIGER, THEN YOU HAVE TO ENTER THE TIGER'S DEN!!

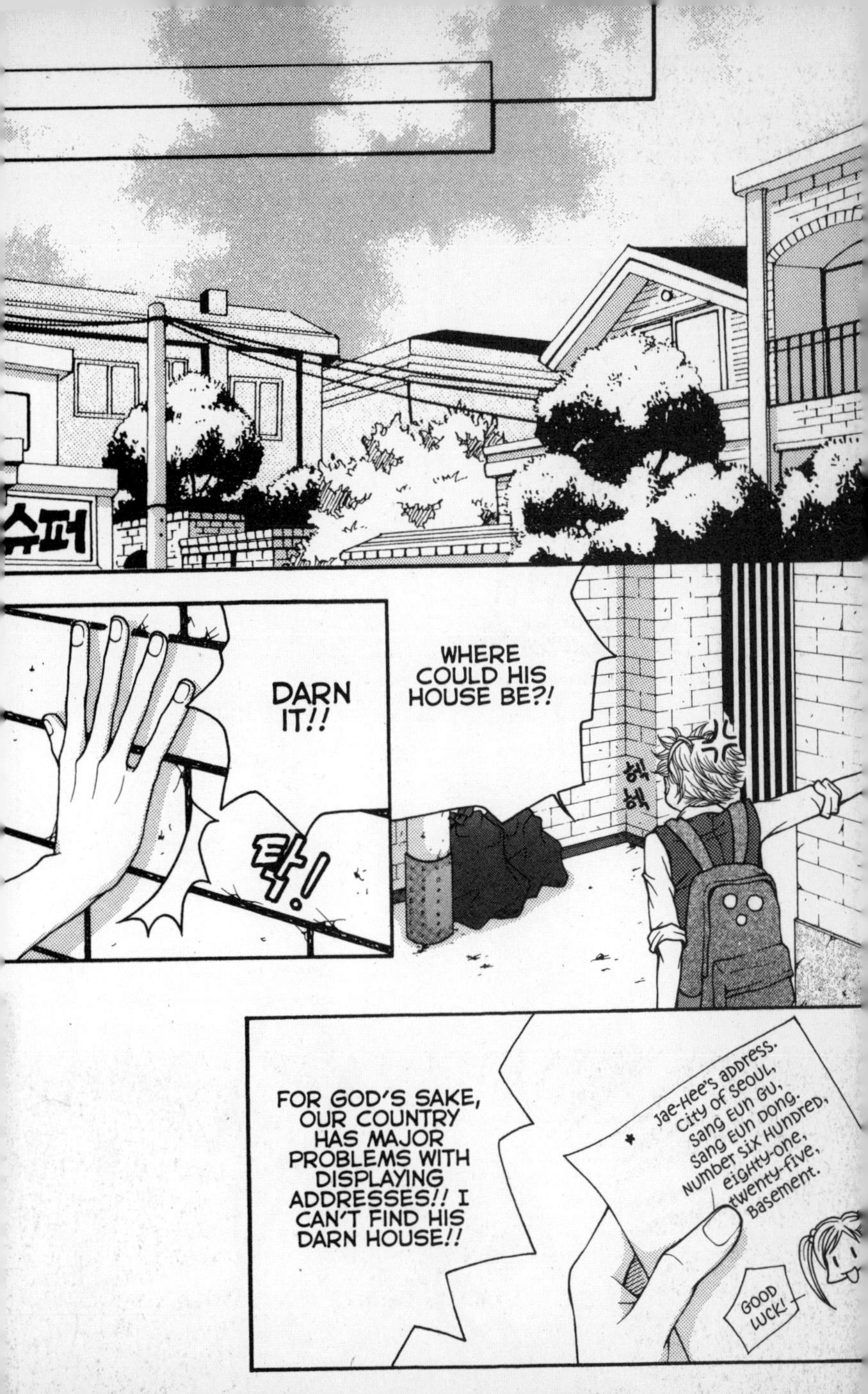
슈퍼
DARN IT!!
탁!
WHERE COULD HIS HOUSE BE?!
헥 헥
FOR GOD'S SAKE, OUR COUNTRY HAS MAJOR PROBLEMS WITH DISPLAYING ADDRESSES!! I CAN'T FIND HIS DARN HOUSE!!
Jae-Hee's address. City of Seoul, Sang Eun Gu, Sang Eun Dong. Number six hundred, eighty-one, twenty-five, Basement.
GOOD LUCK!

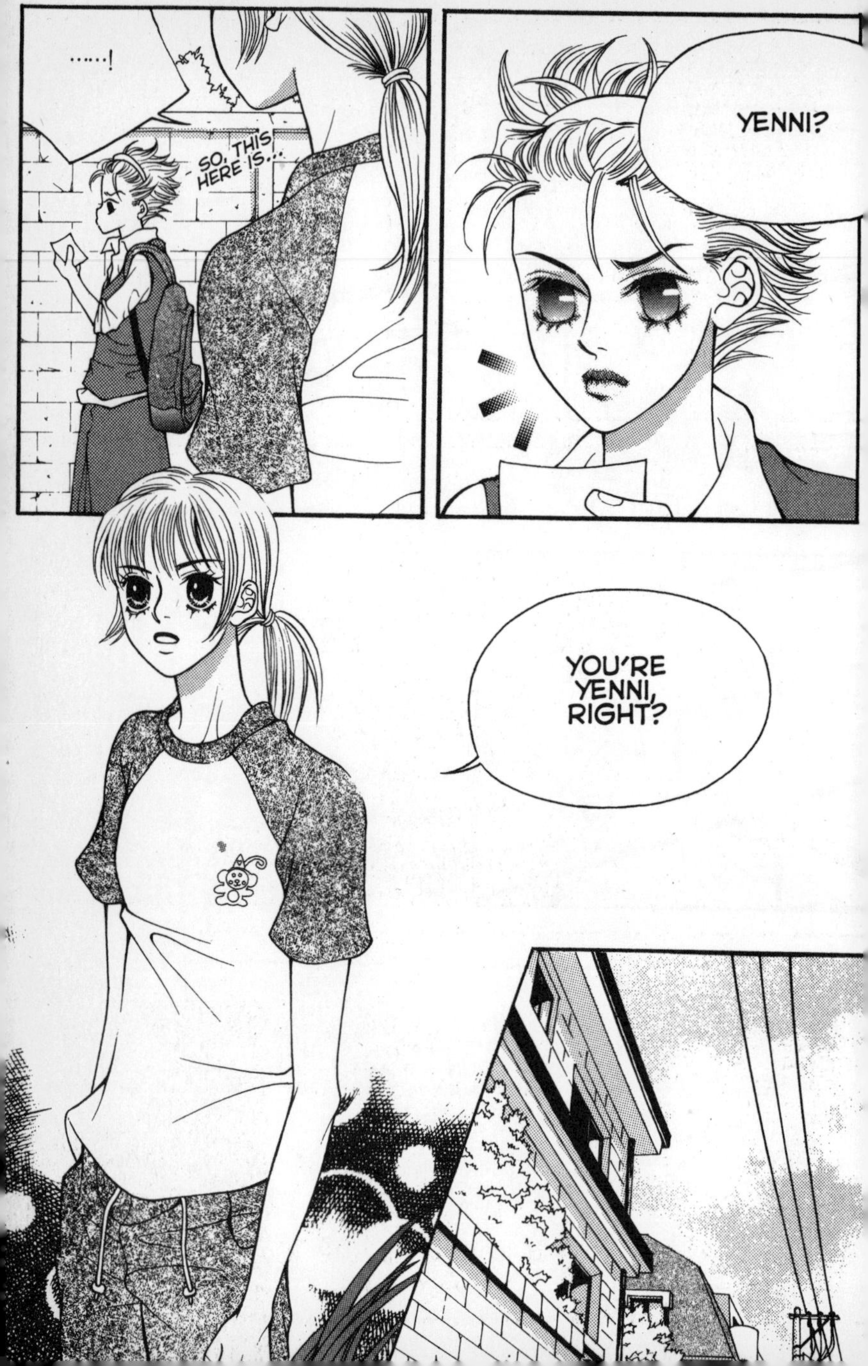
......!
SO, THIS HERE IS...
YENNI?
YOU'RE YENNI, RIGHT?

IT'S BEEN A REALLY LONG TIME, YENNI. YOU'VE GROWN UP SO MUCH SINCE I LAST SAW YOU. YOU'VE BECOME SO PRETTY TOO.

I DON'T REMEMBER YOU AT ALL.

DO... DO YOU KNOW ME?

SHE DOESN'T REMEMBER US, EVEN THOUGH WE WERE NEIGHBORS FOR 10 YEARS...

I KNEW SHE WOULDN'T REMEMBER US.

ONE THING ABOUT YOU THAT HASN'T CHANGED AT ALL IS HOW EASILY YOU FORGET SOMEONE. YOU'RE NICE WHEN YOU MEET THEM, BUT LATER YOU FORGET ALL ABOUT THEM.

BUT IT'S SCARY HOW YOU NEVER FORGOT THE NAME OF EVERY PERSON WHO BORROWED MONEY FROM YOU.

AM I REALLY LIKE THAT?

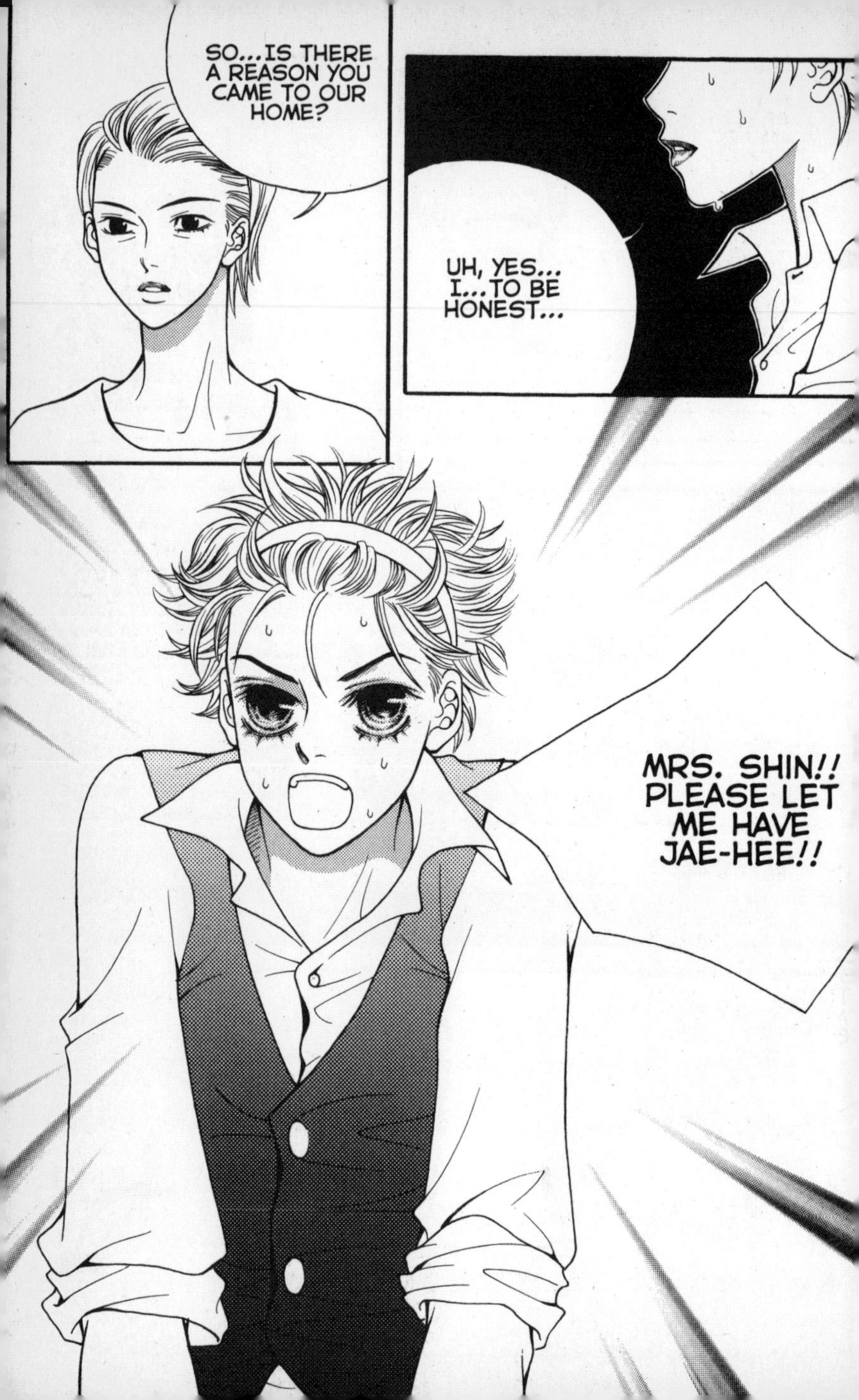
SO...IS THERE A REASON YOU CAME TO OUR HOME?
UH, YES... I...TO BE HONEST...
MRS. SHIN!! PLEASE LET ME HAVE JAE-HEE!!

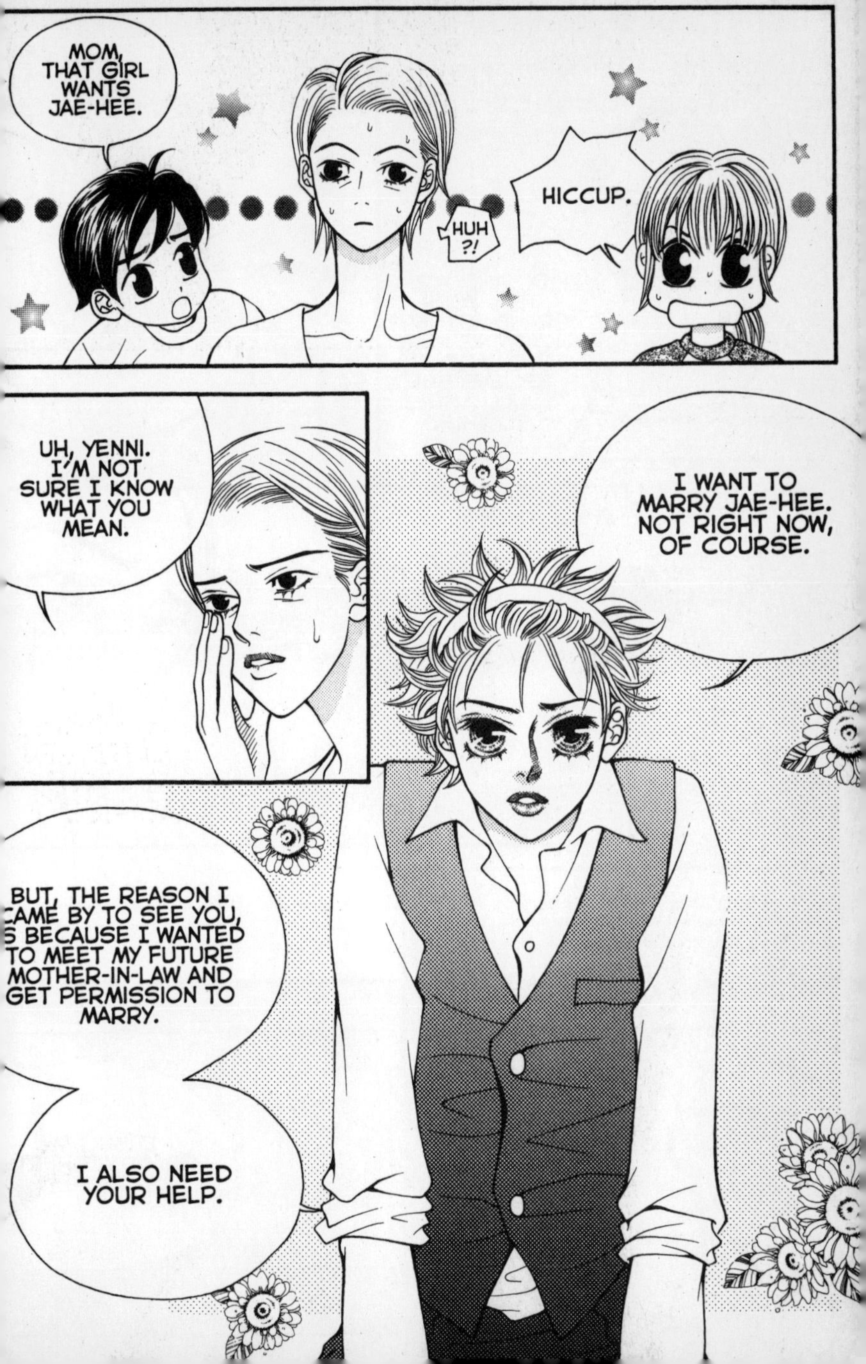
MOM, THAT GIRL WANTS JAE-HEE.
HUH ?!
HICCUP.
UH, YENNI. I'M NOT SURE I KNOW WHAT YOU MEAN.
I WANT TO MARRY JAE-HEE. NOT RIGHT NOW, OF COURSE.
BUT, THE REASON I CAME BY TO SEE YOU, IS BECAUSE I WANTED TO MEET MY FUTURE MOTHER-IN-LAW AND GET PERMISSION TO MARRY.
I ALSO NEED YOUR HELP.

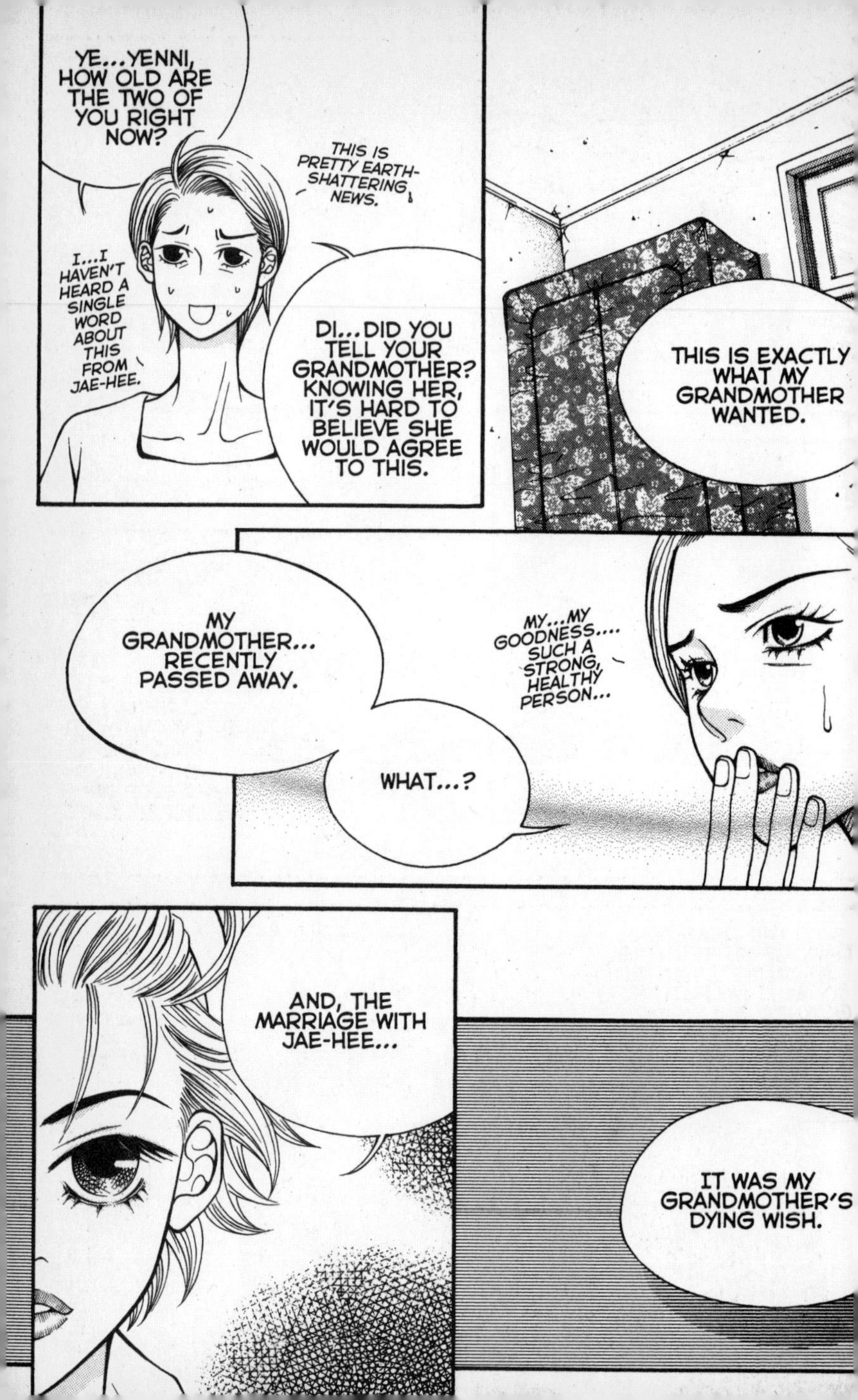
YE...YENNI, HOW OLD ARE THE TWO OF YOU RIGHT NOW?
THIS IS PRETTY EARTH-SHATTERING NEWS.
I...I HAVEN'T HEARD A SINGLE WORD ABOUT THIS FROM JAE-HEE.
DI...DID YOU TELL YOUR GRANDMOTHER? KNOWING HER, IT'S HARD TO BELIEVE SHE WOULD AGREE TO THIS.
THIS IS EXACTLY WHAT MY GRANDMOTHER WANTED.
MY GRANDMOTHER... RECENTLY PASSED AWAY.
WHAT...?
MY...MY GOODNESS.... SUCH A STRONG, HEALTHY PERSON...
AND, THE MARRIAGE WITH JAE-HEE...
IT WAS MY GRANDMOTHER'S DYING WISH.

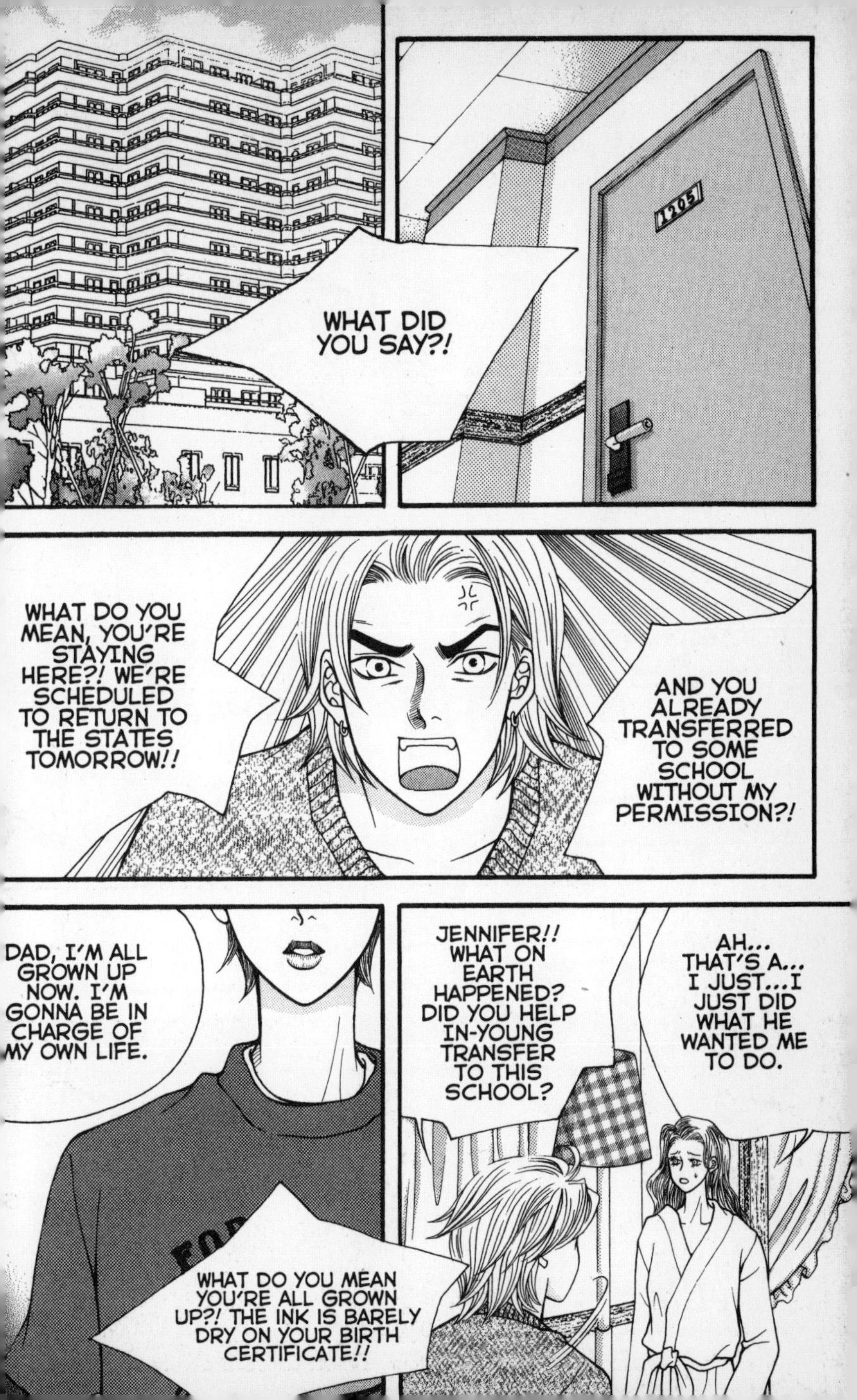
1205
WHAT DID YOU SAY?!
WHAT DO YOU MEAN, YOU'RE STAYING HERE?! WE'RE SCHEDULED TO RETURN TO THE STATES TOMORROW!!
AND YOU ALREADY TRANSFERRED TO SOME SCHOOL WITHOUT MY PERMISSION?!
DAD, I'M ALL GROWN UP NOW. I'M GONNA BE IN CHARGE OF MY OWN LIFE.
WHAT DO YOU MEAN YOU'RE ALL GROWN UP?! THE INK IS BARELY DRY ON YOUR BIRTH CERTIFICATE!!
JENNIFER!! WHAT ON EARTH HAPPENED? DID YOU HELP IN-YOUNG TRANSFER TO THIS SCHOOL?
AH... THAT'S A... I JUST...I JUST DID WHAT HE WANTED ME TO DO.

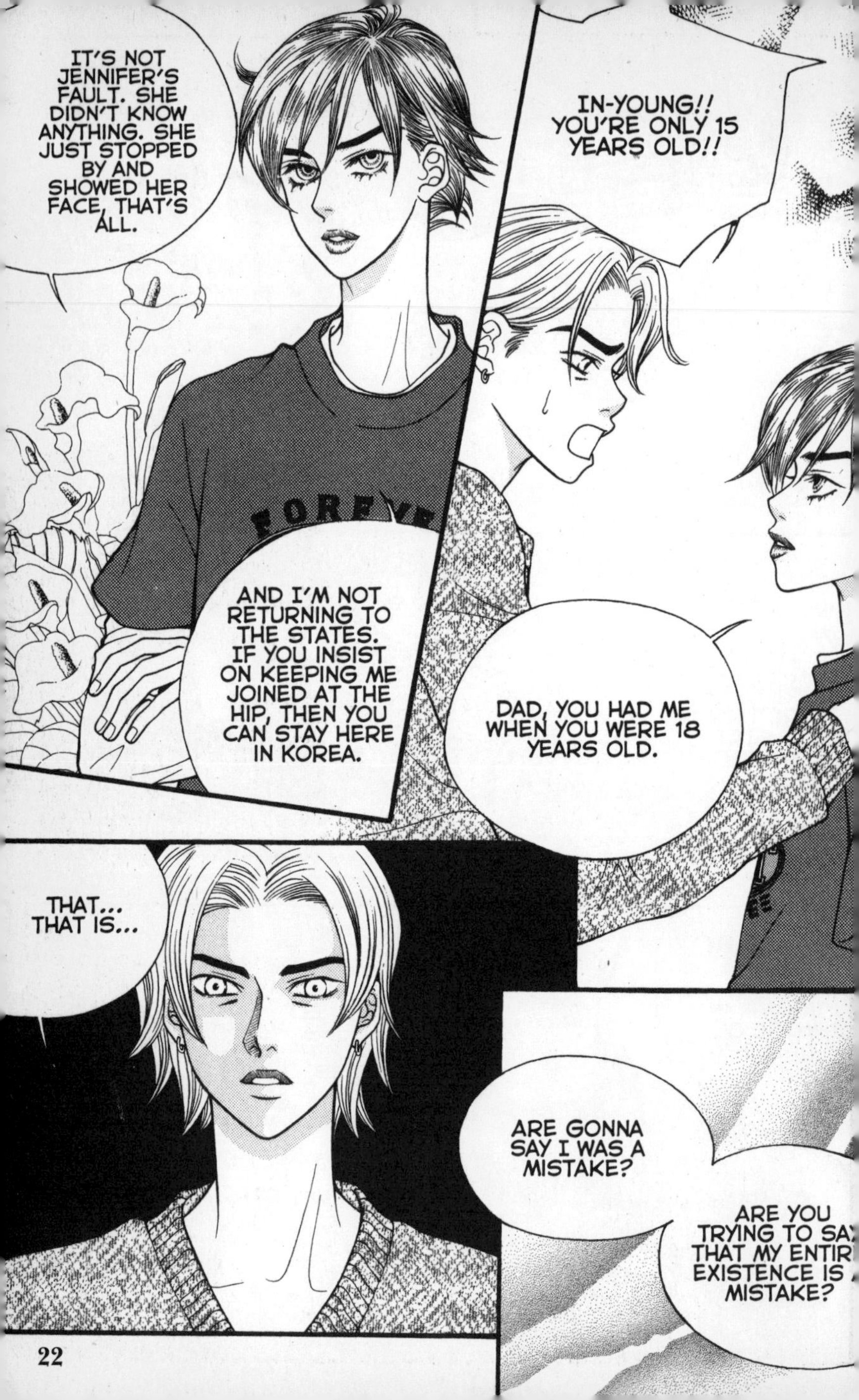
IT'S NOT JENNIFER'S FAULT. SHE DIDN'T KNOW ANYTHING. SHE JUST STOPPED BY AND SHOWED HER FACE, THAT'S ALL.
AND I'M NOT RETURNING TO THE STATES. IF YOU INSIST ON KEEPING ME JOINED AT THE HIP, THEN YOU CAN STAY HERE IN KOREA.
IN-YOUNG!! YOU'RE ONLY 15 YEARS OLD!!
DAD, YOU HAD ME WHEN YOU WERE 18 YEARS OLD.
THAT... THAT IS...
ARE GONNA SAY I WAS A MISTAKE?
ARE YOU TRYING TO SA THAT MY ENTIR EXISTENCE IS MISTAKE?

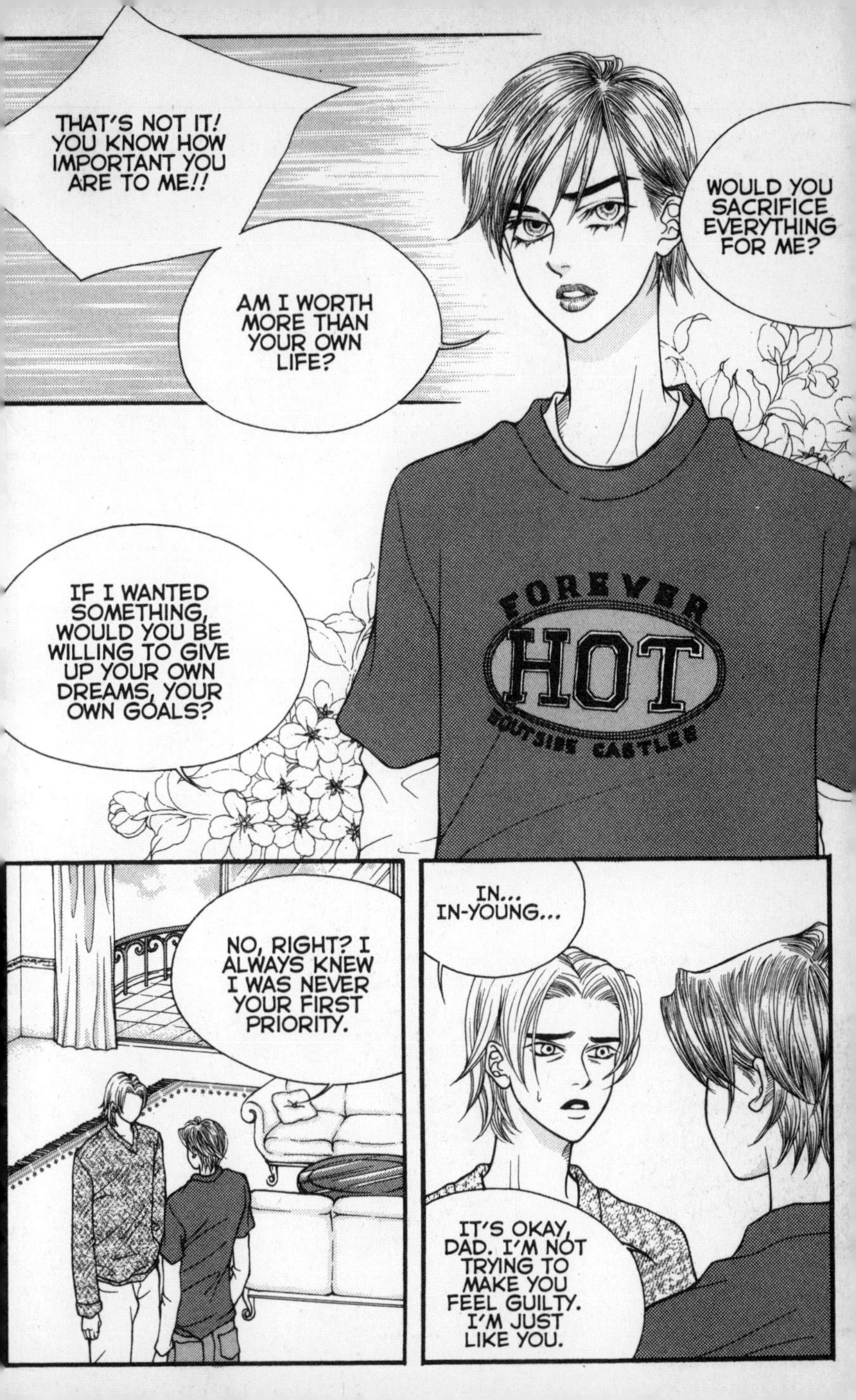
THAT'S NOT IT! YOU KNOW HOW IMPORTANT YOU ARE TO ME!!
WOULD YOU SACRIFICE EVERYTHING FOR ME?
AM I WORTH MORE THAN YOUR OWN LIFE?
FOREVER
HOT
IF I WANTED SOMETHING, WOULD YOU BE WILLING TO GIVE UP YOUR OWN DREAMS, YOUR OWN GOALS?
NO, RIGHT? I ALWAYS KNEW I WAS NEVER YOUR FIRST PRIORITY.
IN... IN-YOUNG...
IT'S OKAY, DAD. I'M NOT TRYING TO MAKE YOU FEEL GUILTY. I'M JUST LIKE YOU.

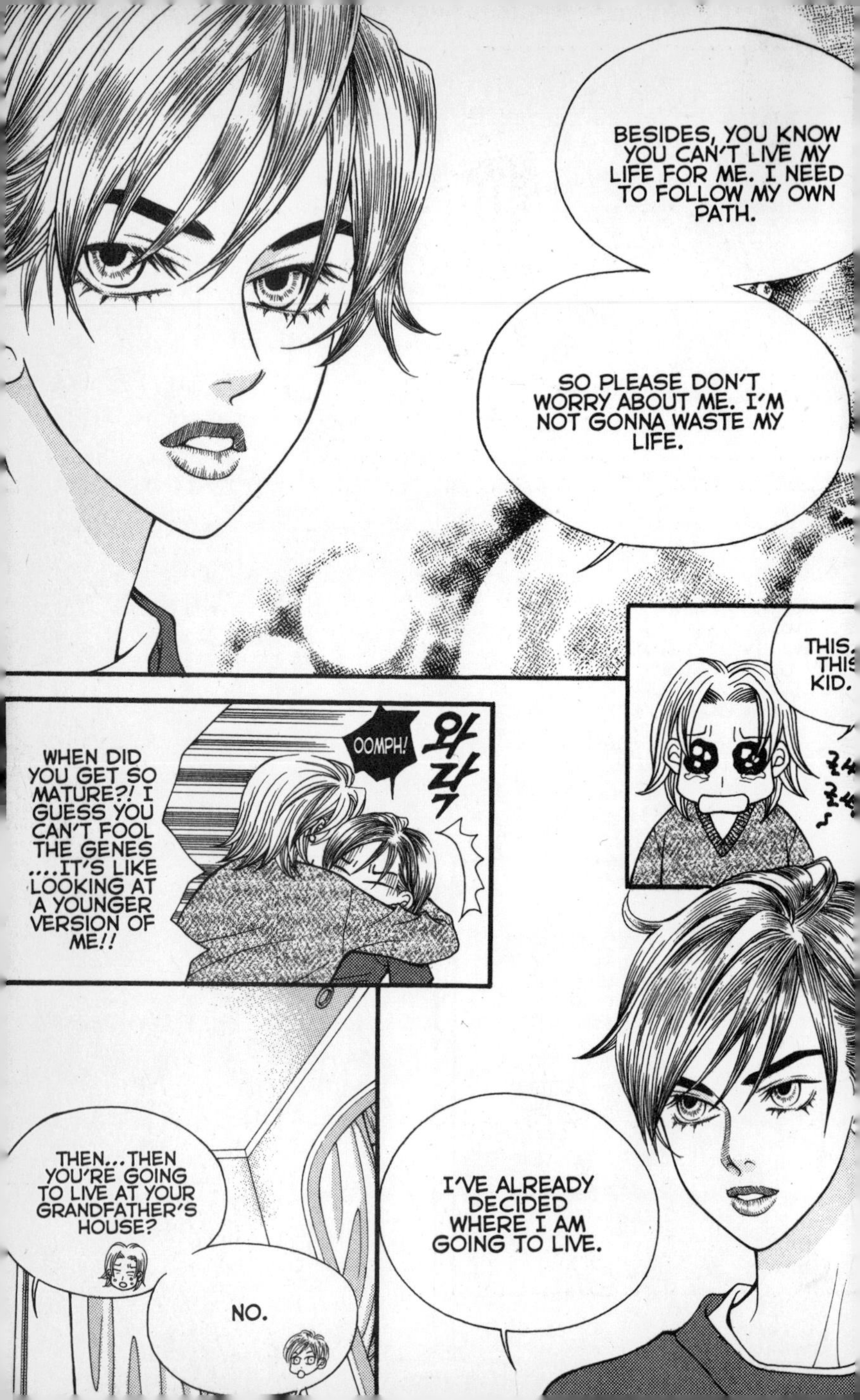
BESIDES, YOU KNOW YOU CAN'T LIVE MY LIFE FOR ME. I NEED TO FOLLOW MY OWN PATH.
SO PLEASE DON'T WORRY ABOUT ME. I'M NOT GONNA WASTE MY LIFE.
THIS. THIS KID.
OOMPH!
와락
WHEN DID YOU GET SO MATURE?! I GUESS YOU CAN'T FOOL THE GENES ....IT'S LIKE LOOKING AT A YOUNGER VERSION OF ME!!
THEN...THEN YOU'RE GOING TO LIVE AT YOUR GRANDFATHER'S HOUSE?
NO.
I'VE ALREADY DECIDED WHERE I AM GOING TO LIVE.

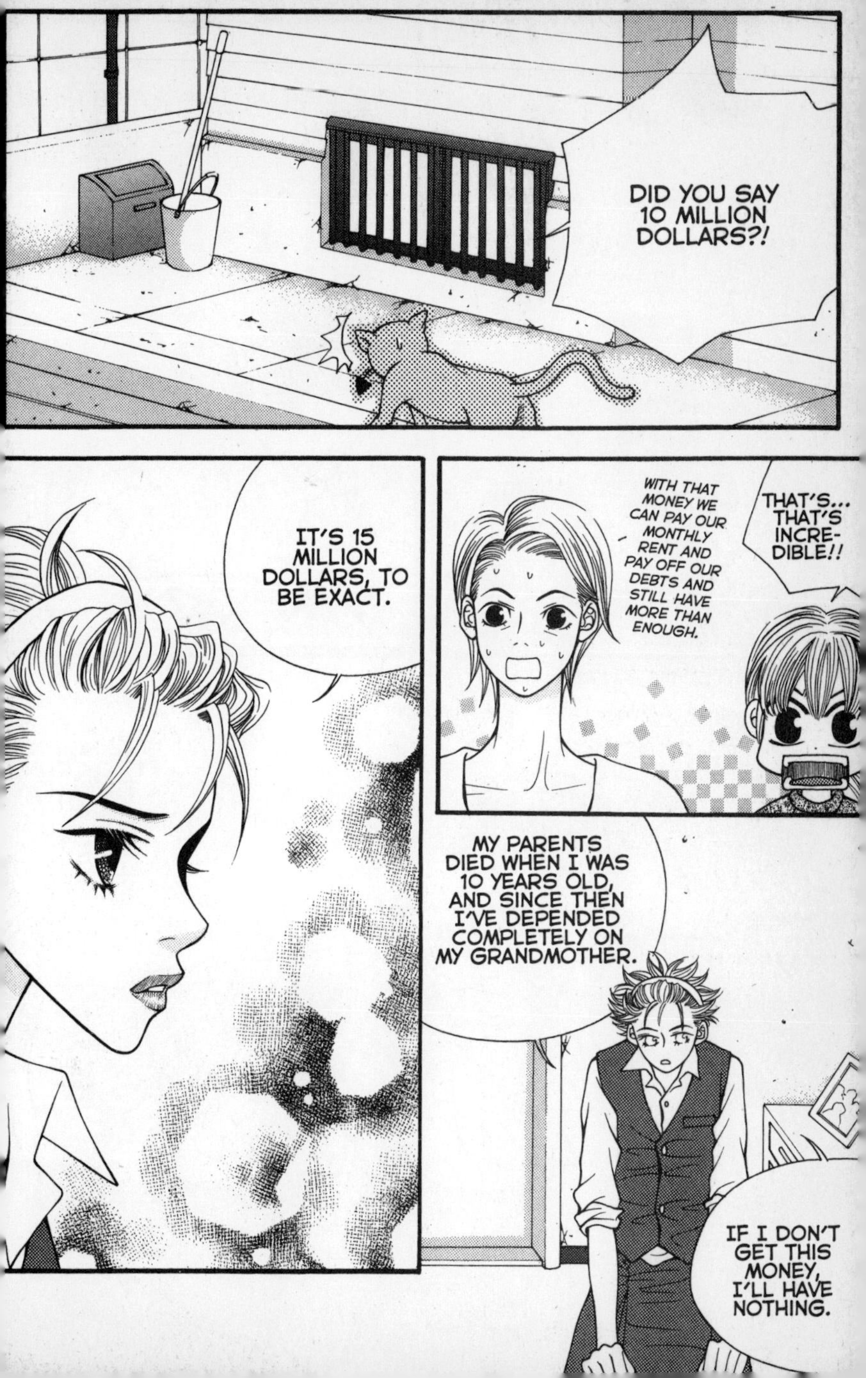
DID YOU SAY 10 MILLION DOLLARS?!
IT'S 15 MILLION DOLLARS, TO BE EXACT.
WITH THAT MONEY WE CAN PAY OUR MONTHLY RENT AND PAY OFF OUR DEBTS AND STILL HAVE MORE THAN ENOUGH.
THAT'S... THAT'S INCRE-DIBLE!!
MY PARENTS DIED WHEN I WAS 10 YEARS OLD, AND SINCE THEN I'VE DEPENDED COMPLETELY ON MY GRANDMOTHER.
IF I DON'T GET THIS MONEY, I'LL HAVE NOTHING.

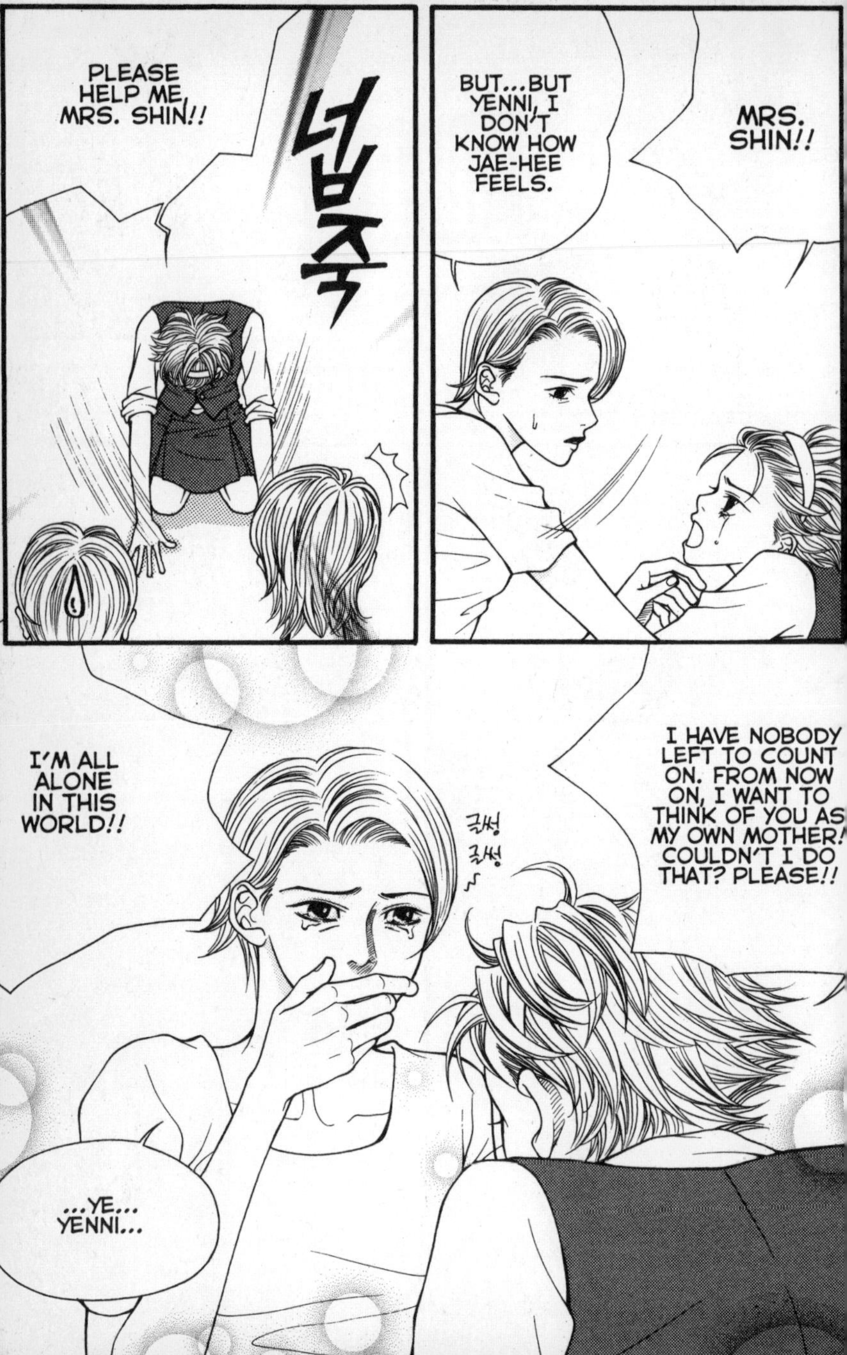
PLEASE HELP ME, MRS. SHIN!!
넙죽
BUT...BUT YENNI, I DON'T KNOW HOW JAE-HEE FEELS.
MRS. SHIN!!
I'M ALL ALONE IN THIS WORLD!!
글썽 글썽
I HAVE NOBODY LEFT TO COUNT ON. FROM NOW ON, I WANT TO THINK OF YOU AS MY OWN MOTHER! COULDN'T I DO THAT? PLEASE!!
...YE... YENNI...

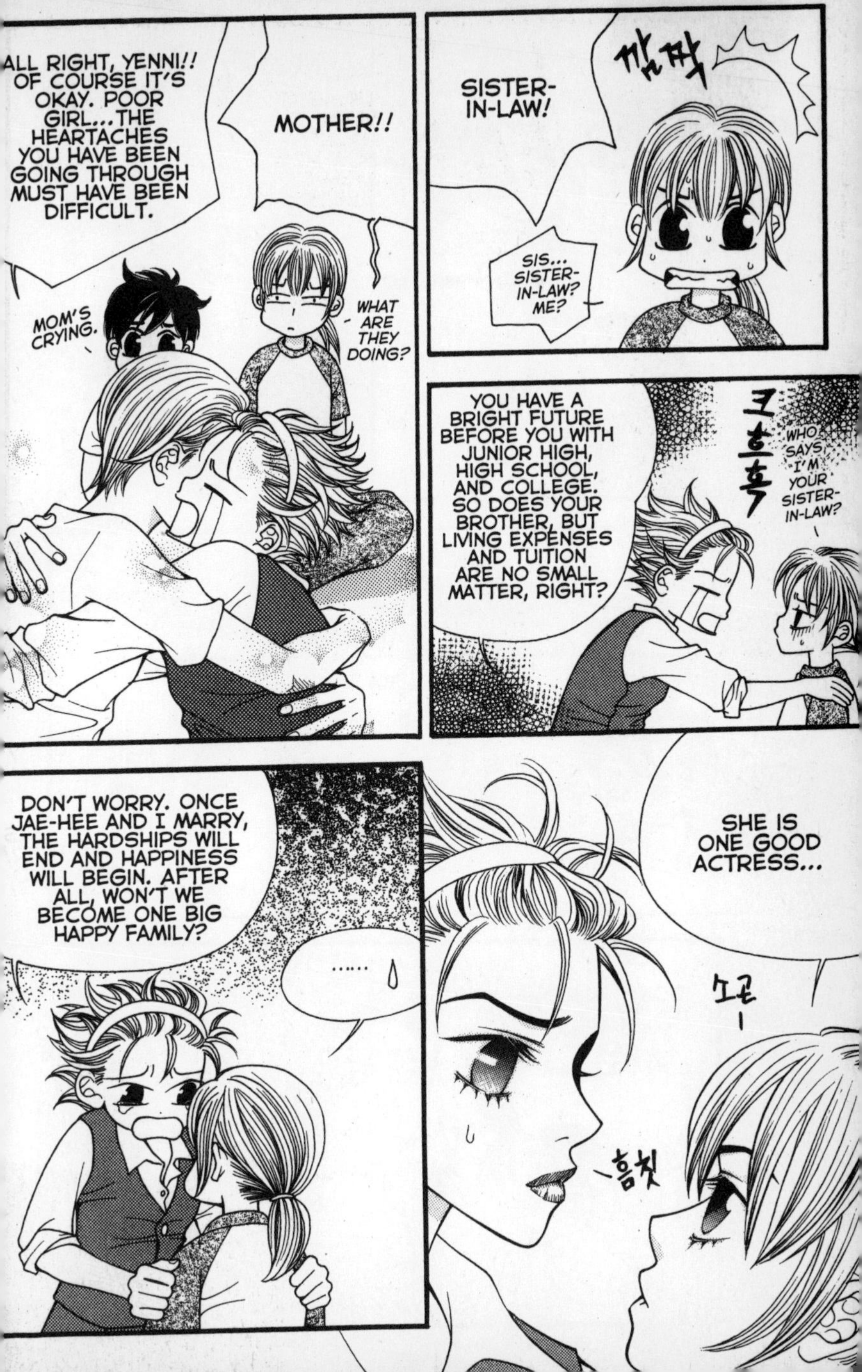
ALL RIGHT, YENNI!! OF COURSE IT'S OKAY. POOR GIRL...THE HEARTACHES YOU HAVE BEEN GOING THROUGH MUST HAVE BEEN DIFFICULT.
MOTHER!!
MOM'S CRYING.
WHAT ARE THEY DOING?
SISTER-IN-LAW!
깜짝
SIS... SISTER-IN-LAW? ME?
YOU HAVE A BRIGHT FUTURE BEFORE YOU WITH JUNIOR HIGH, HIGH SCHOOL, AND COLLEGE. SO DOES YOUR BROTHER, BUT LIVING EXPENSES AND TUITION ARE NO SMALL MATTER, RIGHT?
크흐흑
WHO SAYS I'M YOUR SISTER-IN-LAW?
DON'T WORRY. ONCE JAE-HEE AND I MARRY, THE HARDSHIPS WILL END AND HAPPINESS WILL BEGIN. AFTER ALL, WON'T WE BECOME ONE BIG HAPPY FAMILY?
......
SHE IS ONE GOOD ACTRESS...
소곤
흠칫

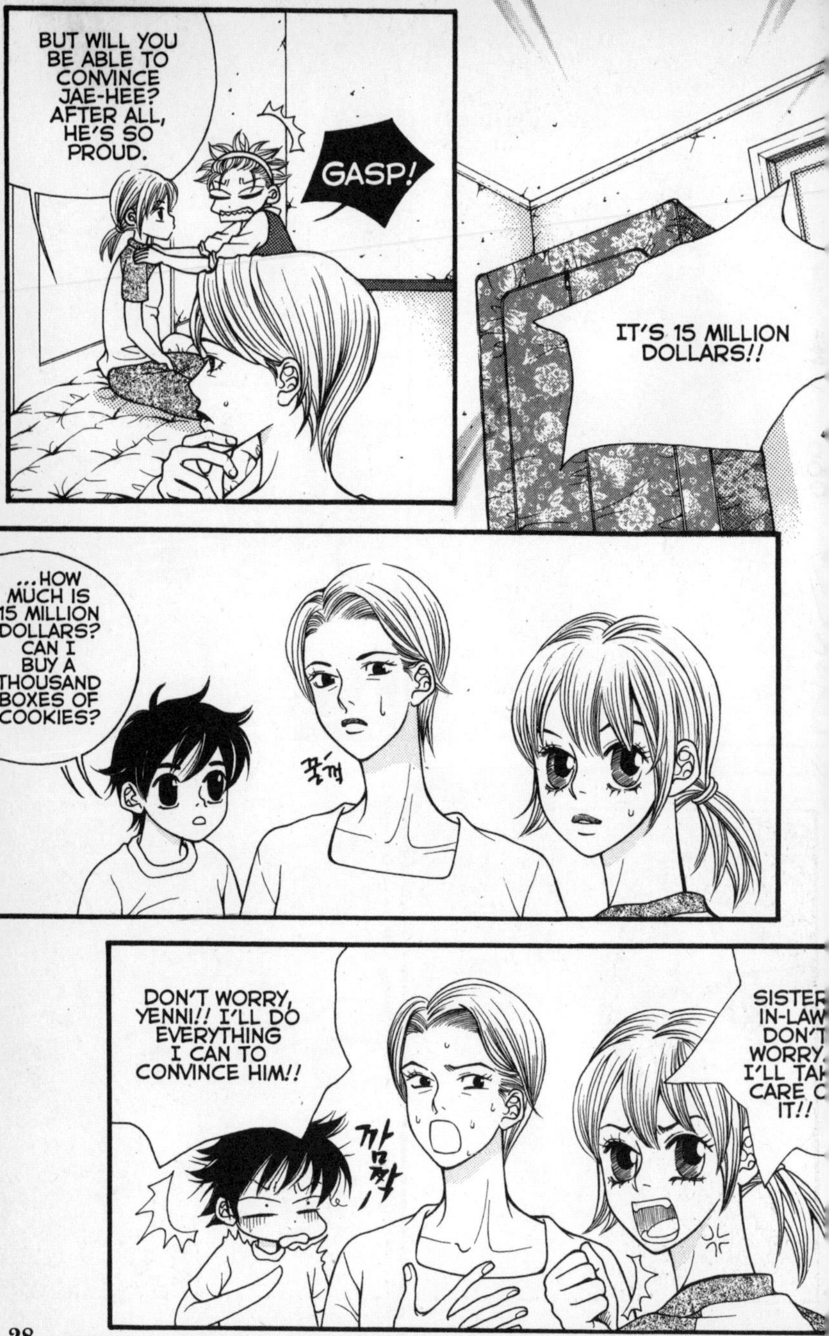
BUT WILL YOU BE ABLE TO CONVINCE JAE-HEE? AFTER ALL, HE'S SO PROUD.
GASP!
IT'S 15 MILLION DOLLARS!!
...HOW MUCH IS 15 MILLION DOLLARS? CAN I BUY A THOUSAND BOXES OF COOKIES?
꿀꺽
DON'T WORRY, YENNI!! I'LL DO EVERYTHING I CAN TO CONVINCE HIM!!
깜짝
SISTER-IN-LAW, DON'T WORRY. I'LL TAKE CARE OF IT!!

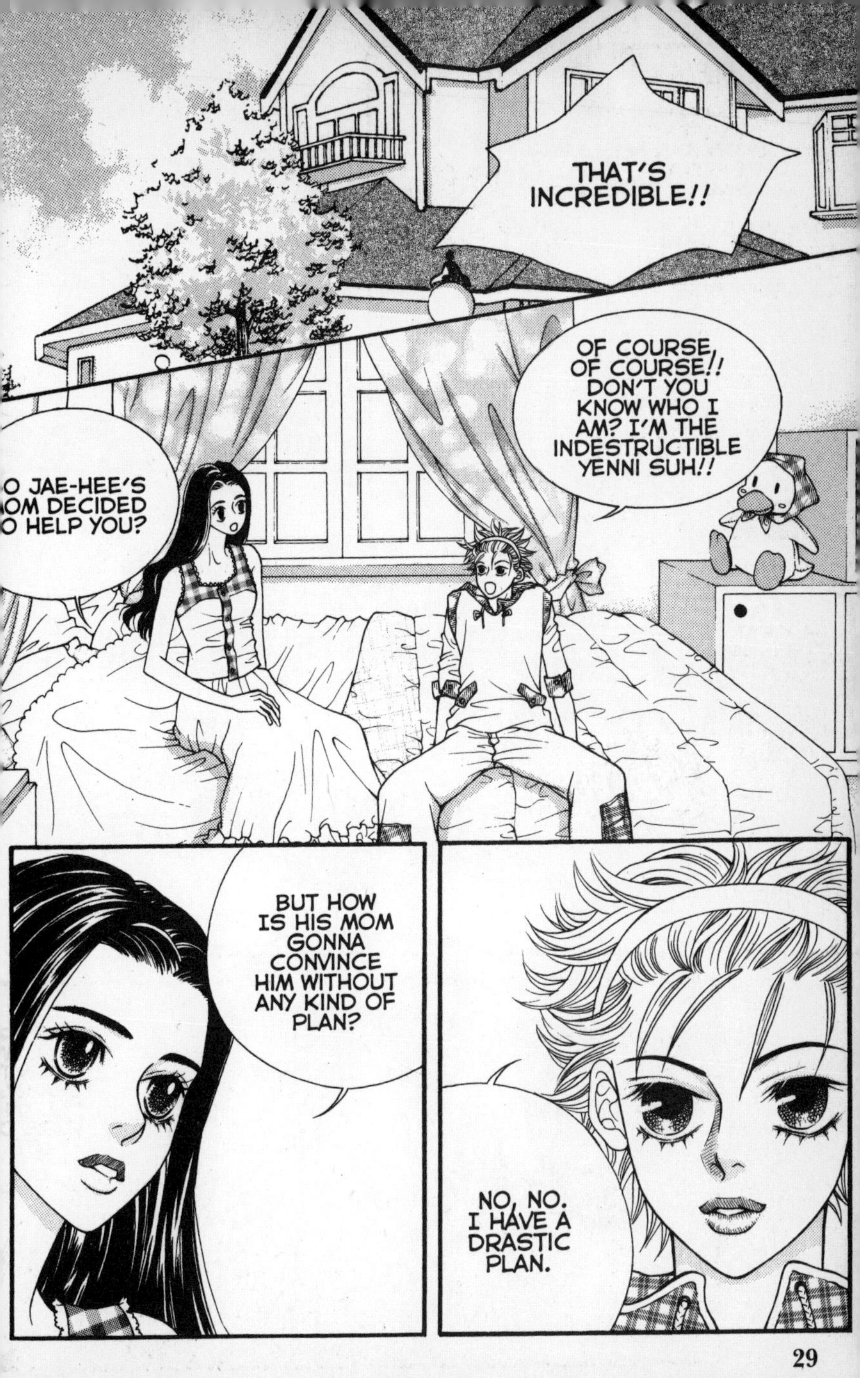
THAT'S INCREDIBLE!!
O JAE-HEE'S OM DECIDED O HELP YOU?
OF COURSE, OF COURSE!! DON'T YOU KNOW WHO I AM? I'M THE INDESTRUCTIBLE YENNI SUH!!
BUT HOW IS HIS MOM GONNA CONVINCE HIM WITHOUT ANY KIND OF PLAN?
NO, NO. I HAVE A DRASTIC PLAN.

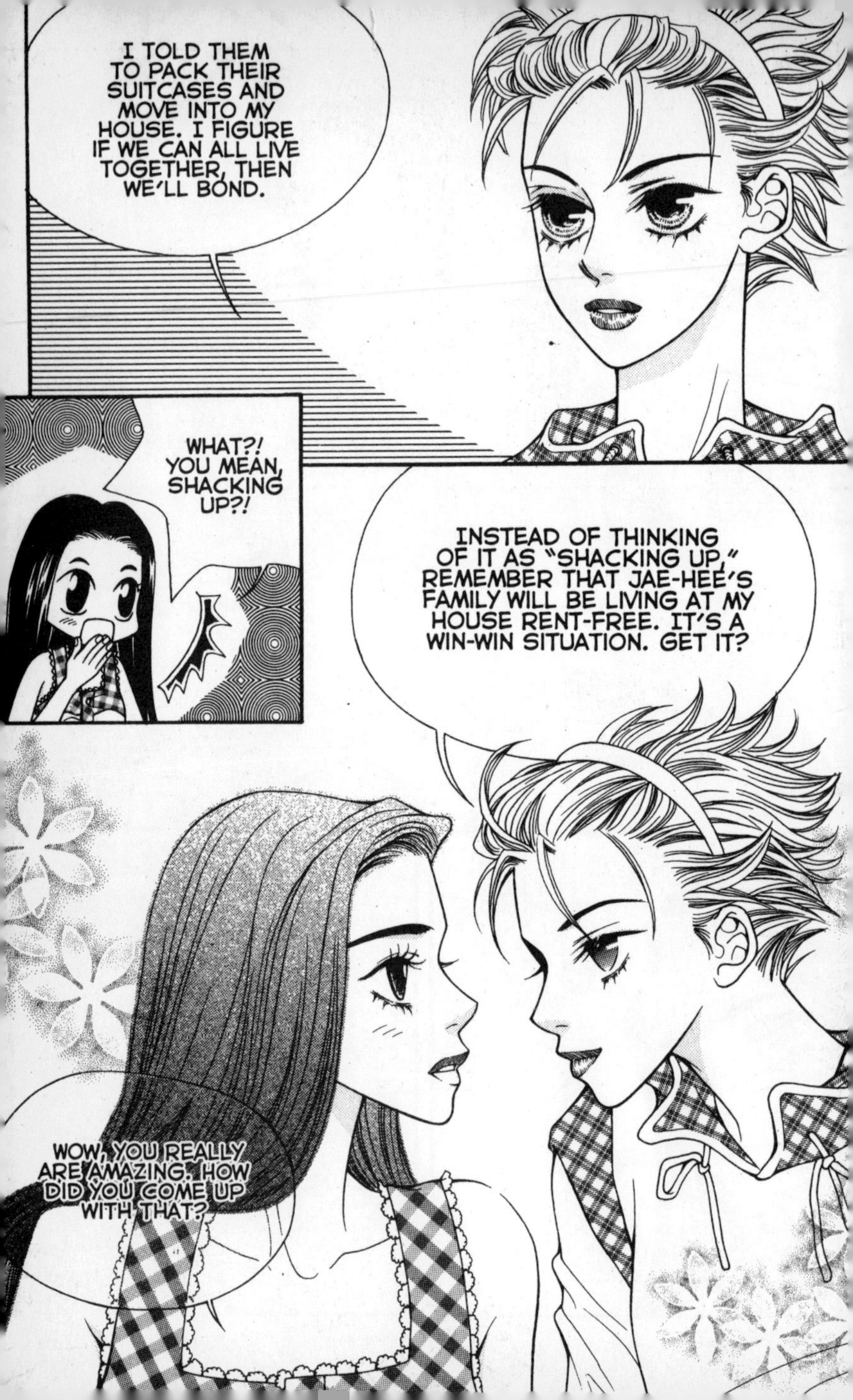
I TOLD THEM TO PACK THEIR SUITCASES AND MOVE INTO MY HOUSE. I FIGURE IF WE CAN ALL LIVE TOGETHER, THEN WE'LL BOND.
WHAT?! YOU MEAN, SHACKING UP?!
INSTEAD OF THINKING OF IT AS "SHACKING UP," REMEMBER THAT JAE-HEE'S FAMILY WILL BE LIVING AT MY HOUSE RENT-FREE. IT'S A WIN-WIN SITUATION. GET IT?
WOW, YOU REALLY ARE AMAZING. HOW DID YOU COME UP WITH THAT?

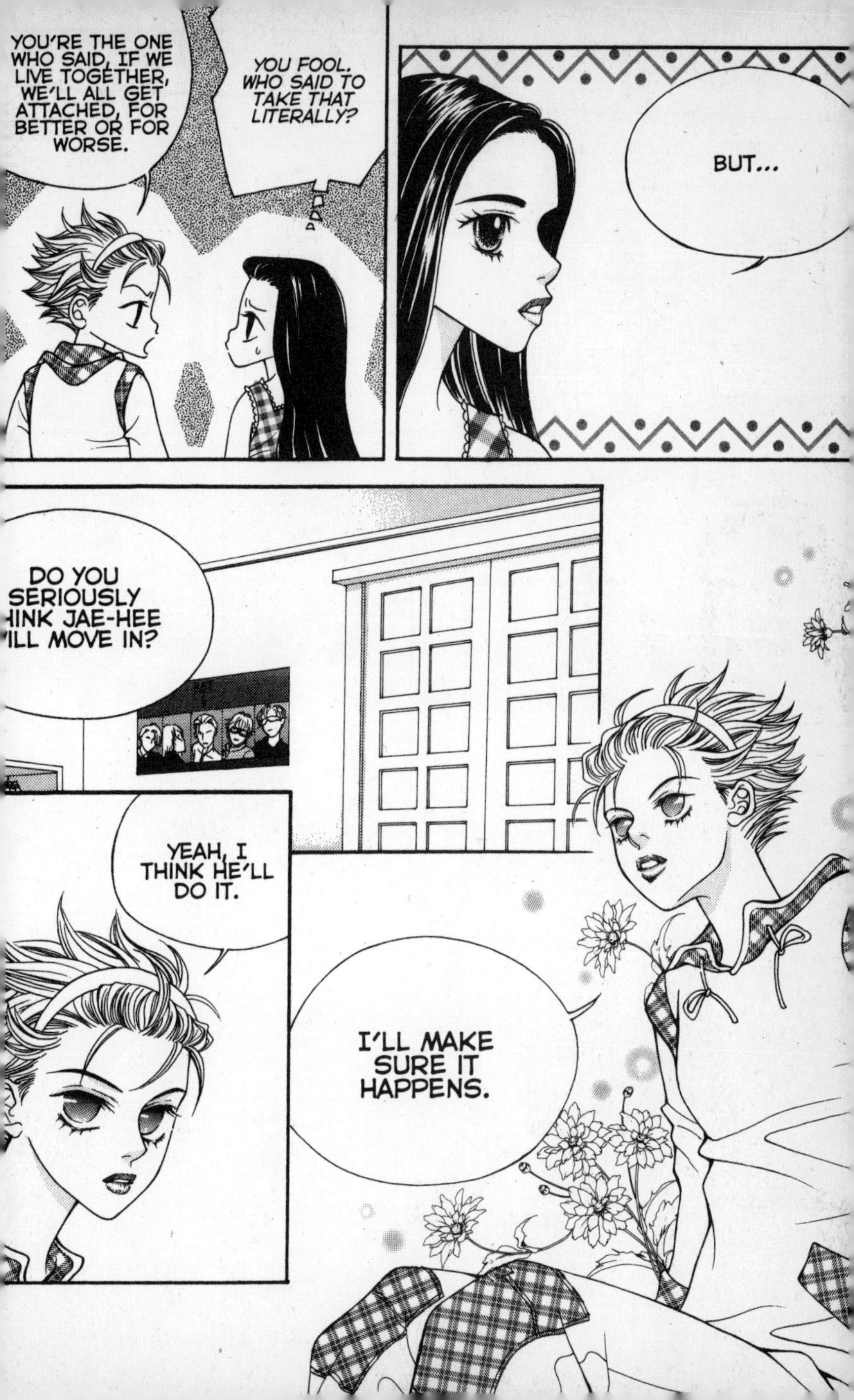

YOU'RE THE ONE WHO SAID, IF WE LIVE TOGETHER, WE'LL ALL GET ATTACHED, FOR BETTER OR FOR WORSE.
YOU FOOL. WHO SAID TO TAKE THAT LITERALLY?
BUT...
DO YOU SERIOUSLY HINK JAE-HEE ILL MOVE IN?
YEAH, I THINK HE'LL DO IT.
I'LL MAKE SURE IT HAPPENS.

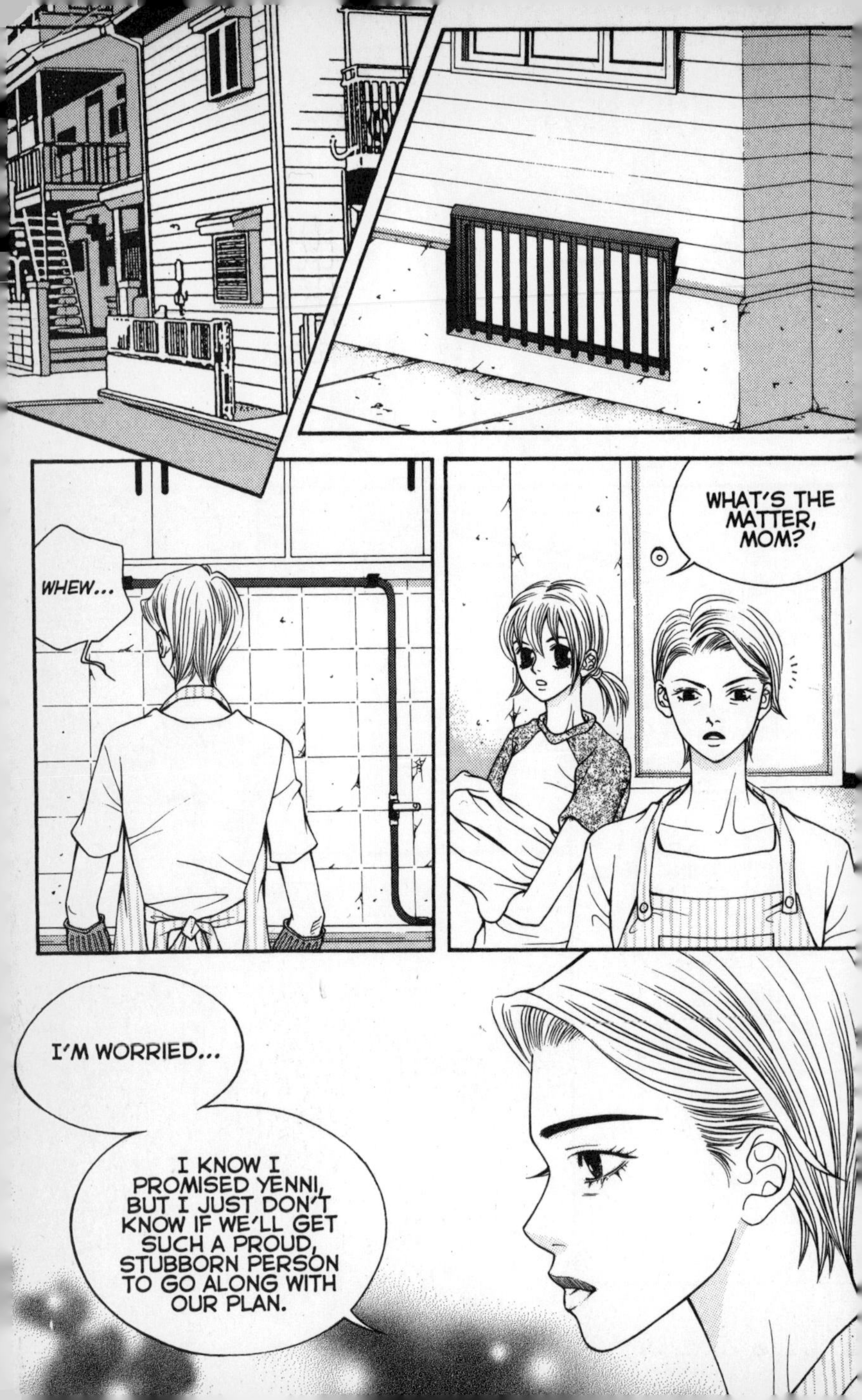
WHEW...
WHAT'S THE MATTER, MOM?
I'M WORRIED...
I KNOW I PROMISED YENNI, BUT I JUST DON'T KNOW IF WE'LL GET SUCH A PROUD, STUBBORN PERSON TO GO ALONG WITH OUR PLAN.

I'M HOME!!

......

WHAT...WHAT SHOULD WE DO, JAE-YUN? JAE...JAE-HEE'S HOME.

DON'T WORRY, MOM. I'LL TELL HIM. YOU JUST GO TAKE YOUR SAUNA.

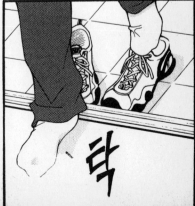

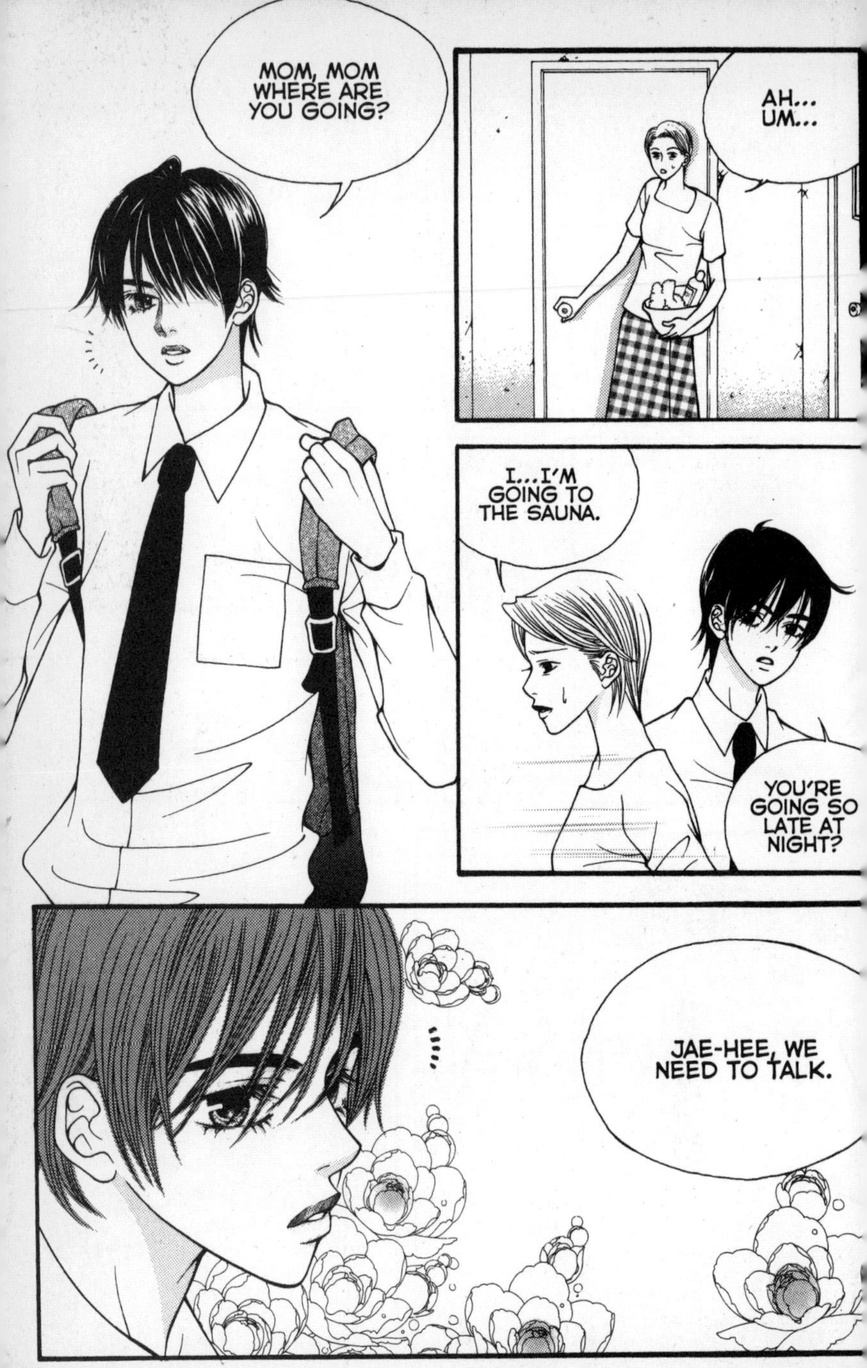
MOM, MOM WHERE ARE YOU GOING?
AH... UM...
I...I'M GOING TO THE SAUNA.
YOU'RE GOING SO LATE AT NIGHT?
JAE-HEE, WE NEED TO TALK.

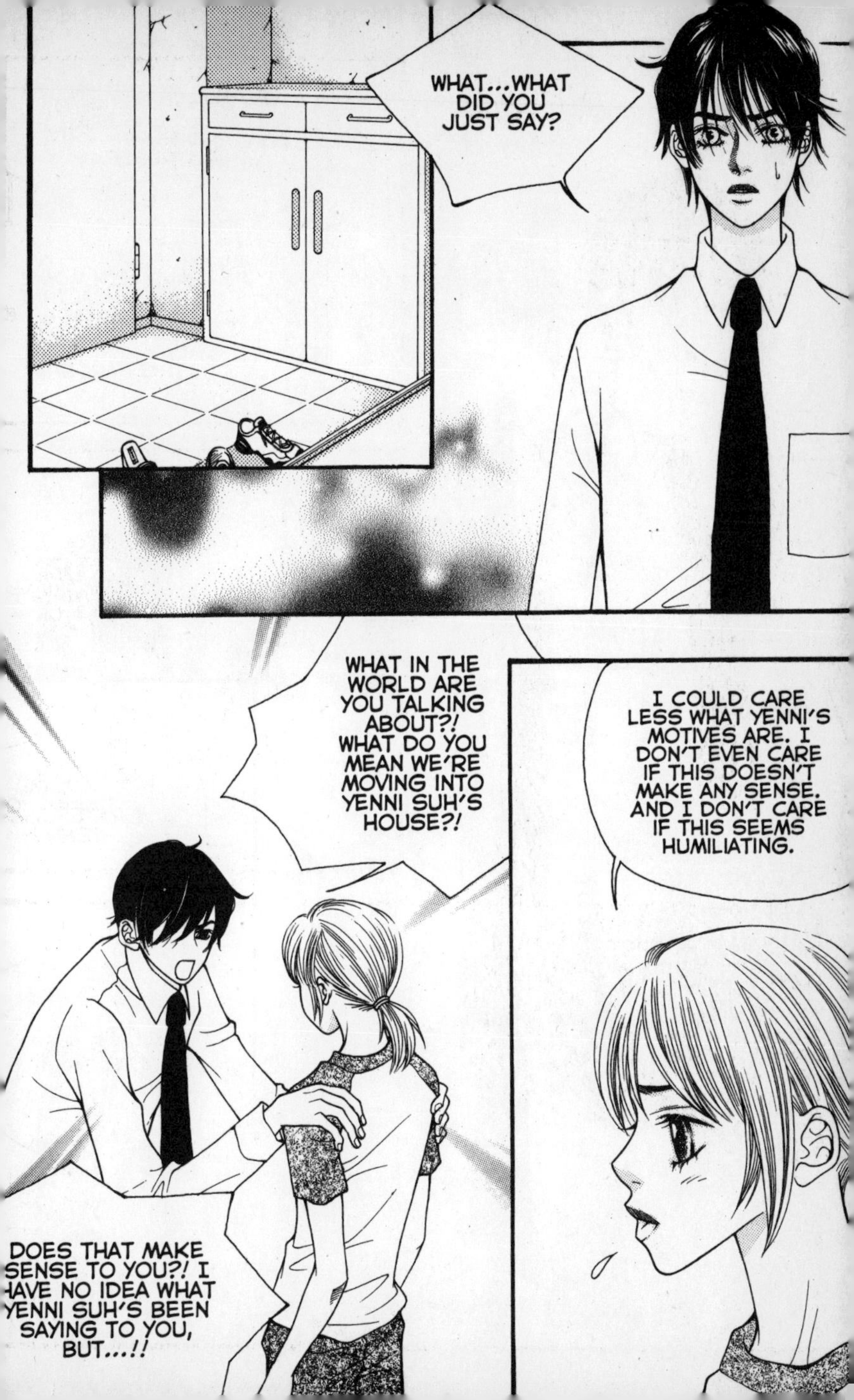
WHAT...WHAT DID YOU JUST SAY?
WHAT IN THE WORLD ARE YOU TALKING ABOUT?! WHAT DO YOU MEAN WE'RE MOVING INTO YENNI SUH'S HOUSE?!
DOES THAT MAKE SENSE TO YOU?! I HAVE NO IDEA WHAT YENNI SUH'S BEEN SAYING TO YOU, BUT...!!
I COULD CARE LESS WHAT YENNI'S MOTIVES ARE. I DON'T EVEN CARE IF THIS DOESN'T MAKE ANY SENSE. AND I DON'T CARE IF THIS SEEMS HUMILIATING.

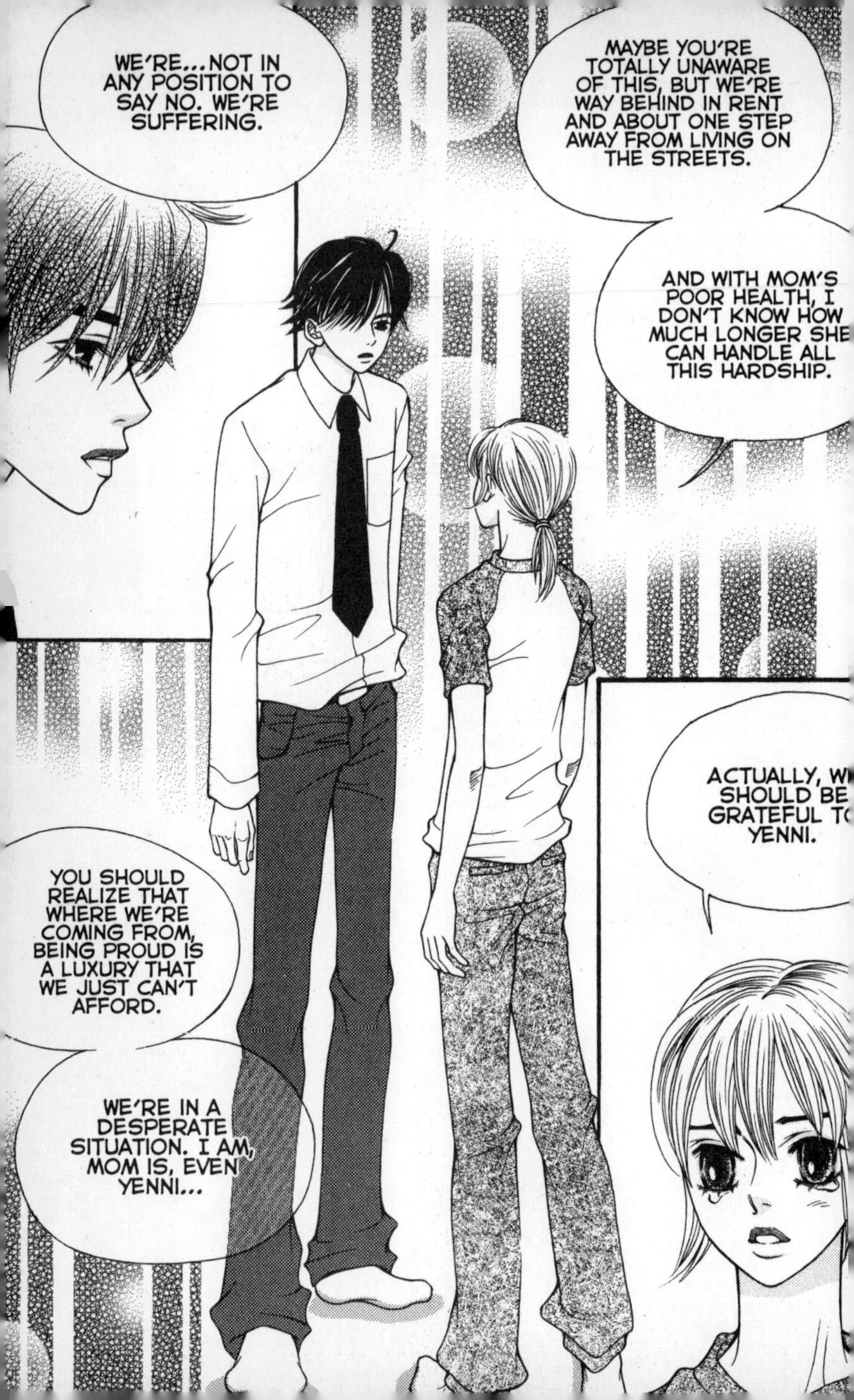
WE'RE...NOT IN ANY POSITION TO SAY NO. WE'RE SUFFERING.
MAYBE YOU'RE TOTALLY UNAWARE OF THIS, BUT WE'RE WAY BEHIND IN RENT AND ABOUT ONE STEP AWAY FROM LIVING ON THE STREETS.
AND WITH MOM'S POOR HEALTH, I DON'T KNOW HOW MUCH LONGER SHE CAN HANDLE ALL THIS HARDSHIP.
YOU SHOULD REALIZE THAT WHERE WE'RE COMING FROM, BEING PROUD IS A LUXURY THAT WE JUST CAN'T AFFORD.
WE'RE IN A DESPERATE SITUATION. I AM, MOM IS, EVEN YENNI...
ACTUALLY, W SHOULD BE GRATEFUL T YENNI.

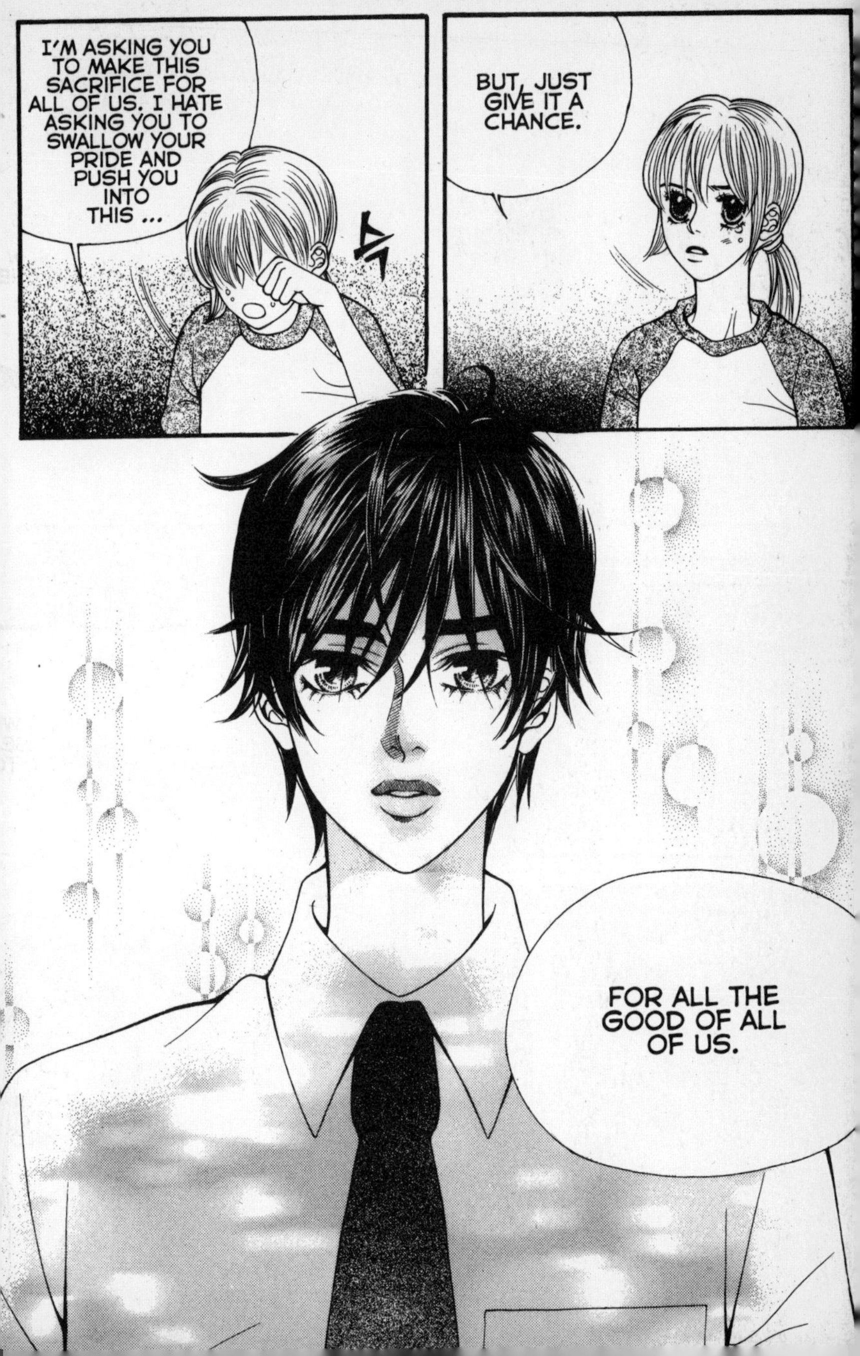
I'M ASKING YOU TO MAKE THIS SACRIFICE FOR ALL OF US. I HATE ASKING YOU TO SWALLOW YOUR PRIDE AND PUSH YOU INTO THIS ...
BUT, JUST GIVE IT A CHANCE.
FOR ALL THE GOOD OF ALL OF US.

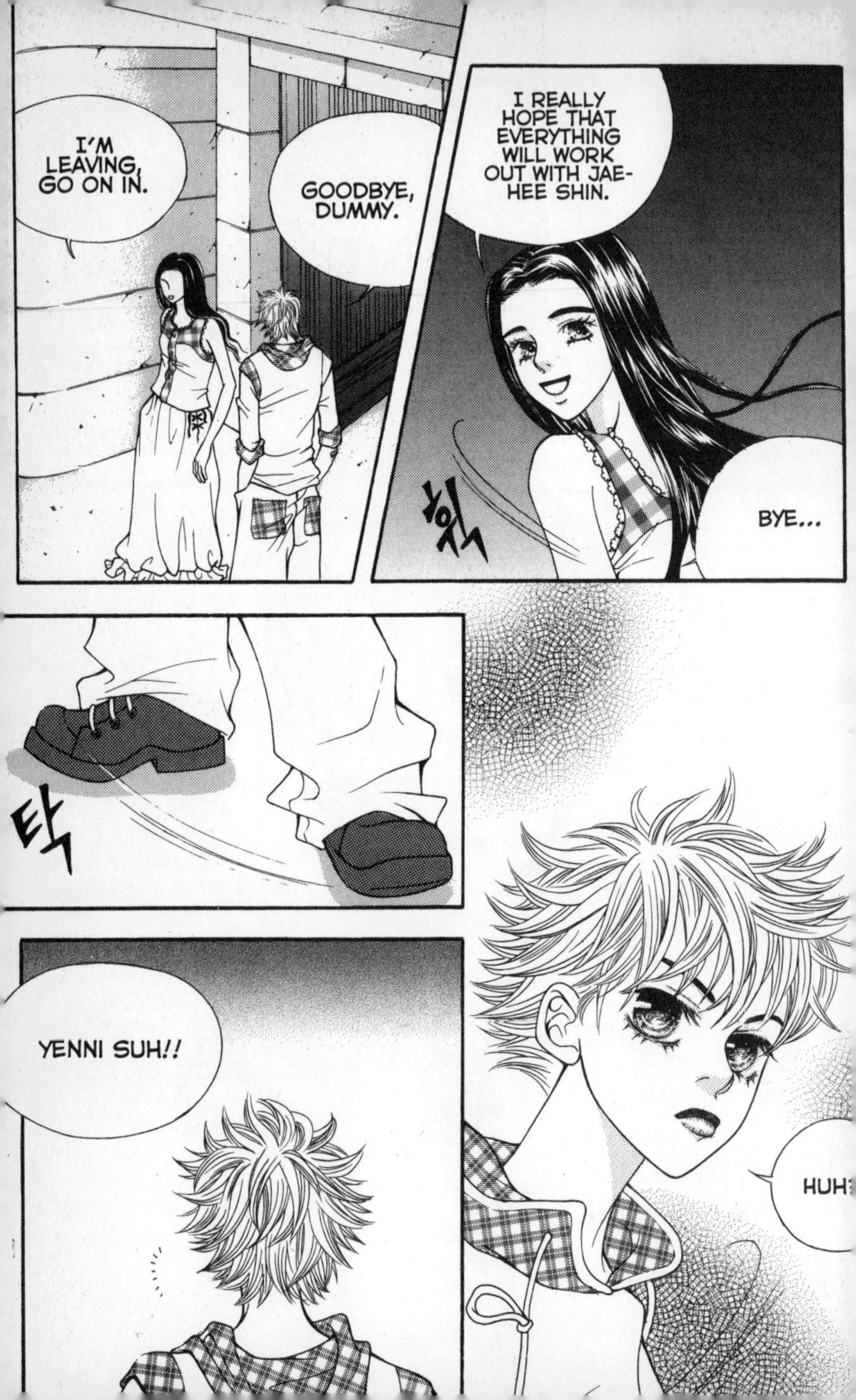
I'M LEAVING, GO ON IN.
GOODBYE, DUMMY.
I REALLY HOPE THAT EVERYTHING WILL WORK OUT WITH JAE-HEE SHIN.
BYE...
탁
YENNI SUH!!
HUH

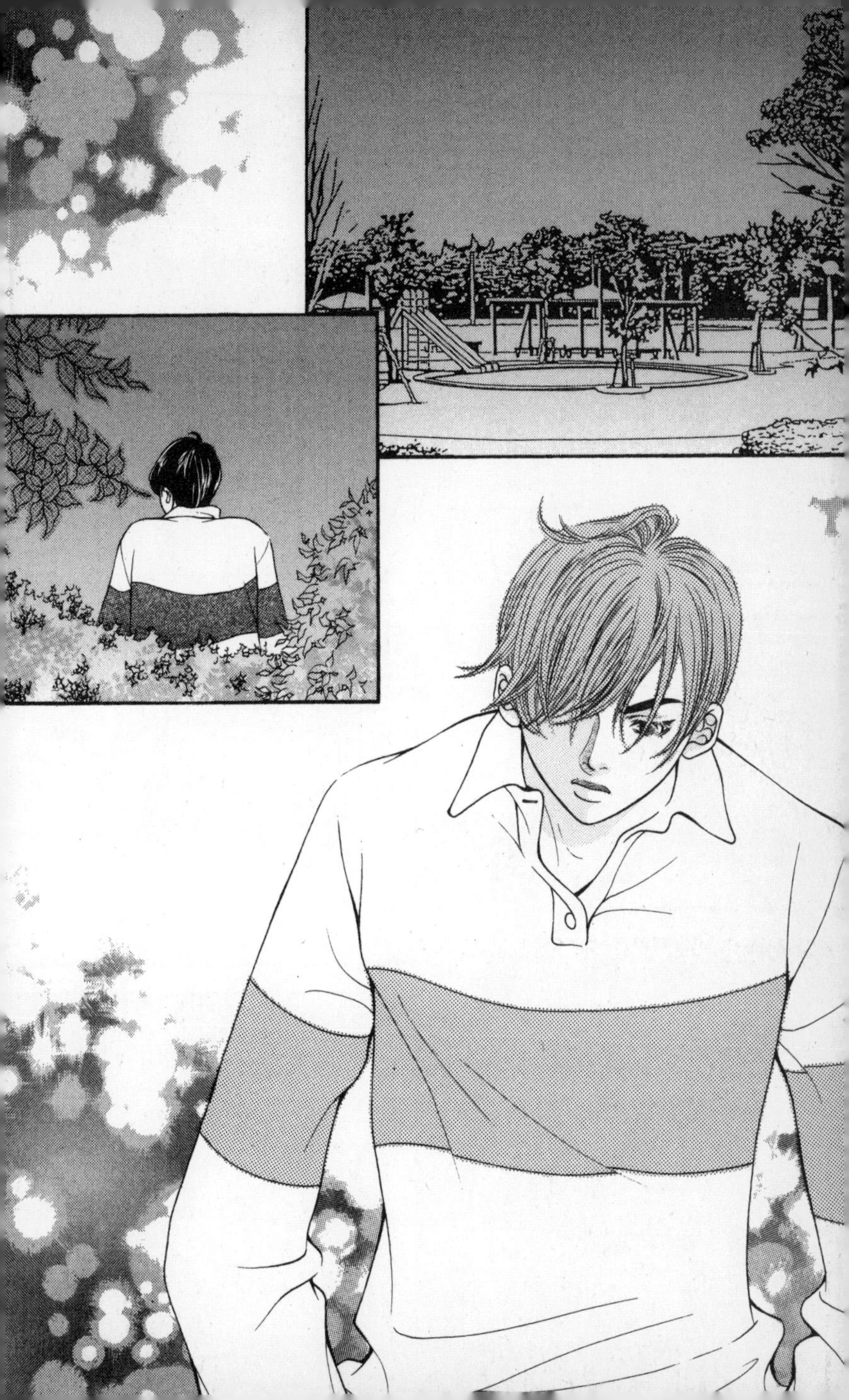

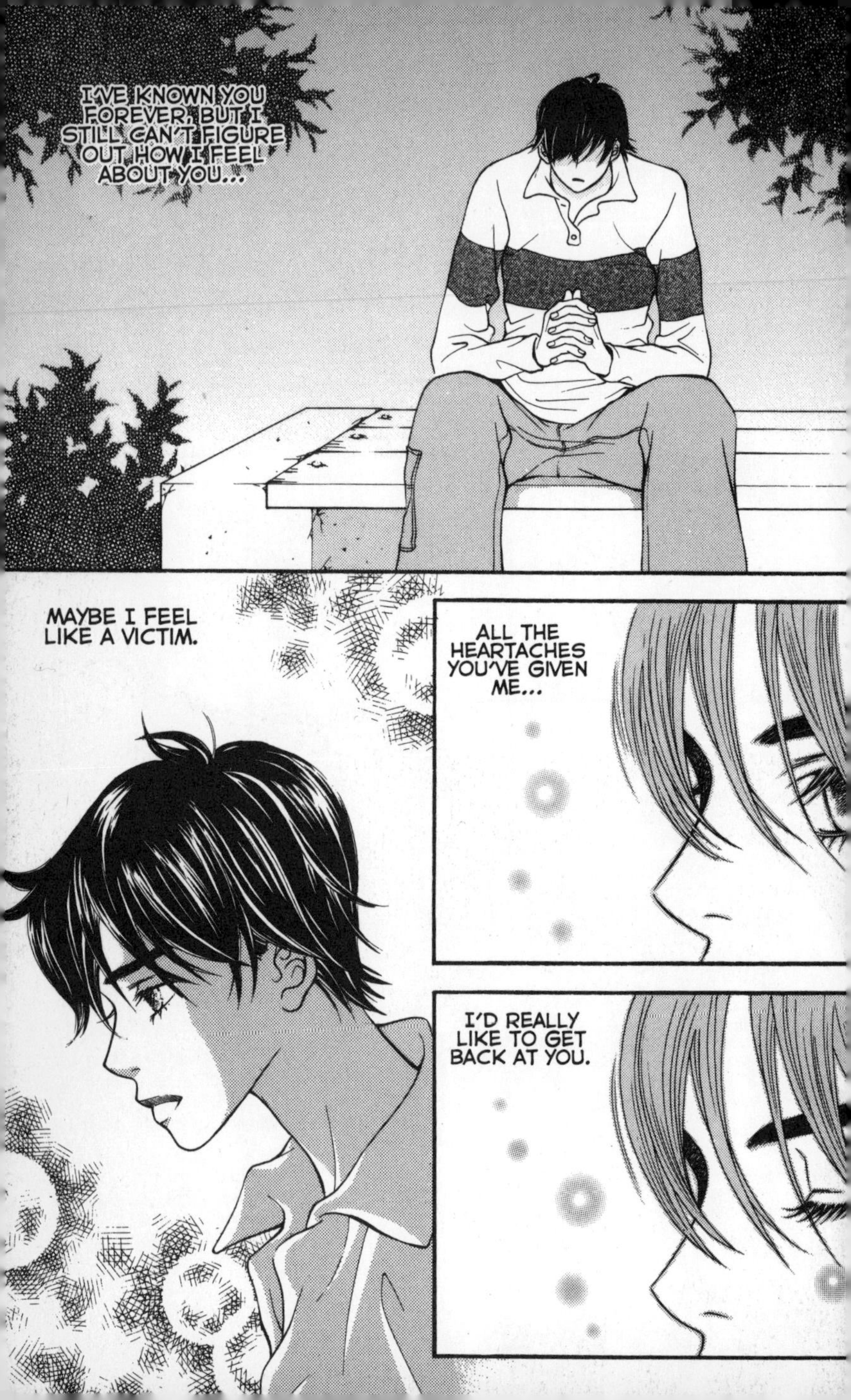
I'VE KNOWN YOU FOREVER, BUT I STILL CAN'T FIGURE OUT HOW I FEEL ABOUT YOU...
ALL THE HEARTACHES YOU'VE GIVEN ME...
I'D REALLY LIKE TO GET BACK AT YOU.
MAYBE I FEEL LIKE A VICTIM.

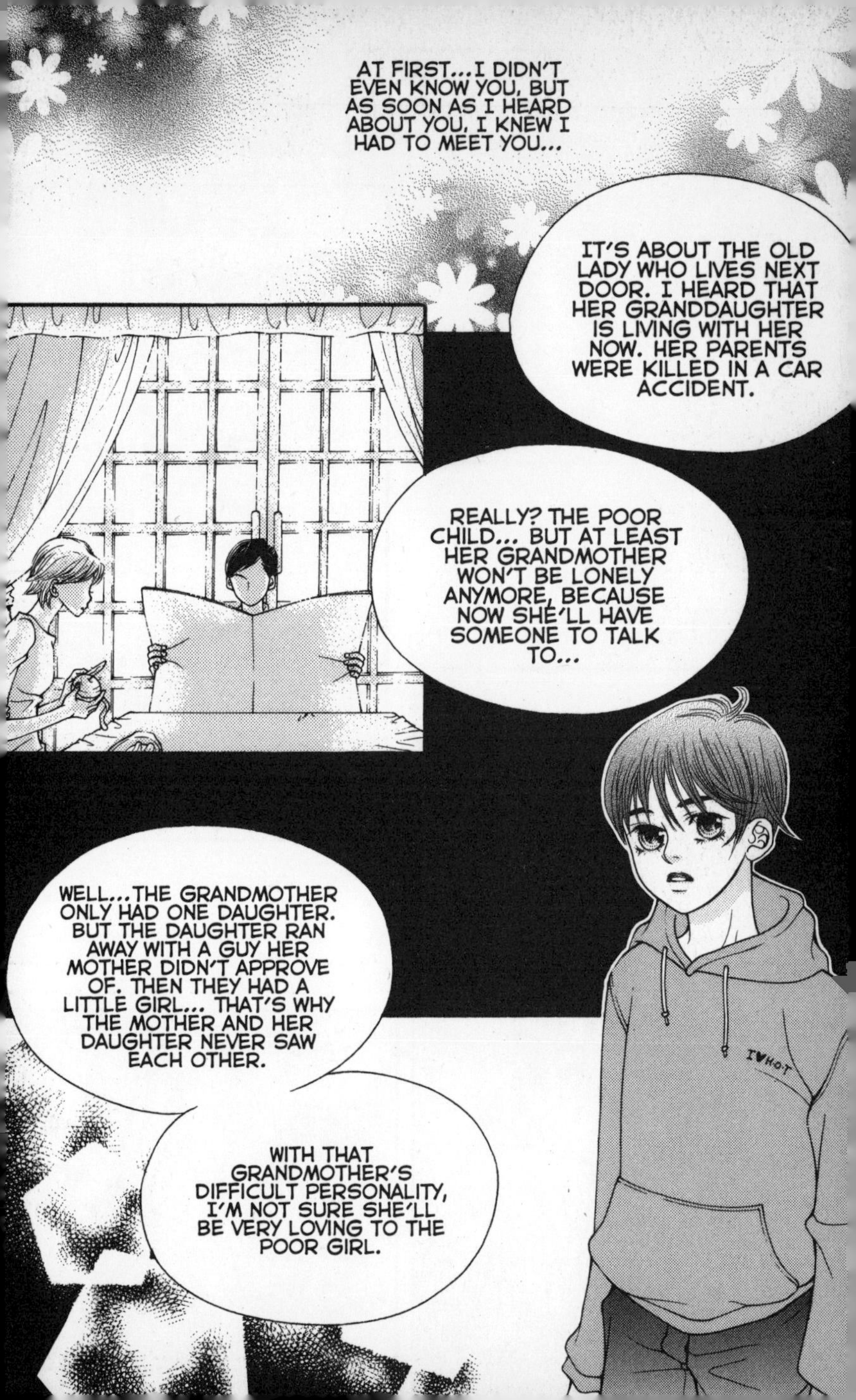
AT FIRST...I DIDN'T EVEN KNOW YOU, BUT AS SOON AS I HEARD ABOUT YOU, I KNEW I HAD TO MEET YOU...
IT'S ABOUT THE OLD LADY WHO LIVES NEXT DOOR. I HEARD THAT HER GRANDDAUGHTER IS LIVING WITH HER NOW. HER PARENTS WERE KILLED IN A CAR ACCIDENT.
REALLY? THE POOR CHILD... BUT AT LEAST HER GRANDMOTHER WON'T BE LONELY ANYMORE, BECAUSE NOW SHE'LL HAVE SOMEONE TO TALK TO...
WELL...THE GRANDMOTHER ONLY HAD ONE DAUGHTER. BUT THE DAUGHTER RAN AWAY WITH A GUY HER MOTHER DIDN'T APPROVE OF. THEN THEY HAD A LITTLE GIRL... THAT'S WHY THE MOTHER AND HER DAUGHTER NEVER SAW EACH OTHER.
I♥H.O.T
WITH THAT GRANDMOTHER'S DIFFICULT PERSONALITY, I'M NOT SURE SHE'LL BE VERY LOVING TO THE POOR GIRL.

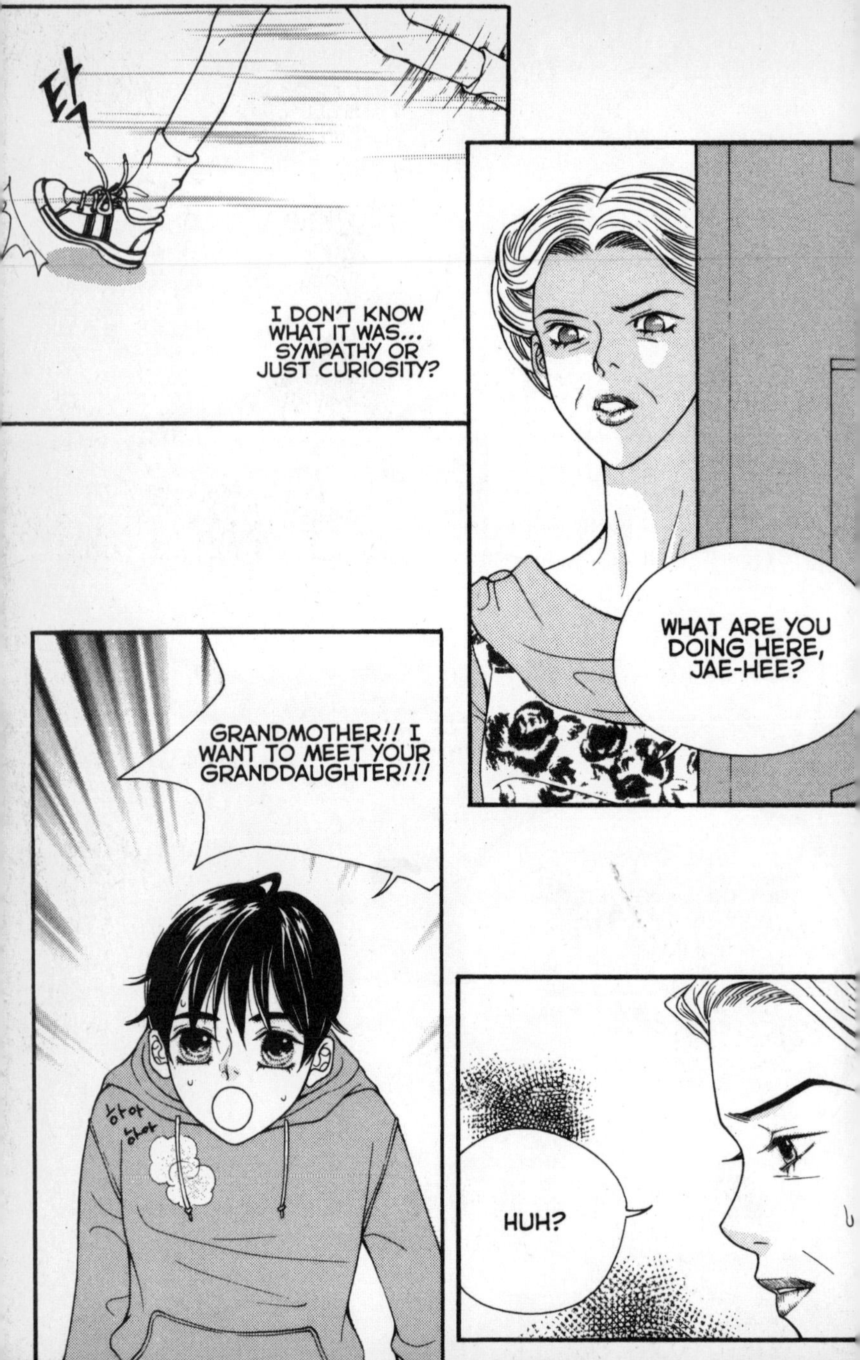
탁
I DON'T KNOW WHAT IT WAS... SYMPATHY OR JUST CURIOSITY?
WHAT ARE YOU DOING HERE, JAE-HEE?
GRANDMOTHER!! I WANT TO MEET YOUR GRANDDAUGHTER!!!
HUH?

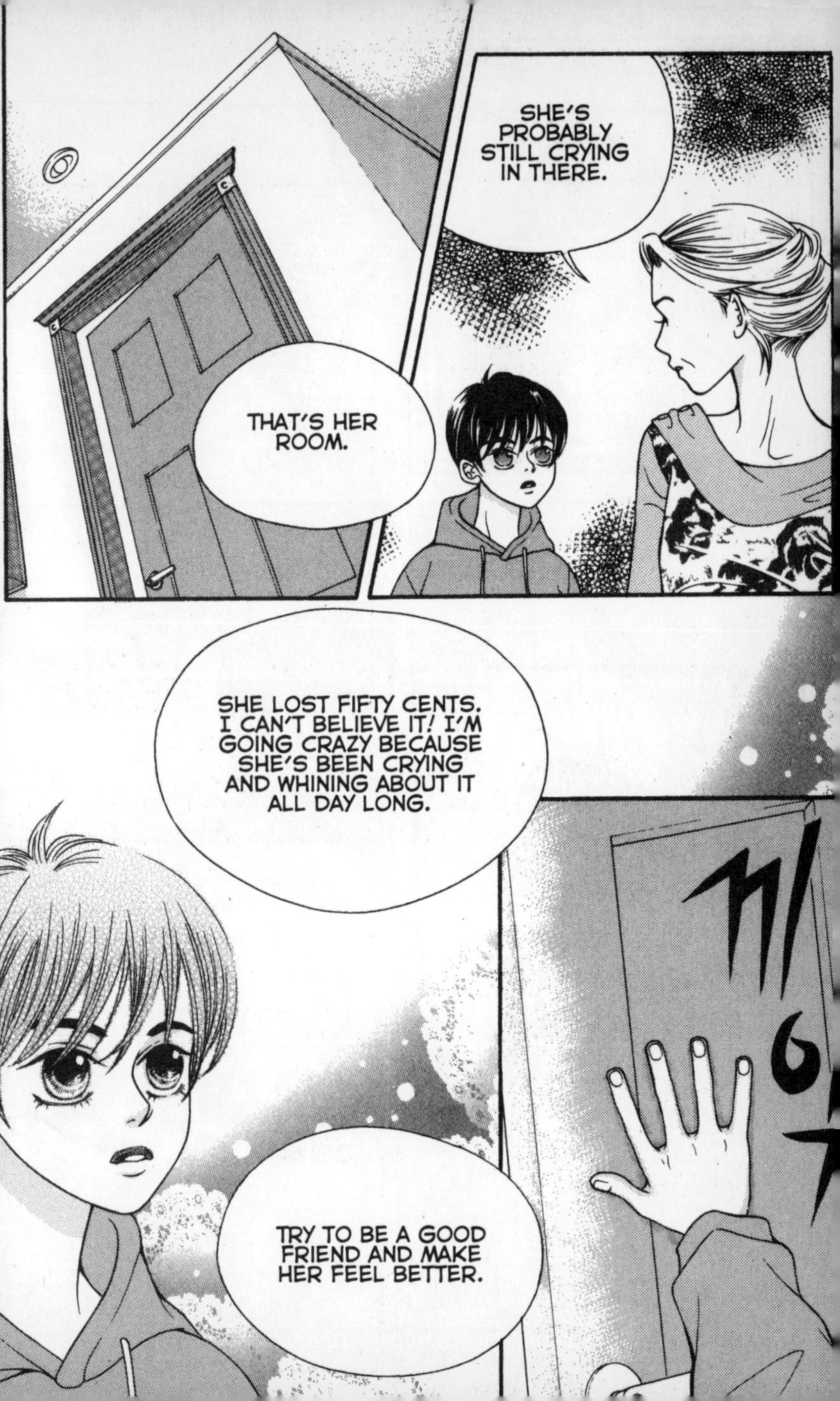
THAT'S HER ROOM.
SHE'S PROBABLY STILL CRYING IN THERE.
SHE LOST FIFTY CENTS. I CAN'T BELIEVE IT! I'M GOING CRAZY BECAUSE SHE'S BEEN CRYING AND WHINING ABOUT IT ALL DAY LONG.
TRY TO BE A GOOD FRIEND AND MAKE HER FEEL BETTER.

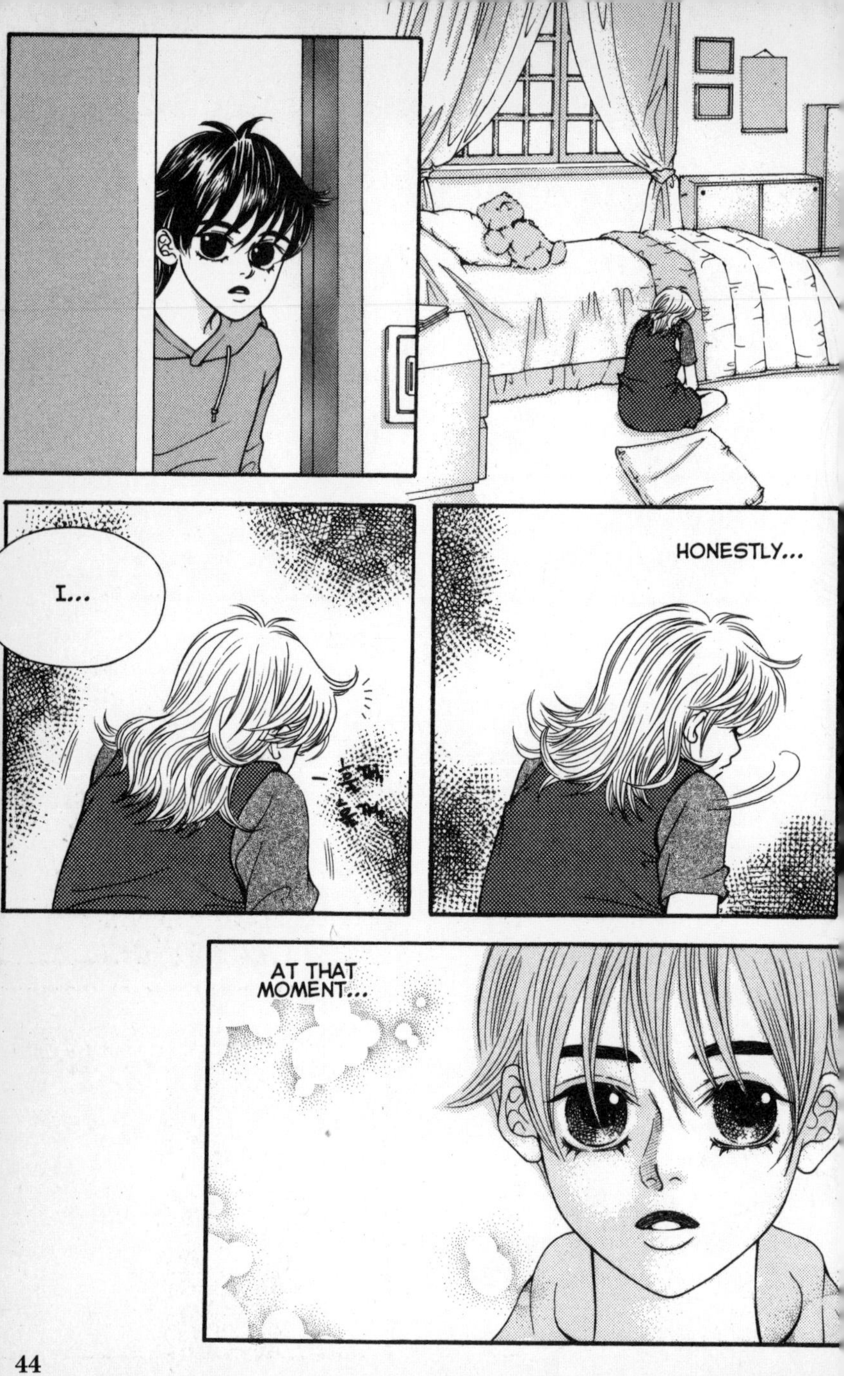
I...
HONESTLY...
AT THAT MOMENT...

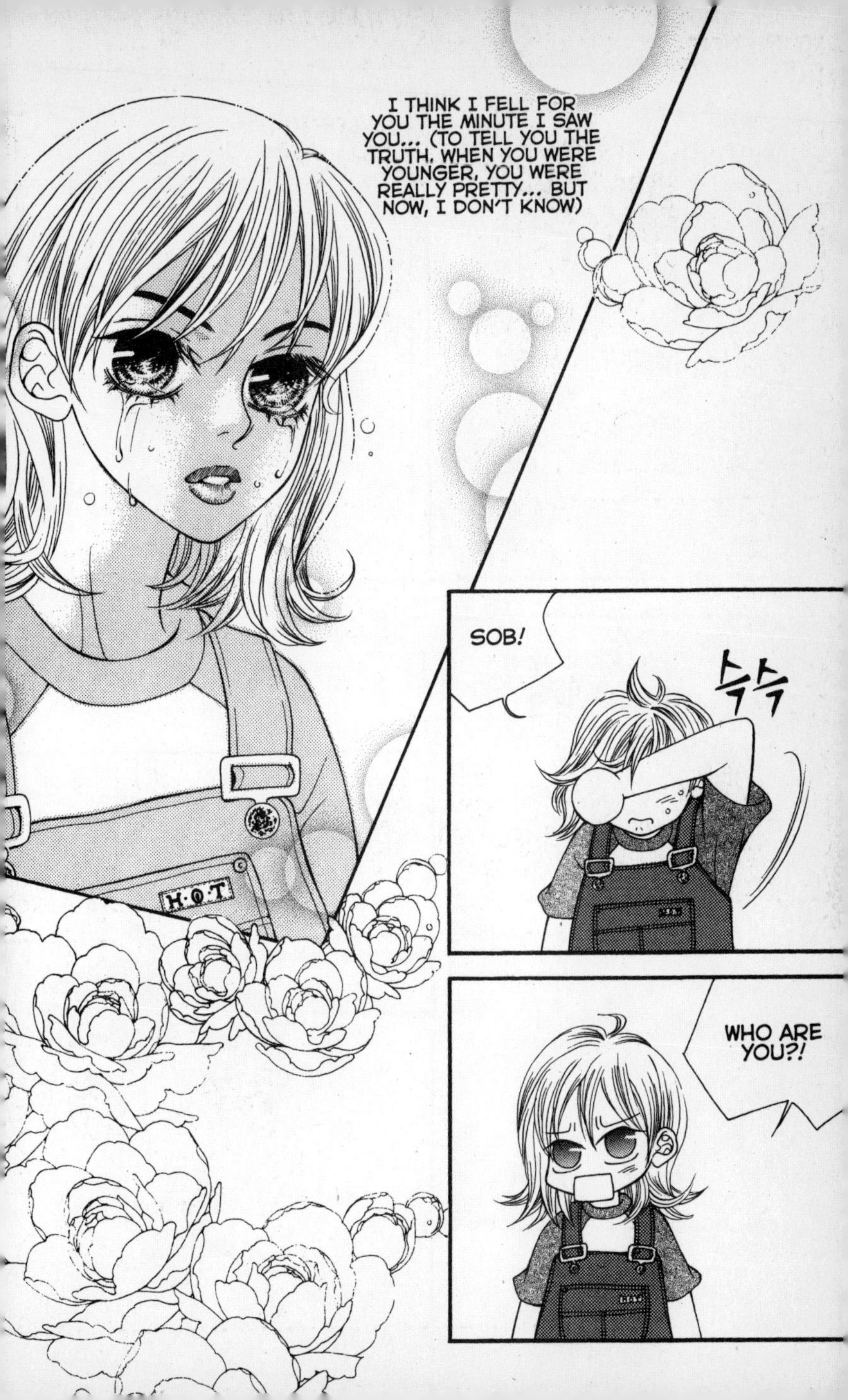
I THINK I FELL FOR YOU THE MINUTE I SAW YOU... (TO TELL YOU THE TRUTH, WHEN YOU WERE YOUNGER, YOU WERE REALLY PRETTY... BUT NOW, I DON'T KNOW)
SOB!
흑흑
WHO ARE YOU?!

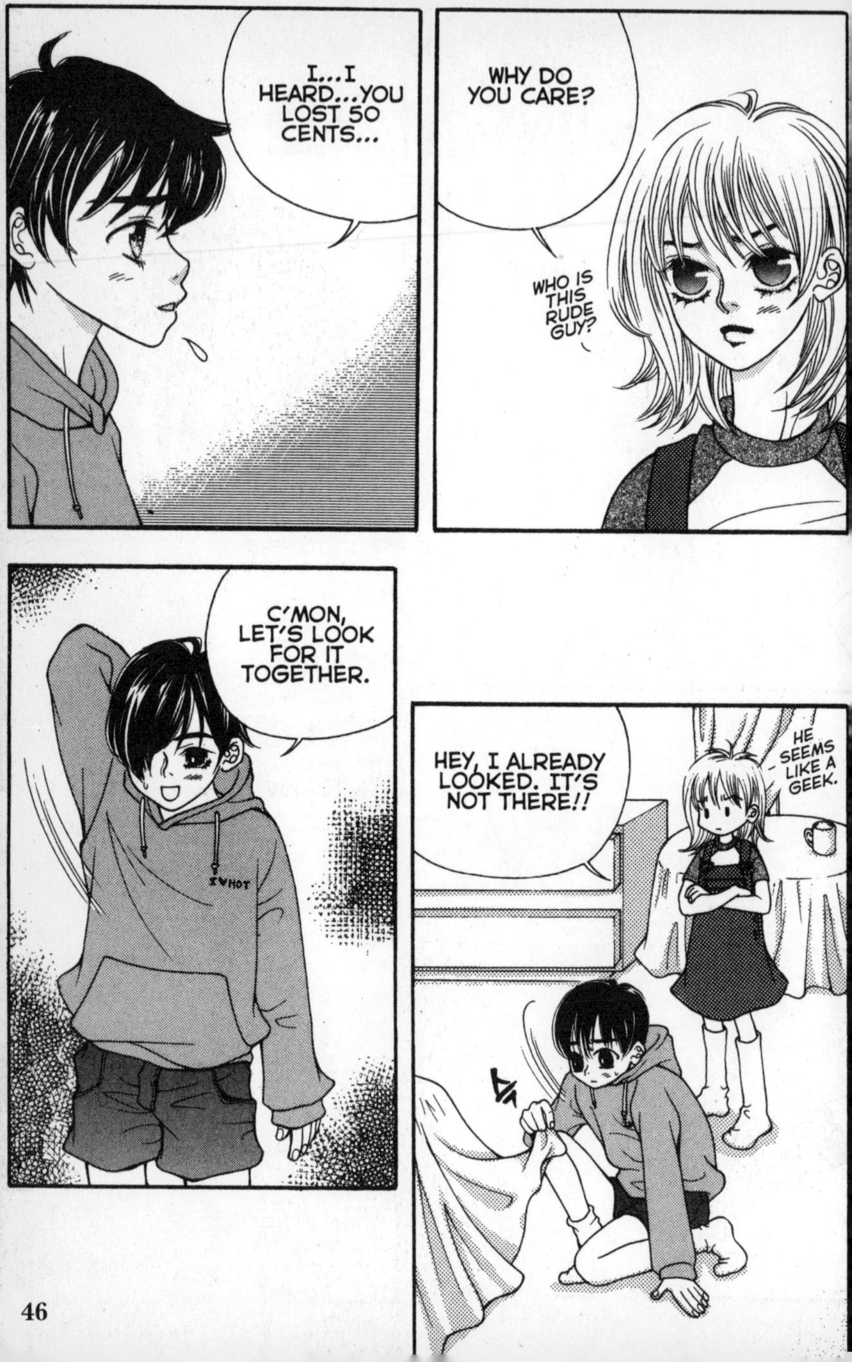
I...I HEARD...YOU LOST 50 CENTS...
WHY DO YOU CARE?
WHO IS THIS RUDE GUY?
C'MON, LET'S LOOK FOR IT TOGETHER.
HEY, I ALREADY LOOKED. IT'S NOT THERE!!
HE SEEMS LIKE A GEEK.

MY GRANDMOTHER THINKS IT'S NO BIG DEAL, BUT IT'S REALLY IMPORTANT TO ME. IT'S MY LUCKY COIN. I REALLY NEED TO FIND IT.

I DON'T KNOW WHAT WAS GOING THROUGH MY MIND, BUT...

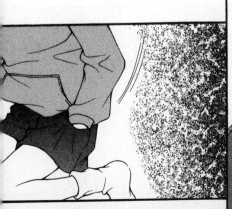

ISN'T, ISN'T THIS IT? I FOUND IT!!

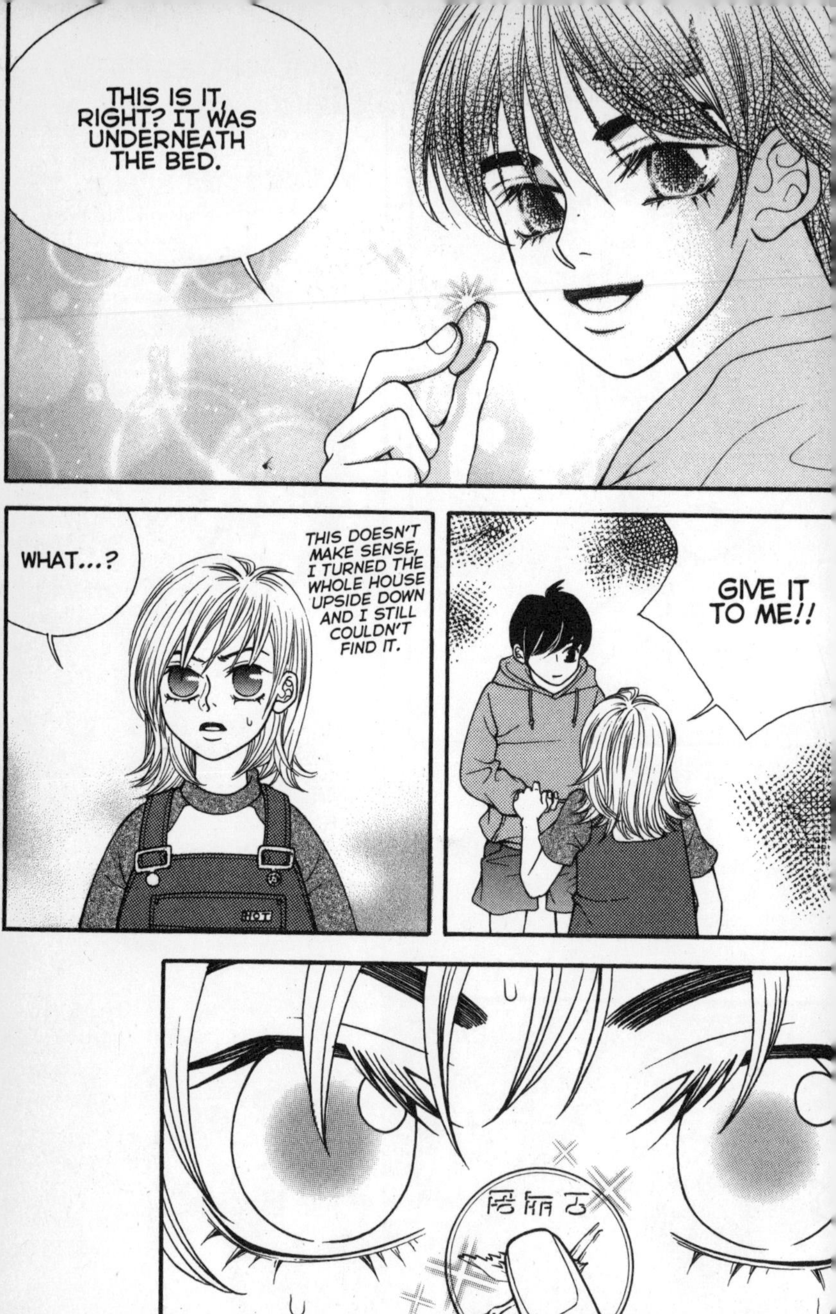
THIS IS IT, RIGHT? IT WAS UNDERNEATH THE BED.
WHAT...?
THIS DOESN'T MAKE SENSE, I TURNED THE WHOLE HOUSE UPSIDE DOWN AND I STILL COULDN'T FIND IT.
GIVE IT TO ME!!

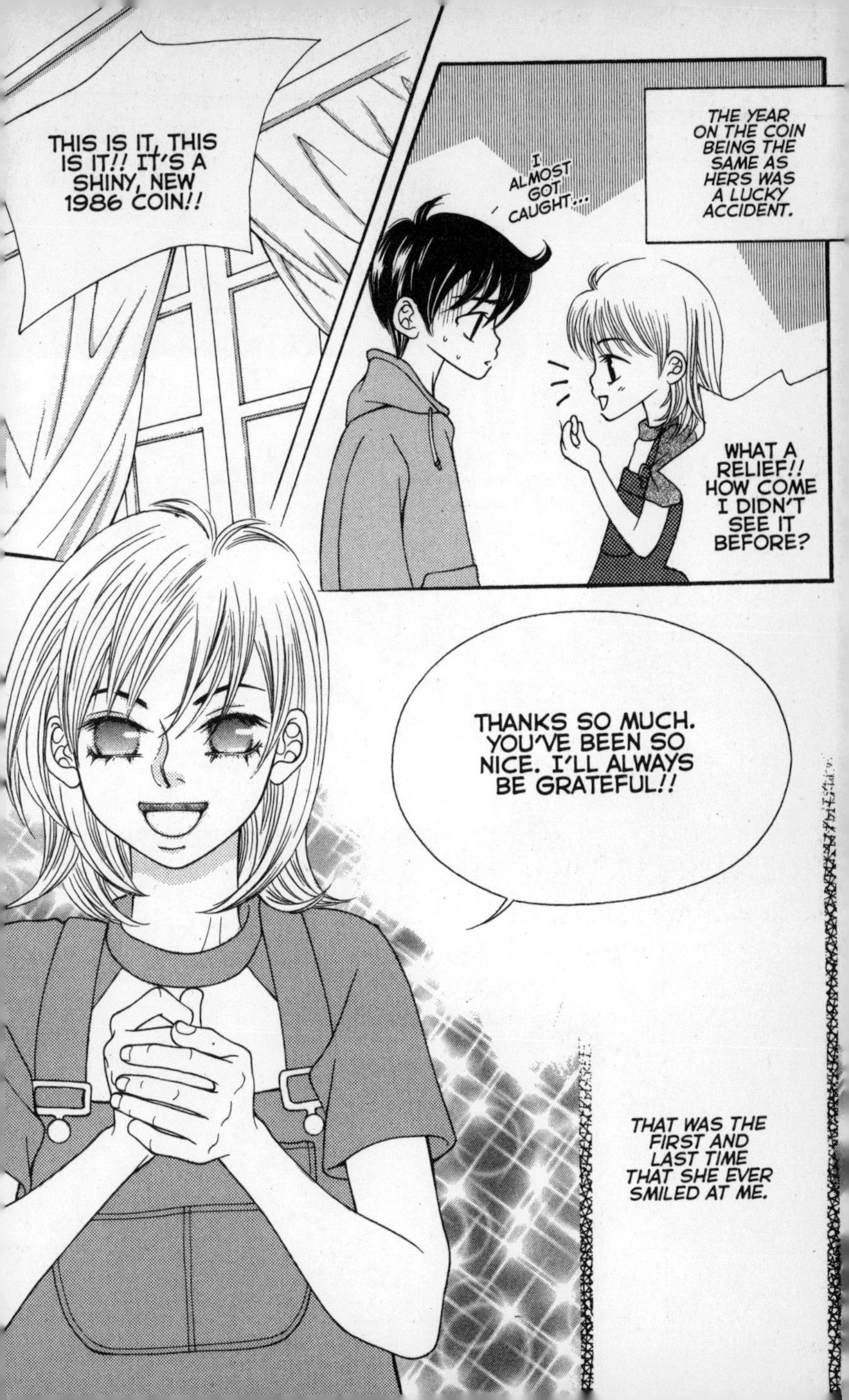
THIS IS IT, THIS IS IT!! IT'S A SHINY, NEW 1986 COIN!!
THE YEAR ON THE COIN BEING THE SAME AS HERS WAS A LUCKY ACCIDENT.
I ALMOST GOT CAUGHT...
WHAT A RELIEF!! HOW COME I DIDN'T SEE IT BEFORE?
THANKS SO MUCH. YOU'VE BEEN SO NICE. I'LL ALWAYS BE GRATEFUL!!
THAT WAS THE FIRST AND LAST TIME THAT SHE EVER SMILED AT ME.

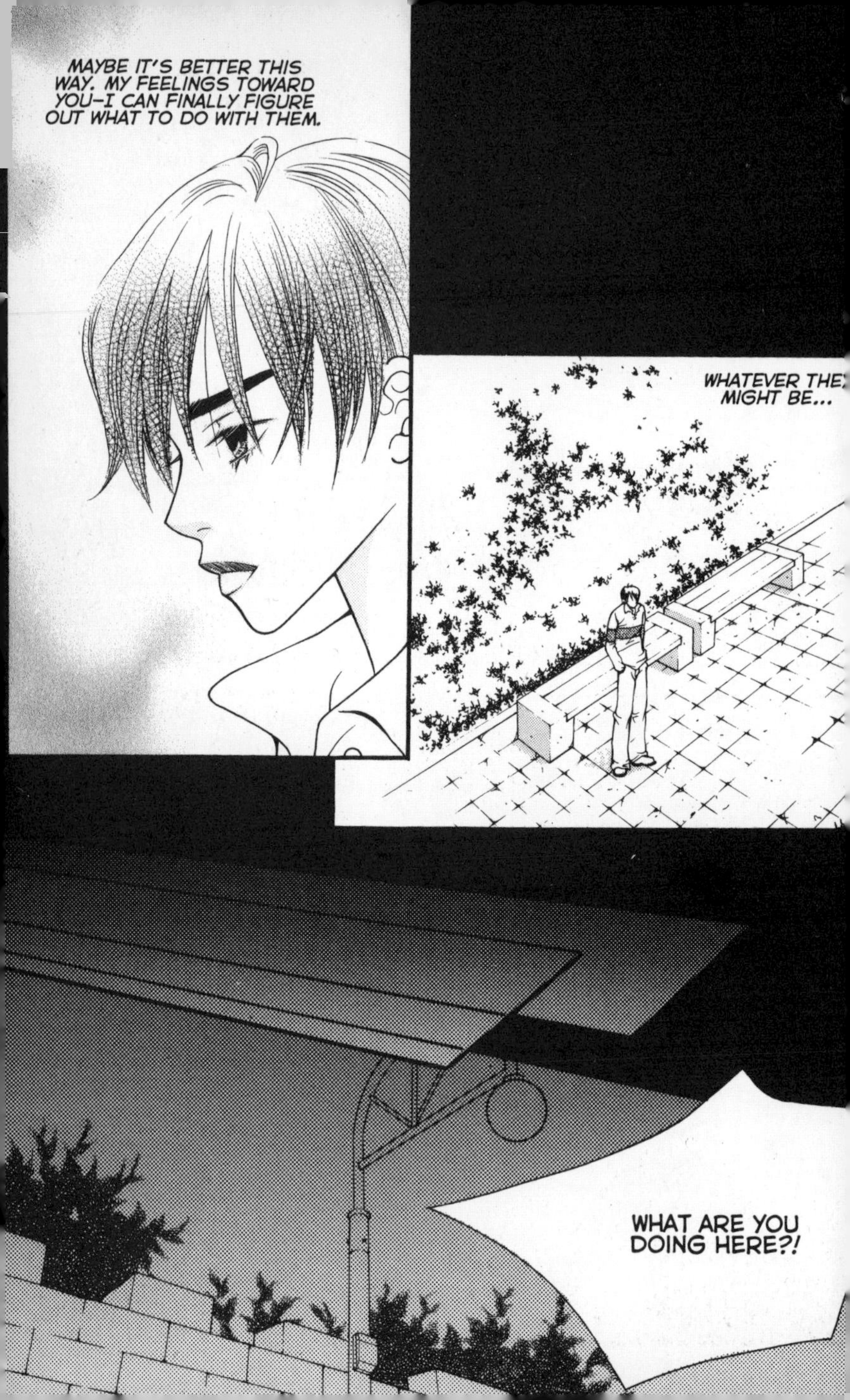
MAYBE IT'S BETTER THIS WAY. MY FEELINGS TOWARD YOU–I CAN FINALLY FIGURE OUT WHAT TO DO WITH THEM.
MIGHT BE...
WHAT ARE YOU DOING HERE?!

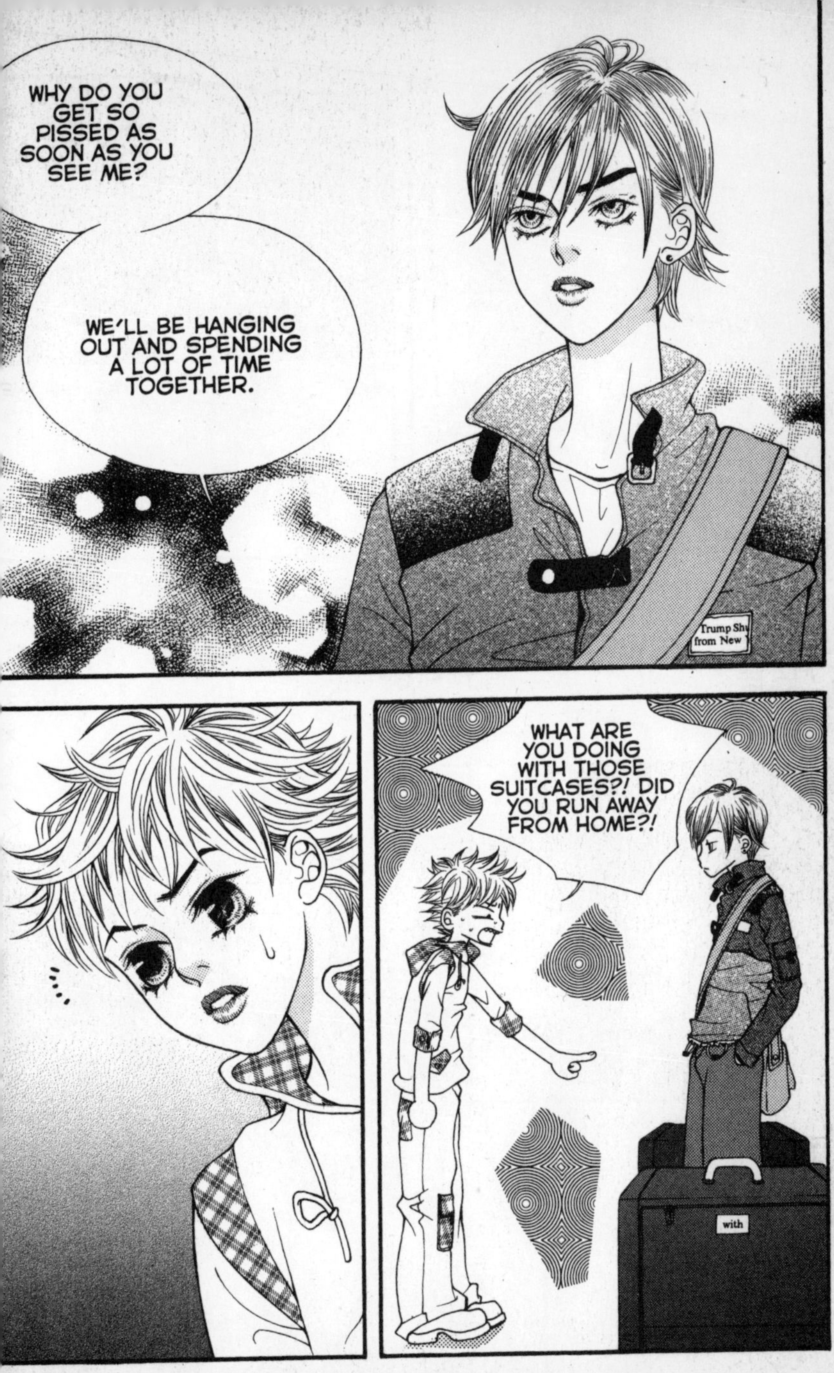
WHY DO YOU GET SO PISSED AS SOON AS YOU SEE ME?
WE'LL BE HANGING OUT AND SPENDING A LOT OF TIME TOGETHER.
Trump Sh from New
...
WHAT ARE YOU DOING WITH THOSE SUITCASES?! DID YOU RUN AWAY FROM HOME?!
with

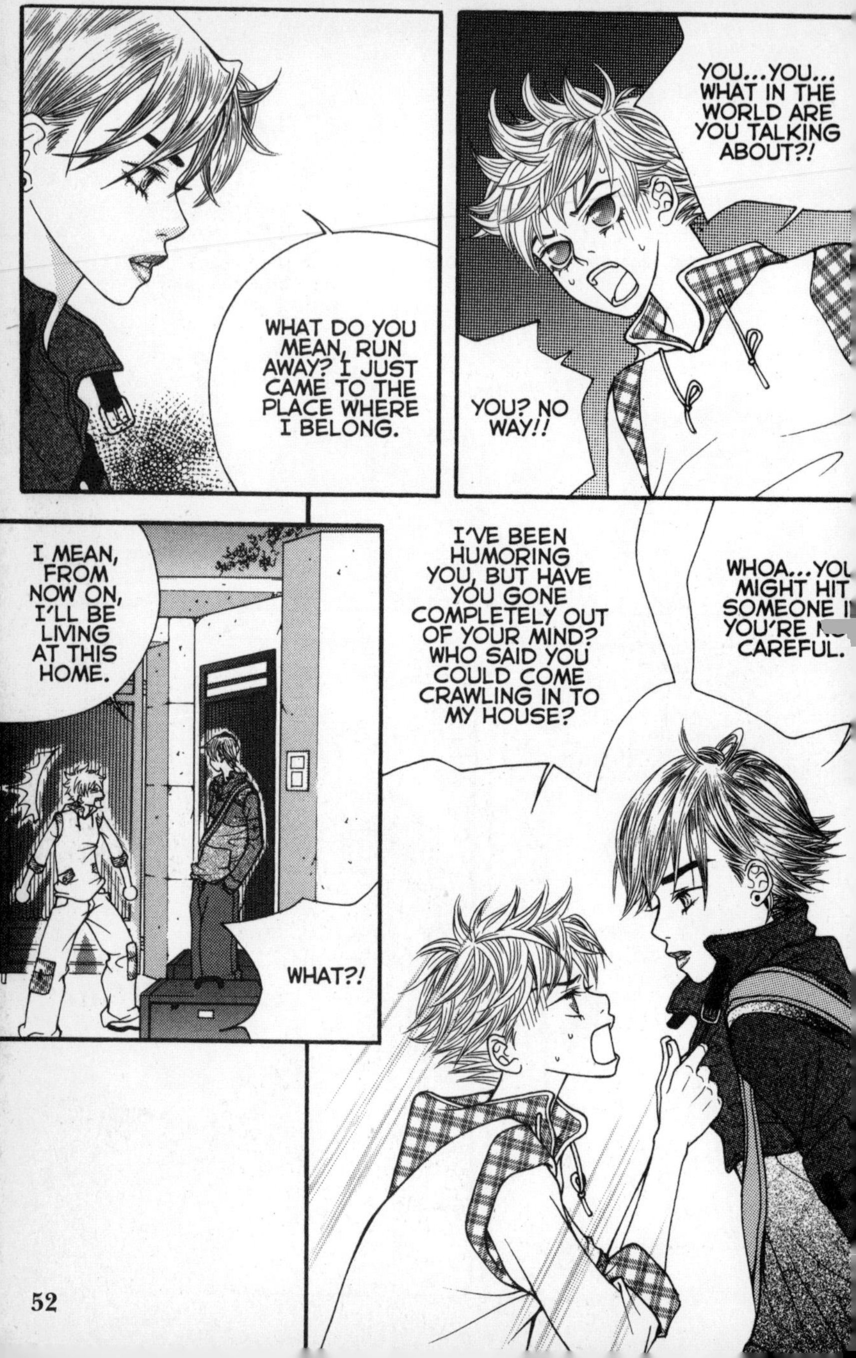
WHAT DO YOU MEAN, RUN AWAY? I JUST CAME TO THE PLACE WHERE I BELONG.
YOU...YOU... WHAT IN THE WORLD ARE YOU TALKING ABOUT?!
YOU? NO WAY!!
I MEAN, FROM NOW ON, I'LL BE LIVING AT THIS HOME.
WHAT?!
I'VE BEEN HUMORING YOU, BUT HAVE YOU GONE COMPLETELY OUT OF YOUR MIND? WHO SAID YOU COULD COME CRAWLING IN TO MY HOUSE?
WHOA...YOU MIGHT HIT SOMEONE I YOU'RE N CAREFUL.

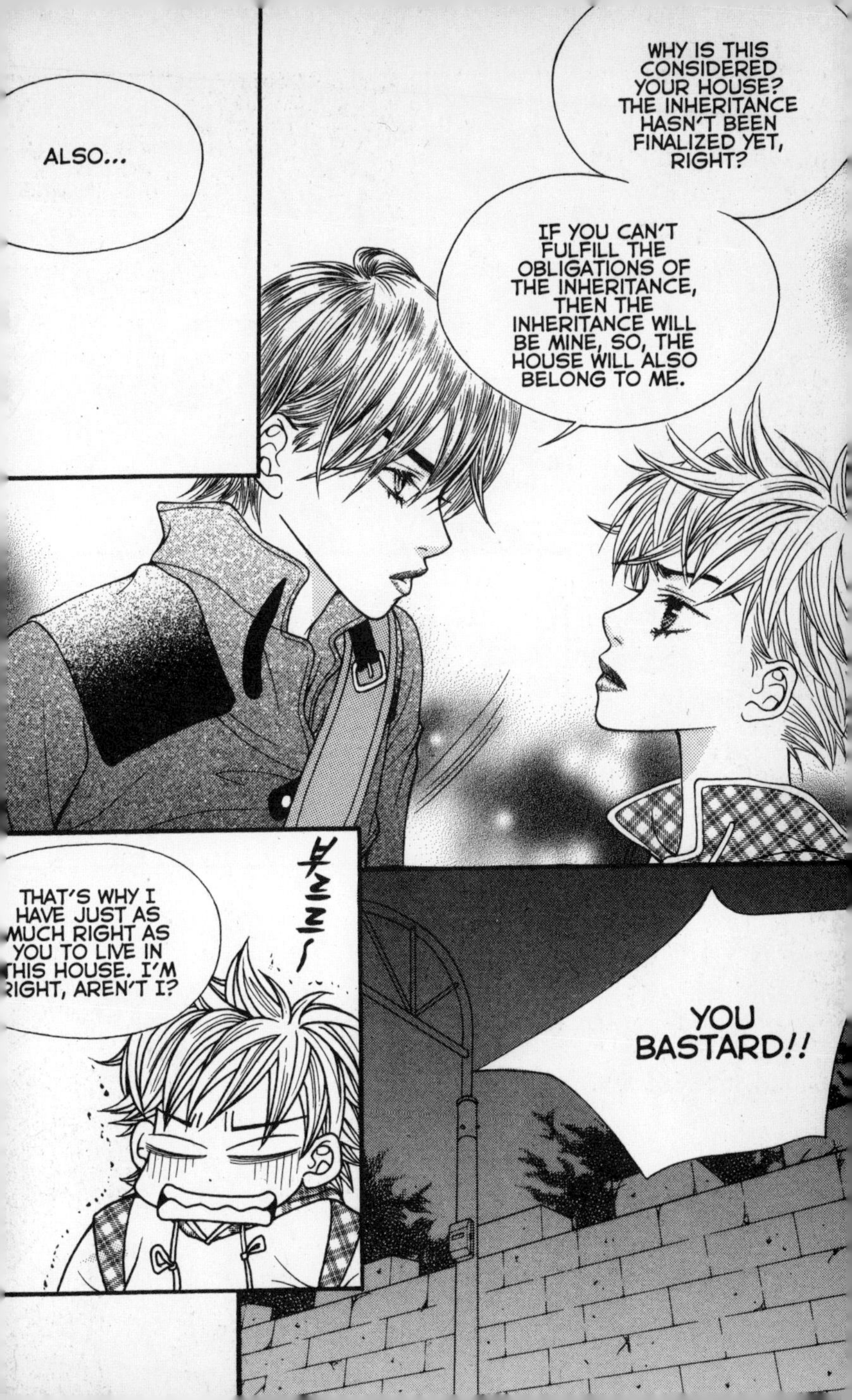
ALSO...
WHY IS THIS CONSIDERED YOUR HOUSE? THE INHERITANCE HASN'T BEEN FINALIZED YET, RIGHT?
IF YOU CAN'T FULFILL THE OBLIGATIONS OF THE INHERITANCE, THEN THE INHERITANCE WILL BE MINE, SO, THE HOUSE WILL ALSO BELONG TO ME.
THAT'S WHY I HAVE JUST AS MUCH RIGHT AS YOU TO LIVE IN THIS HOUSE. I'M RIGHT, AREN'T I?
YOU BASTARD!!

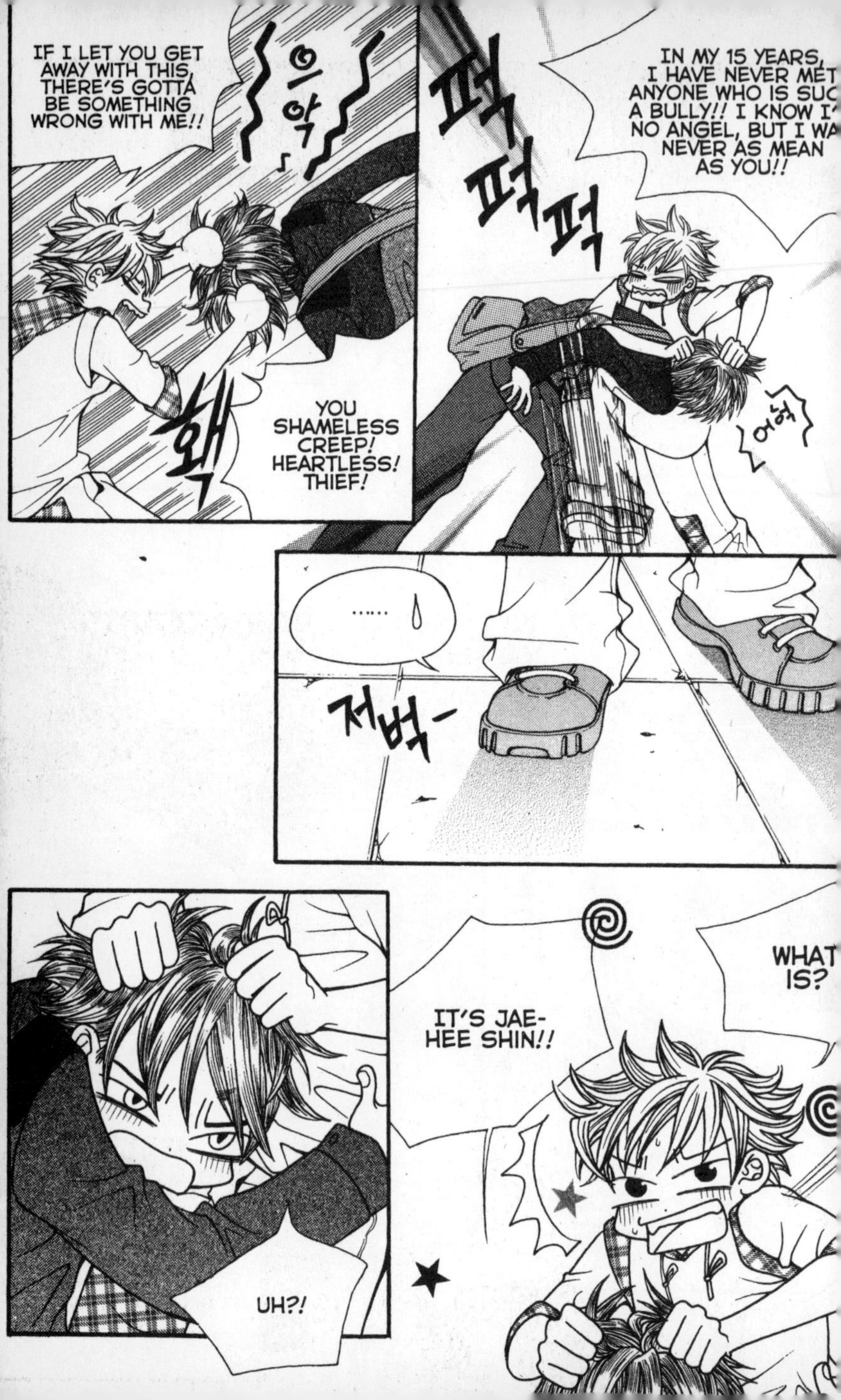

IF I LET YOU GET AWAY WITH THIS, THERE'S GOTTA BE SOMETHING WRONG WITH ME!!
으악
휙
YOU SHAMELESS CREEP! HEARTLESS! THIEF!
퍽 퍽 퍽
IN MY 15 YEARS, I HAVE NEVER MET ANYONE WHO IS SUC A BULLY!! I KNOW I' NO ANGEL, BUT I WA NEVER AS MEAN AS YOU!!
......
저벅-
UH?!
IT'S JAE-HEE SHIN!!
WHAT IS?

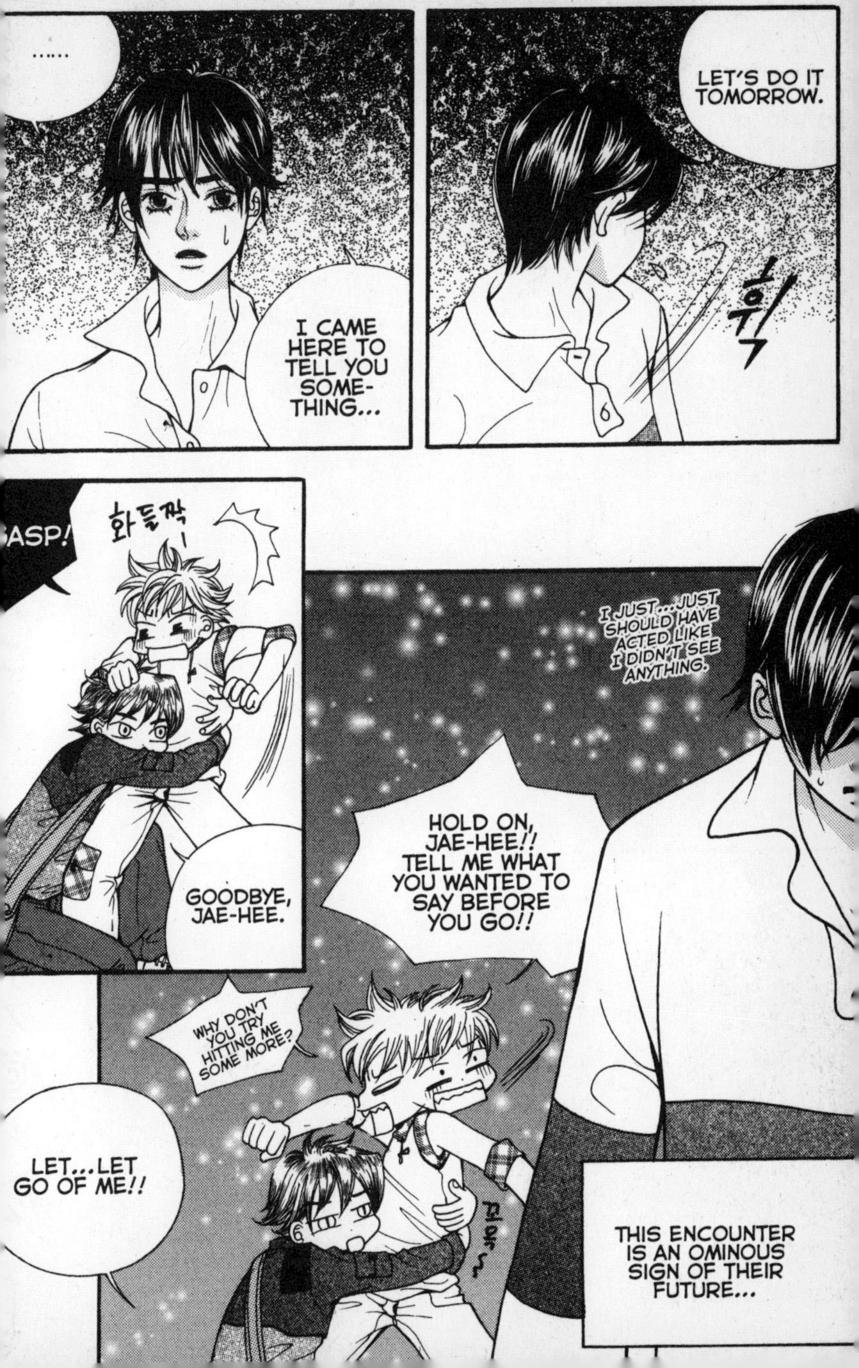
……
I CAME HERE TO TELL YOU SOME-THING...
LET'S DO IT TOMORROW.
휙
ASP!
화들짝
GOODBYE, JAE-HEE.
I JUST...JUST SHOULD HAVE ACTED LIKE I DIDN'T SEE ANYTHING.
HOLD ON, JAE-HEE!! TELL ME WHAT YOU WANTED TO SAY BEFORE YOU GO!!
WHY DON'T YOU TRY HITTING ME SOME MORE?
LET...LET GO OF ME!!
THIS ENCOUNTER IS AN OMINOUS SIGN OF THEIR FUTURE...

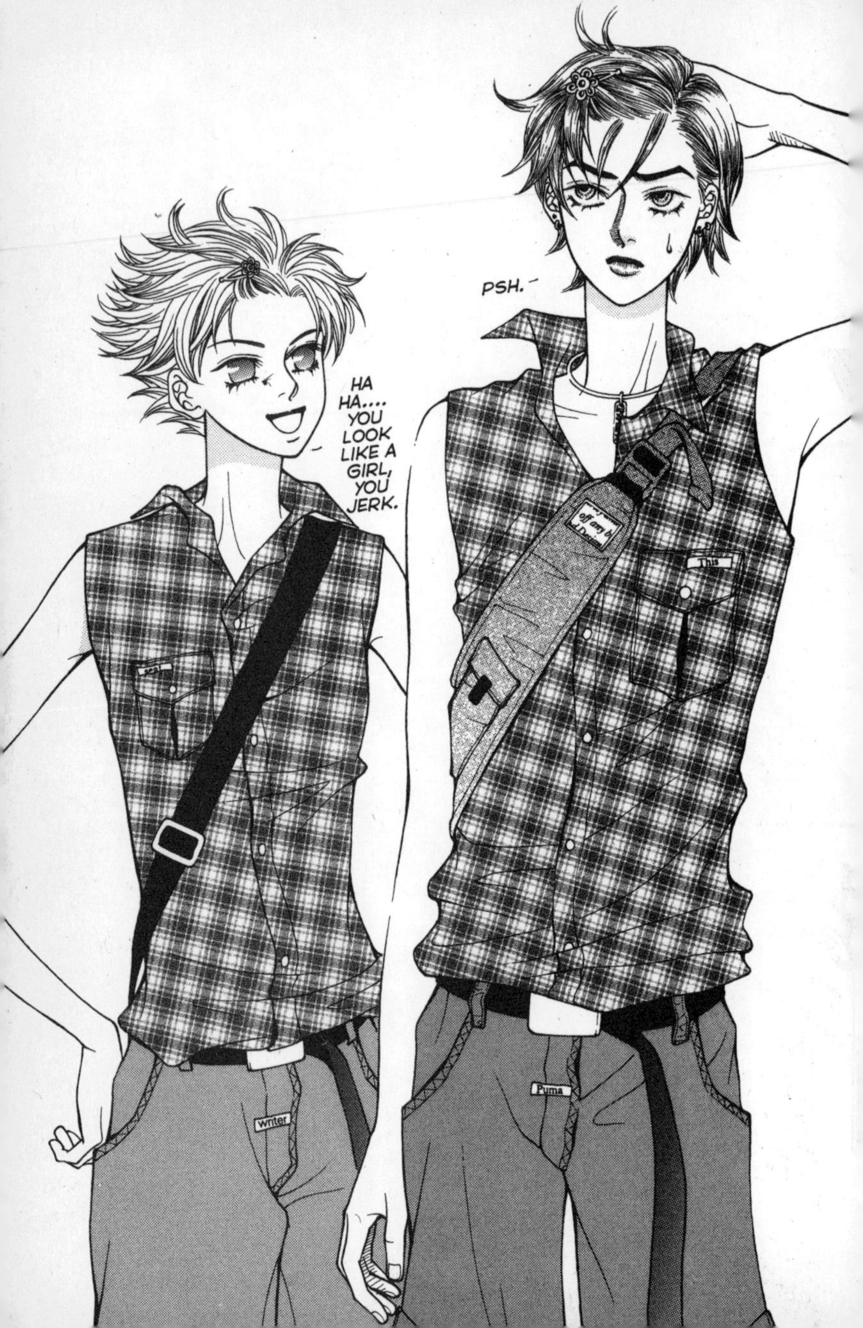
HA HA.... YOU LOOK LIKE A GIRL, YOU JERK.
PSH.

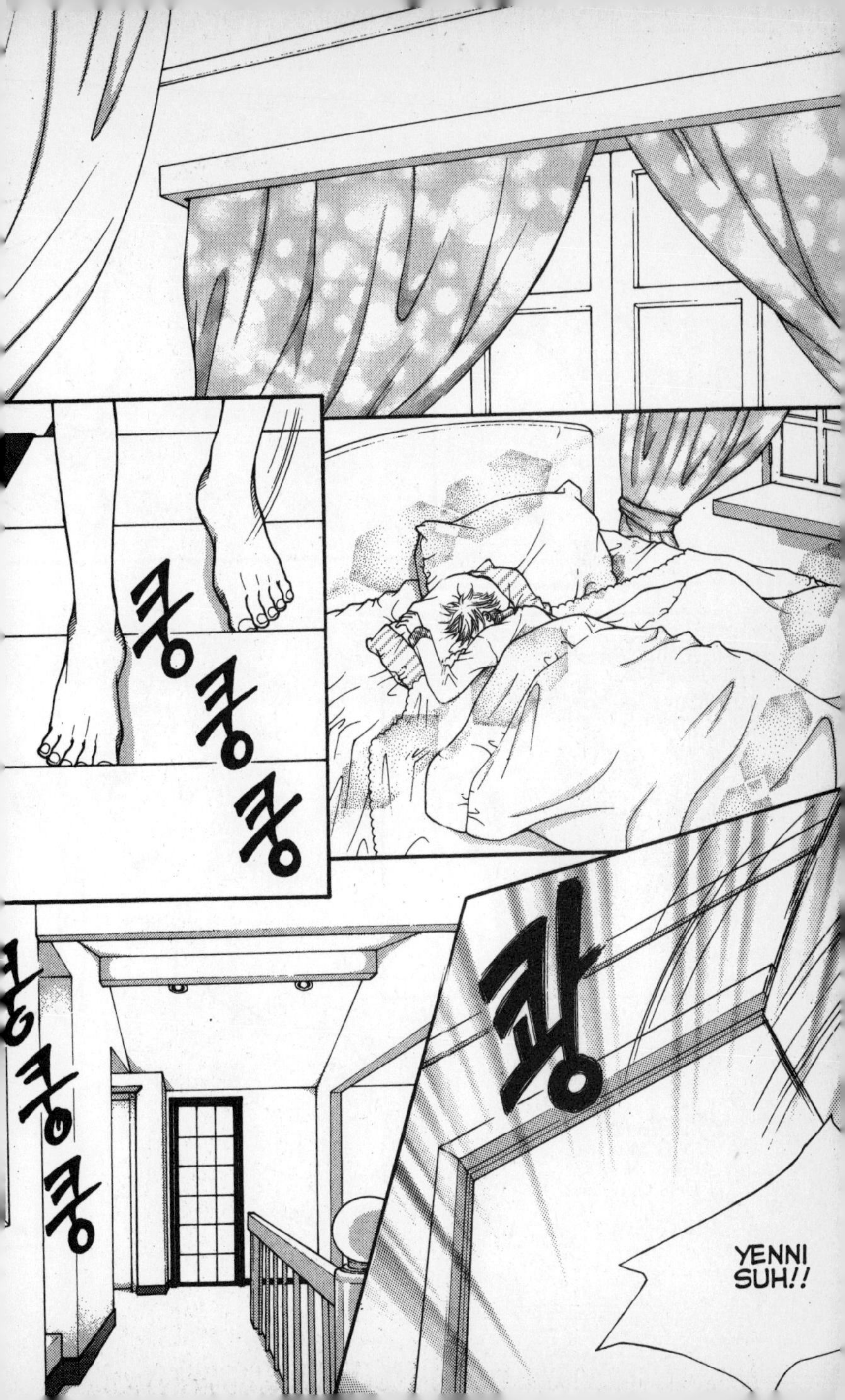
쿵
쿵
쿵
쿵
쿵
쿵
쾅
YENNI SUH!!

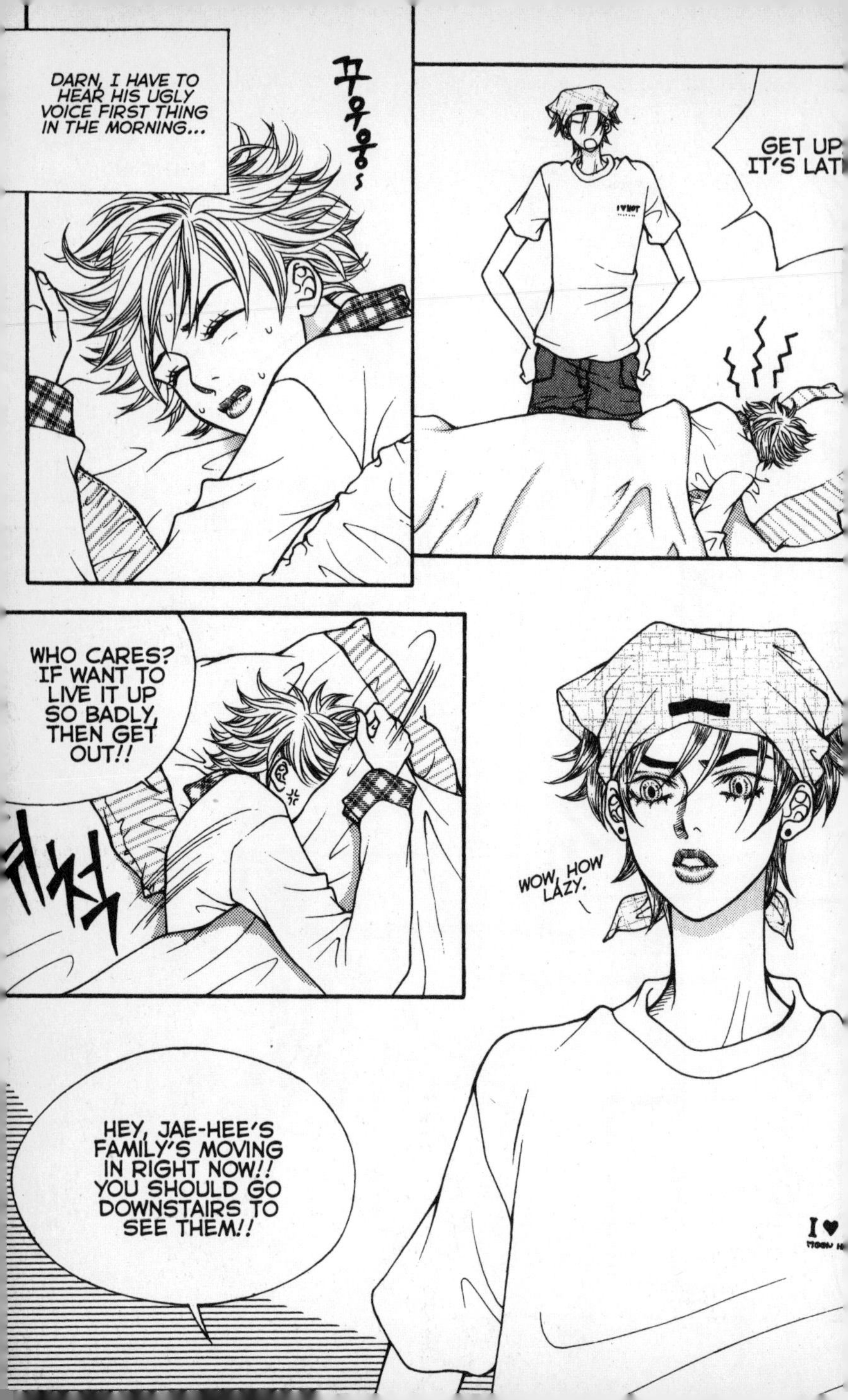
DARN, I HAVE TO HEAR HIS UGLY VOICE FIRST THING IN THE MORNING...
꾸우웅~
GET UP IT'S LAT
WHO CARES? IF WANT TO LIVE IT UP SO BADLY, THEN GET OUT!!
WOW, HOW LAZY.
HEY, JAE-HEE'S FAMILY'S MOVING IN RIGHT NOW!! YOU SHOULD GO DOWNSTAIRS TO SEE THEM!!

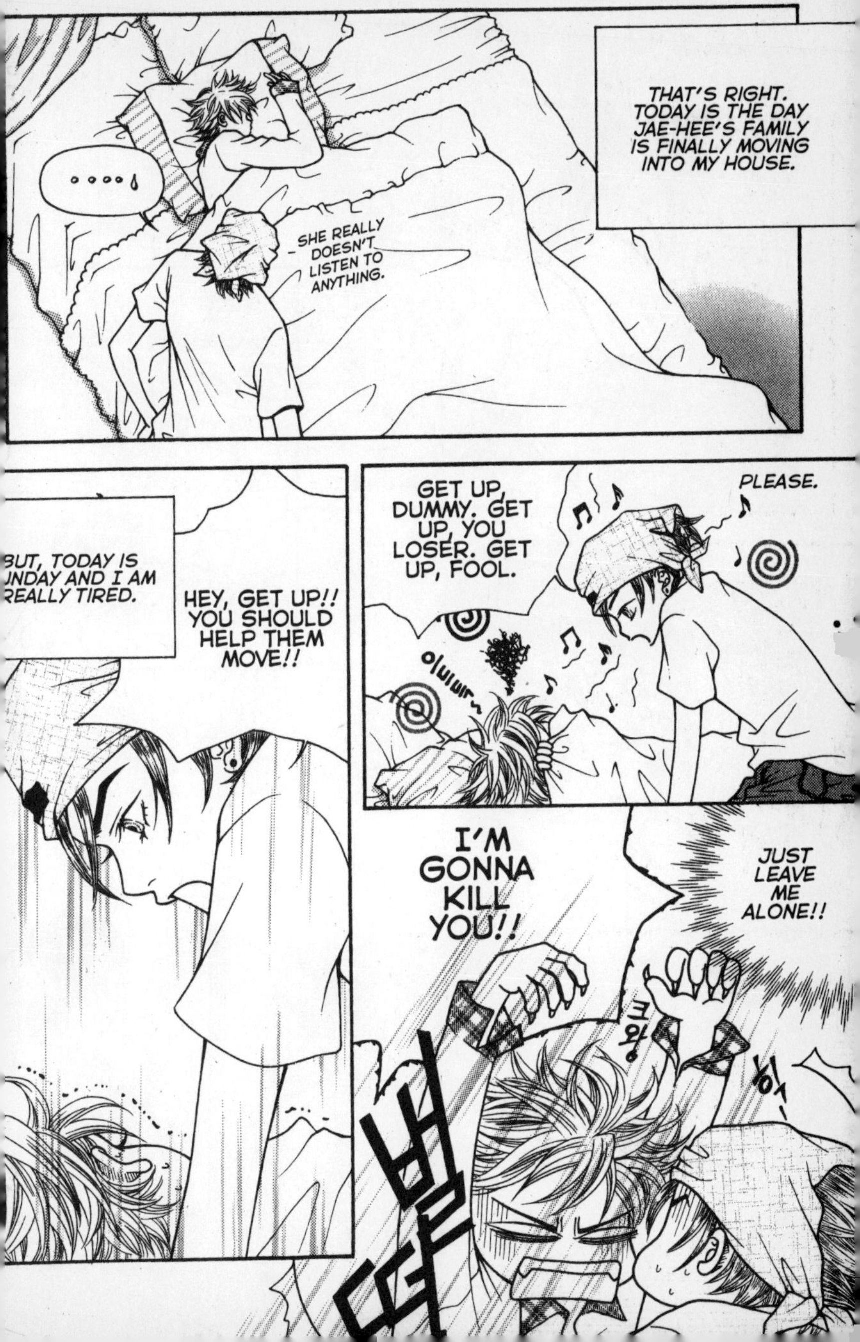
....
THAT'S RIGHT. TODAY IS THE DAY JAE-HEE'S FAMILY IS FINALLY MOVING INTO MY HOUSE.
SHE REALLY DOESN'T LISTEN TO ANYTHING.
BUT, TODAY IS UNDAY AND I AM REALLY TIRED.
HEY, GET UP!! YOU SHOULD HELP THEM MOVE!!
GET UP, DUMMY. GET UP, YOU LOSER. GET UP, FOOL.
PLEASE.
I'M GONNA KILL YOU!!
JUST LEAVE ME ALONE!!
크앙
벌떡

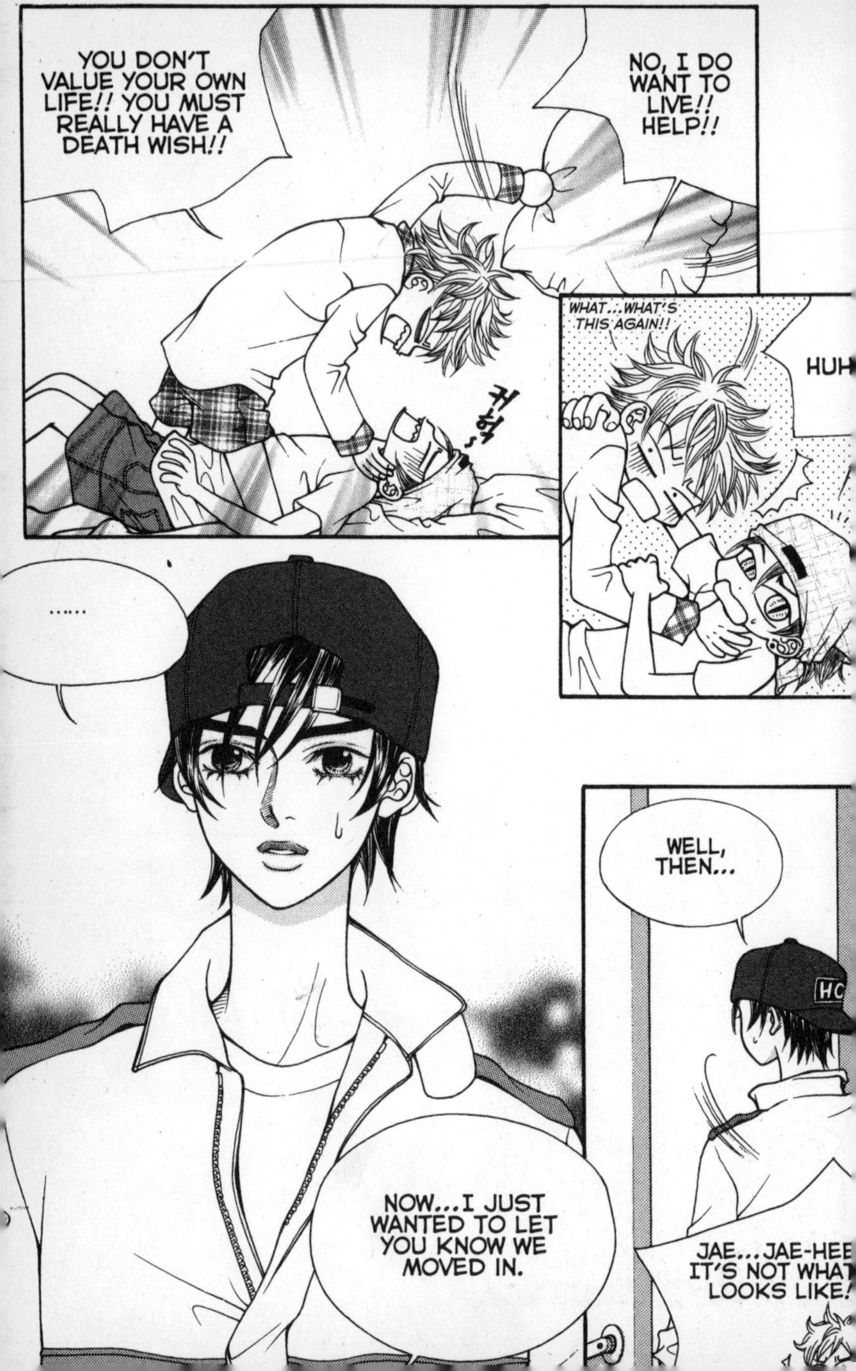
YOU DON'T VALUE YOUR OWN LIFE!! YOU MUST REALLY HAVE A DEATH WISH!!
NO, I DO WANT TO LIVE!! HELP!!
WHAT...WHAT'S THIS AGAIN!!
HUH
......
NOW...I JUST WANTED TO LET YOU KNOW WE MOVED IN.
WELL, THEN...
JAE...JAE-HEE IT'S NOT WHAT LOOKS LIKE!

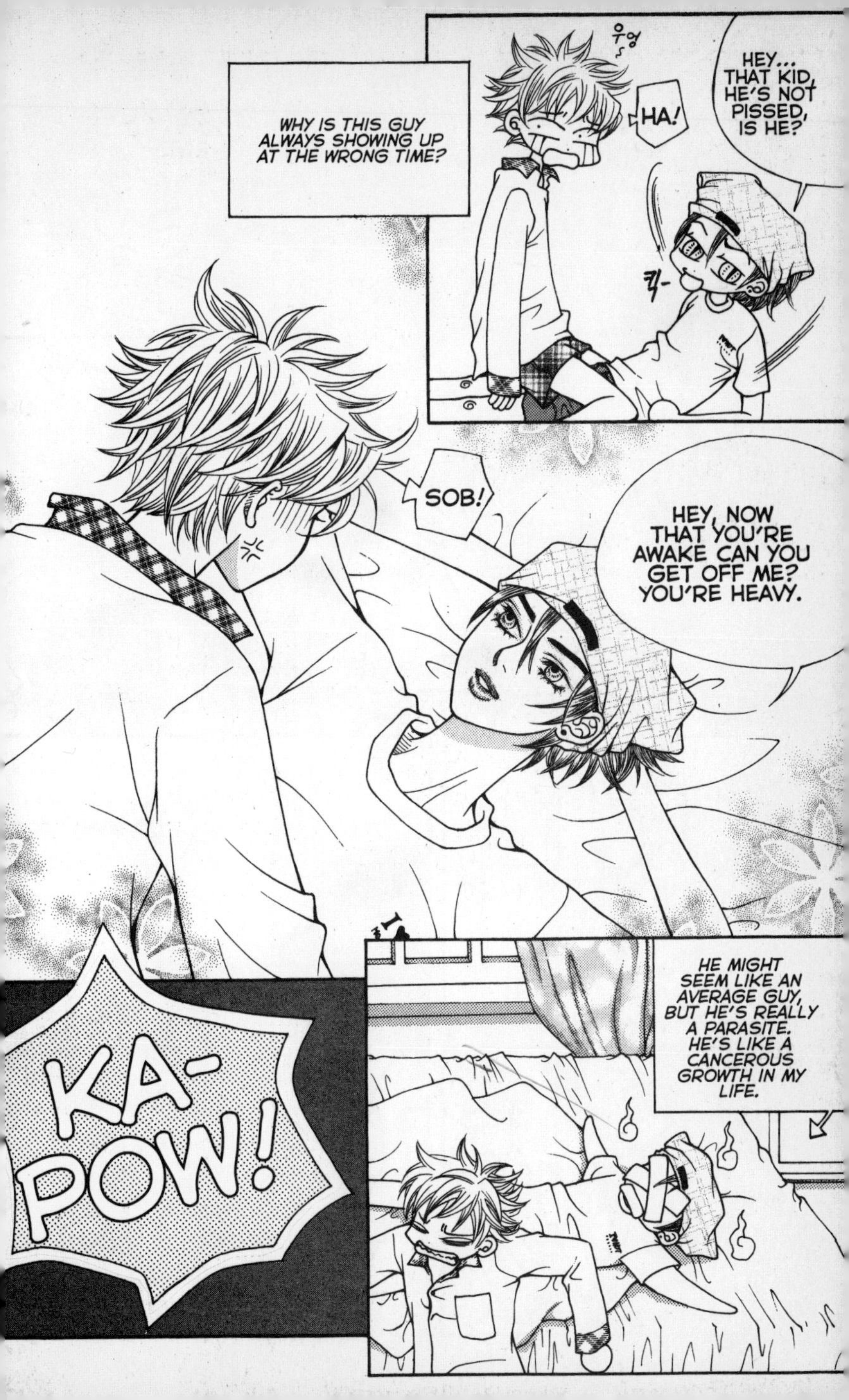
WHY IS THIS GUY ALWAYS SHOWING UP AT THE WRONG TIME?
우엉~
HA!
HEY... THAT KID, HE'S NOT PISSED, IS HE?
킥-
SOB!
HEY, NOW THAT YOU'RE AWAKE CAN YOU GET OFF ME? YOU'RE HEAVY.
KA-POW!
HE MIGHT SEEM LIKE AN AVERAGE GUY, BUT HE'S REALLY A PARASITE. HE'S LIKE A CANCEROUS GROWTH IN MY LIFE.

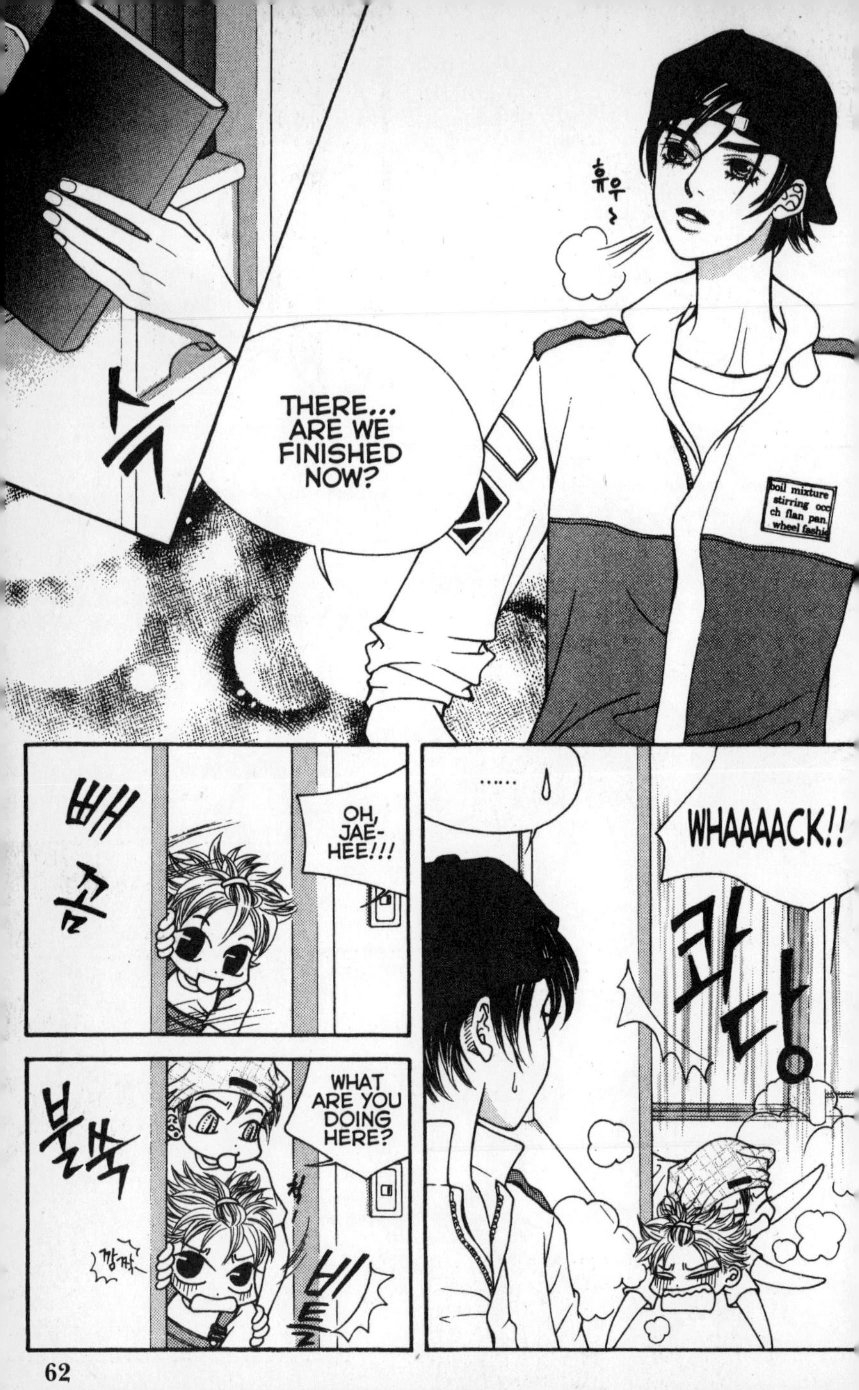

휴우~
THERE... ARE WE FINISHED NOW?
빼꼼
OH, JAE-HEE!!!
불쑥
WHAT ARE YOU DOING HERE?
......
WHAAAACK!!
콰당!

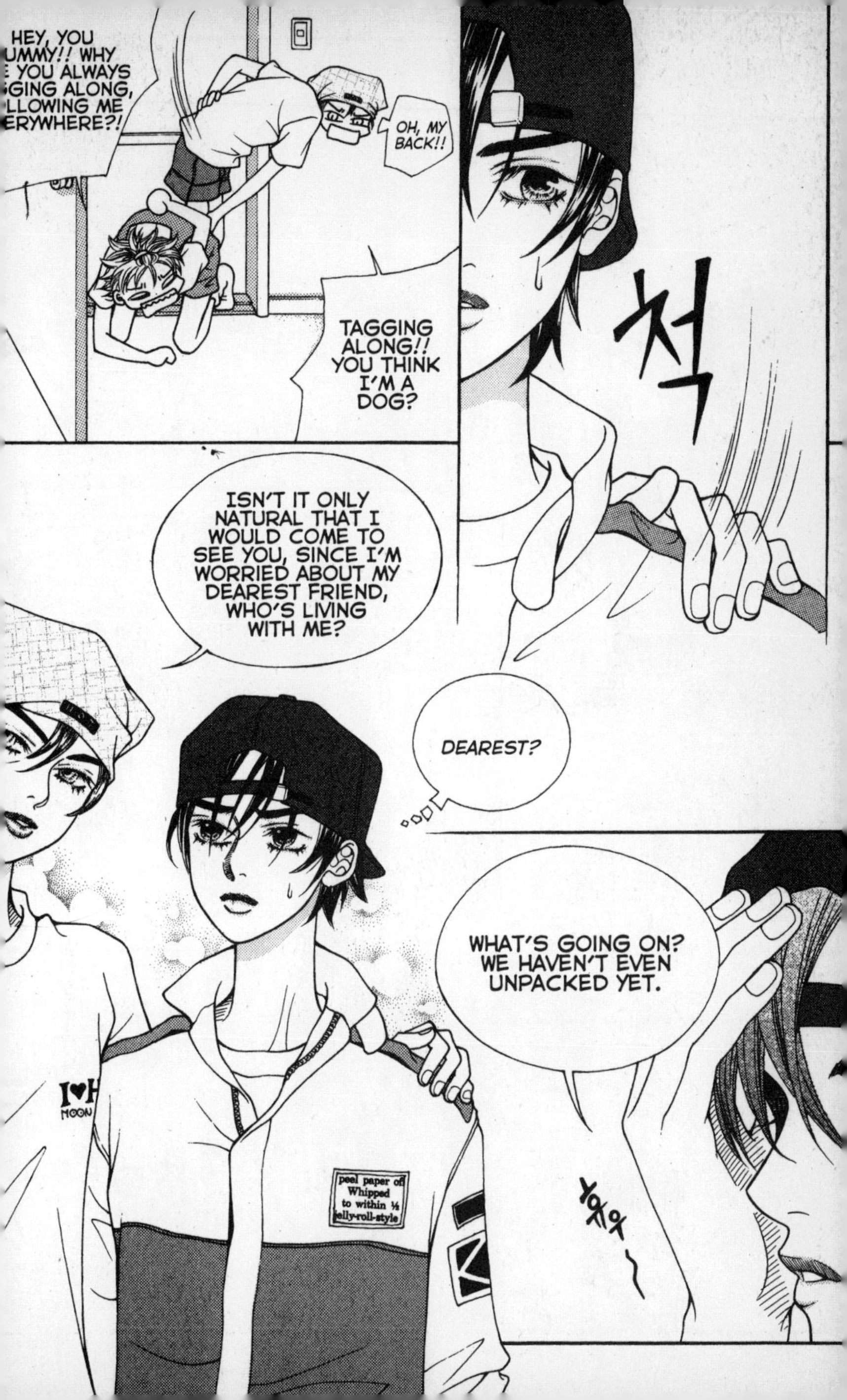
HEY, YOU UMMY!! WHY E YOU ALWAYS GGING ALONG, LLOWING ME ERYWHERE?!
OH, MY BACK!!
TAGGING ALONG!! YOU THINK I'M A DOG?
척
ISN'T IT ONLY NATURAL THAT I WOULD COME TO SEE YOU, SINCE I'M WORRIED ABOUT MY DEAREST FRIEND, WHO'S LIVING WITH ME?
DEAREST?
I♥H MOON
peel paper off Whipped to within ½ jelly-roll-style
WHAT'S GOING ON? WE HAVEN'T EVEN UNPACKED YET.

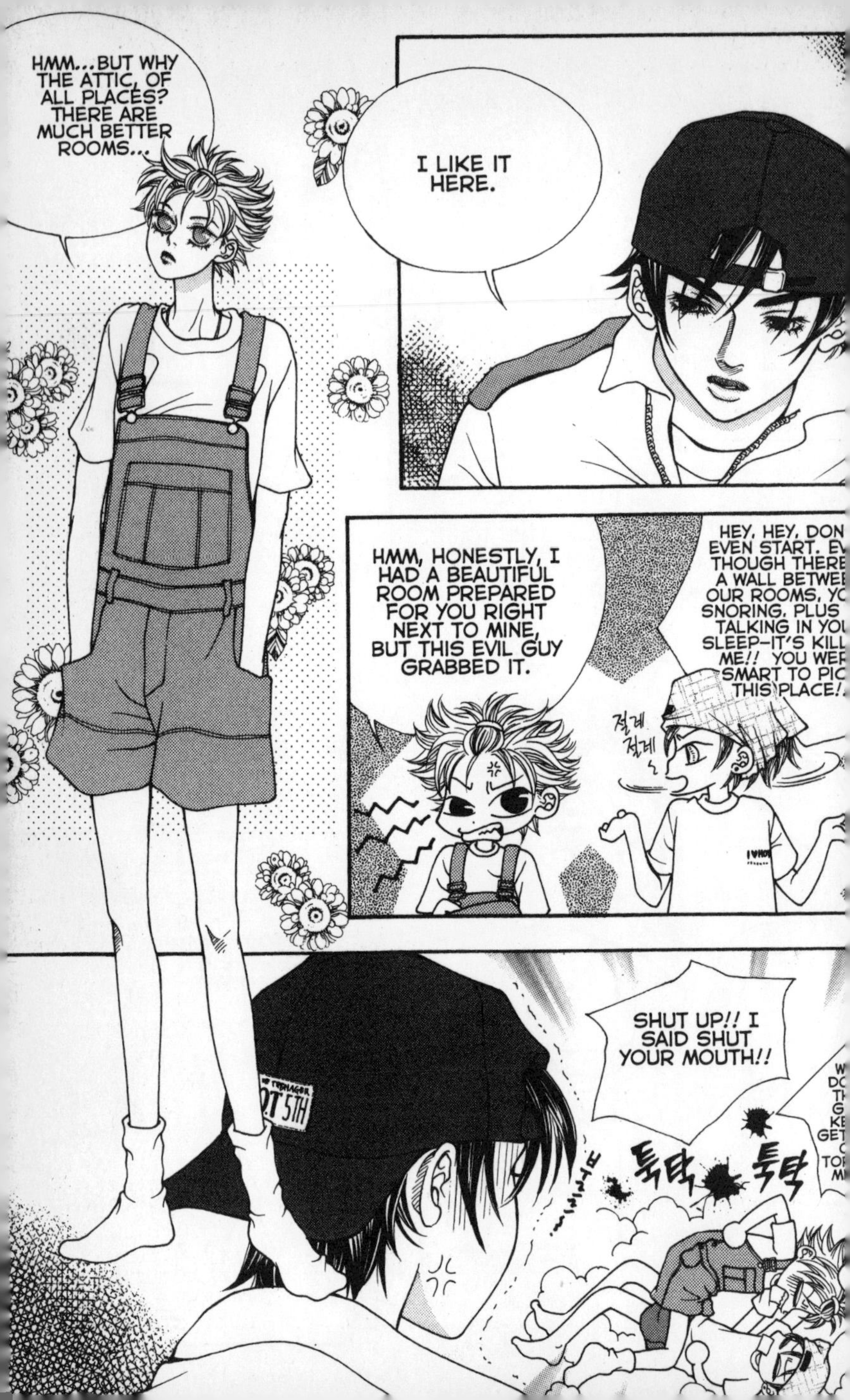
HMM...BUT WHY THE ATTIC, OF ALL PLACES? THERE ARE MUCH BETTER ROOMS...
I LIKE IT HERE.
HMM, HONESTLY, I HAD A BEAUTIFUL ROOM PREPARED FOR YOU RIGHT NEXT TO MINE, BUT THIS EVIL GUY GRABBED IT.
HEY, HEY, DON EVEN START. EV THOUGH THERE A WALL BETWE OUR ROOMS, YO SNORING. PLUS TALKING IN YOU SLEEP–IT'S KILL ME!! YOU WER SMART TO PIC THIS PLACE!
절레 절레
SHUT UP!! I SAID SHUT YOUR MOUTH!!
툭탁 툭탁

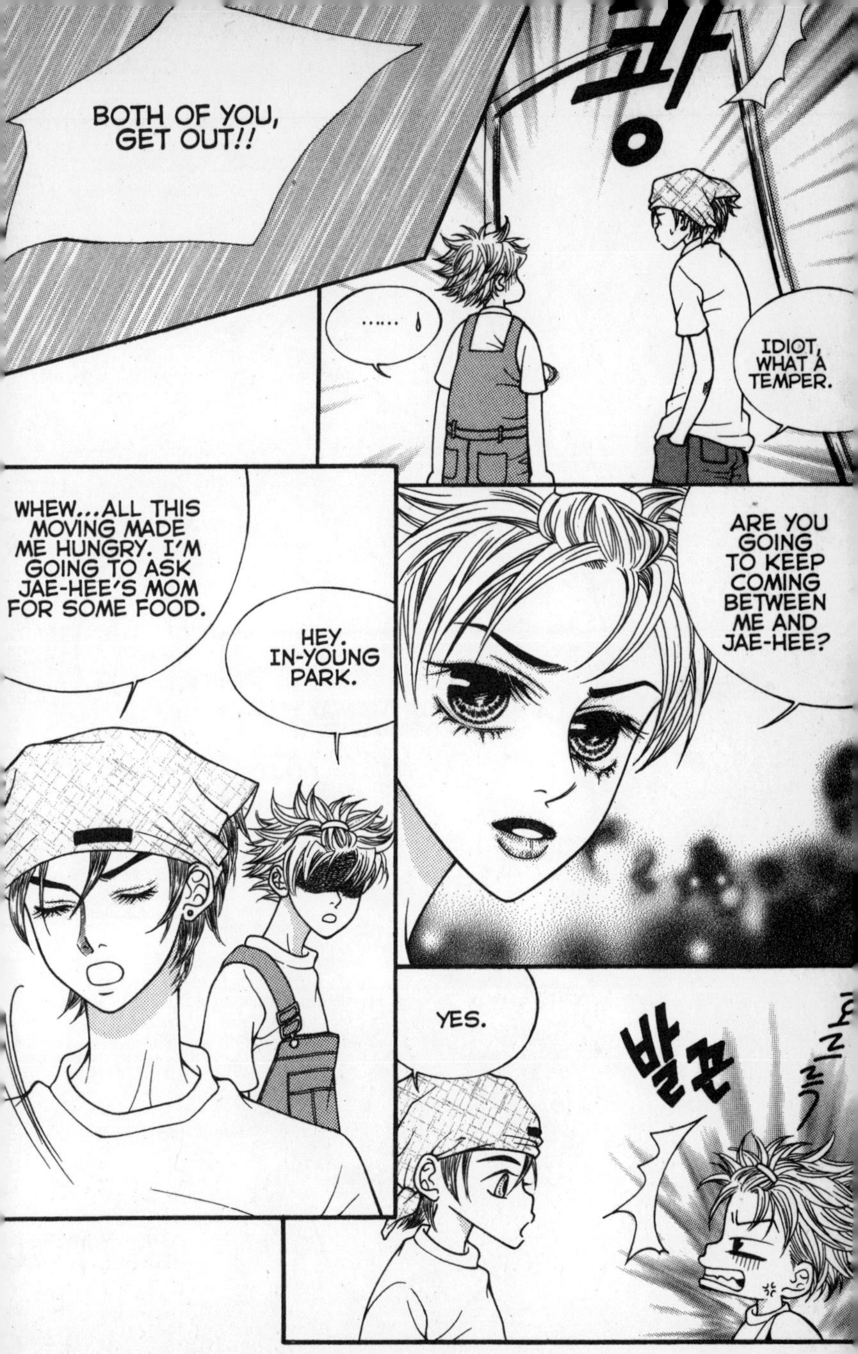
BOTH OF YOU, GET OUT!!
쾅
......
IDIOT, WHAT A TEMPER.
WHEW...ALL THIS MOVING MADE ME HUNGRY. I'M GOING TO ASK JAE-HEE'S MOM FOR SOME FOOD.
HEY. IN-YOUNG PARK.
ARE YOU GOING TO KEEP COMING BETWEEN ME AND JAE-HEE?
YES.
발끈

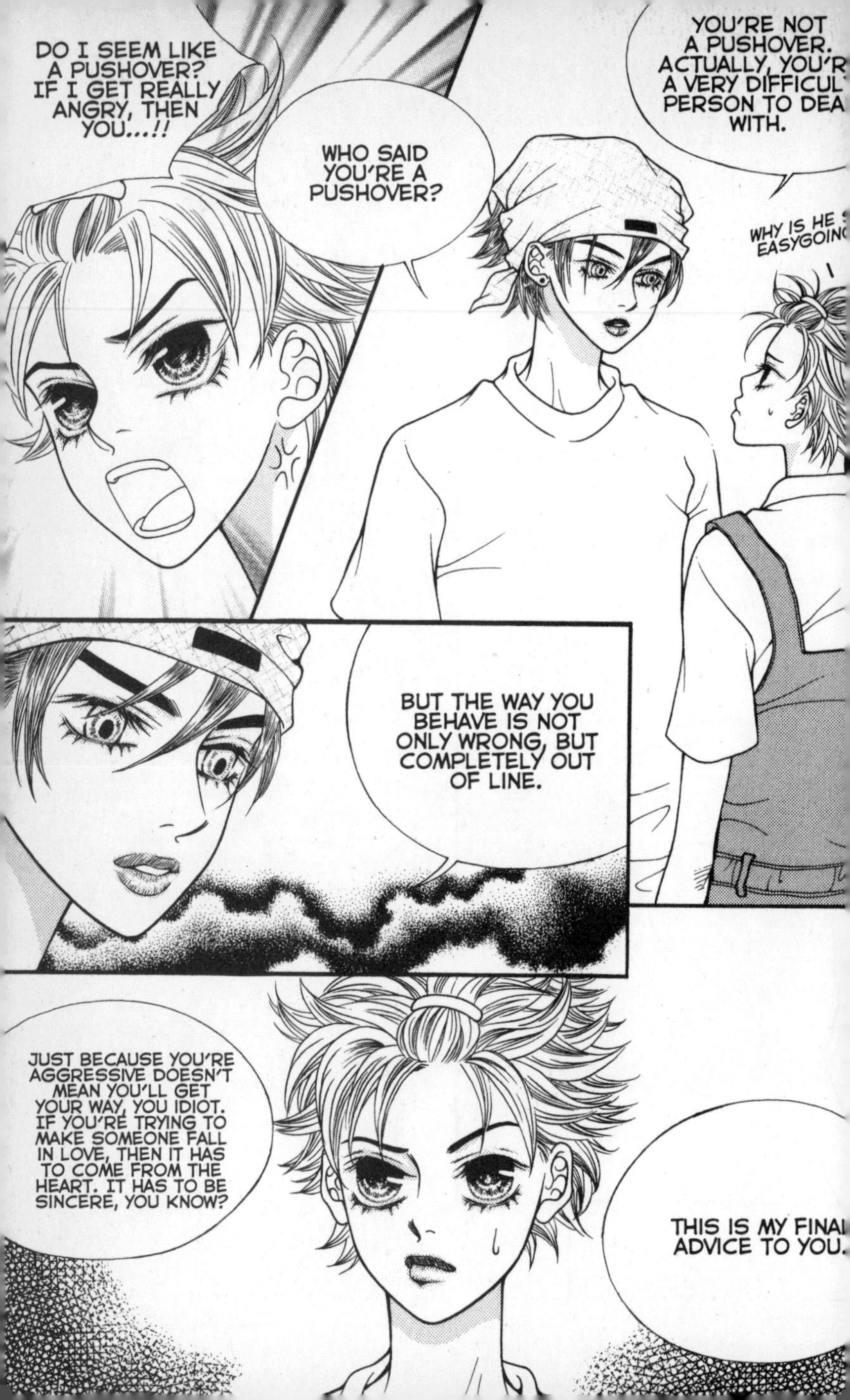
DO I SEEM LIKE A PUSHOVER? IF I GET REALLY ANGRY, THEN YOU...!!
WHO SAID YOU'RE A PUSHOVER?
YOU'RE NOT A PUSHOVER. ACTUALLY, YOU'R A VERY DIFFICUL PERSON TO DEA WITH.
WHY IS HE S EASYGOIN
BUT THE WAY YOU BEHAVE IS NOT ONLY WRONG, BUT COMPLETELY OUT OF LINE.
JUST BECAUSE YOU'RE AGGRESSIVE DOESN'T MEAN YOU'LL GET YOUR WAY, YOU IDIOT. IF YOU'RE TRYING TO MAKE SOMEONE FALL IN LOVE, THEN IT HAS TO COME FROM THE HEART. IT HAS TO BE SINCERE, YOU KNOW?
THIS IS MY FINA ADVICE TO YOU.

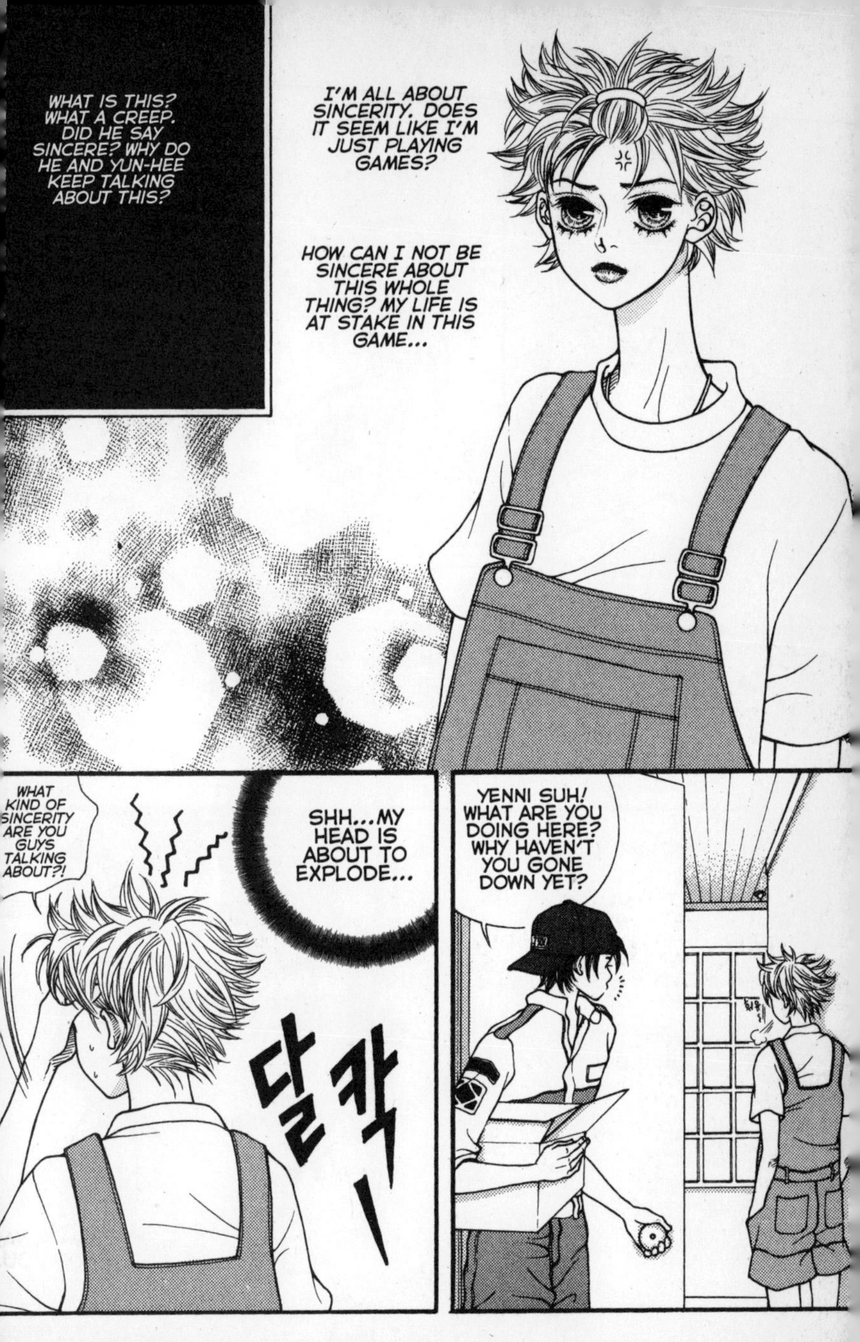
WHAT IS THIS? WHAT A CREEP. DID HE SAY SINCERE? WHY DO HE AND YUN-HEE KEEP TALKING ABOUT THIS?
I'M ALL ABOUT SINCERITY. DOES IT SEEM LIKE I'M JUST PLAYING GAMES?
HOW CAN I NOT BE SINCERE ABOUT THIS WHOLE THING? MY LIFE IS AT STAKE IN THIS GAME...
WHAT KIND OF SINCERITY ARE YOU GUYS TALKING ABOUT?!
SHH...MY HEAD IS ABOUT TO EXPLODE...
달칵
YENNI SUH! WHAT ARE YOU DOING HERE? WHY HAVEN'T YOU GONE DOWN YET?

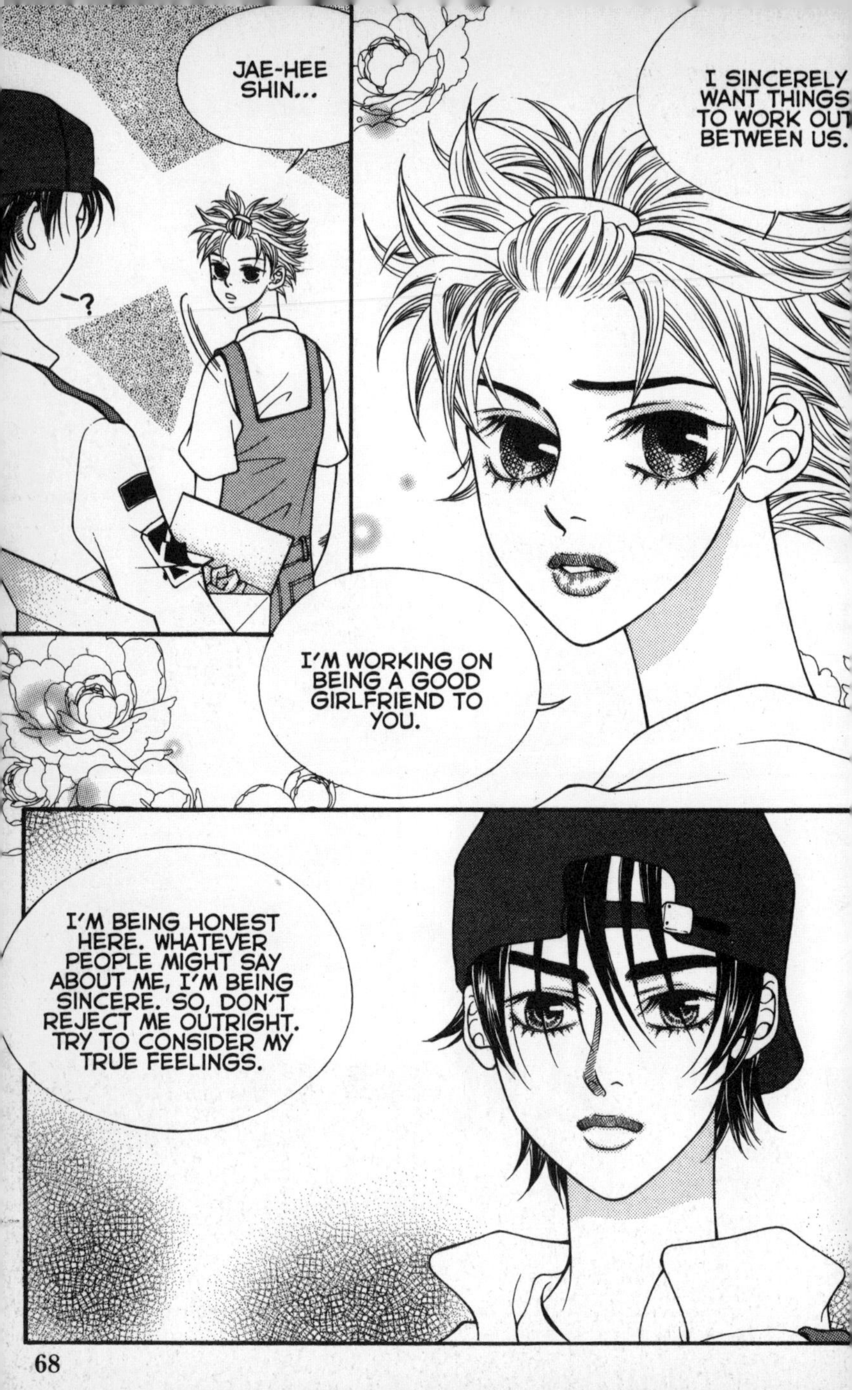

JAE-HEE SHIN...
?
I SINCERELY WANT THINGS TO WORK OUT BETWEEN US.
I'M WORKING ON BEING A GOOD GIRLFRIEND TO YOU.
I'M BEING HONEST HERE. WHATEVER PEOPLE MIGHT SAY ABOUT ME, I'M BEING SINCERE. SO, DON'T REJECT ME OUTRIGHT. TRY TO CONSIDER MY TRUE FEELINGS.

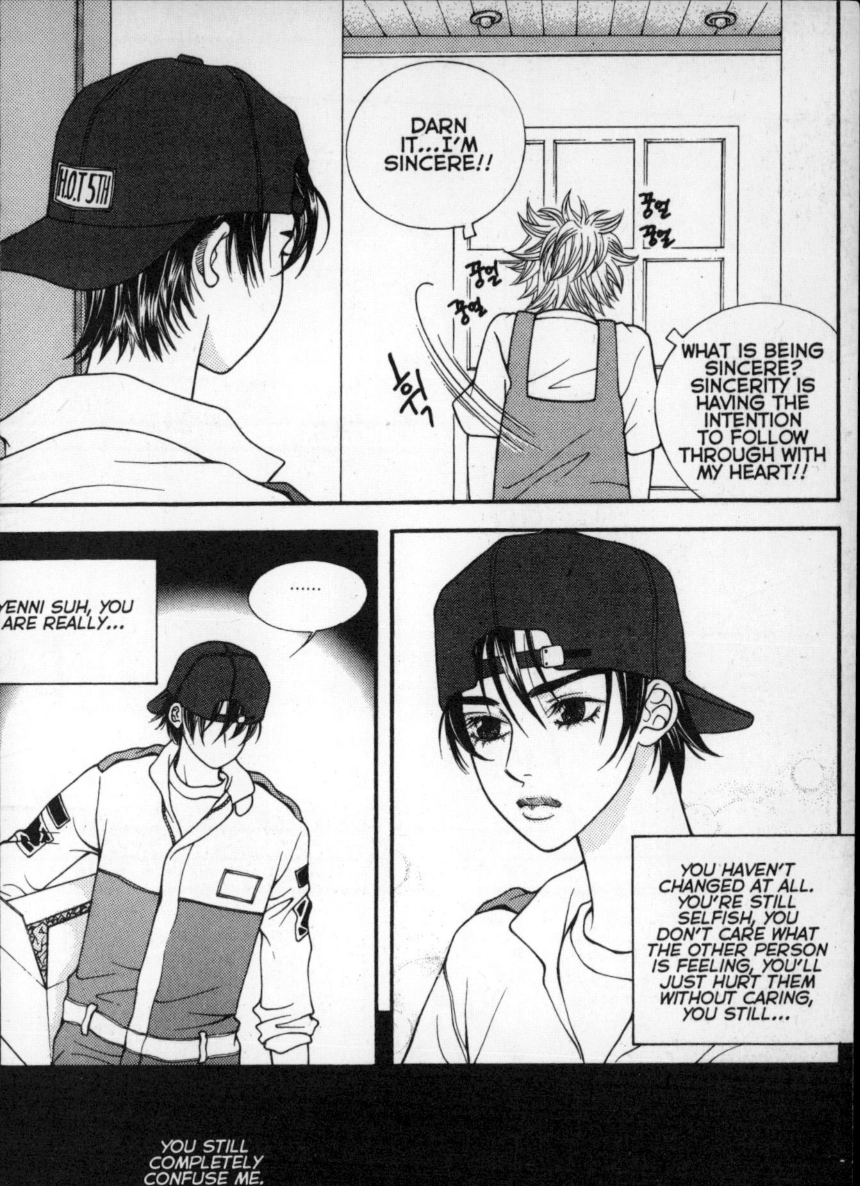
DARN IT...I'M SINCERE!!
WHAT IS BEING SINCERE? SINCERITY IS HAVING THE INTENTION TO FOLLOW THROUGH WITH MY HEART!!
YENNI SUH, YOU ARE REALLY...
......
YOU HAVEN'T CHANGED AT ALL. YOU'RE STILL SELFISH, YOU DON'T CARE WHAT THE OTHER PERSON IS FEELING, YOU'LL JUST HURT THEM WITHOUT CARING, YOU STILL...
YOU STILL COMPLETELY CONFUSE ME.

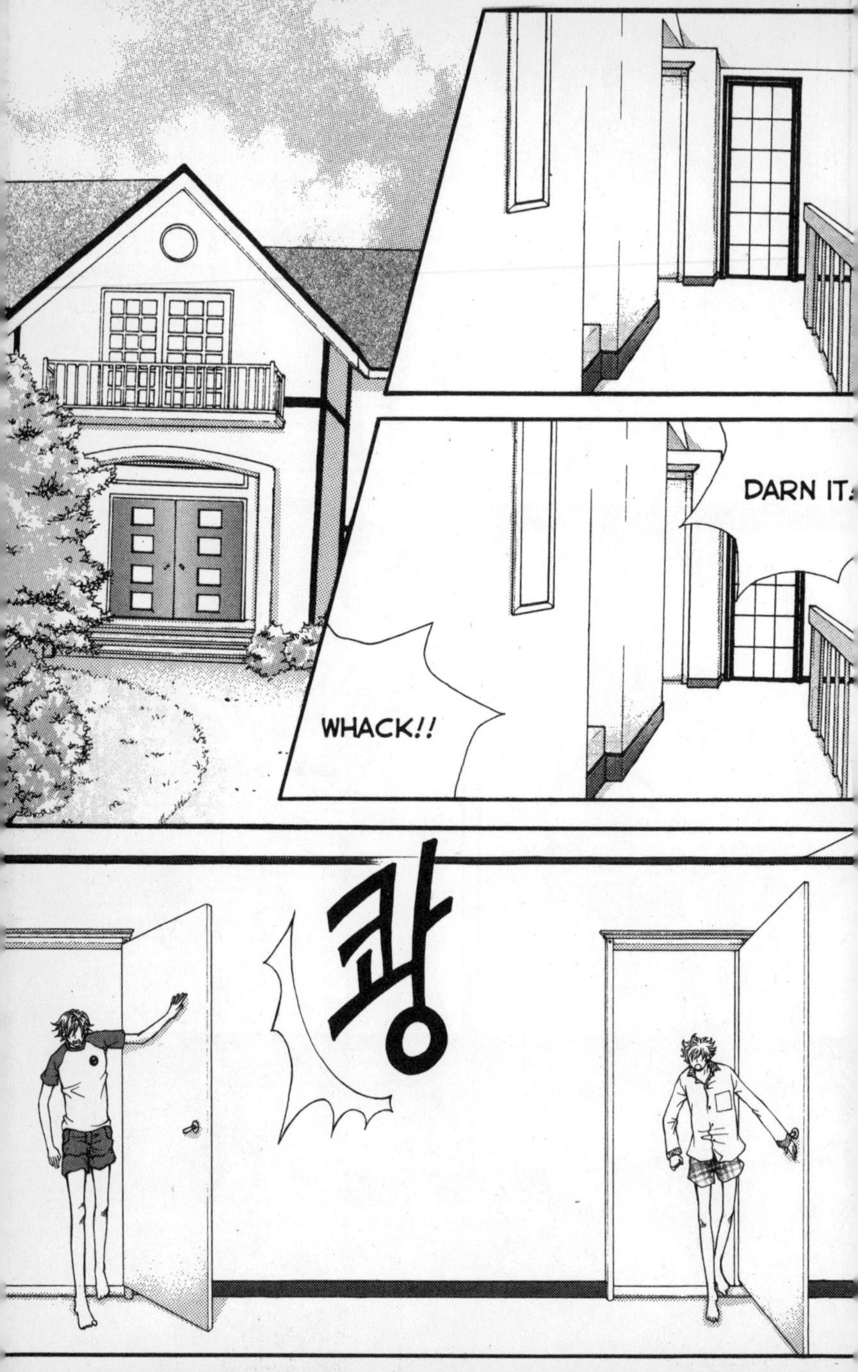
WHACK!!
DARN IT.
쾅

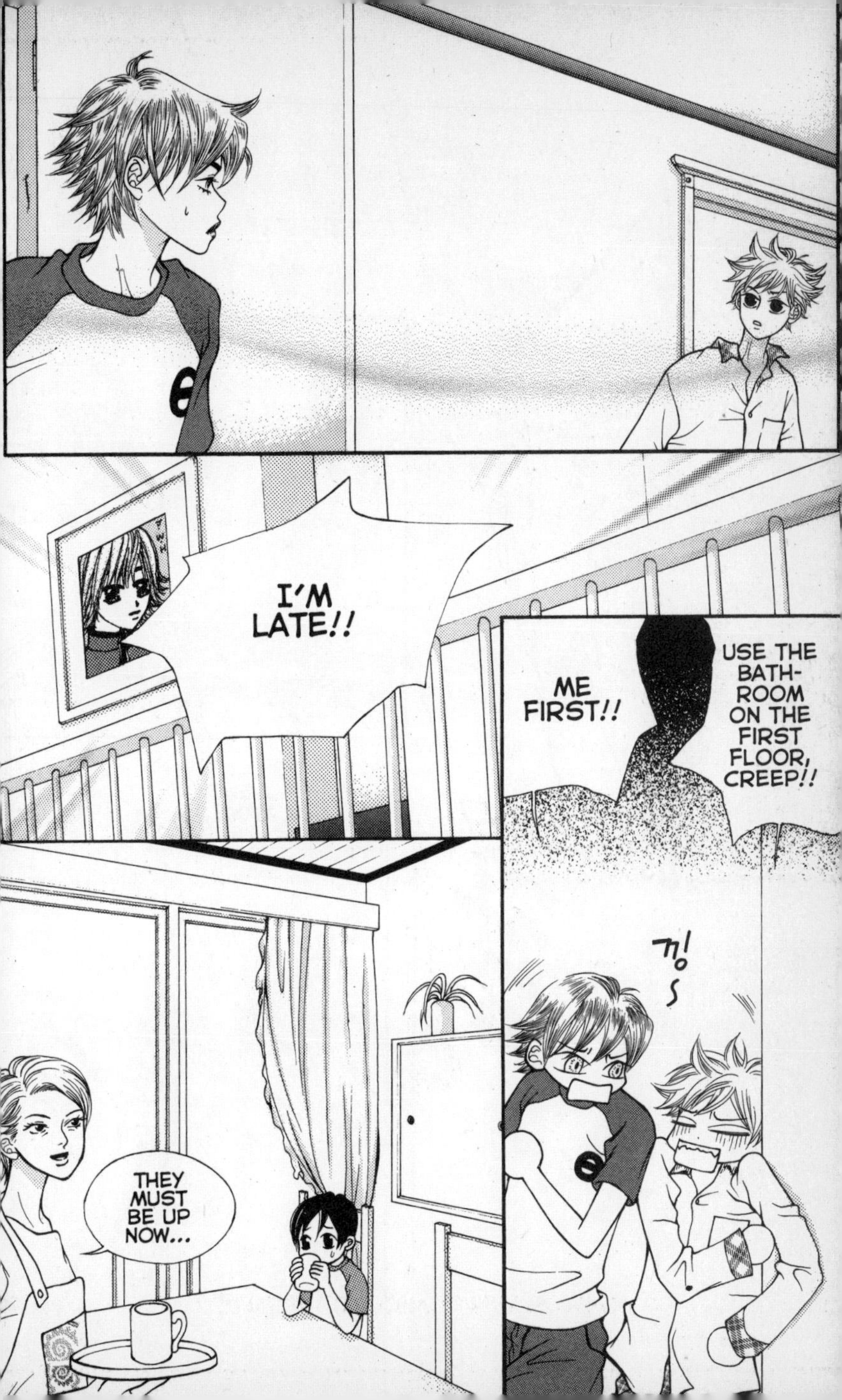
I'M LATE!!
THEY MUST BE UP NOW...
ME FIRST!!
USE THE BATH-ROOM ON THE FIRST FLOOR, CREEP!!
끼잉

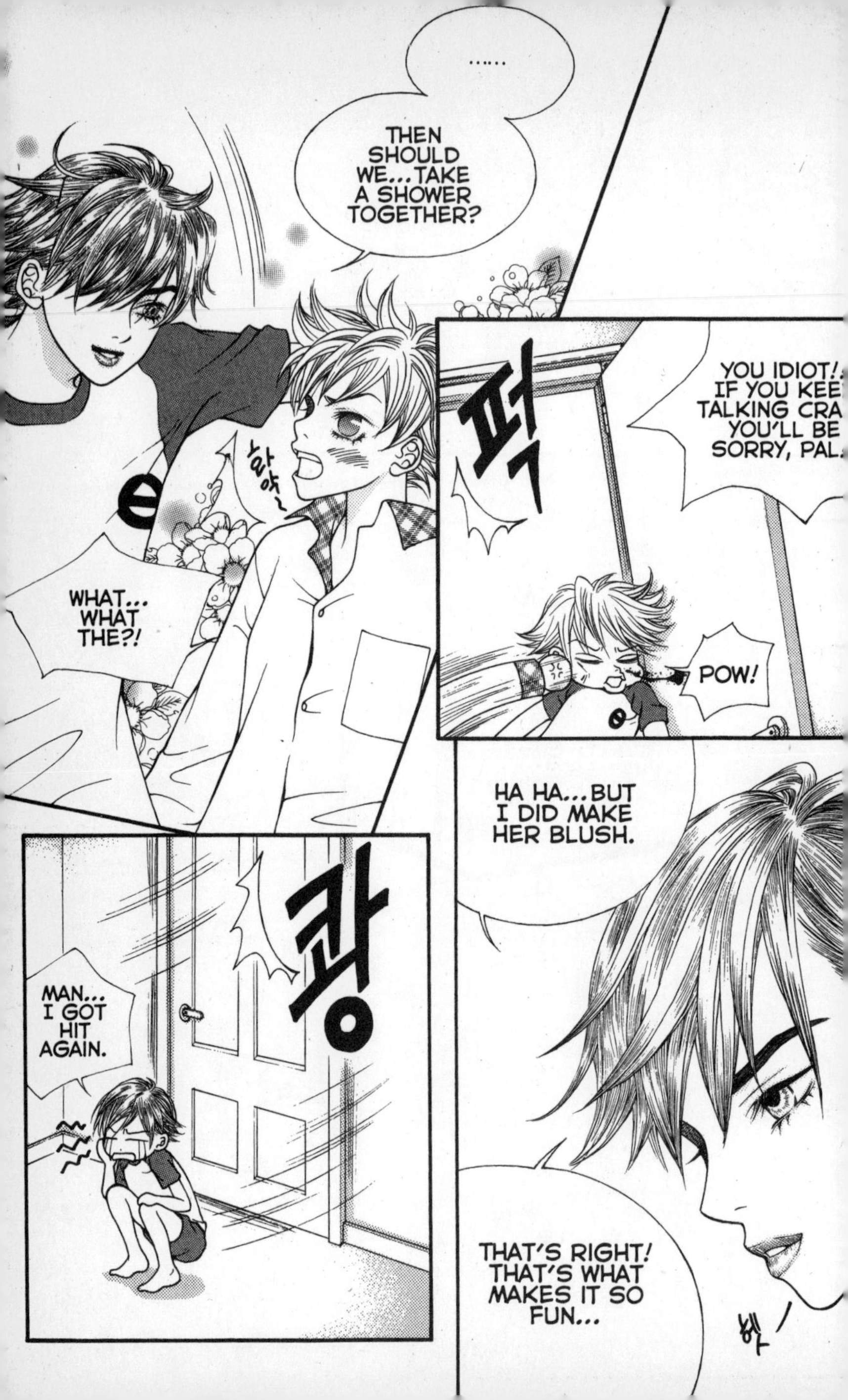
......
THEN SHOULD WE...TAKE A SHOWER TOGETHER?
WHAT... WHAT THE?!
퍽
YOU IDIOT!. IF YOU KEE TALKING CRA YOU'LL BE SORRY, PAL.
POW!
MAN... I GOT HIT AGAIN.
쾅
HA HA...BUT I DID MAKE HER BLUSH.
THAT'S RIGHT! THAT'S WHAT MAKES IT SO FUN...

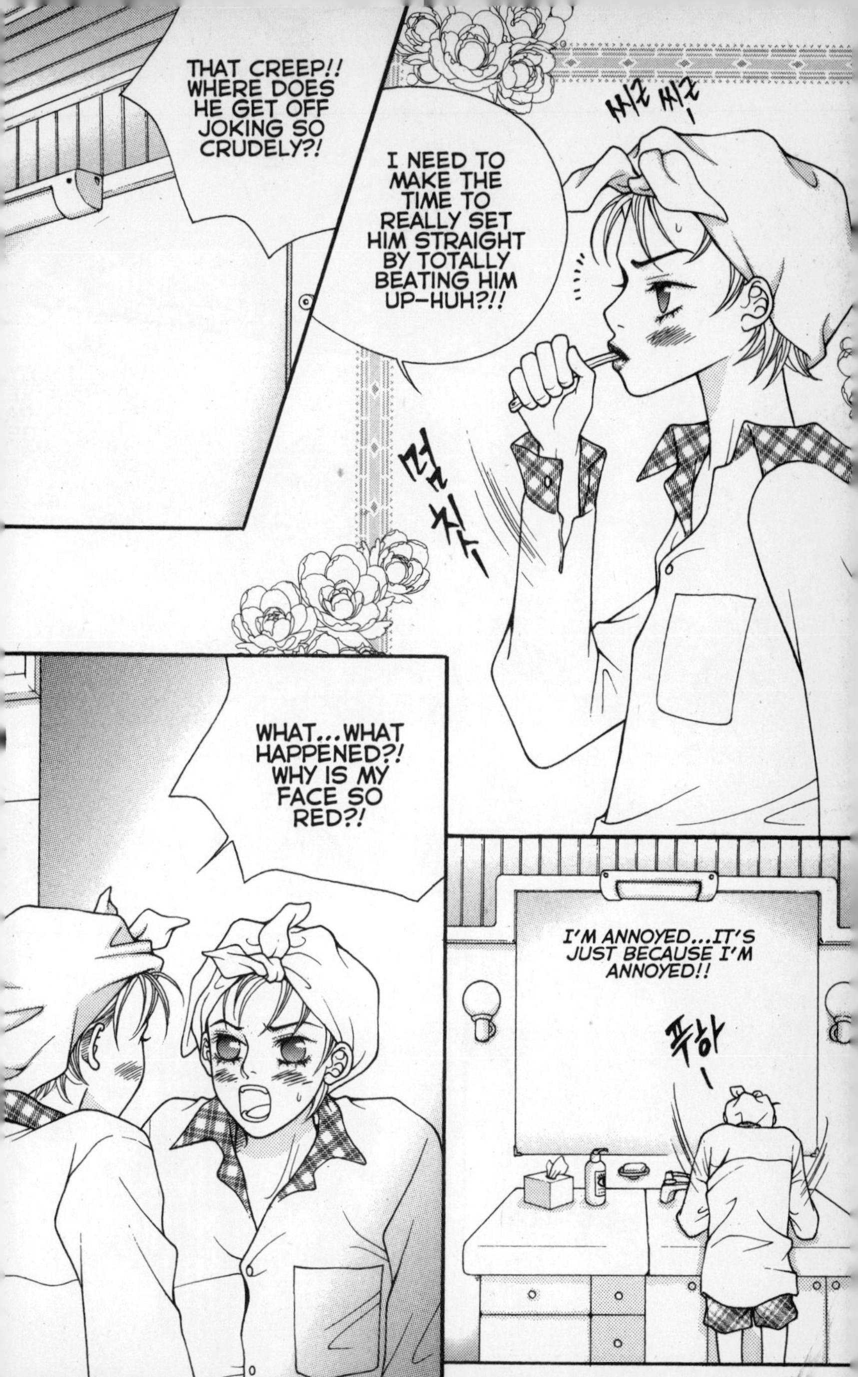
THAT CREEP!! WHERE DOES HE GET OFF JOKING SO CRUDELY?!
I NEED TO MAKE THE TIME TO REALLY SET HIM STRAIGHT BY TOTALLY BEATING HIM UP—HUH?!!
WHAT...WHAT HAPPENED?! WHY IS MY FACE SO RED?!
I'M ANNOYED...IT'S JUST BECAUSE I'M ANNOYED!!
푸하

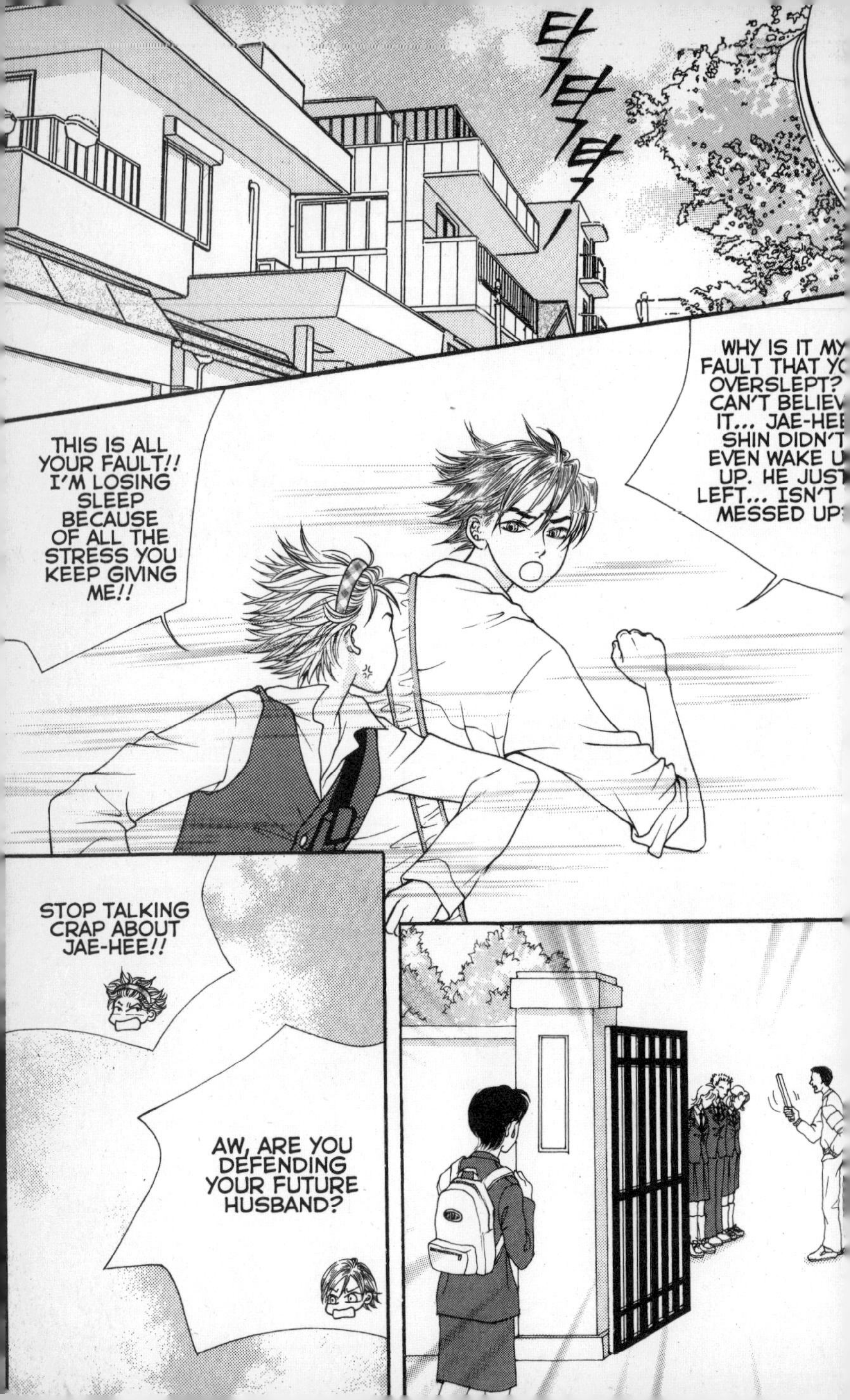

타닥타닥!
THIS IS ALL YOUR FAULT!! I'M LOSING SLEEP BECAUSE OF ALL THE STRESS YOU KEEP GIVING ME!!
WHY IS IT MY FAULT THAT YO OVERSLEPT? CAN'T BELIEV IT... JAE-HEE SHIN DIDN'T EVEN WAKE U UP. HE JUST LEFT... ISN'T MESSED UP
STOP TALKING CRAP ABOUT JAE-HEE!!
AW, ARE YOU DEFENDING YOUR FUTURE HUSBAND?

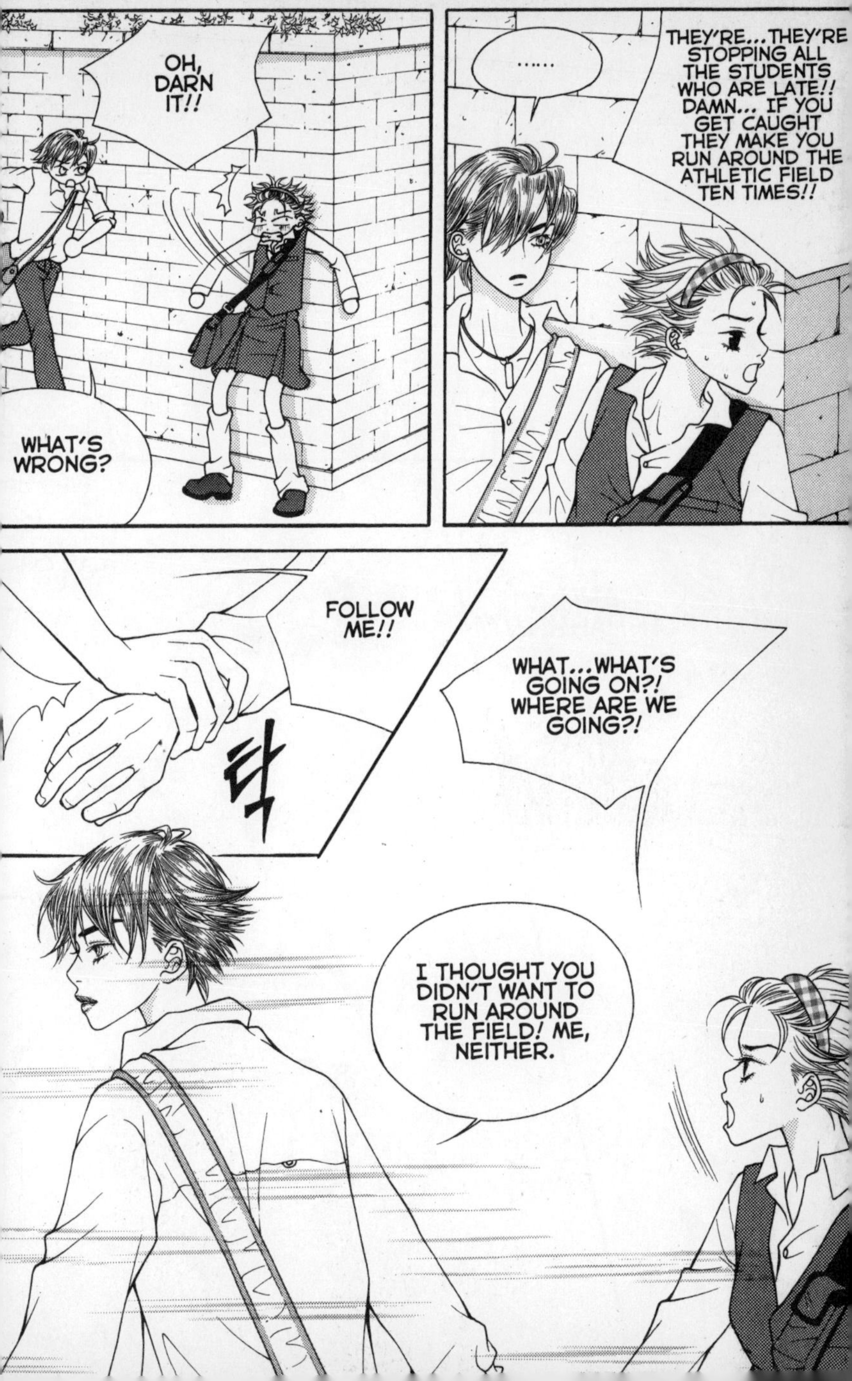
OH, DARN IT!!
WHAT'S WRONG?
......
THEY'RE...THEY'RE STOPPING ALL THE STUDENTS WHO ARE LATE!! DAMN... IF YOU GET CAUGHT THEY MAKE YOU RUN AROUND THE ATHLETIC FIELD TEN TIMES!!
FOLLOW ME!!
탁
WHAT...WHAT'S GOING ON?! WHERE ARE WE GOING?!
I THOUGHT YOU DIDN'T WANT TO RUN AROUND THE FIELD! ME, NEITHER.

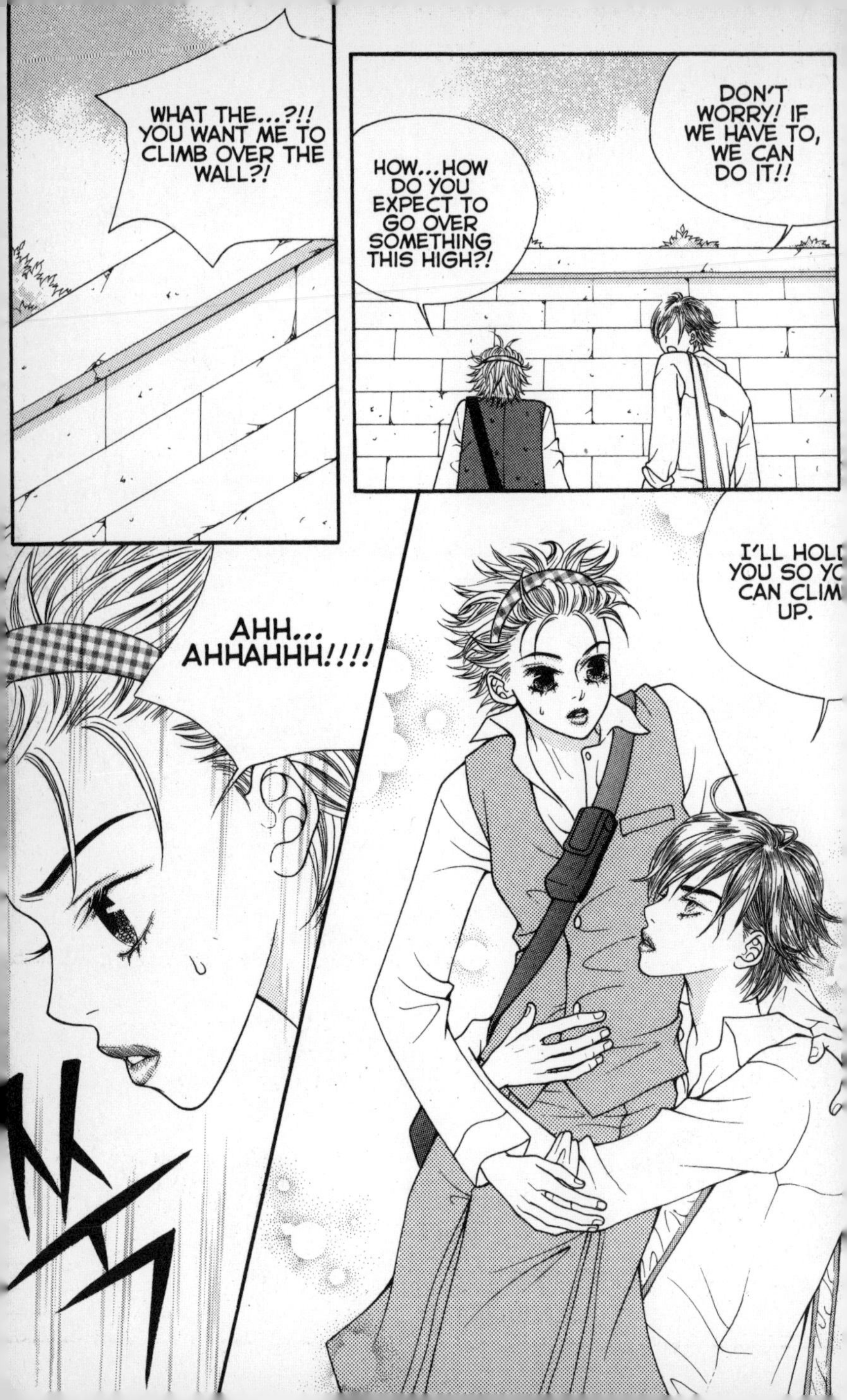
WHAT THE...?!! YOU WANT ME TO CLIMB OVER THE WALL?!
HOW...HOW DO YOU EXPECT TO GO OVER SOMETHING THIS HIGH?!
DON'T WORRY! IF WE HAVE TO, WE CAN DO IT!!
AHH... AHHAHHH!!!!
I'LL HOLD YOU SO YO CAN CLIM UP.

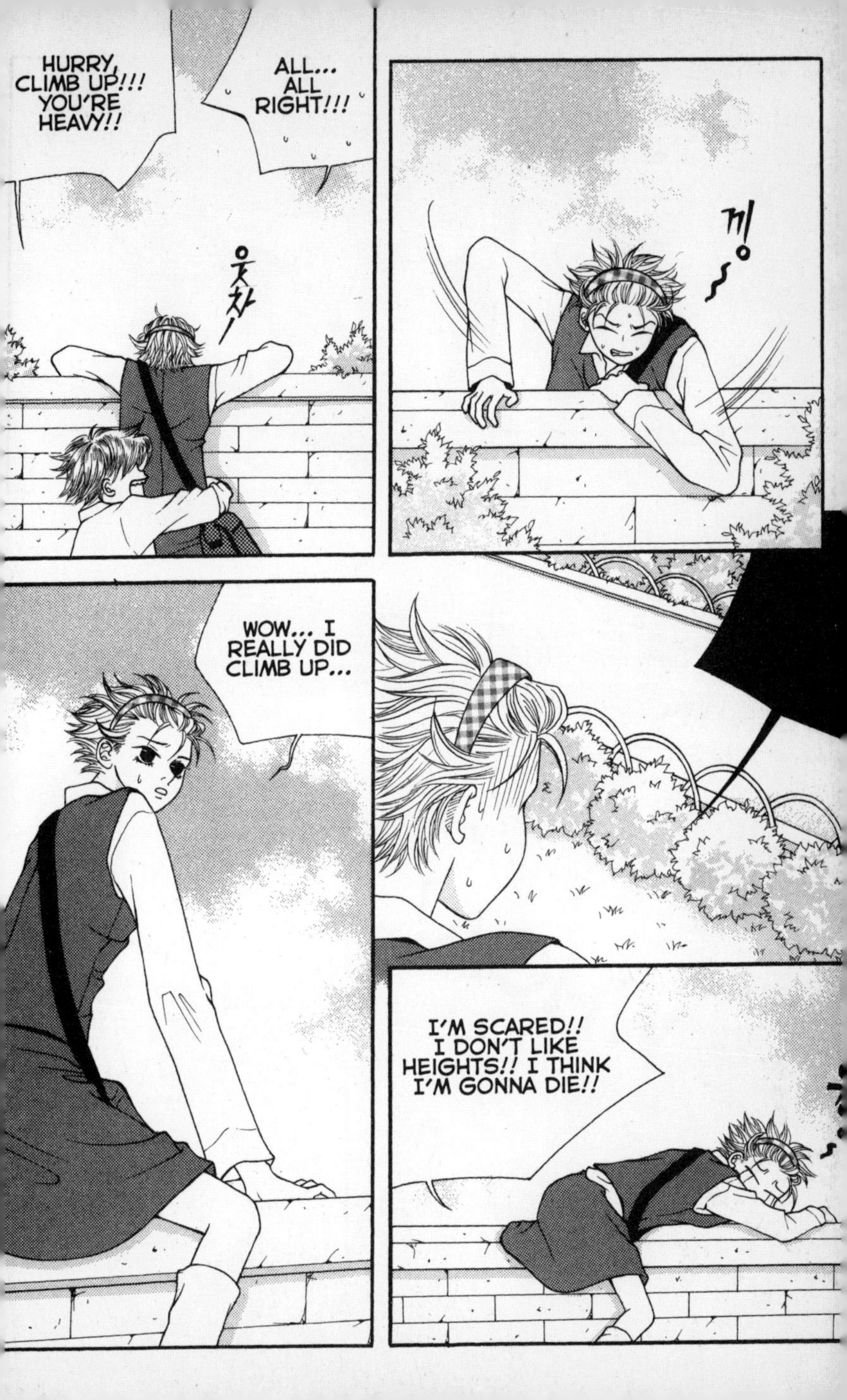
HURRY, CLIMB UP!!! YOU'RE HEAVY!!
ALL... ALL RIGHT!!!
읏차
낑~
WOW... I REALLY DID CLIMB UP...
I'M SCARED!! I DON'T LIKE HEIGHTS!! I THINK I'M GONNA DIE!!

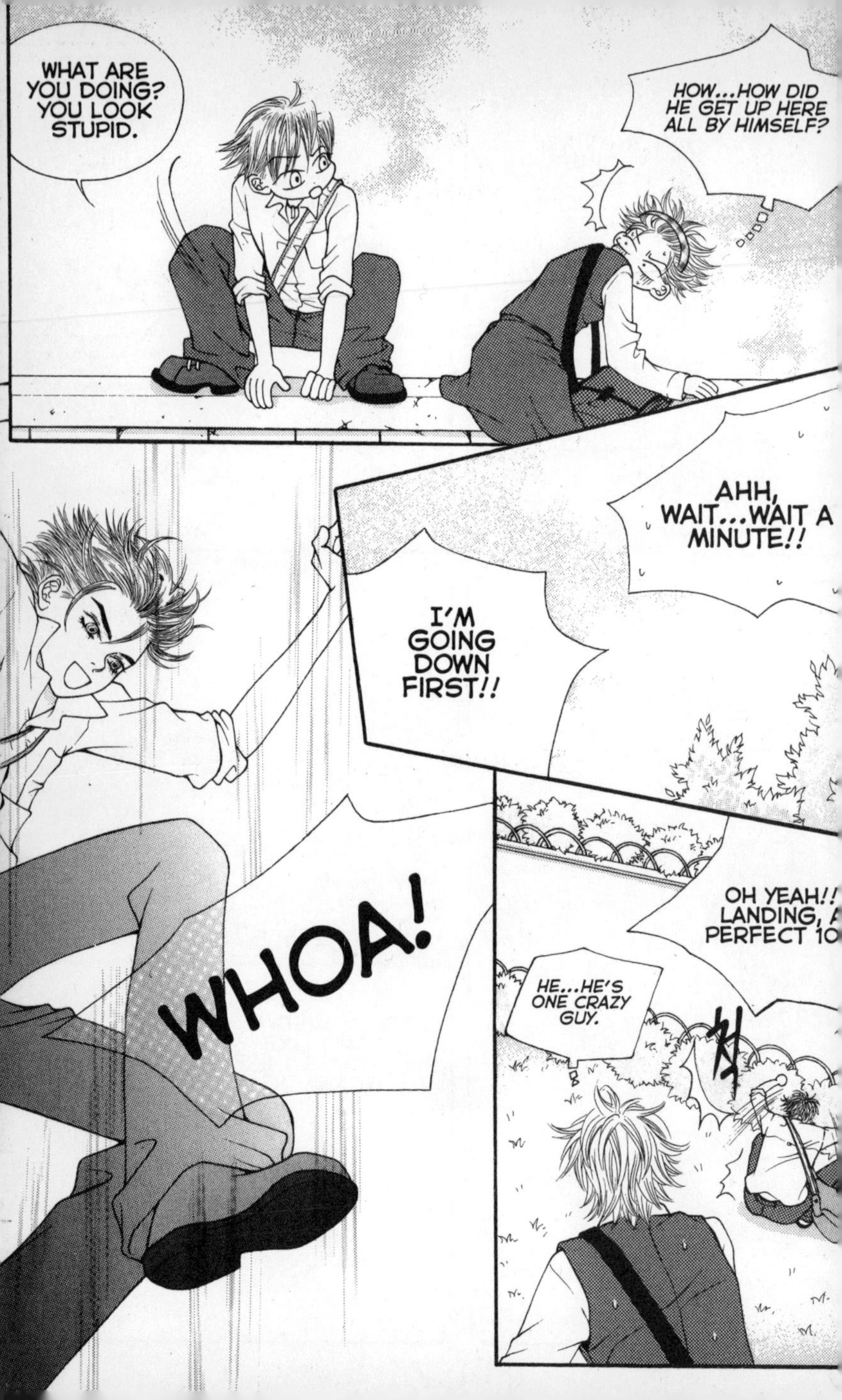
HOW...HOW DID HE GET UP HERE ALL BY HIMSELF?
WHAT ARE YOU DOING? YOU LOOK STUPID.
AHH, WAIT...WAIT A MINUTE!!
I'M GOING DOWN FIRST!!
OH YEAH!! LANDING, A PERFECT 10
HE...HE'S ONE CRAZY GUY.
WHOA!

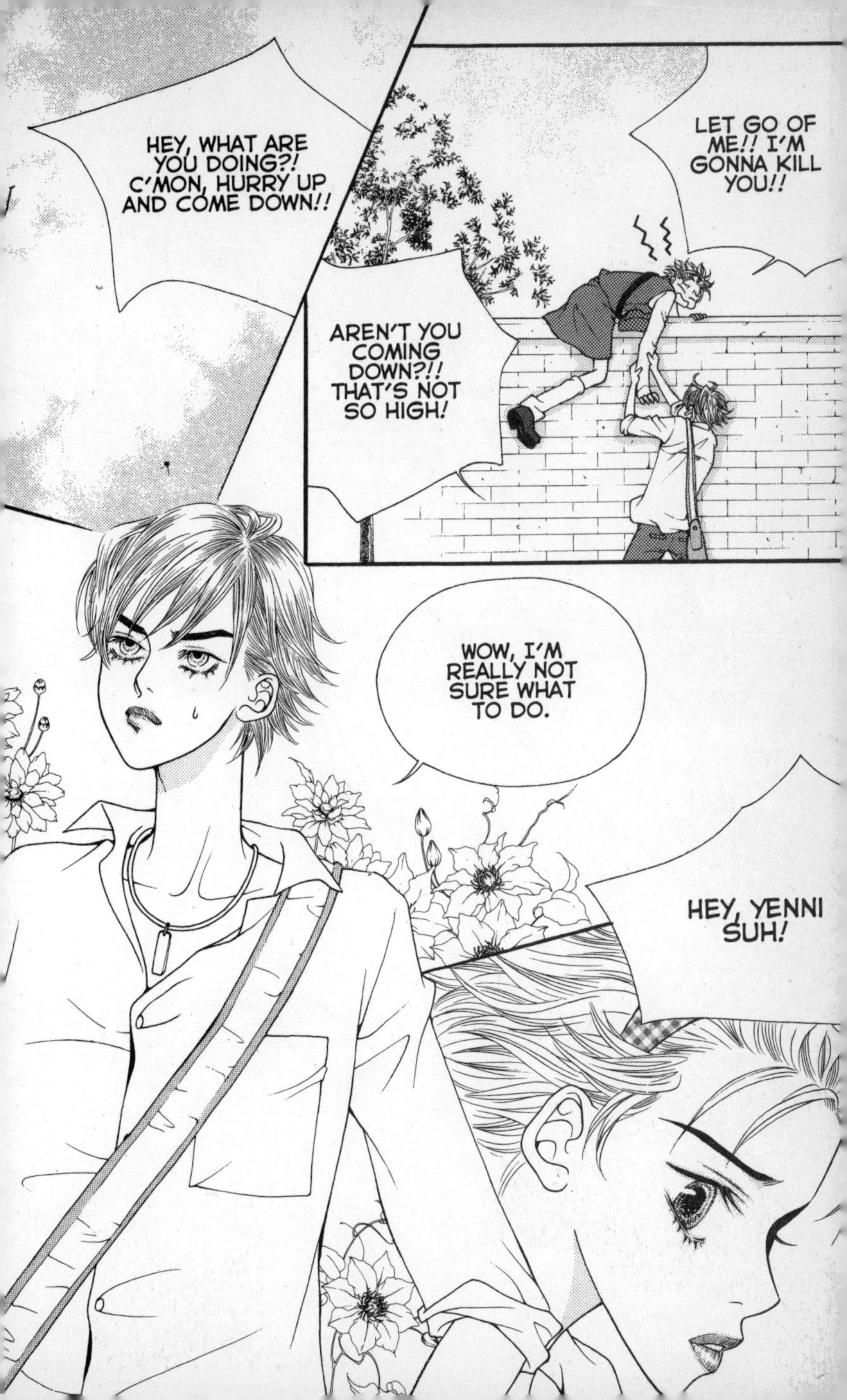
HEY, WHAT ARE YOU DOING?! C'MON, HURRY UP AND COME DOWN!!
LET GO OF ME!! I'M GONNA KILL YOU!!
AREN'T YOU COMING DOWN?!! THAT'S NOT SO HIGH!
WOW, I'M REALLY NOT SURE WHAT TO DO.
HEY, YENNI SUH!

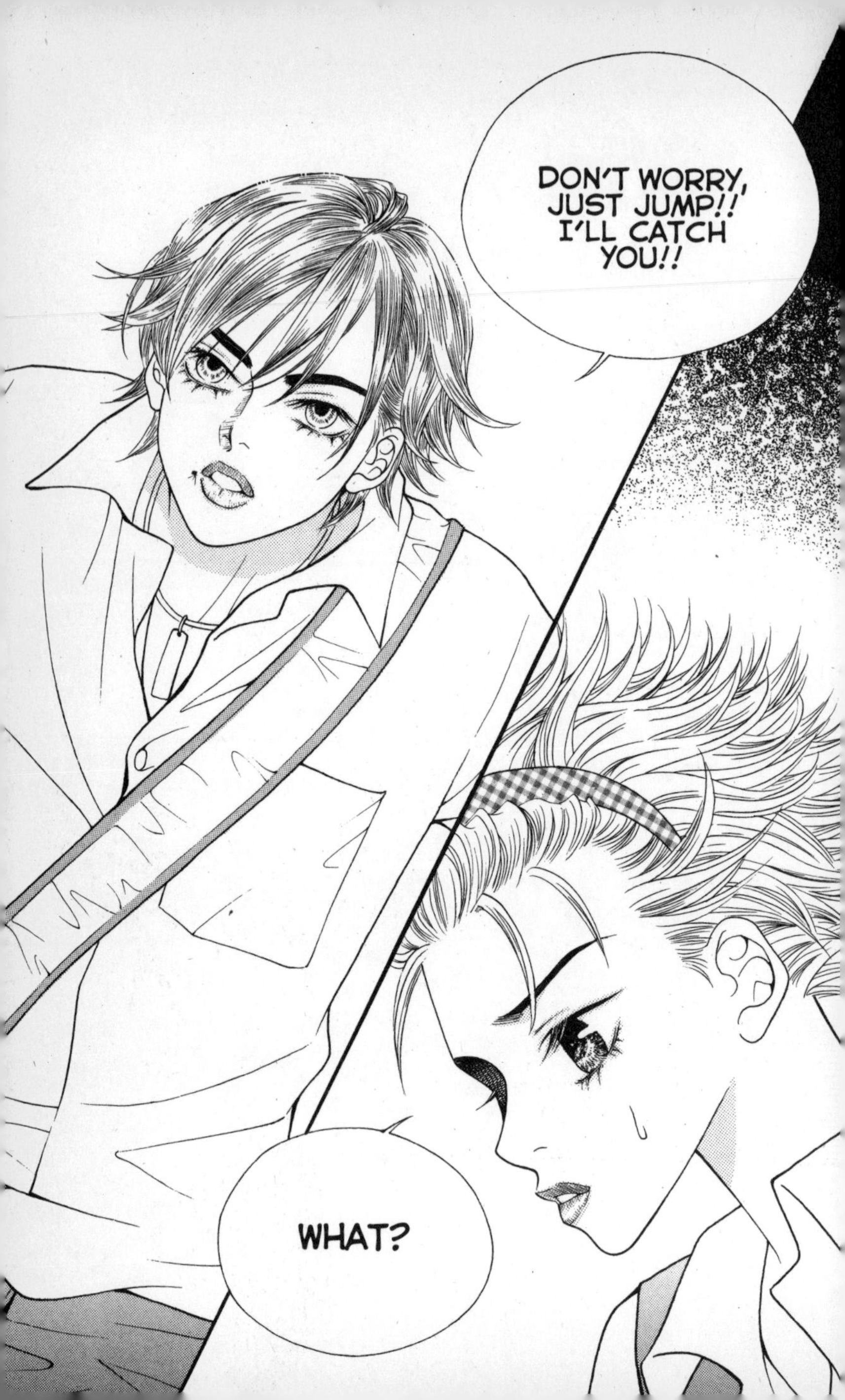
DON'T WORRY, JUST JUMP!! I'LL CATCH YOU!!
WHAT?

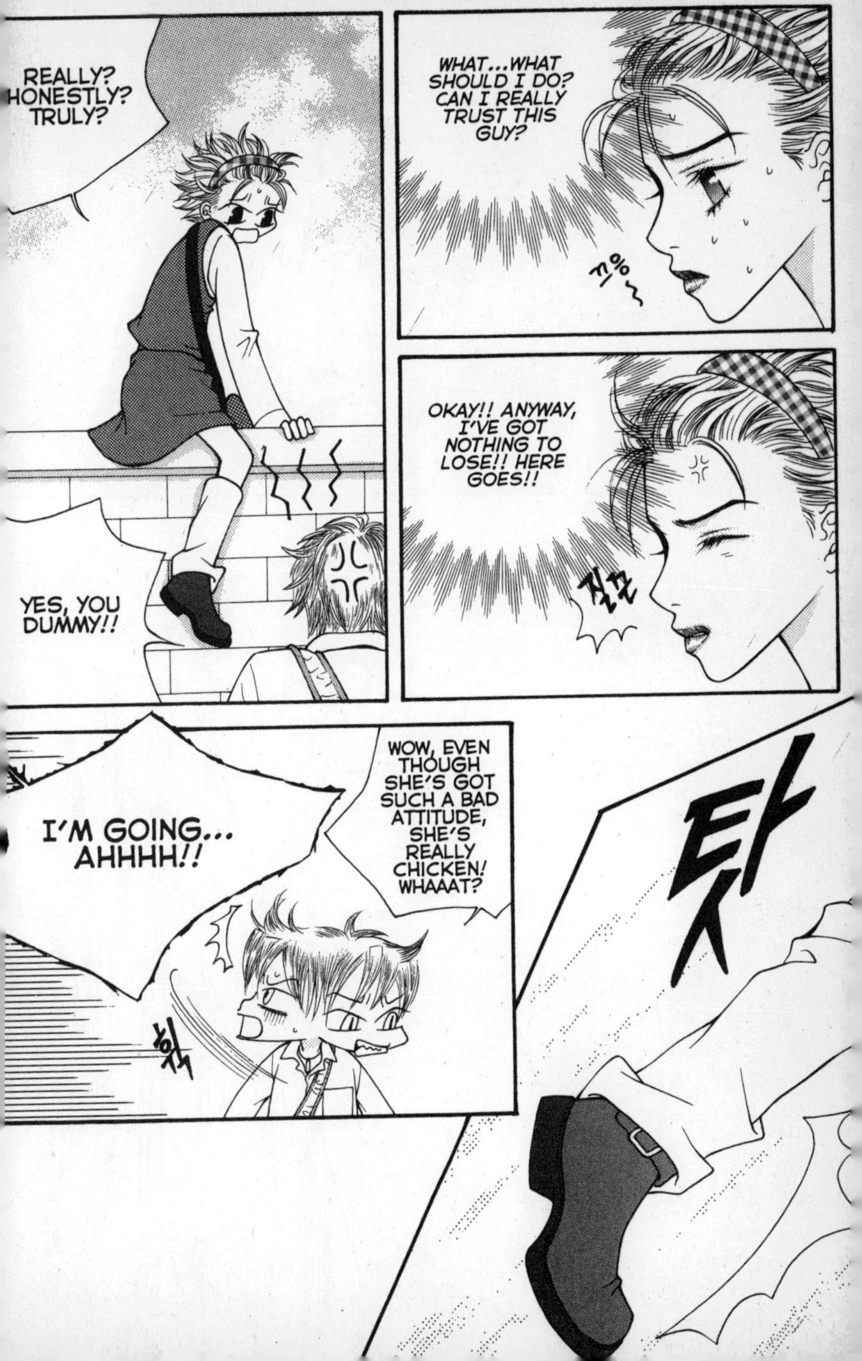
REALLY? HONESTLY? TRULY?
YES, YOU DUMMY!!
WHAT...WHAT SHOULD I DO? CAN I REALLY TRUST THIS GUY?
OKAY!! ANYWAY, I'VE GOT NOTHING TO LOSE!! HERE GOES!!
I'M GOING... AHHHH!!
WOW, EVEN THOUGH SHE'S GOT SUCH A BAD ATTITUDE, SHE'S REALLY CHICKEN! WHAAAT?

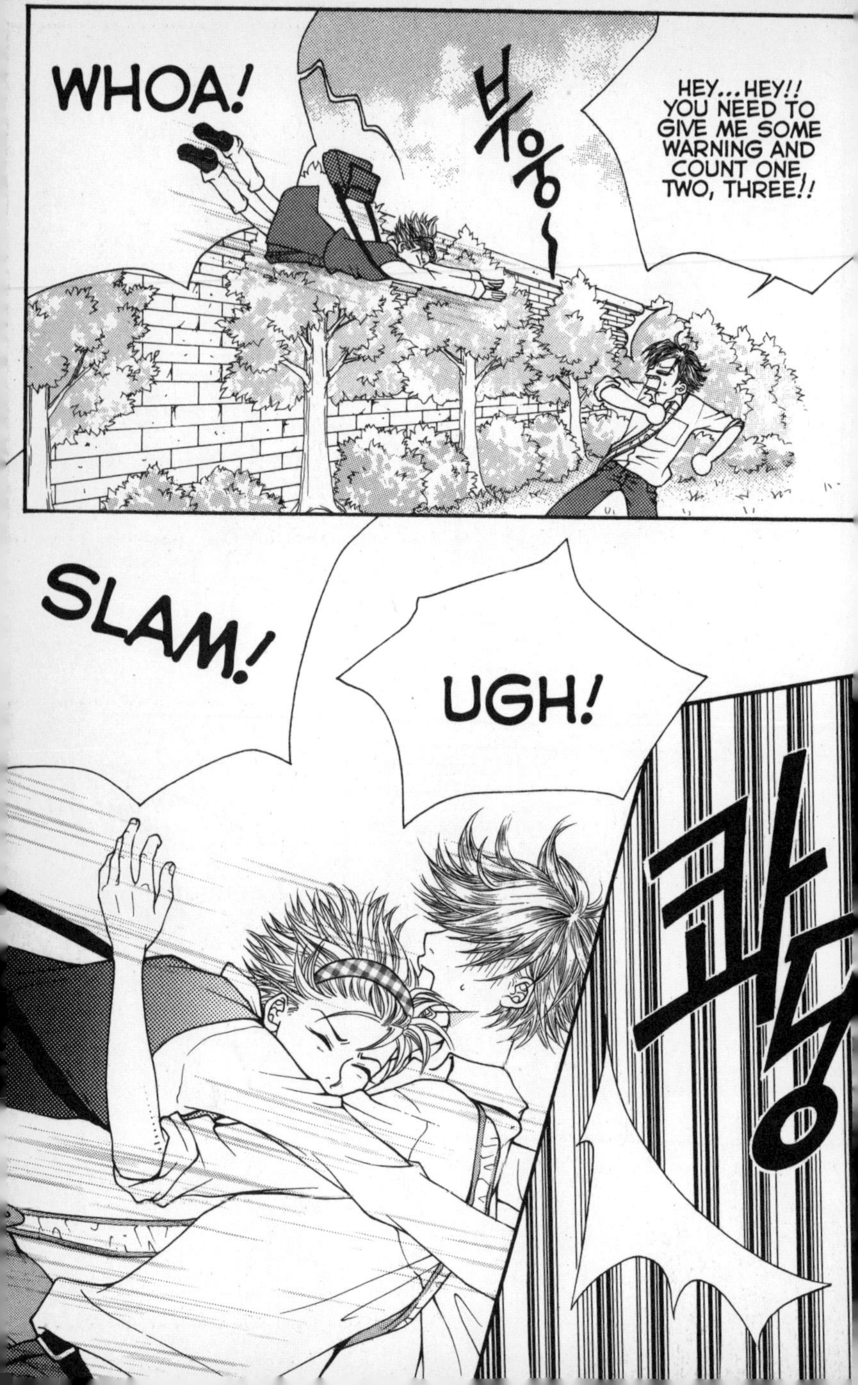
WHOA!
HEY...HEY!! YOU NEED TO GIVE ME SOME WARNING AND COUNT ONE, TWO, THREE!!
SLAM!
UGH!

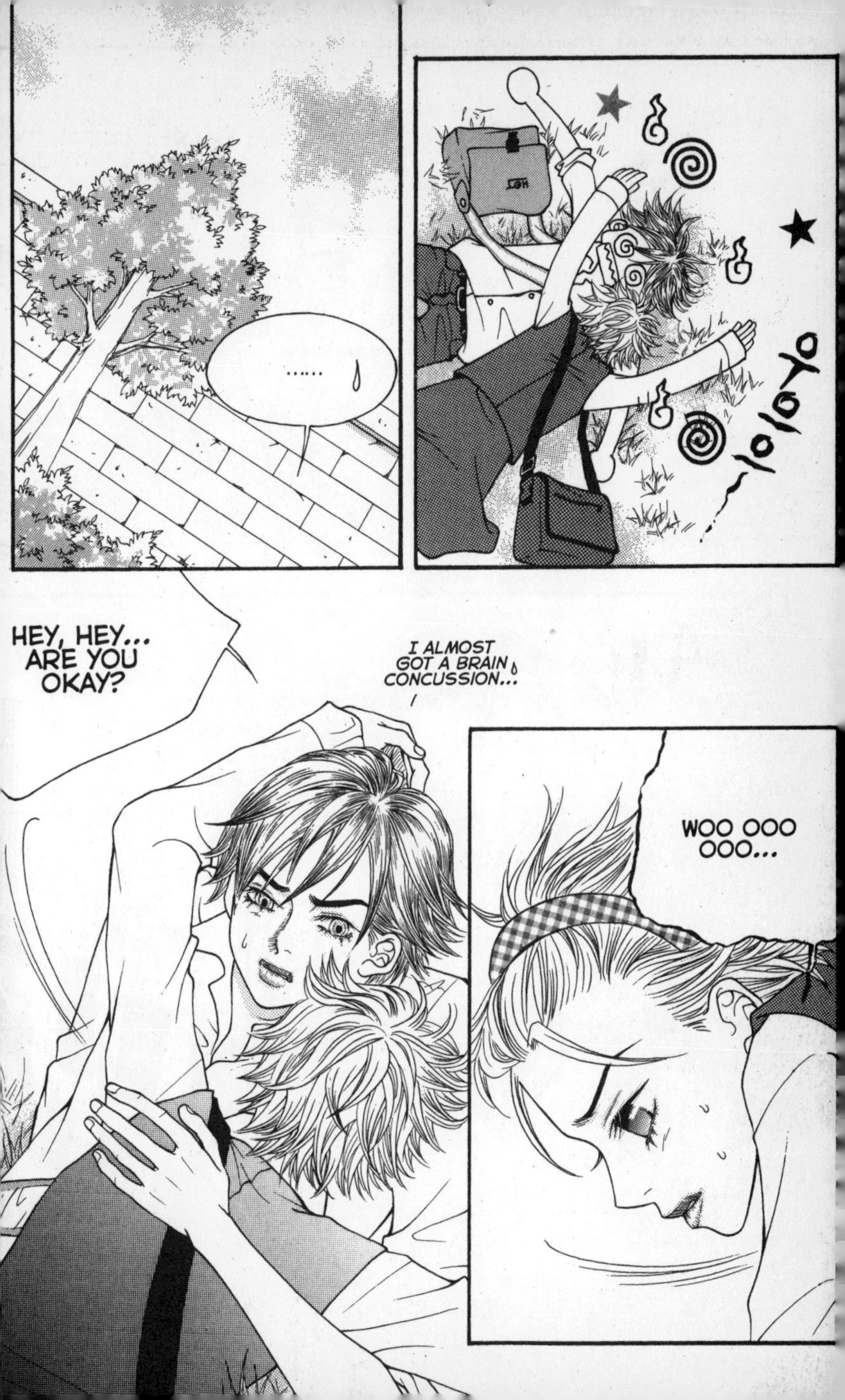
......
HEY, HEY... ARE YOU OKAY?
I ALMOST GOT A BRAIN CONCUSSION...
WOO OOO OOO...

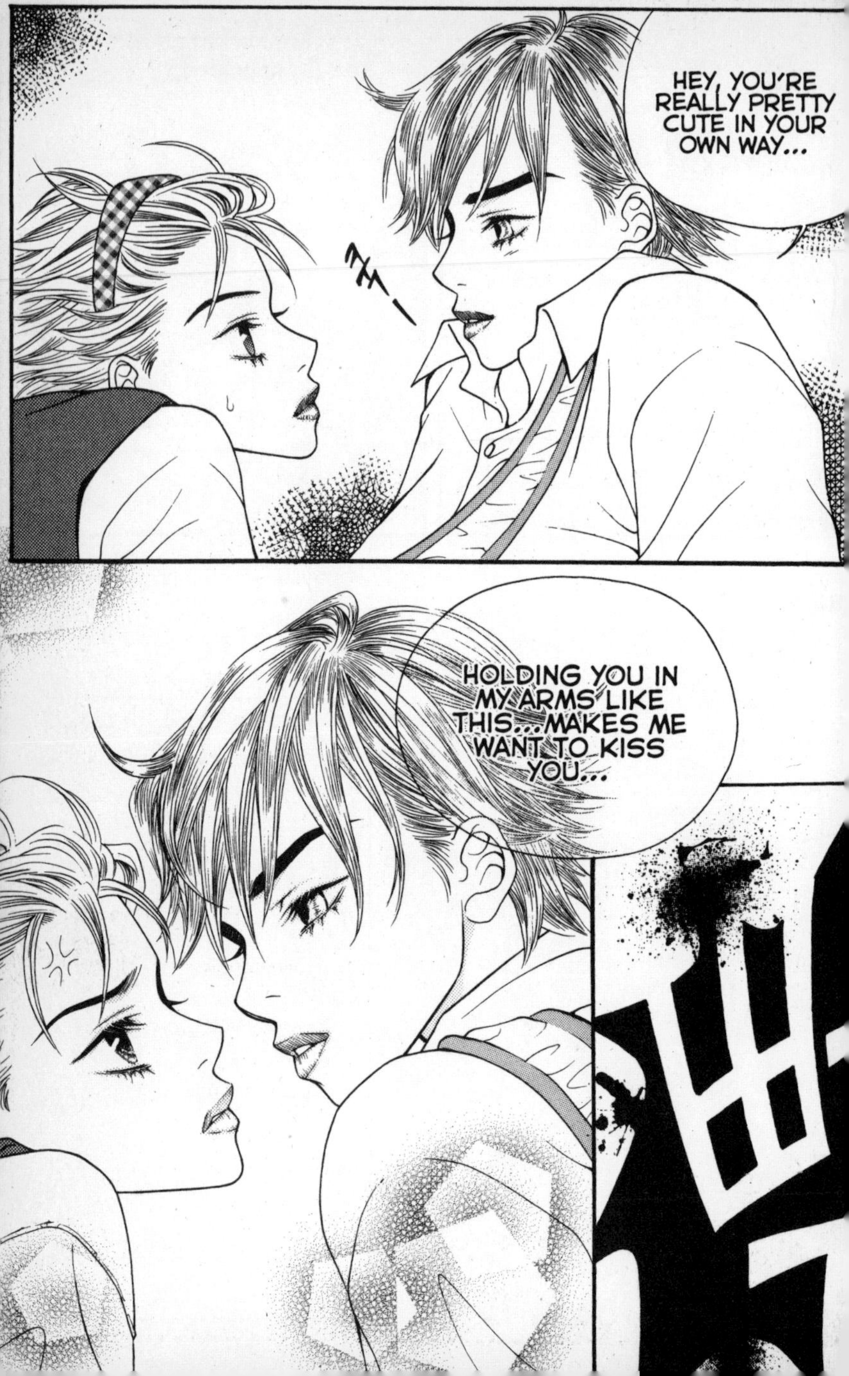
HEY, YOU'RE REALLY PRETTY CUTE IN YOUR OWN WAY...
HOLDING YOU IN MY ARMS LIKE THIS...MAKES ME WANT TO KISS YOU...

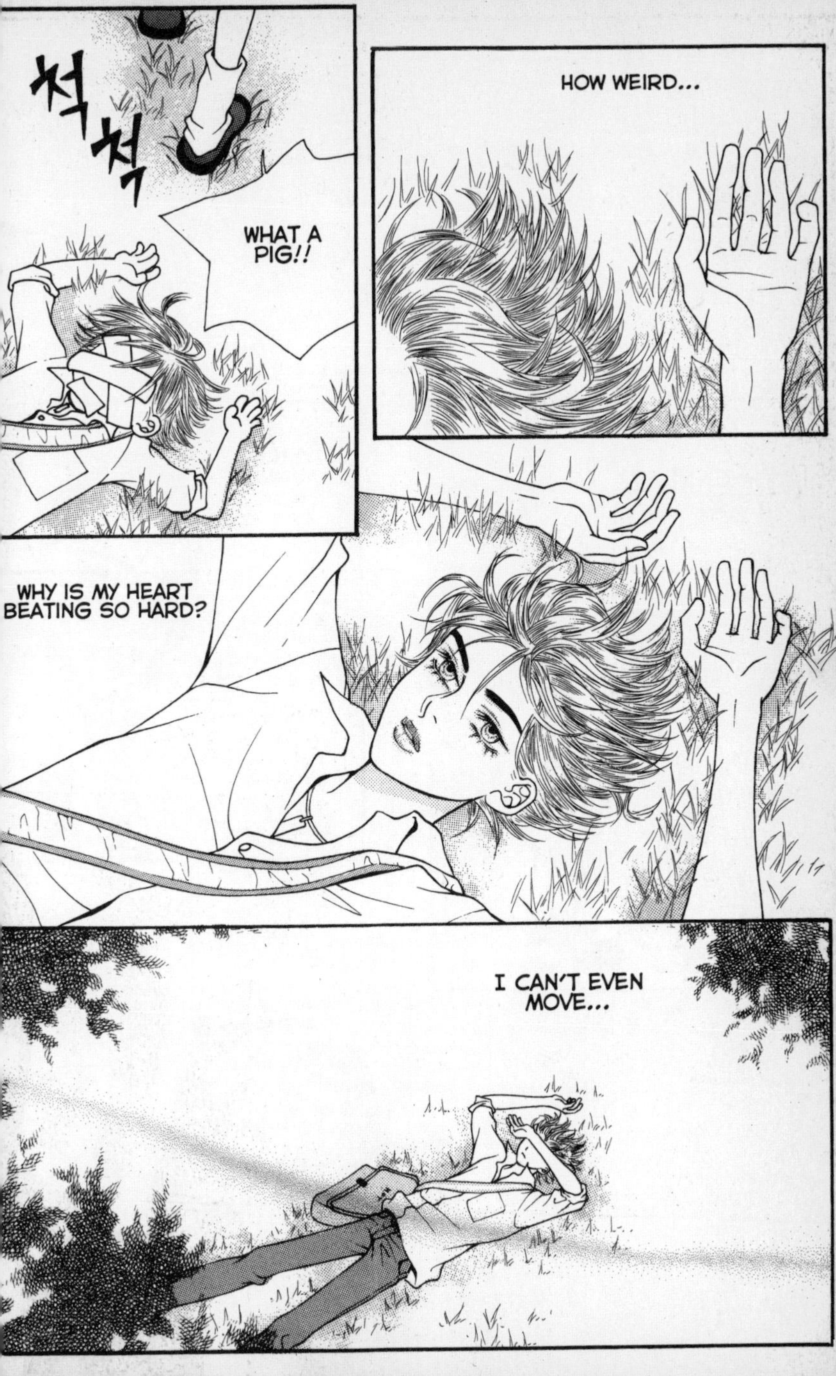
척 척
WHAT A PIG!!
HOW WEIRD...
WHY IS MY HEART BEATING SO HARD?
I CAN'T EVEN MOVE...

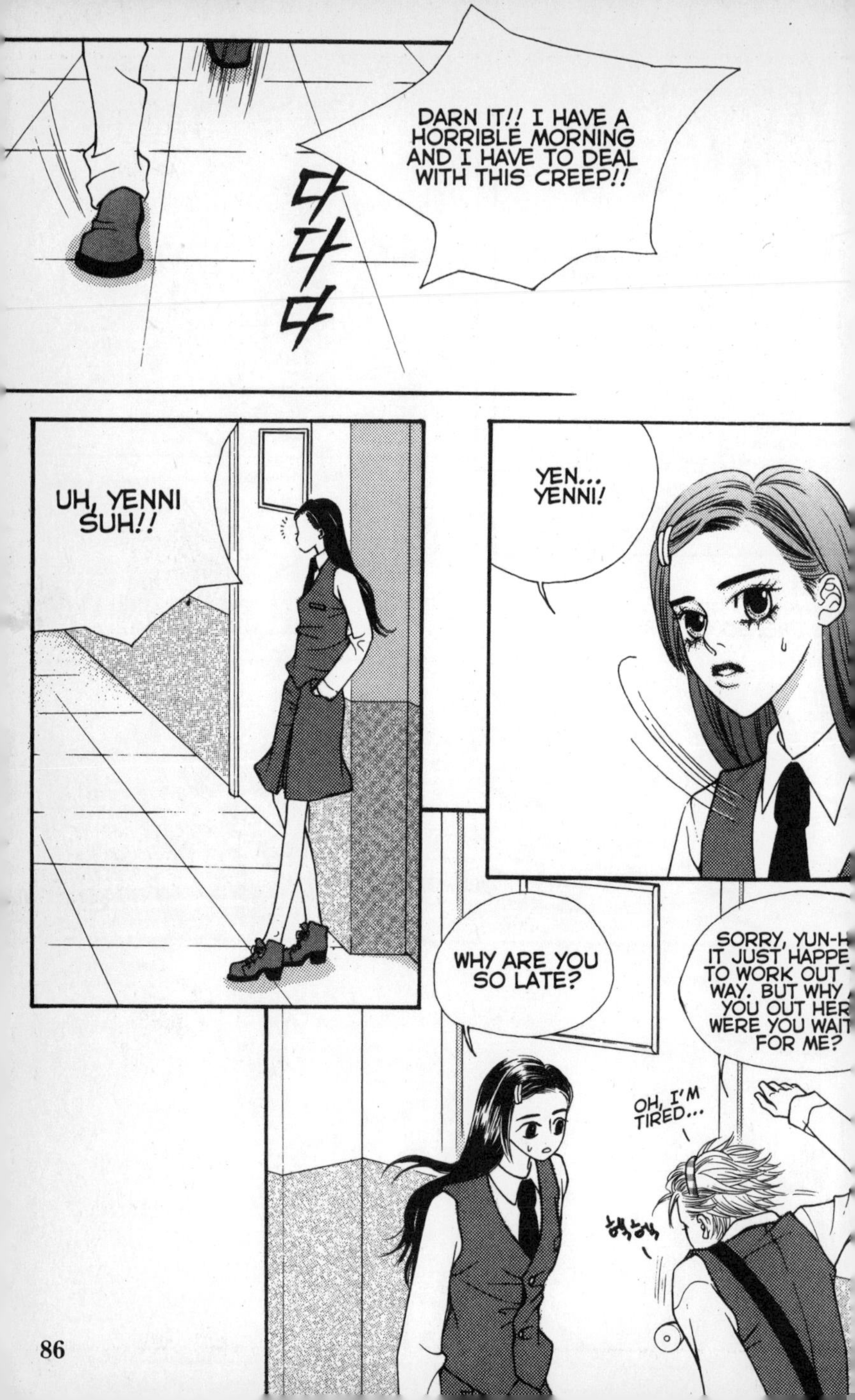
DARN IT!! I HAVE A HORRIBLE MORNING AND I HAVE TO DEAL WITH THIS CREEP!!
다다다
UH, YENNI SUH!!
YEN... YENNI!
WHY ARE YOU SO LATE?
SORRY, YUN-H IT JUST HAPPE TO WORK OUT WAY. BUT WHY YOU OUT HER WERE YOU WAIT FOR ME?
OH, I'M TIRED...
헉헉

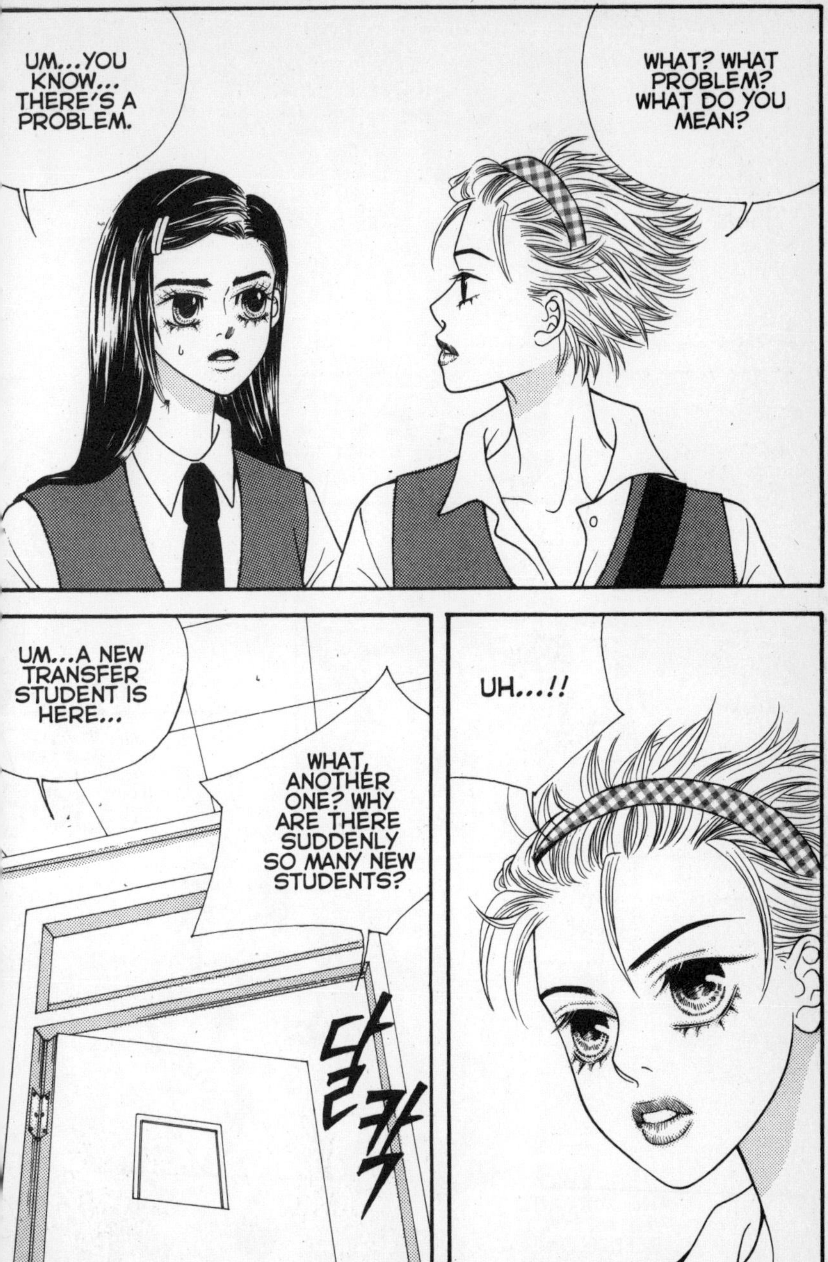
UM...YOU KNOW... THERE'S A PROBLEM.
WHAT? WHAT PROBLEM? WHAT DO YOU MEAN?
UM...A NEW TRANSFER STUDENT IS HERE...
WHAT, ANOTHER ONE? WHY ARE THERE SUDDENLY SO MANY NEW STUDENTS?
달칵
UH...!!

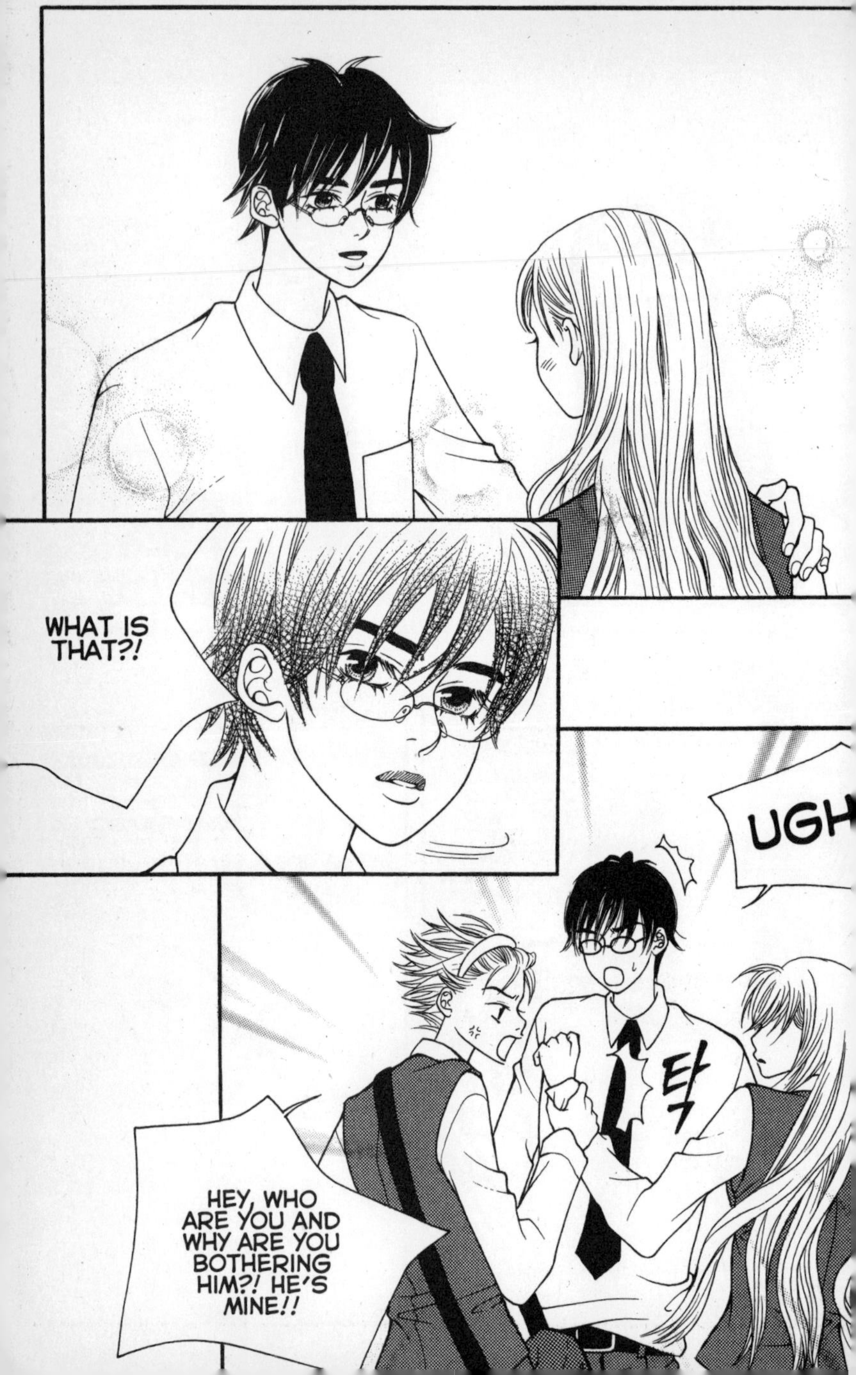
WHAT IS THAT?!
UGH
탁
HEY, WHO ARE YOU AND WHY ARE YOU BOTHERING HIM?! HE'S MINE!!

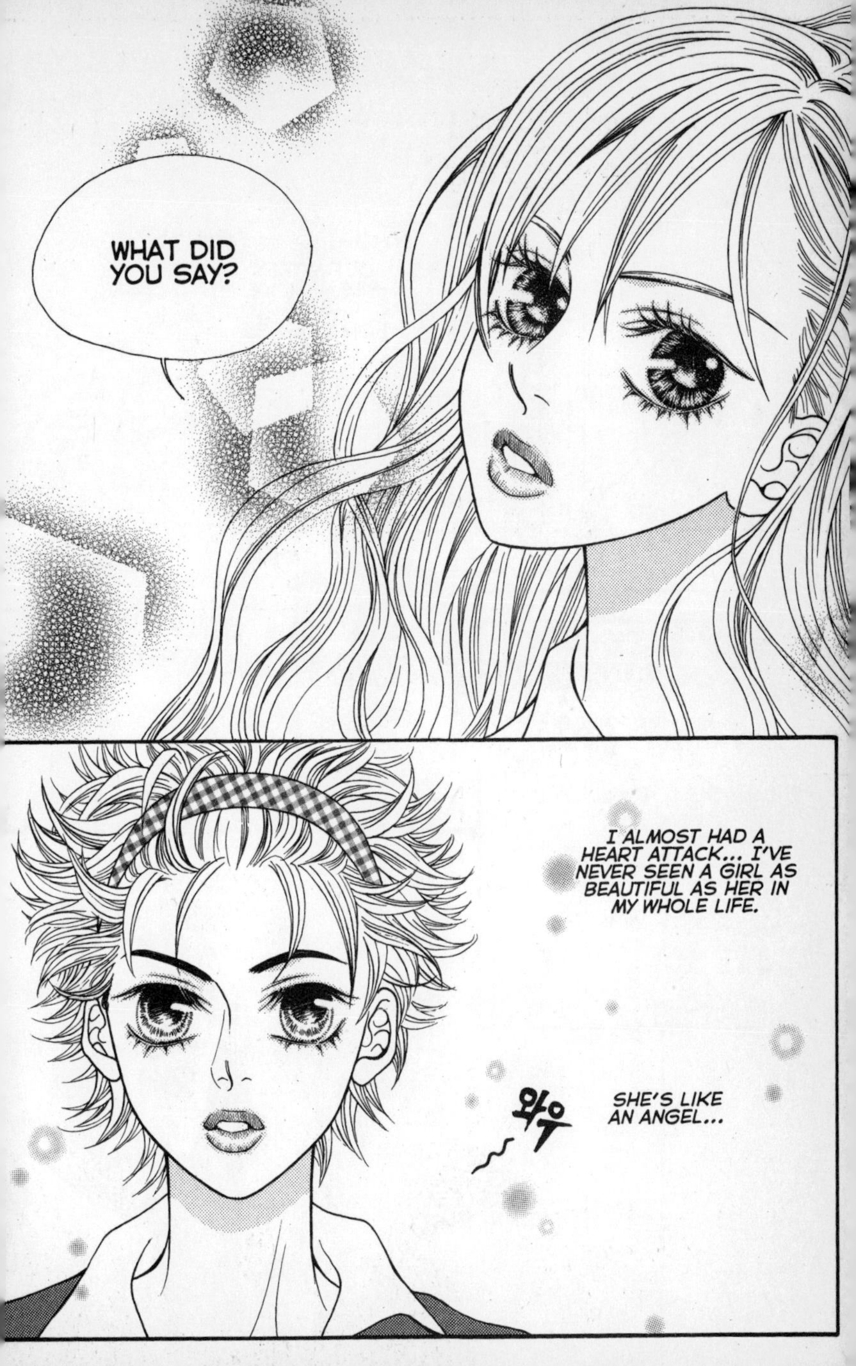
WHAT DID YOU SAY?
I ALMOST HAD A HEART ATTACK... I'VE NEVER SEEN A GIRL AS BEAUTIFUL AS HER IN MY WHOLE LIFE.
와우
SHE'S LIKE AN ANGEL...

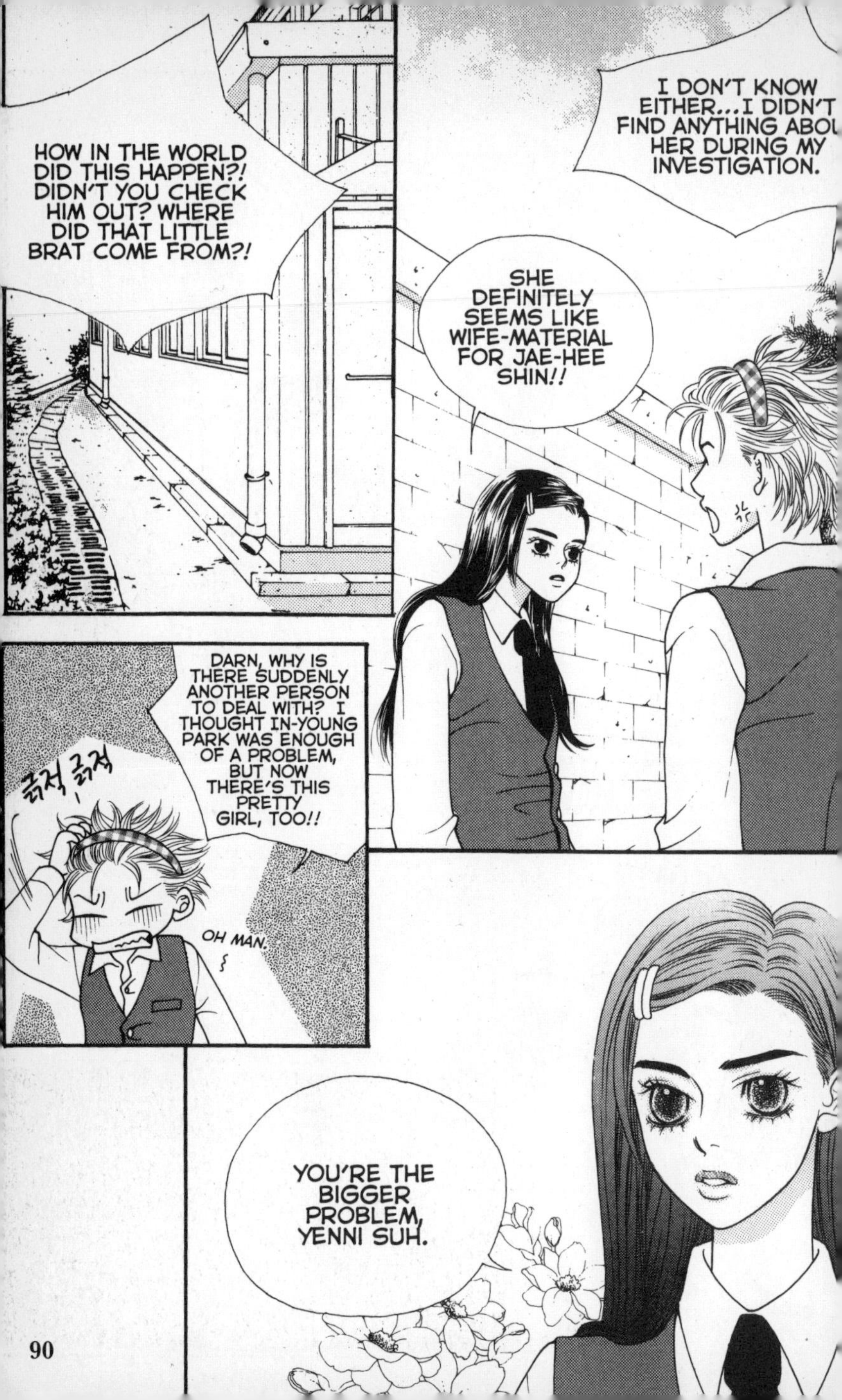
HOW IN THE WORLD DID THIS HAPPEN?! DIDN'T YOU CHECK HIM OUT? WHERE DID THAT LITTLE BRAT COME FROM?!
I DON'T KNOW EITHER...I DIDN'T FIND ANYTHING ABOU HER DURING MY INVESTIGATION.
SHE DEFINITELY SEEMS LIKE WIFE-MATERIAL FOR JAE-HEE SHIN!!
DARN, WHY IS THERE SUDDENLY ANOTHER PERSON TO DEAL WITH? I THOUGHT IN-YOUNG PARK WAS ENOUGH OF A PROBLEM, BUT NOW THERE'S THIS PRETTY GIRL, TOO!!
긁적, 긁적
OH MAN.
YOU'RE THE BIGGER PROBLEM, YENNI SUH.

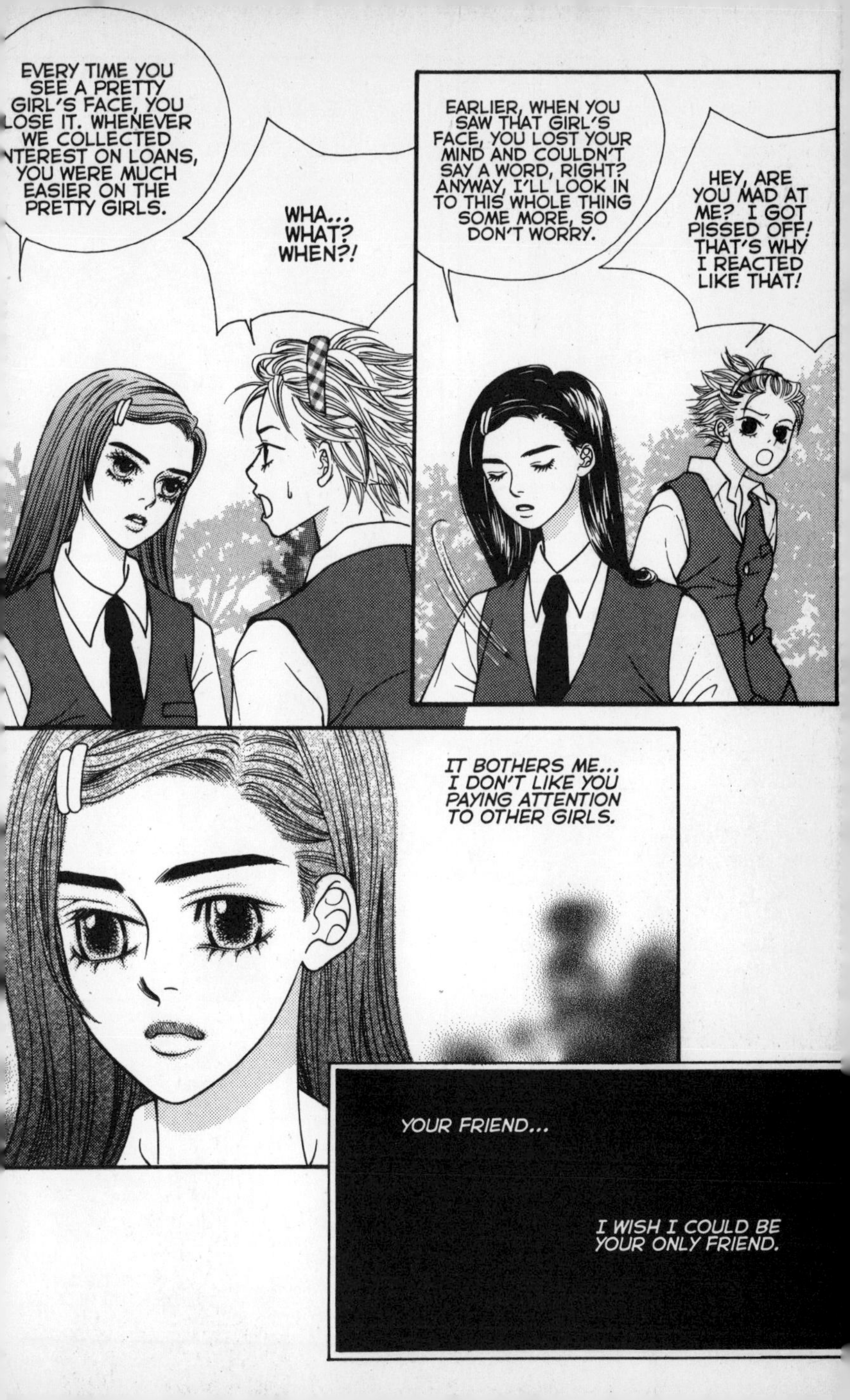

EVERY TIME YOU SEE A PRETTY GIRL'S FACE, YOU LOSE IT. WHENEVER WE COLLECTED INTEREST ON LOANS, YOU WERE MUCH EASIER ON THE PRETTY GIRLS.
WHA... WHAT? WHEN?!
EARLIER, WHEN YOU SAW THAT GIRL'S FACE, YOU LOST YOUR MIND AND COULDN'T SAY A WORD, RIGHT? ANYWAY, I'LL LOOK IN TO THIS WHOLE THING SOME MORE, SO DON'T WORRY.
HEY, ARE YOU MAD AT ME? I GOT PISSED OFF! THAT'S WHY I REACTED LIKE THAT!
IT BOTHERS ME... I DON'T LIKE YOU PAYING ATTENTION TO OTHER GIRLS.
YOUR FRIEND...
I WISH I COULD BE YOUR ONLY FRIEND.

WHY AM I SO DIZZY? I FEEL SO WEAK. I SHOULD HAVE ASKED JAE-HEE TO TAKE ME TO THE NURSE'S OFFICE.

Nurse's office

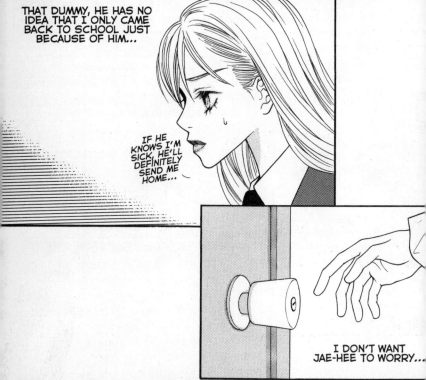

THAT DUMMY, HE HAS NO IDEA THAT I ONLY CAME BACK TO SCHOOL JUST BECAUSE OF HIM...

IF HE KNOWS I'M SICK, HE'LL DEFINITELY SEND ME HOME...

I DON'T WANT JAE-HEE TO WORRY...

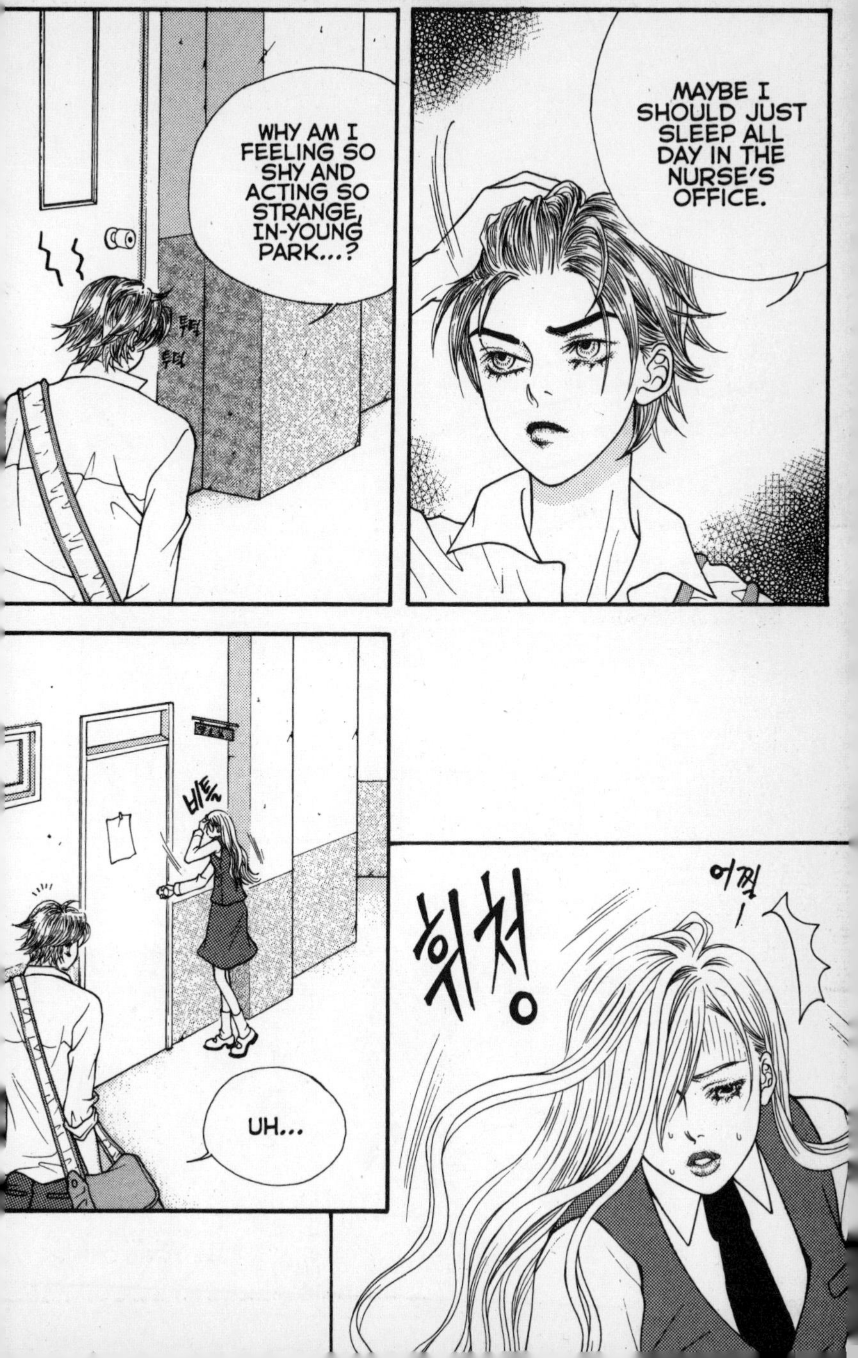
WHY AM I FEELING SO SHY AND ACTING SO STRANGE, IN-YOUNG PARK...?
MAYBE I SHOULD JUST SLEEP ALL DAY IN THE NURSE'S OFFICE.
UH...
휘청
어찔

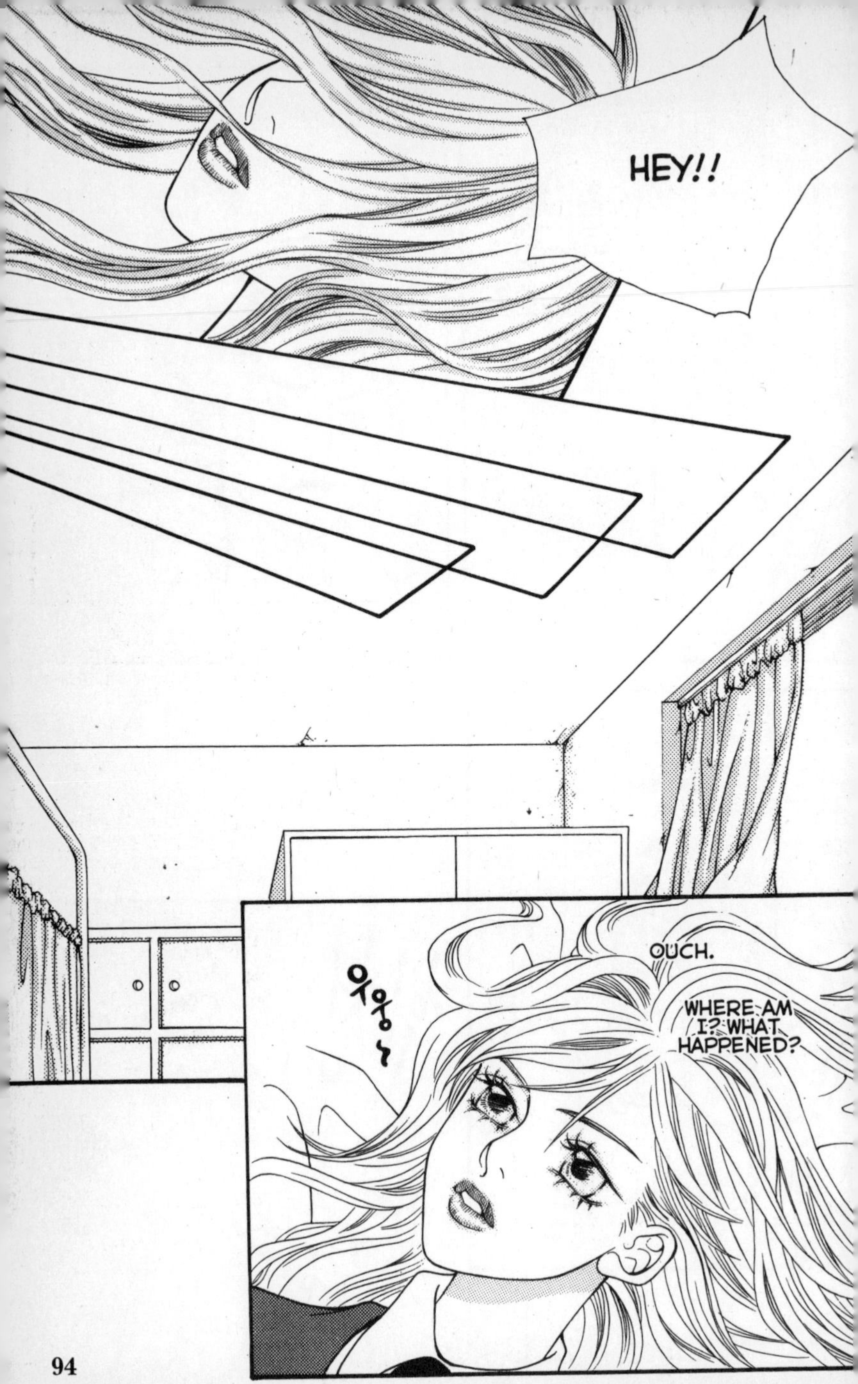
HEY!!
우웅~
OUCH.
WHERE AM I? WHAT HAPPENED?

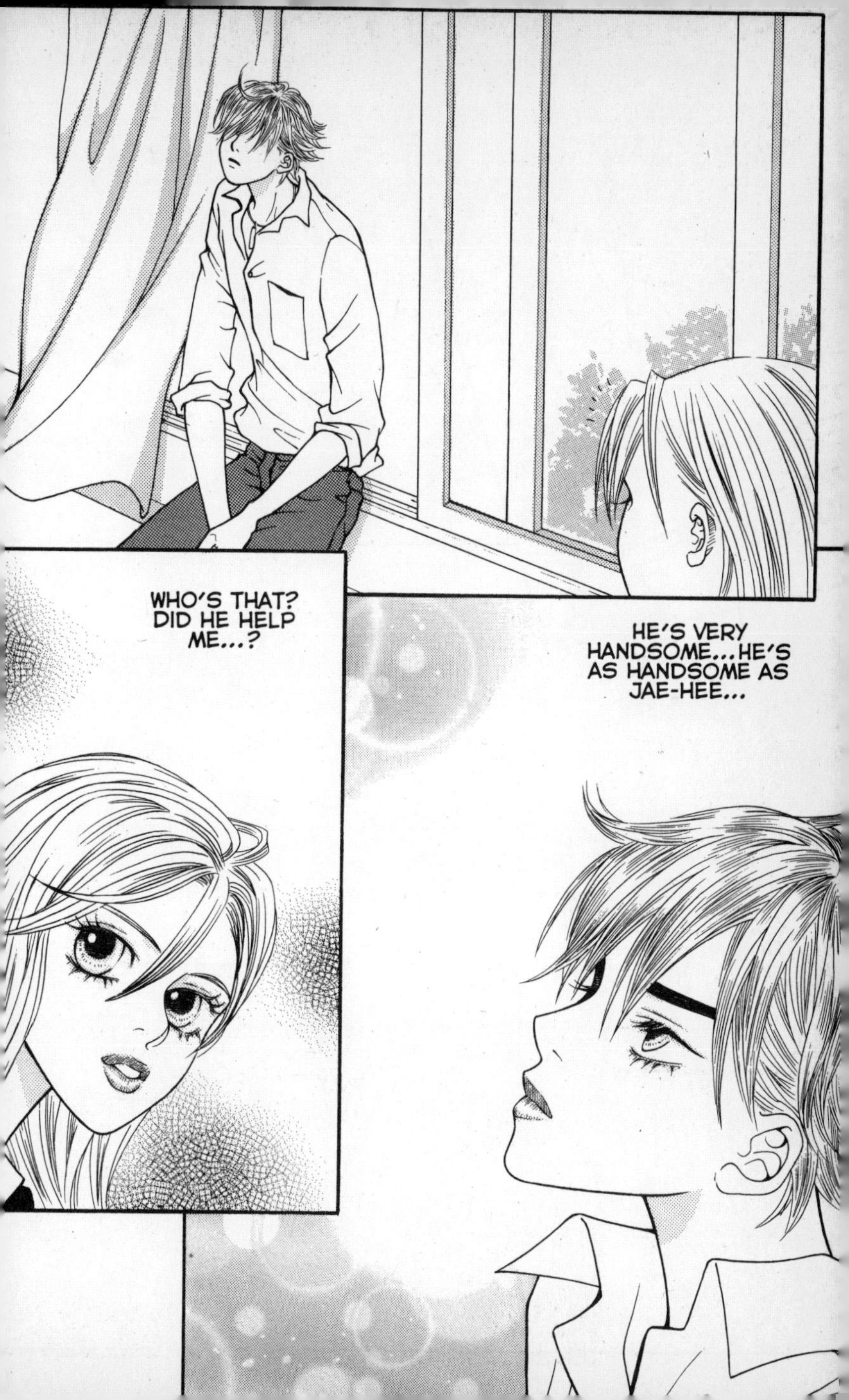
WHO'S THAT? DID HE HELP ME...?
HE'S VERY HANDSOME...HE'S AS HANDSOME AS JAE-HEE...

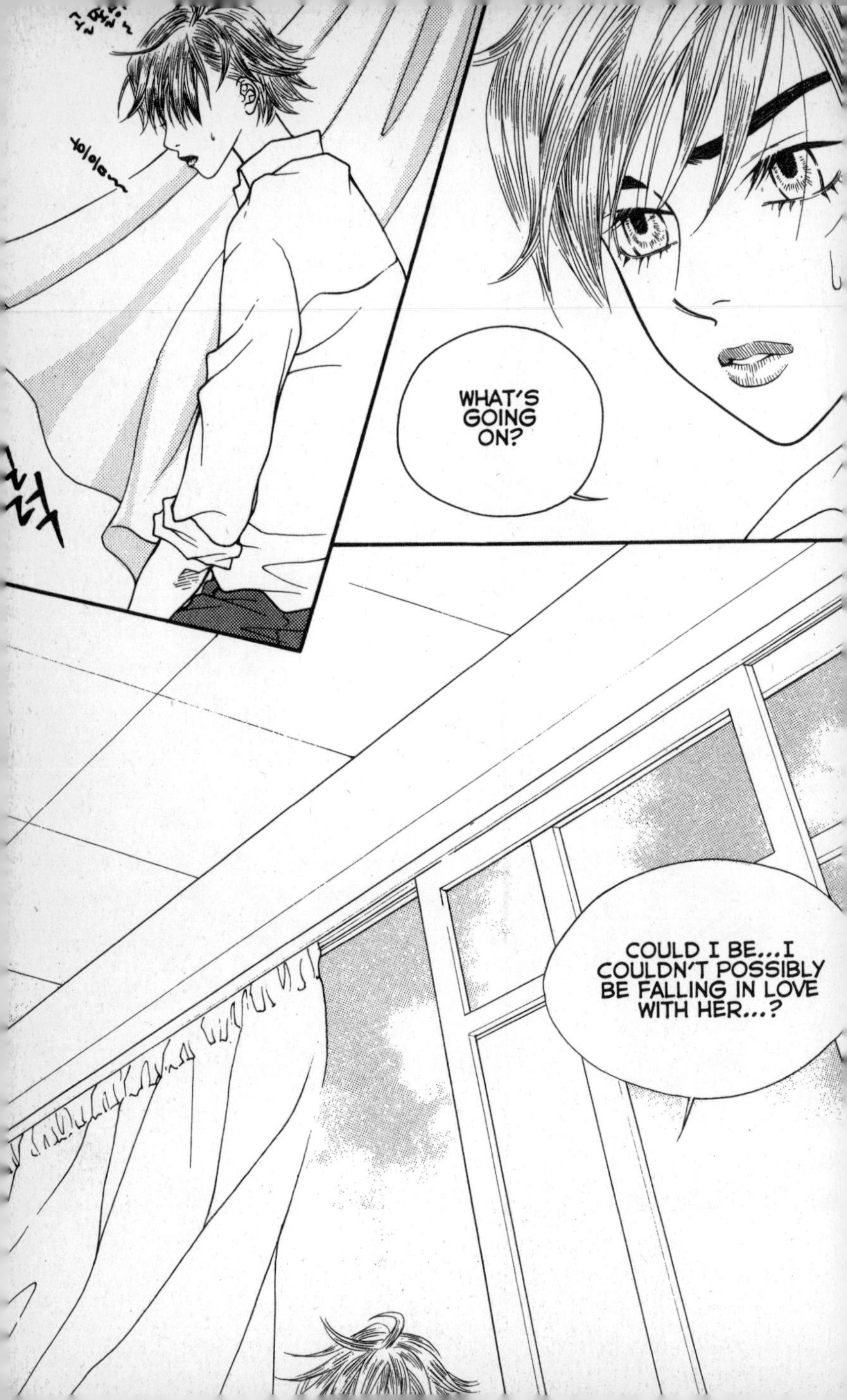
WHAT'S GOING ON?
COULD I BE...I COULDN'T POSSIBLY BE FALLING IN LOVE WITH HER...?

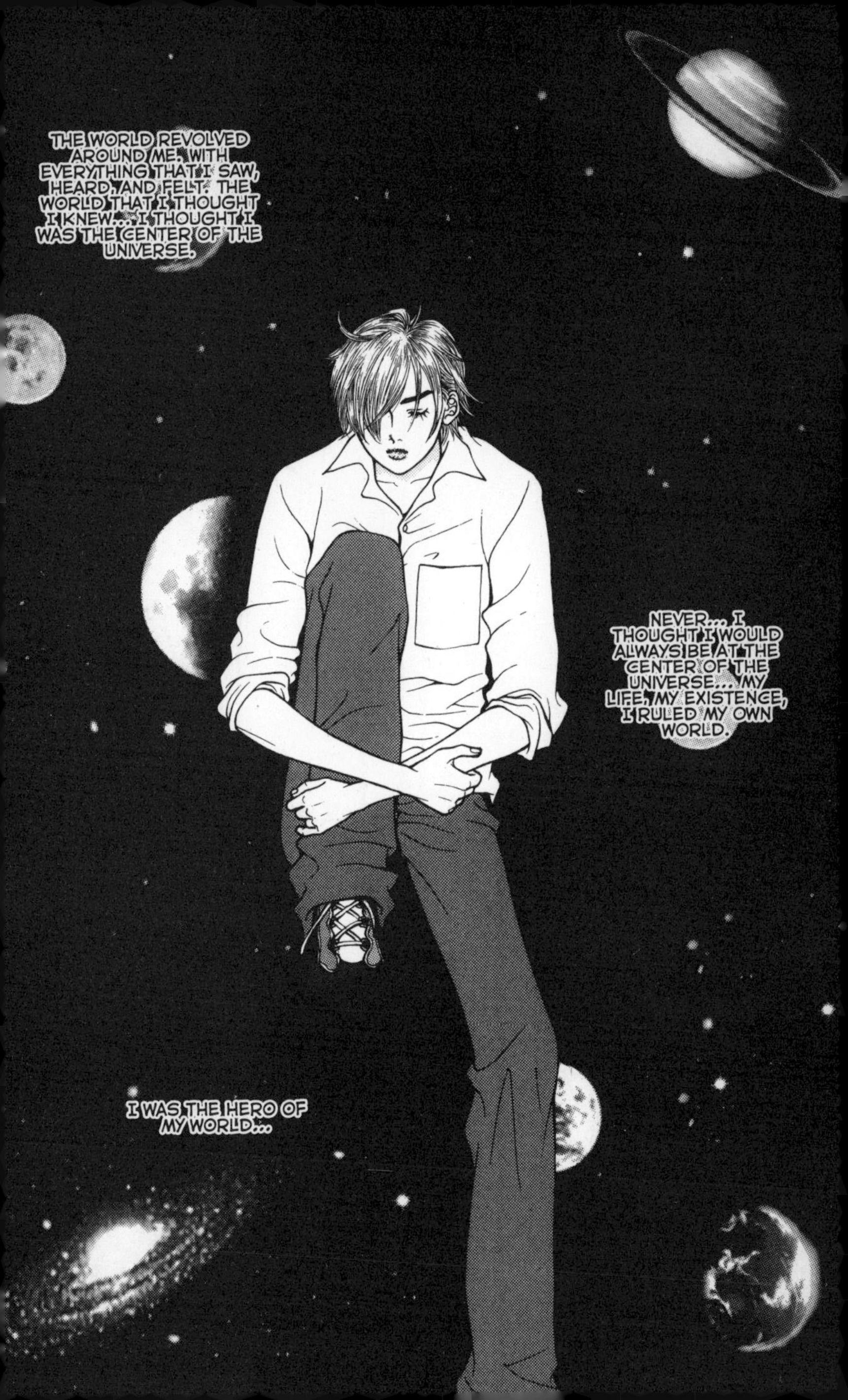
THE WORLD REVOLVED AROUND ME, WITH EVERYTHING THAT I SAW, HEARD AND FELT. THE WORLD THAT I THOUGHT I KNEW... I THOUGHT I WAS THE CENTER OF THE UNIVERSE.
NEVER... I THOUGHT I WOULD ALWAYS BE AT THE CENTER OF THE UNIVERSE... MY LIFE, MY EXISTENCE, I RULED MY OWN WORLD.
I WAS THE HERO OF MY WORLD...

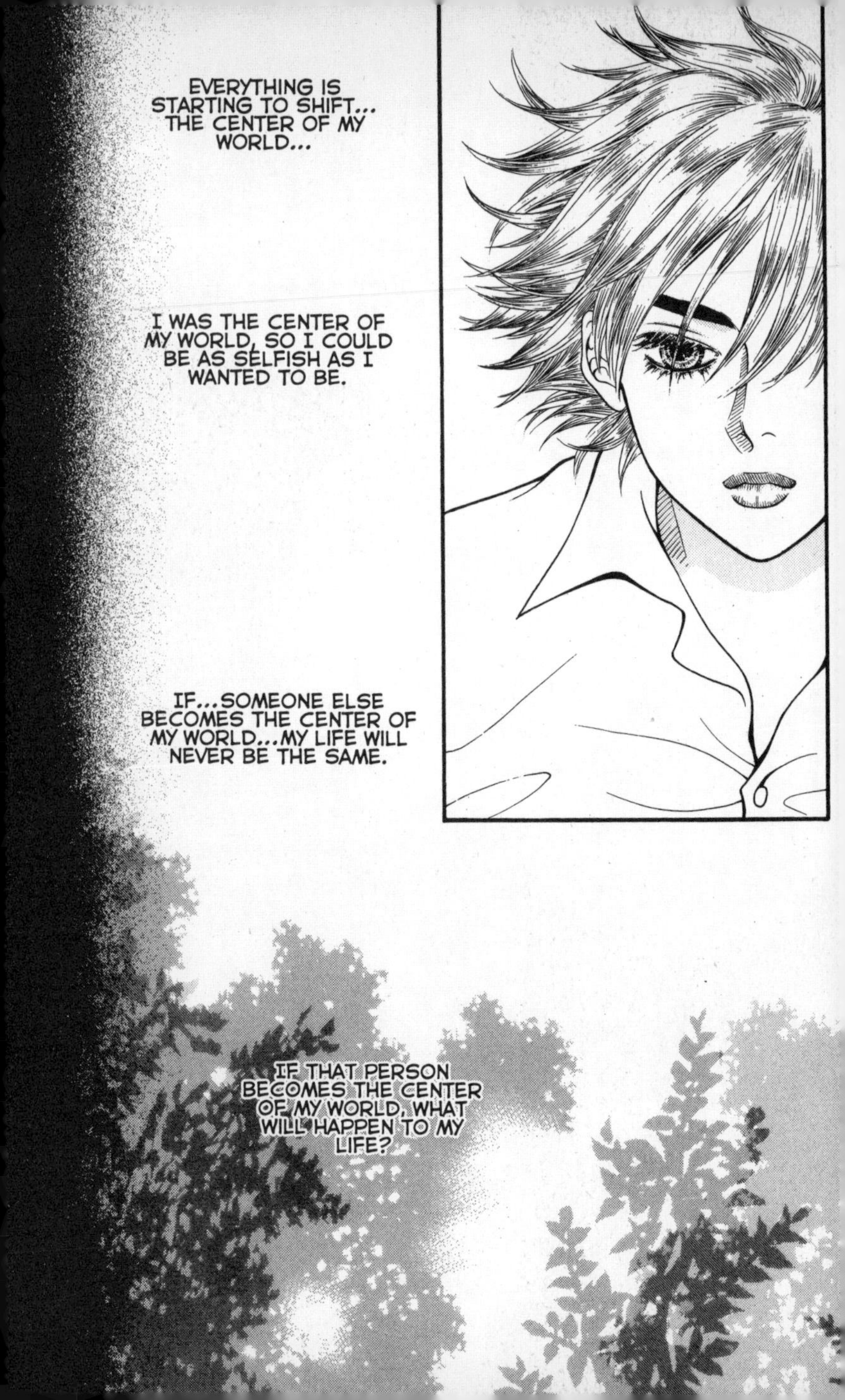
EVERYTHING IS STARTING TO SHIFT... THE CENTER OF MY WORLD...
I WAS THE CENTER OF MY WORLD, SO I COULD BE AS SELFISH AS I WANTED TO BE.
IF...SOMEONE ELSE BECOMES THE CENTER OF MY WORLD...MY LIFE WILL NEVER BE THE SAME.
IF THAT PERSON BECOMES THE CENTER OF MY WORLD, WHAT WILL HAPPEN TO MY LIFE?

BUT, NOW THE WORLD NO LONGER REVOLVES AROUND ME.

ALL OF A SUDDEN...THE CENTER OF MY WORLD IS BECOMING...

I'M SCARED...

TO LIVE, NOT JUST FOR MYSELF BUT FOR SOMEONE ELSE TOO.

I WANT TO BE SELFISH...I WANT TO BE SELFISH...I ONLY WANT TO LOVE MYSELF.

WHAT KIND OF CORNY NARRATION IS THIS?!

NO WAY! THERE'S NO REASON FOR THIS TO HAPPEN!! ME AND THAT AWFUL SPOILED BRAT...

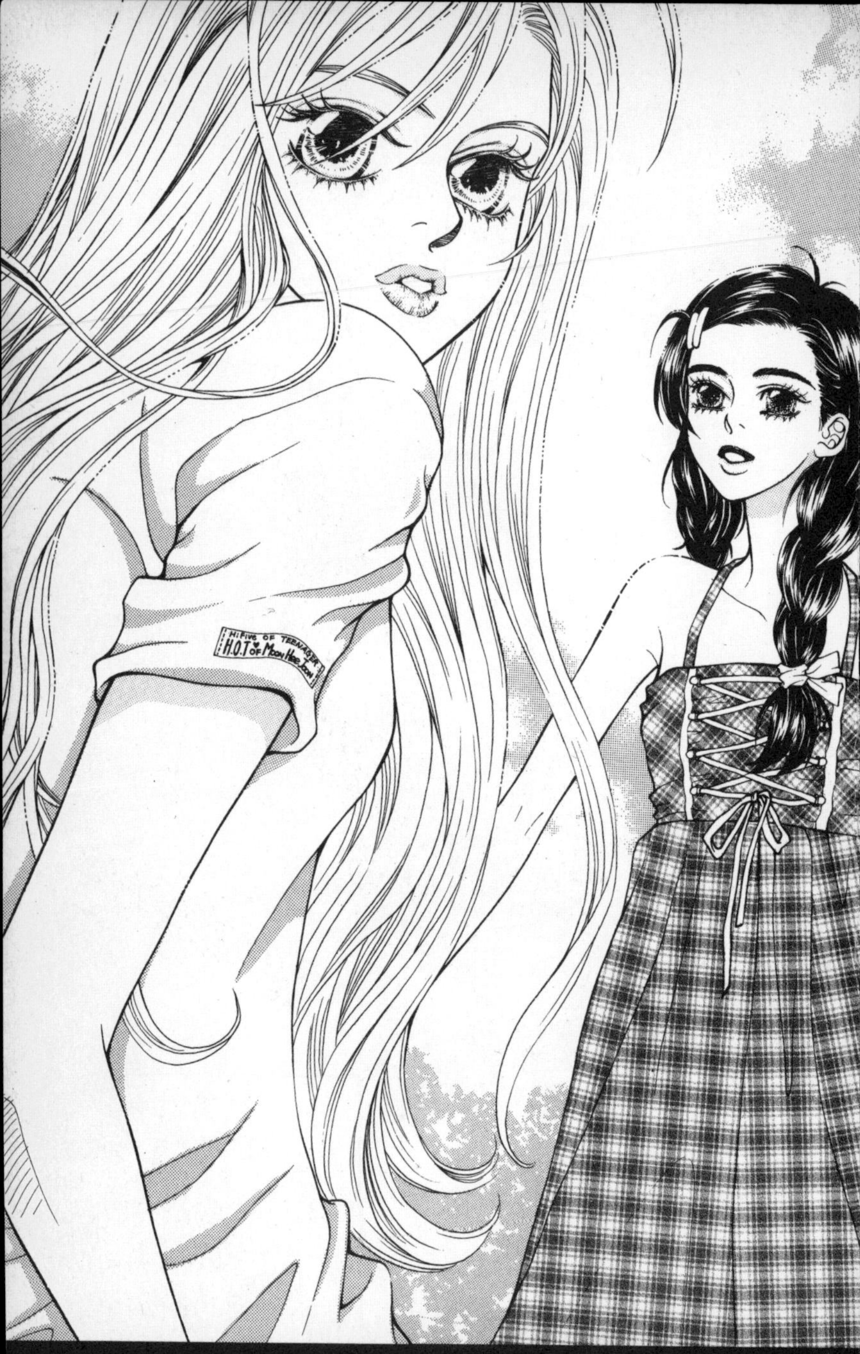

Hi Five OF TEENAGER
H.O.T ♥ OF Moon Hee Joon

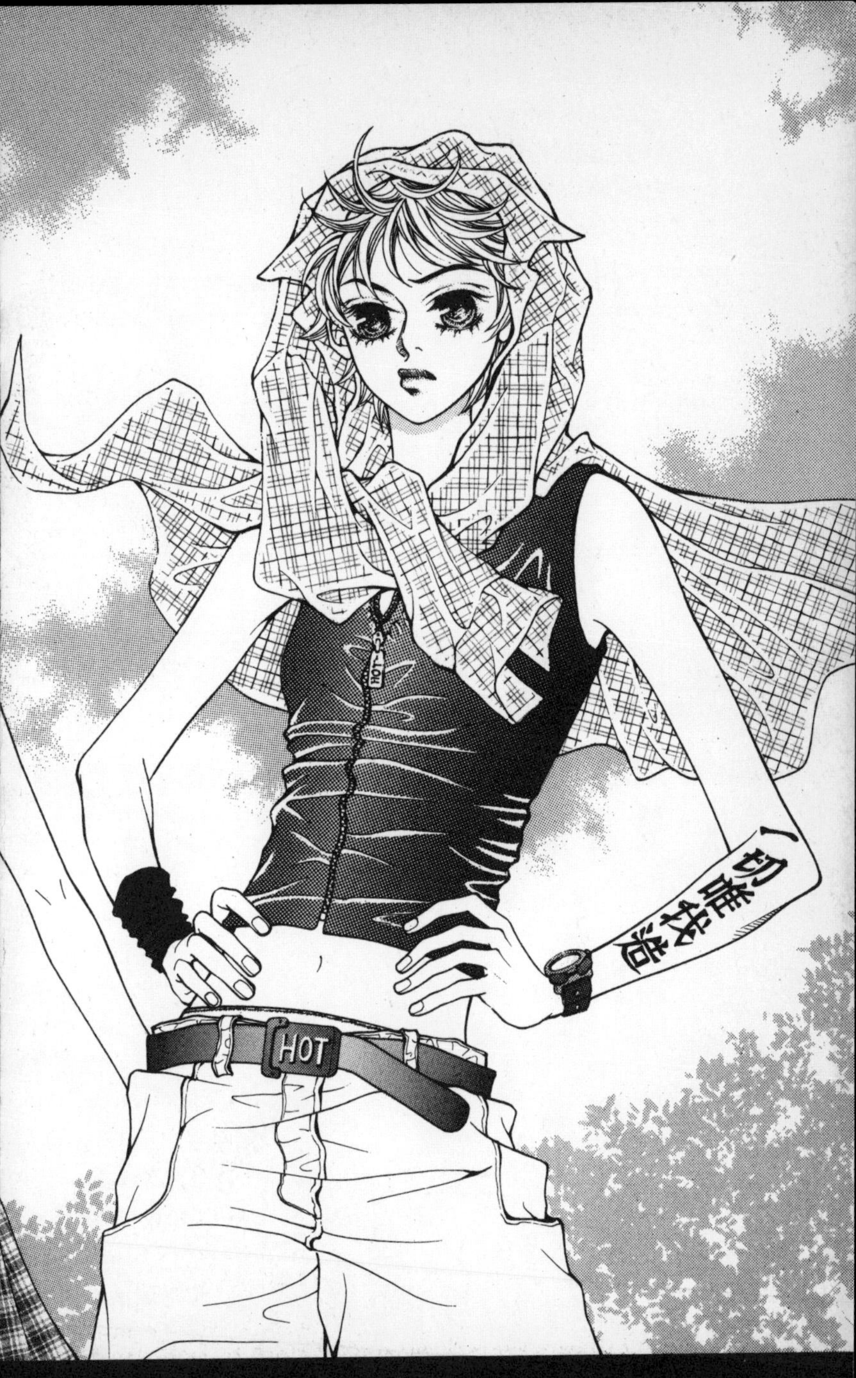
HOT

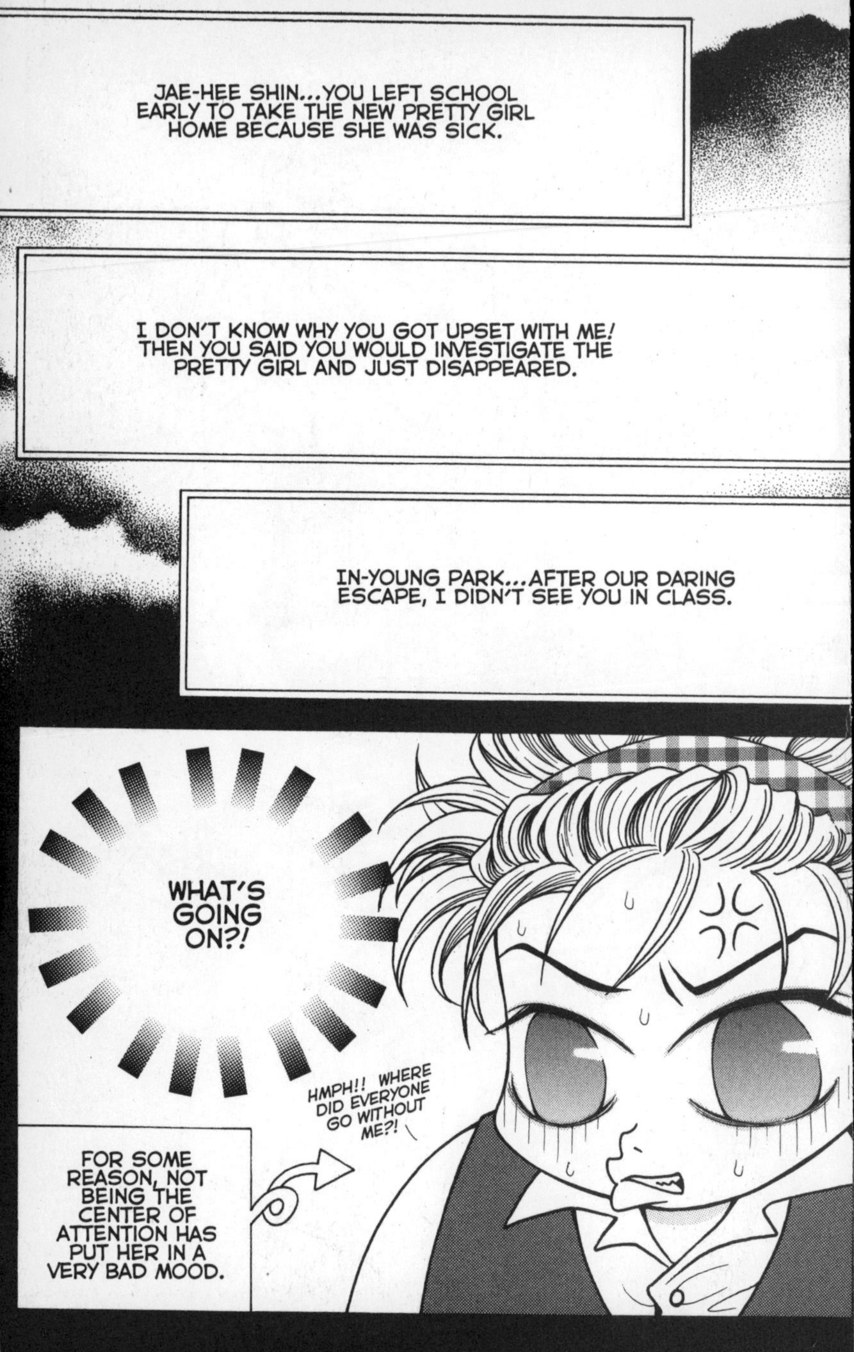
JAE-HEE SHIN...YOU LEFT SCHOOL EARLY TO TAKE THE NEW PRETTY GIRL HOME BECAUSE SHE WAS SICK.
I DON'T KNOW WHY YOU GOT UPSET WITH ME! THEN YOU SAID YOU WOULD INVESTIGATE THE PRETTY GIRL AND JUST DISAPPEARED.
IN-YOUNG PARK...AFTER OUR DARING ESCAPE, I DIDN'T SEE YOU IN CLASS.
WHAT'S GOING ON?!
HMPH!! WHERE DID EVERYONE GO WITHOUT ME?!
FOR SOME REASON, NOT BEING THE CENTER OF ATTENTION HAS PUT HER IN A VERY BAD MOOD.

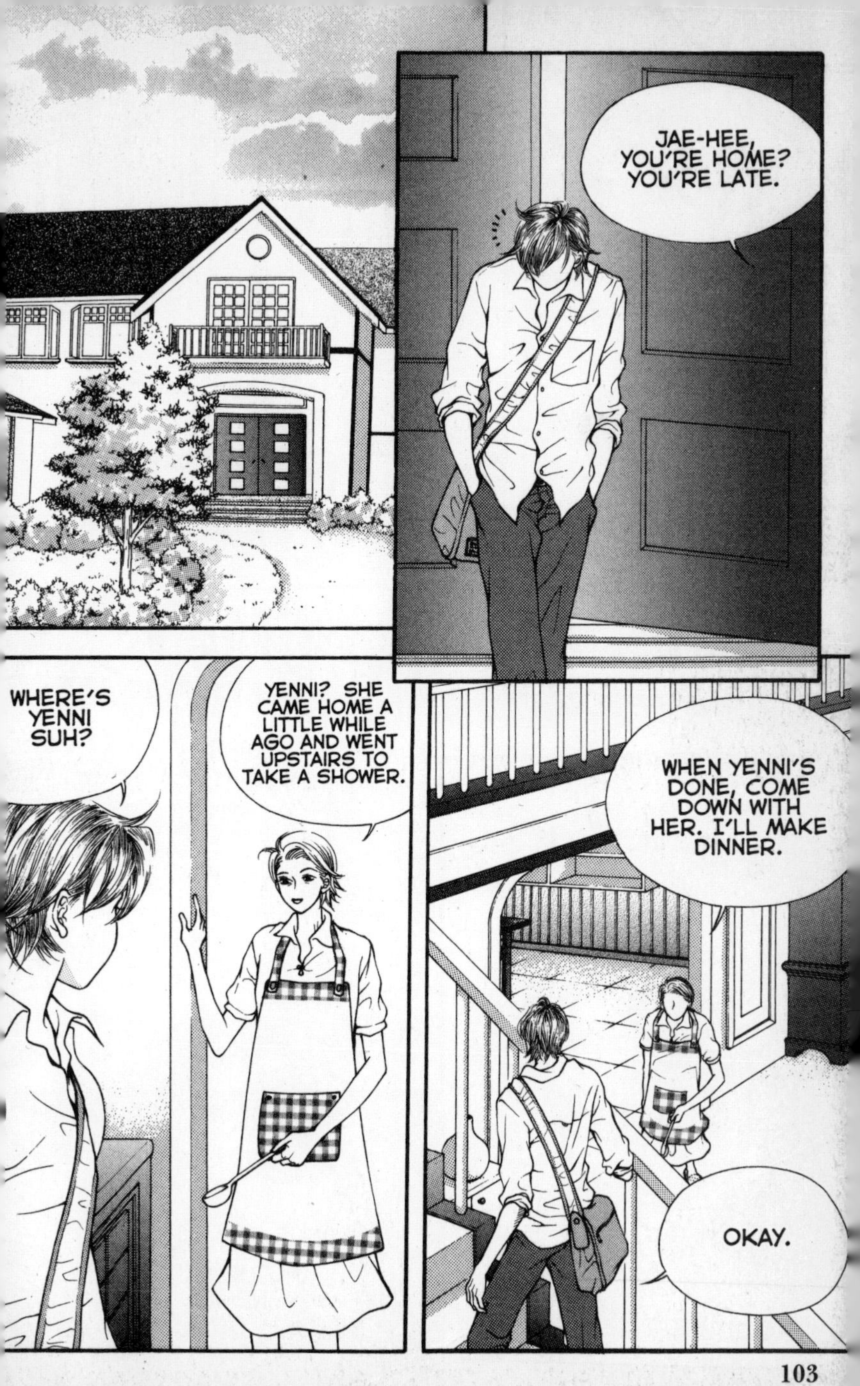
JAE-HEE, YOU'RE HOME? YOU'RE LATE.
WHERE'S YENNI SUH?
YENNI? SHE CAME HOME A LITTLE WHILE AGO AND WENT UPSTAIRS TO TAKE A SHOWER.
WHEN YENNI'S DONE, COME DOWN WITH HER. I'LL MAKE DINNER.
OKAY.

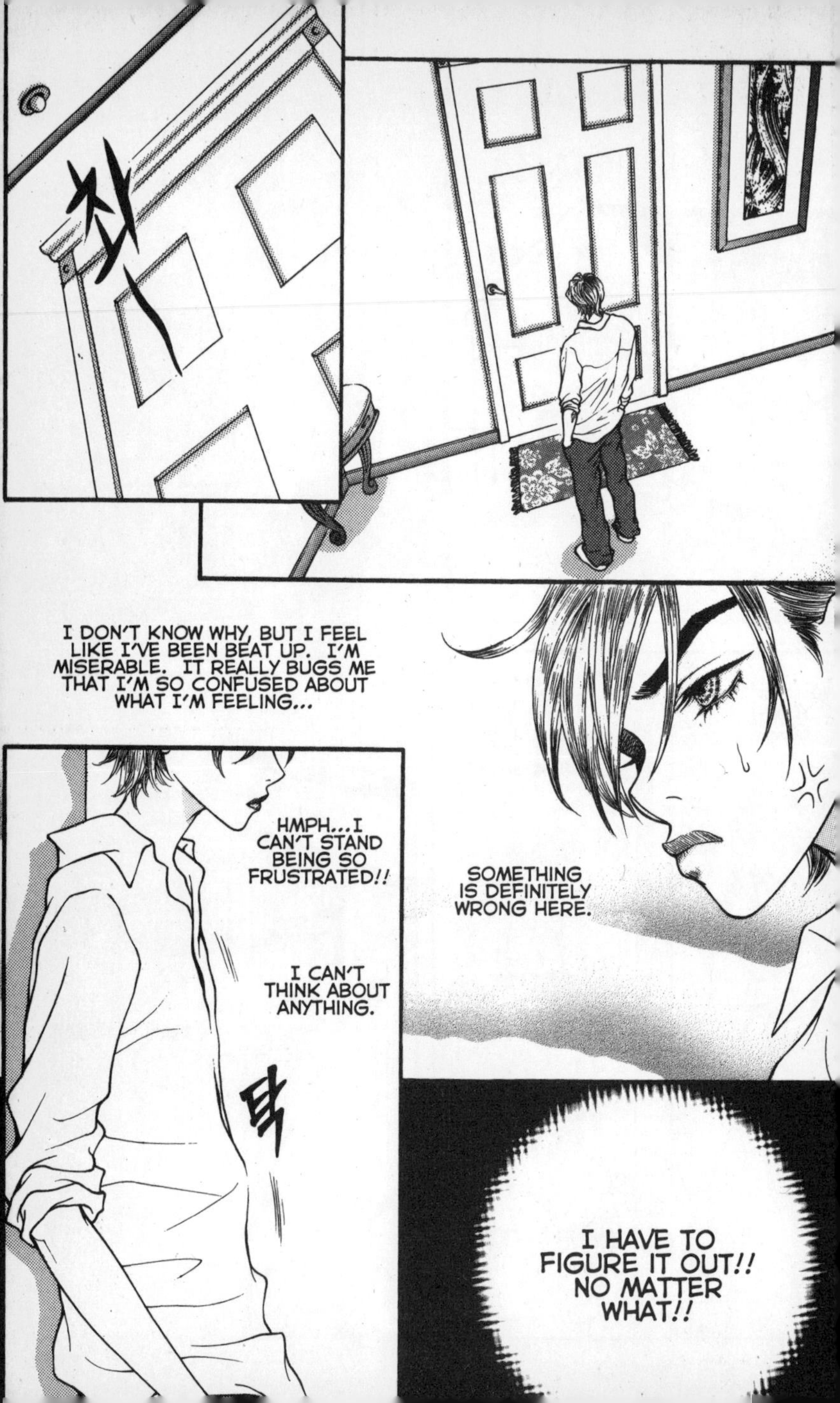
I DON'T KNOW WHY, BUT I FEEL LIKE I'VE BEEN BEAT UP. I'M MISERABLE. IT REALLY BUGS ME THAT I'M SO CONFUSED ABOUT WHAT I'M FEELING...
SOMETHING IS DEFINITELY WRONG HERE.
HMPH...I CAN'T STAND BEING SO FRUSTRATED!!
I CAN'T THINK ABOUT ANYTHING.
탁
I HAVE TO FIGURE IT OUT!! NO MATTER WHAT!!

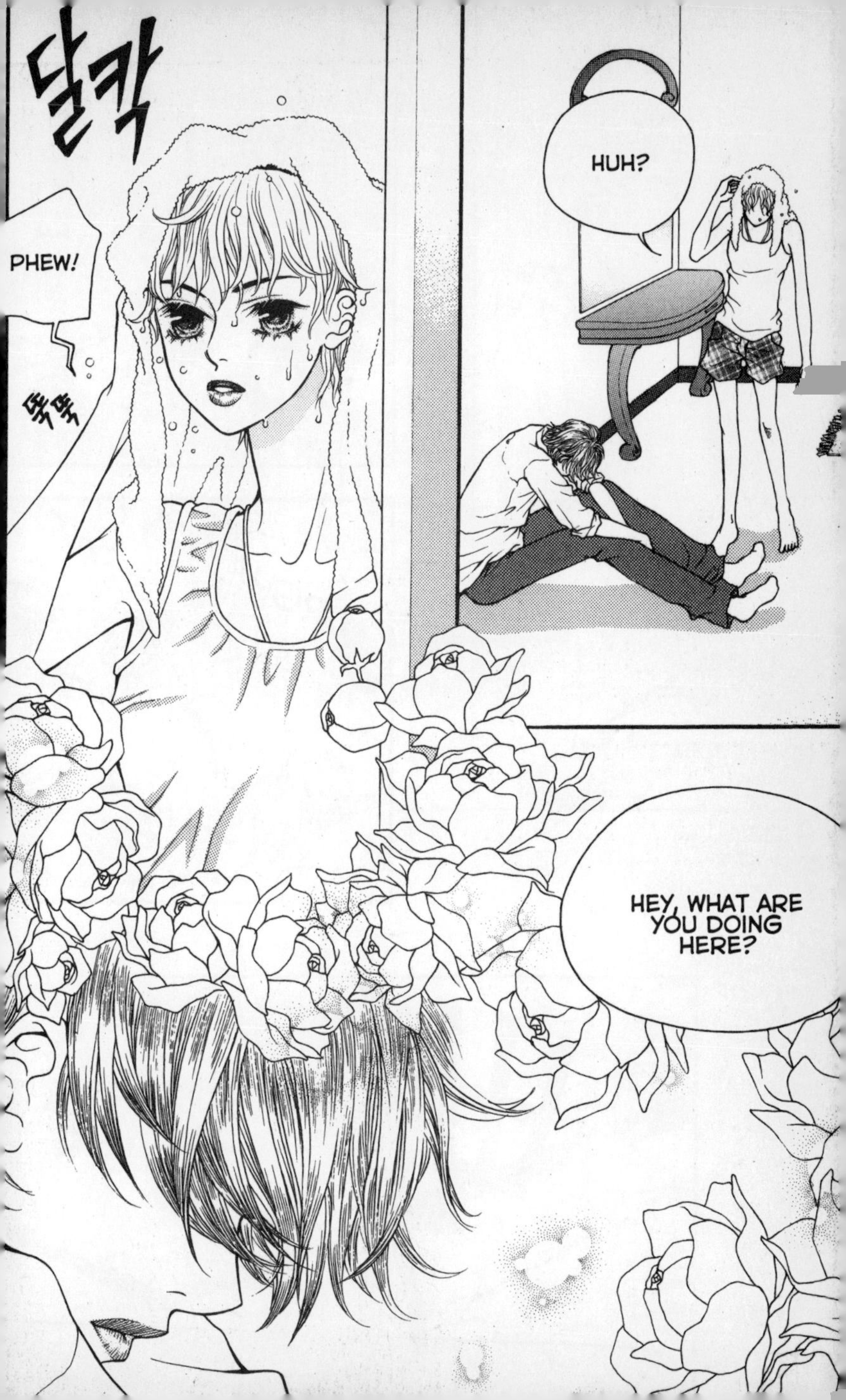
달칵
PHEW!
뚝뚝
HUH?
HEY, WHAT ARE YOU DOING HERE?

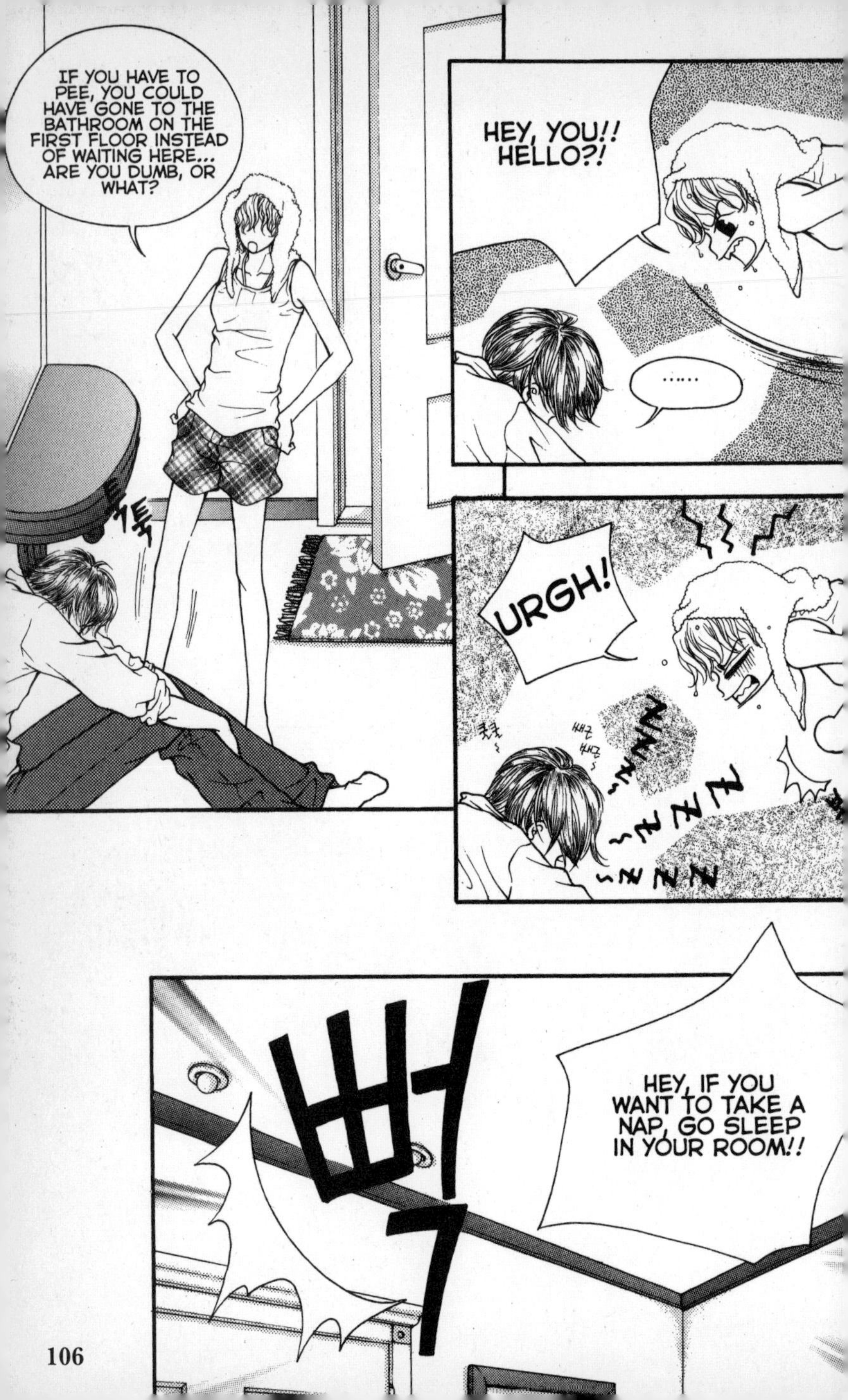
IF YOU HAVE TO PEE, YOU COULD HAVE GONE TO THE BATHROOM ON THE FIRST FLOOR INSTEAD OF WAITING HERE... ARE YOU DUMB, OR WHAT?
HEY, YOU!! HELLO?!
......
URGH!
NNNN...
ZZZ~
ZZZ~
HEY, IF YOU WANT TO TAKE A NAP, GO SLEEP IN YOUR ROOM!!

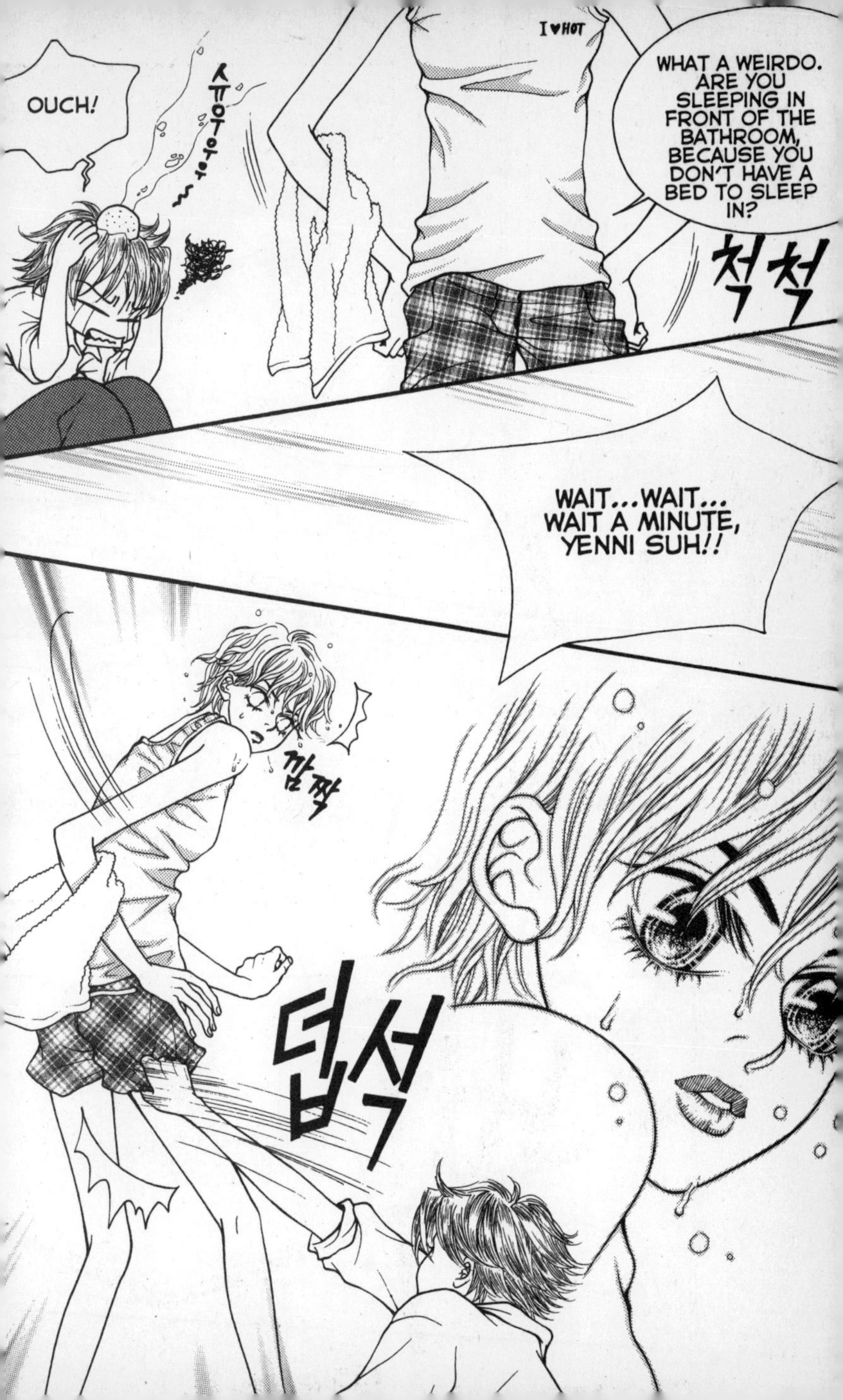
OUCH!
I ♥ HOT
WHAT A WEIRDO. ARE YOU SLEEPING IN FRONT OF THE BATHROOM, BECAUSE YOU DON'T HAVE A BED TO SLEEP IN?
척척
WAIT...WAIT... WAIT A MINUTE, YENNI SUH!!
깜짝
덥석

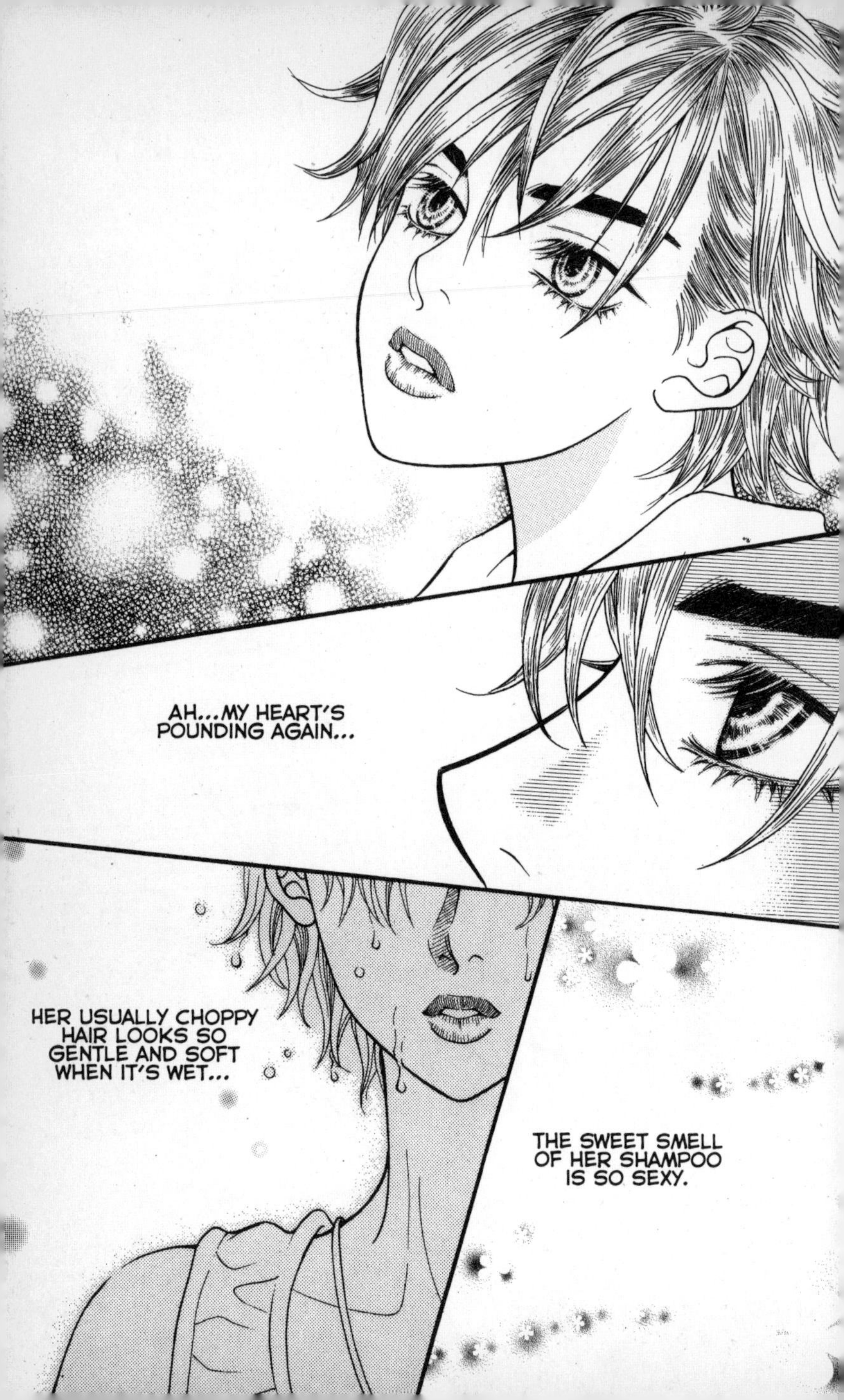
AH...MY HEART'S POUNDING AGAIN...
HER USUALLY CHOPPY HAIR LOOKS SO GENTLE AND SOFT WHEN IT'S WET...
THE SWEET SMELL OF HER SHAMPOO IS SO SEXY.

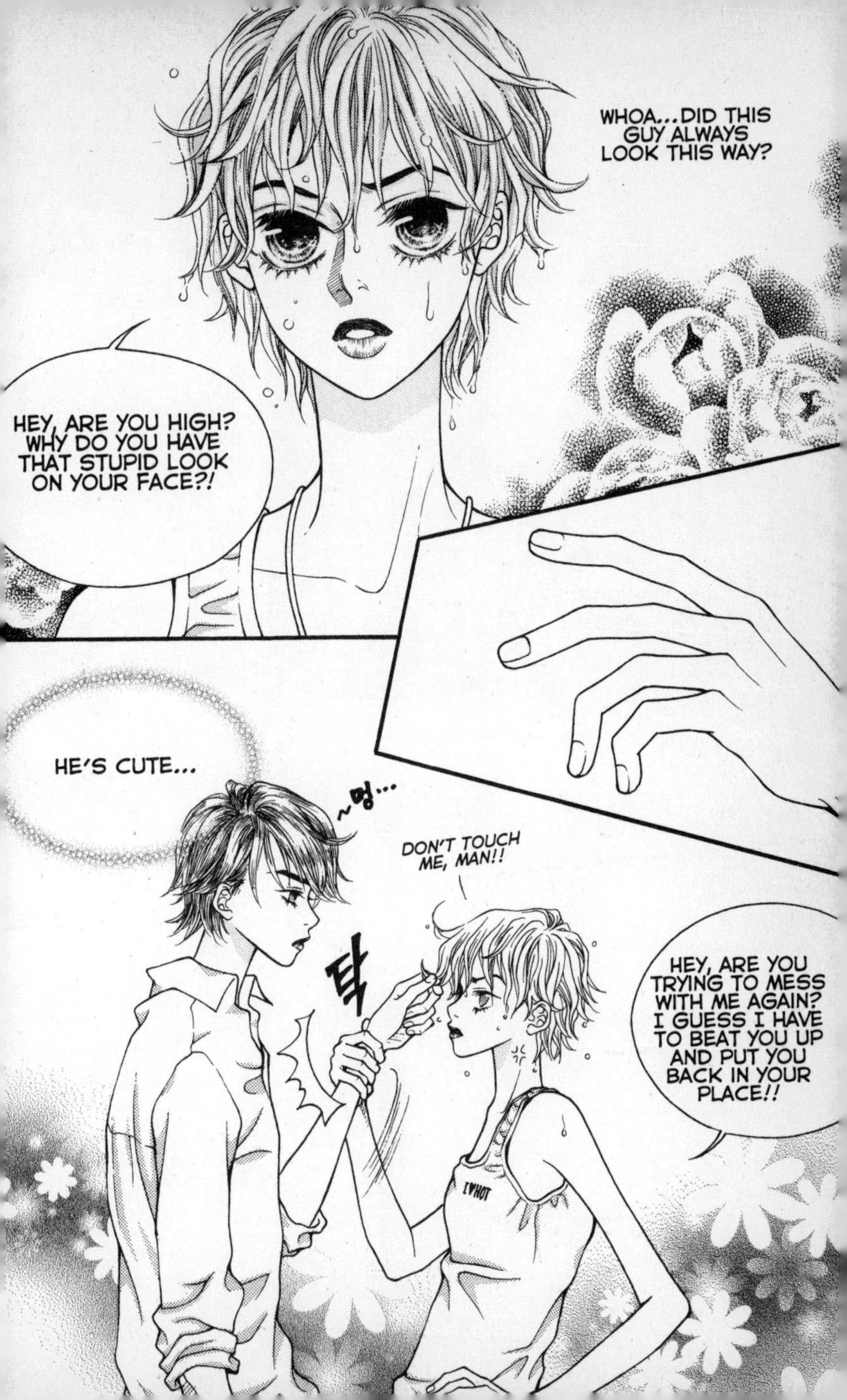
WHOA...DID THIS GUY ALWAYS LOOK THIS WAY?
HEY, ARE YOU HIGH? WHY DO YOU HAVE THAT STUPID LOOK ON YOUR FACE?!
HE'S CUTE...
~멍...
탁
DON'T TOUCH ME, MAN!!
HEY, ARE YOU TRYING TO MESS WITH ME AGAIN? I GUESS I HAVE TO BEAT YOU UP AND PUT YOU BACK IN YOUR PLACE!!
I♥HOT

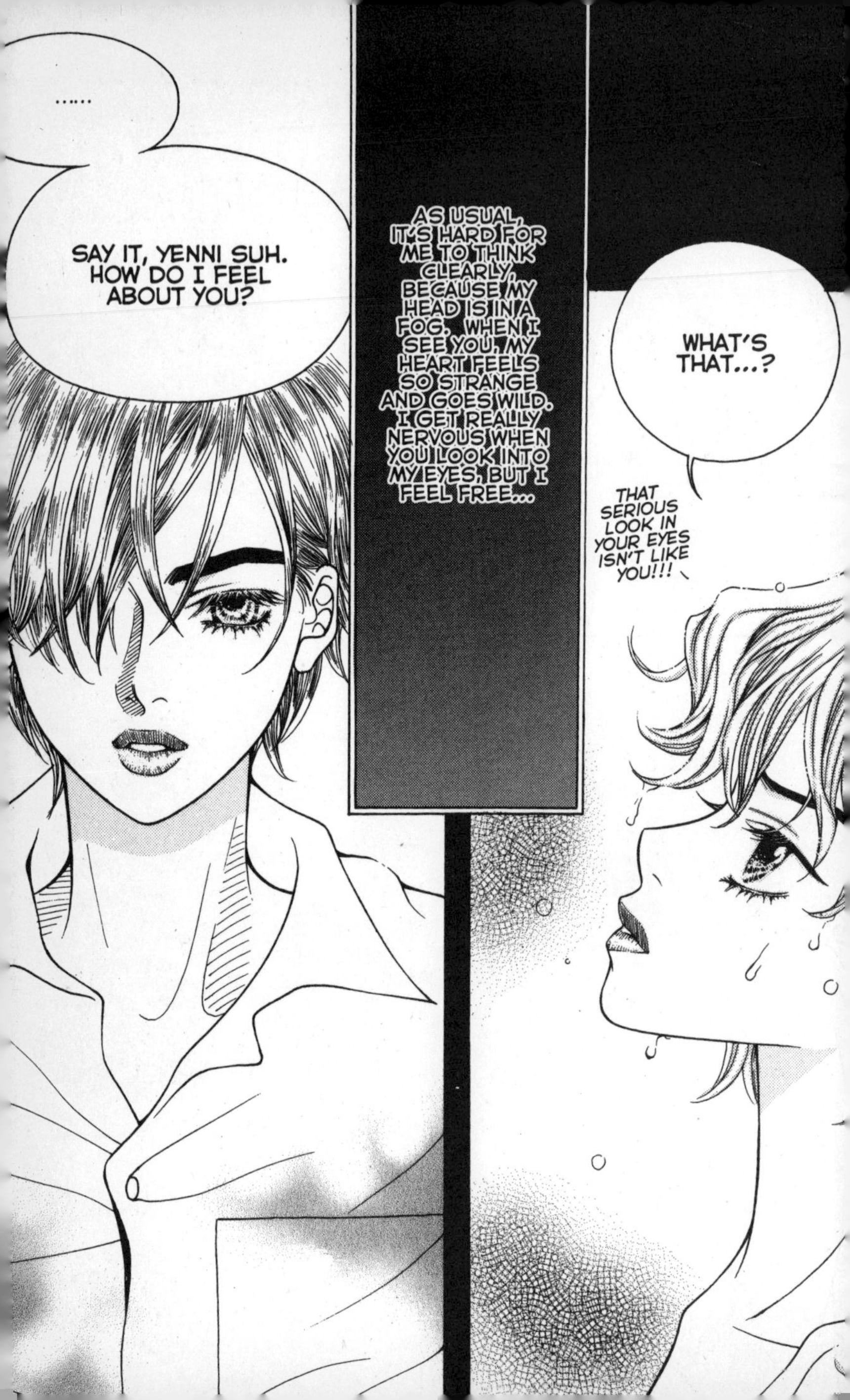
......
SAY IT, YENNI SUH. HOW DO I FEEL ABOUT YOU?
AS USUAL, IT'S HARD FOR ME TO THINK CLEARLY, BECAUSE MY HEAD IS IN A FOG. WHEN I SEE YOU, MY HEART FEELS SO STRANGE AND GOES WILD. I GET REALLY NERVOUS WHEN YOU LOOK INTO MY EYES, BUT I FEEL FREE...
WHAT'S THAT...?
THAT SERIOUS LOOK IN YOUR EYES ISN'T LIKE YOU!!!

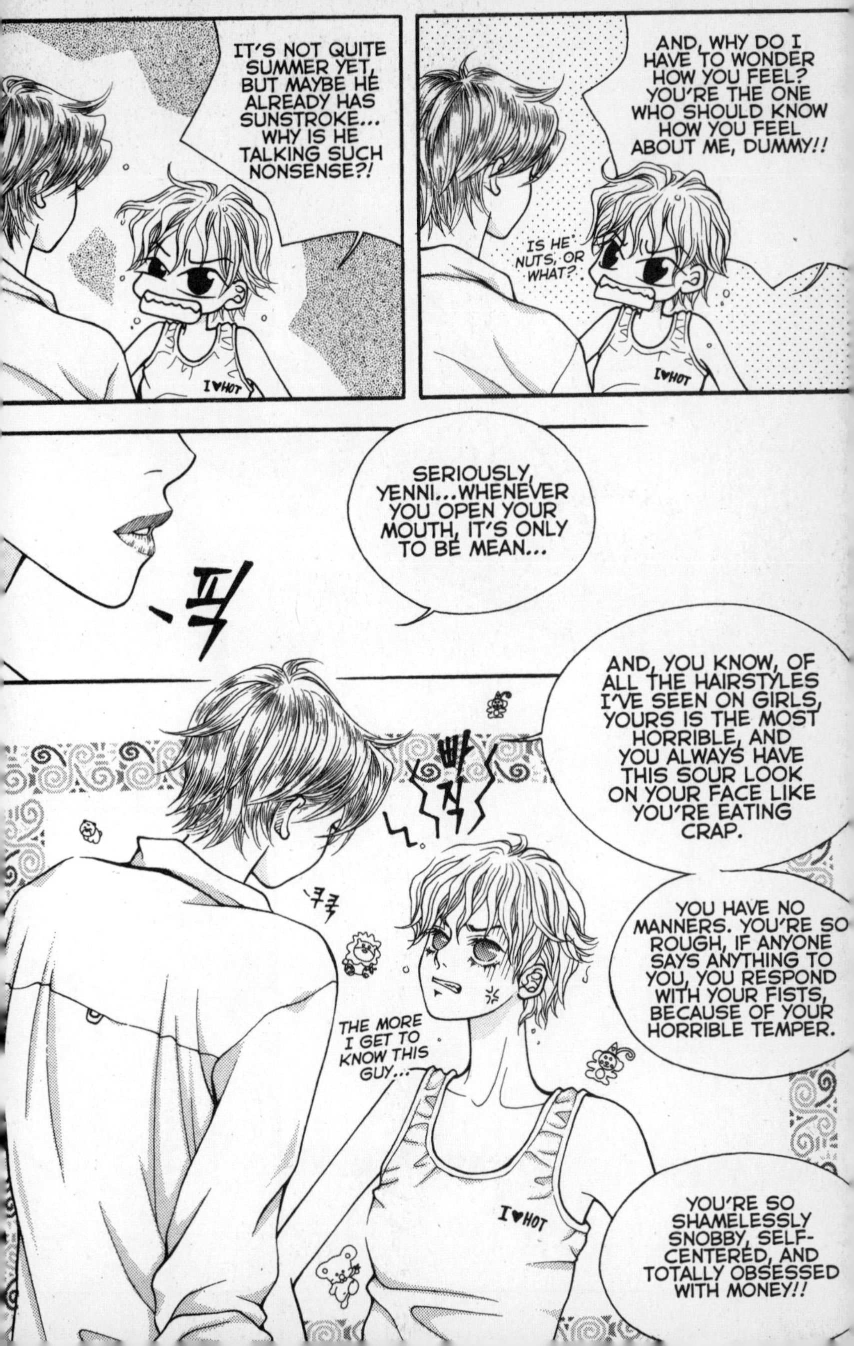

IT'S NOT QUITE SUMMER YET, BUT MAYBE HE ALREADY HAS SUNSTROKE... WHY IS HE TALKING SUCH NONSENSE?!
I♥HOT
AND, WHY DO I HAVE TO WONDER HOW YOU FEEL? YOU'RE THE ONE WHO SHOULD KNOW HOW YOU FEEL ABOUT ME, DUMMY!!
IS HE NUTS, OR WHAT?
I♥HOT
SERIOUSLY, YENNI...WHENEVER YOU OPEN YOUR MOUTH, IT'S ONLY TO BE MEAN...
픽
빠직
AND, YOU KNOW, OF ALL THE HAIRSTYLES I'VE SEEN ON GIRLS, YOURS IS THE MOST HORRIBLE, AND YOU ALWAYS HAVE THIS SOUR LOOK ON YOUR FACE LIKE YOU'RE EATING CRAP.
YOU HAVE NO MANNERS. YOU'RE SO ROUGH, IF ANYONE SAYS ANYTHING TO YOU, YOU RESPOND WITH YOUR FISTS, BECAUSE OF YOUR HORRIBLE TEMPER.
THE MORE I GET TO KNOW THIS GUY...
I♥HOT
YOU'RE SO SHAMELESSLY SNOBBY, SELF-CENTERED, AND TOTALLY OBSESSED WITH MONEY!!

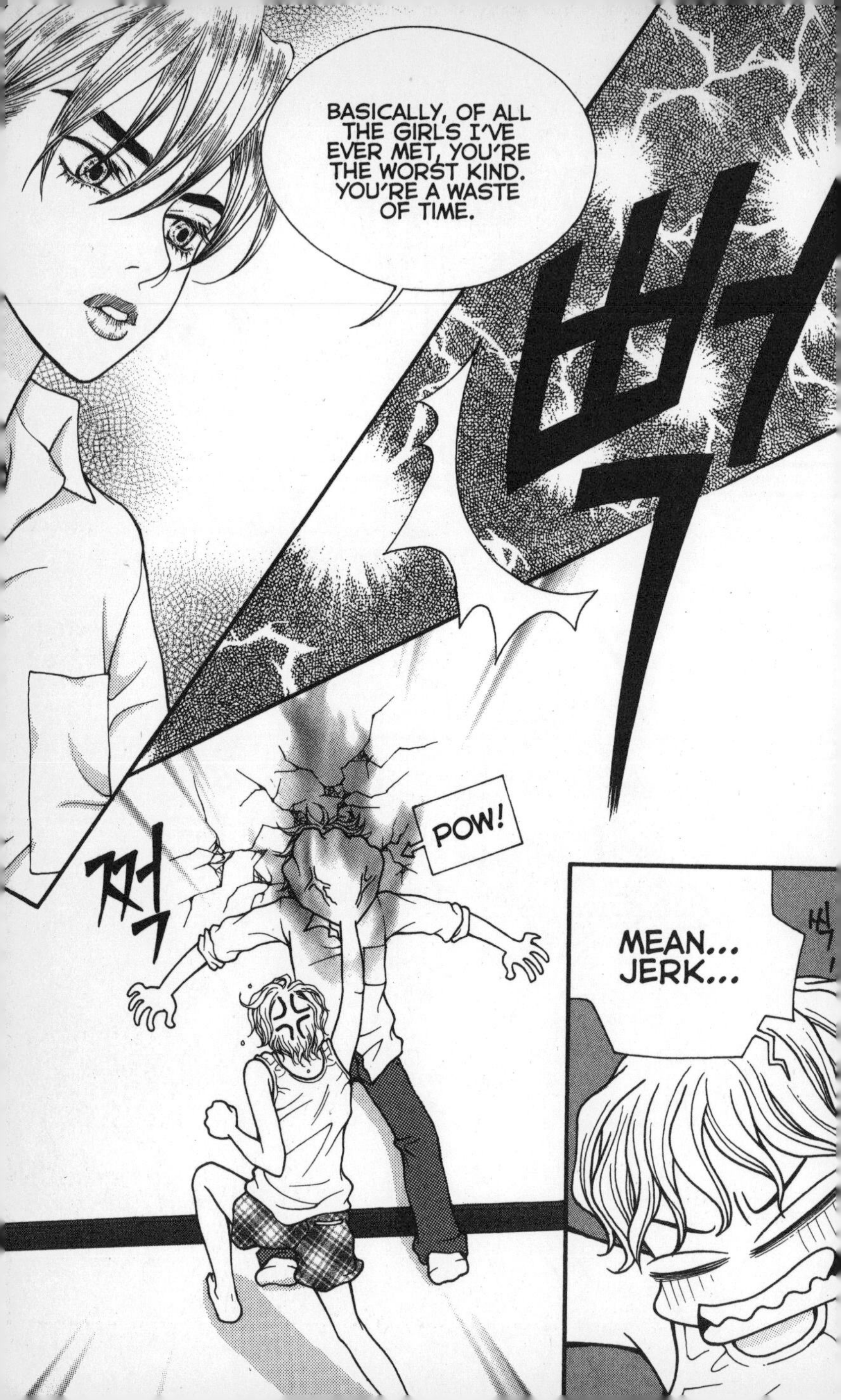
BASICALLY, OF ALL THE GIRLS I'VE EVER MET, YOU'RE THE WORST KIND. YOU'RE A WASTE OF TIME.
빡
POW!
MEAN... JERK...

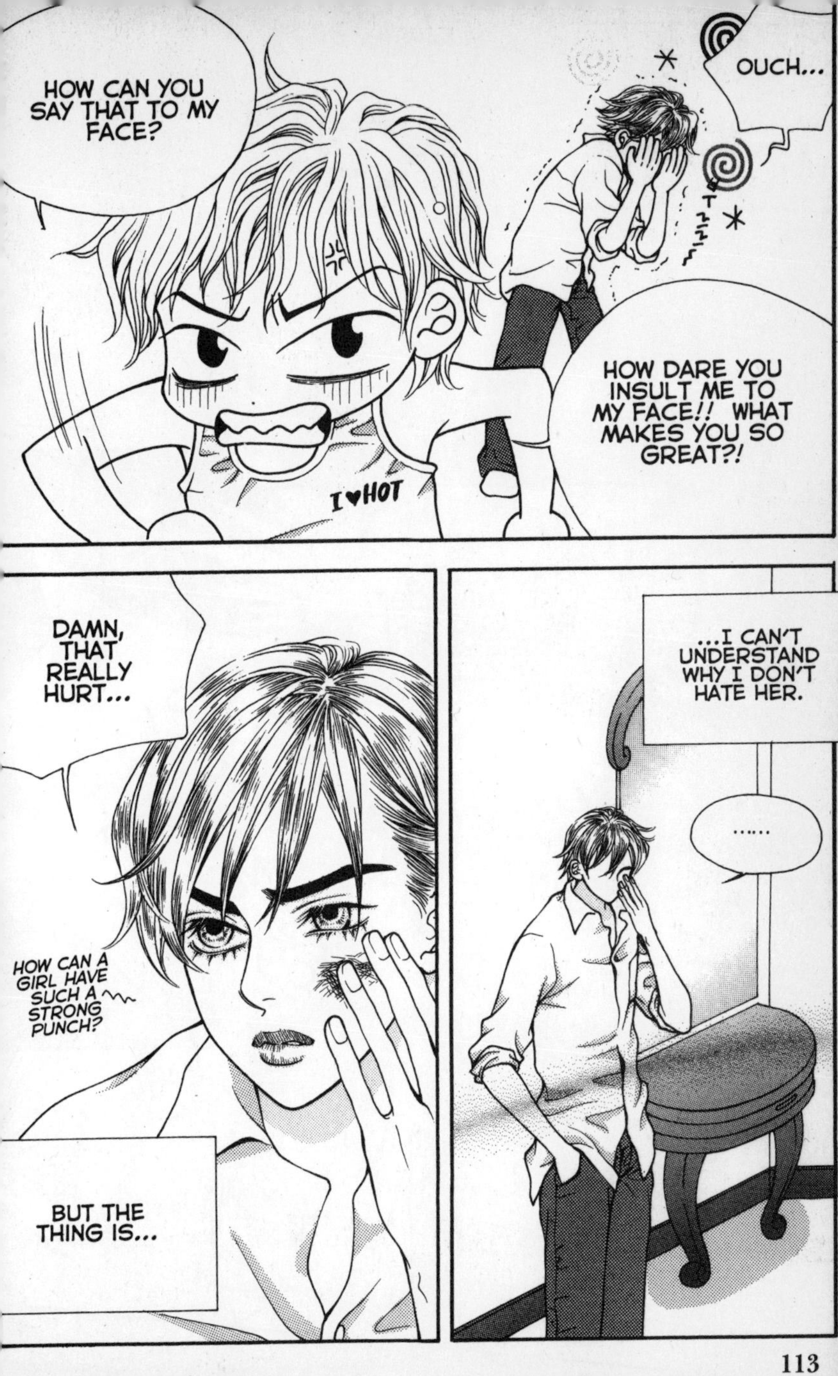
HOW CAN YOU SAY THAT TO MY FACE?
OUCH...
HOW DARE YOU INSULT ME TO MY FACE!! WHAT MAKES YOU SO GREAT?!
I ♥ HOT
DAMN, THAT REALLY HURT...
HOW CAN A GIRL HAVE SUCH A STRONG PUNCH?
BUT THE THING IS...
...I CAN'T UNDERSTAND WHY I DON'T HATE HER.
......

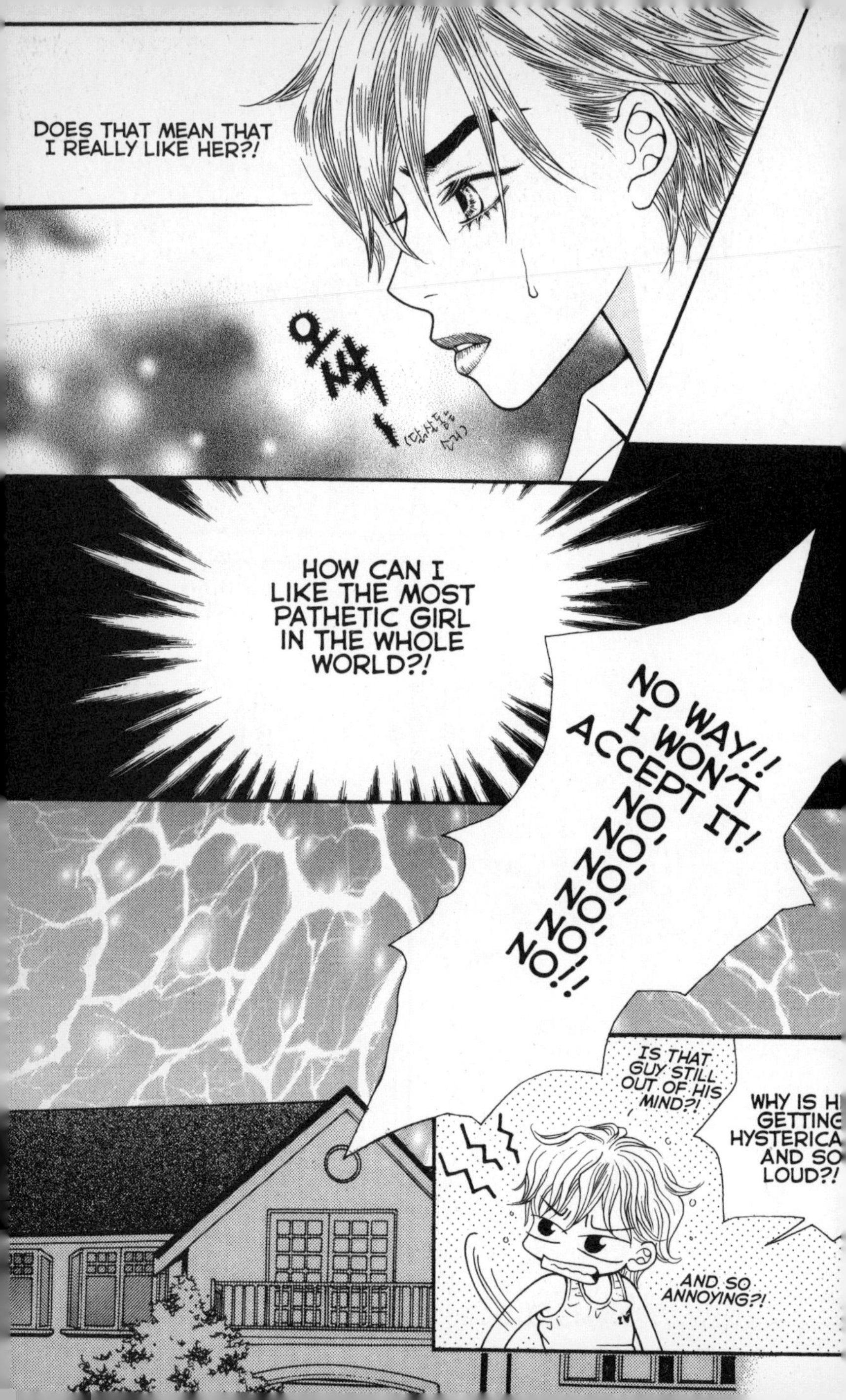
DOES THAT MEAN THAT I REALLY LIKE HER?!
HOW CAN I LIKE THE MOST PATHETIC GIRL IN THE WHOLE WORLD?!
NO WAY!! I WON'T ACCEPT IT! NO, NO, NO, NO, NO, NO!!
IS THAT GUY STILL OUT OF HIS MIND?!
WHY IS HI GETTING HYSTERICA AND SO LOUD?!
AND SO ANNOYING?!

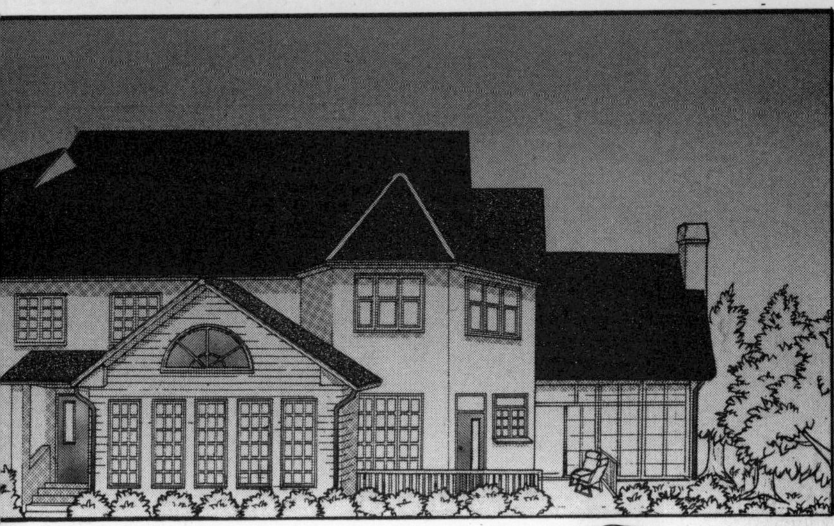

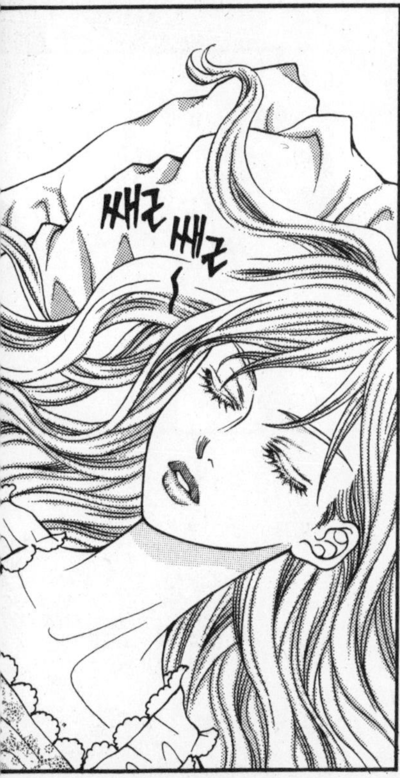
쌔근 쌔근~

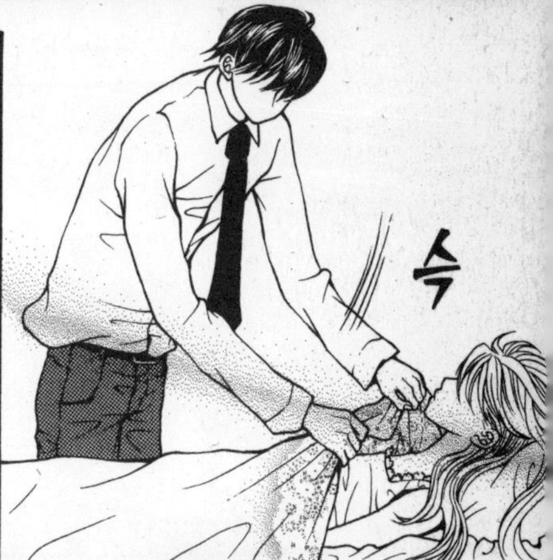
슥

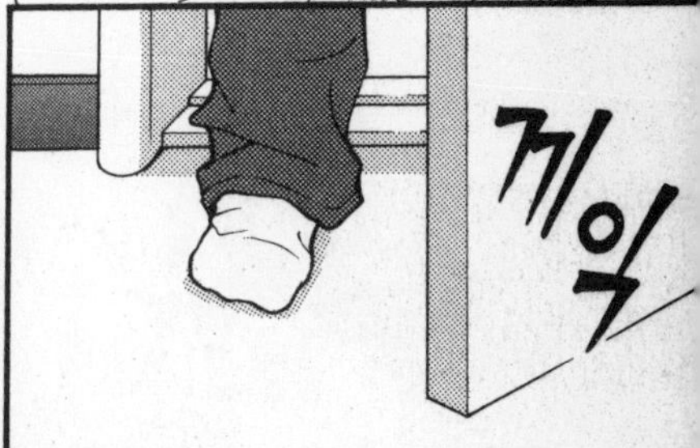
끼익

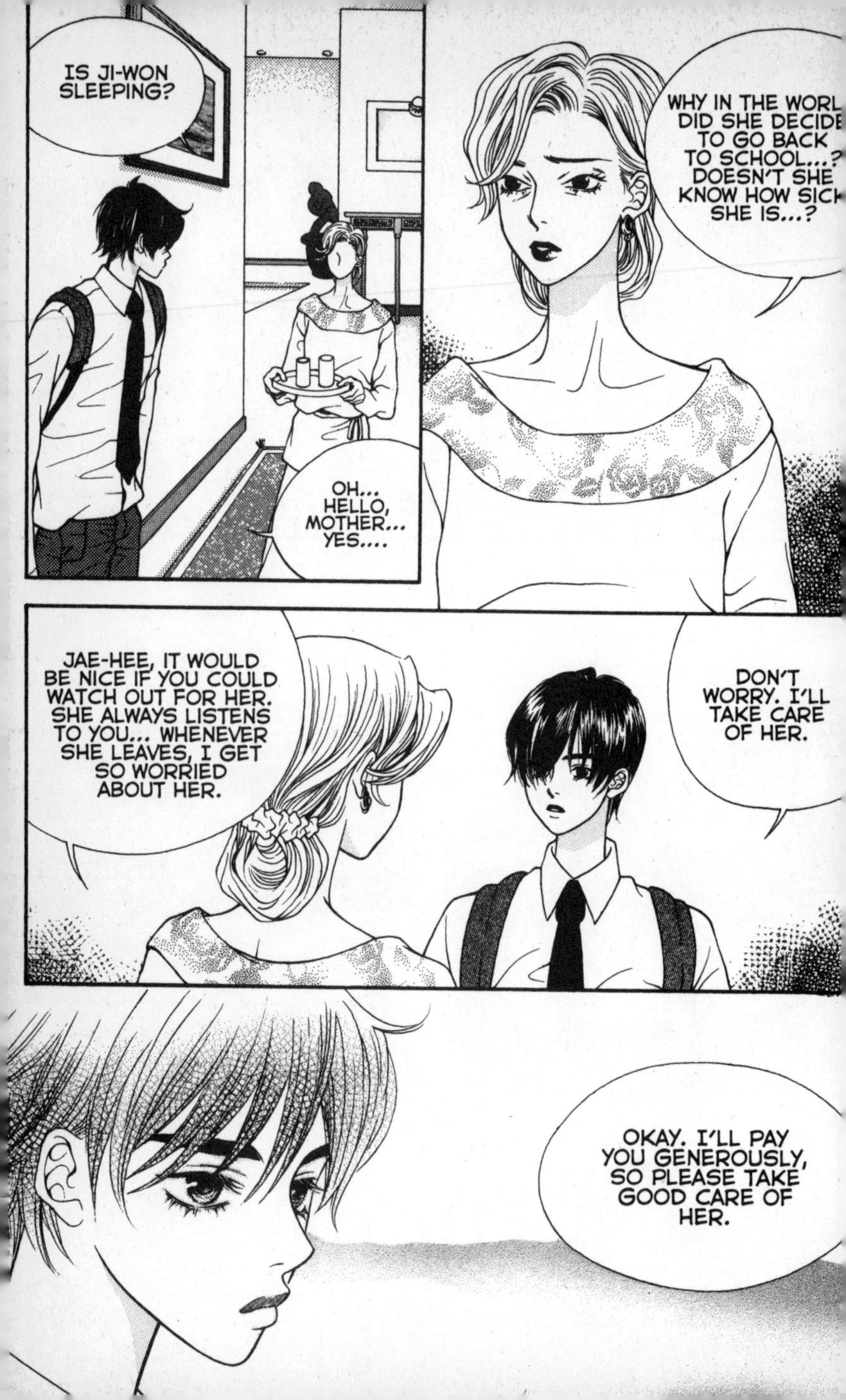
IS JI-WON SLEEPING?
OH... HELLO, MOTHER... YES....
WHY IN THE WORL DID SHE DECIDE TO GO BACK TO SCHOOL...? DOESN'T SHE KNOW HOW SICK SHE IS...?
JAE-HEE, IT WOULD BE NICE IF YOU COULD WATCH OUT FOR HER. SHE ALWAYS LISTENS TO YOU... WHENEVER SHE LEAVES, I GET SO WORRIED ABOUT HER.
DON'T WORRY. I'LL TAKE CARE OF HER.
OKAY. I'LL PAY YOU GENEROUSLY, SO PLEASE TAKE GOOD CARE OF HER.

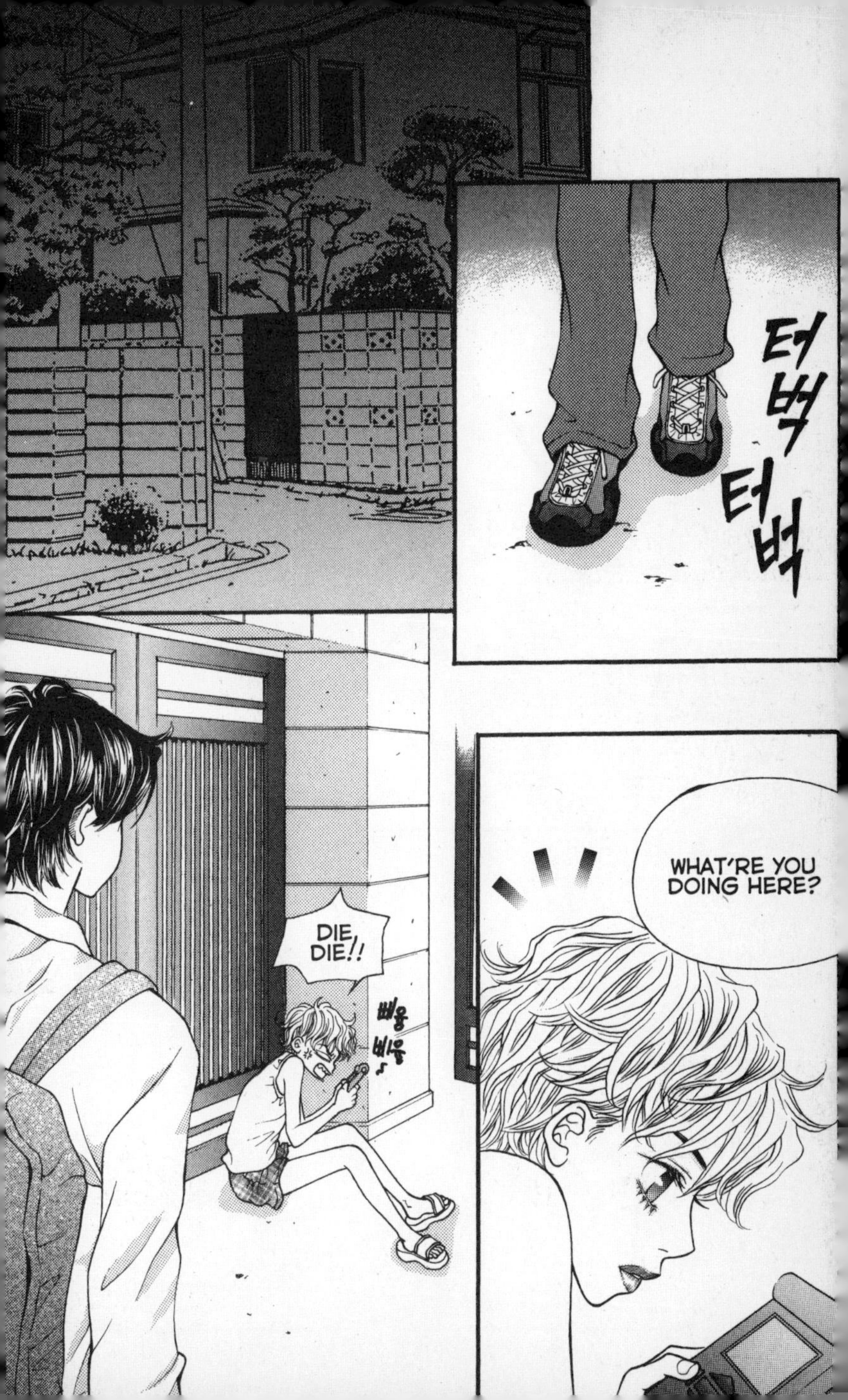
터벅
터벅
DIE, DIE!!
삐융
삐융
WHAT'RE YOU DOING HERE?

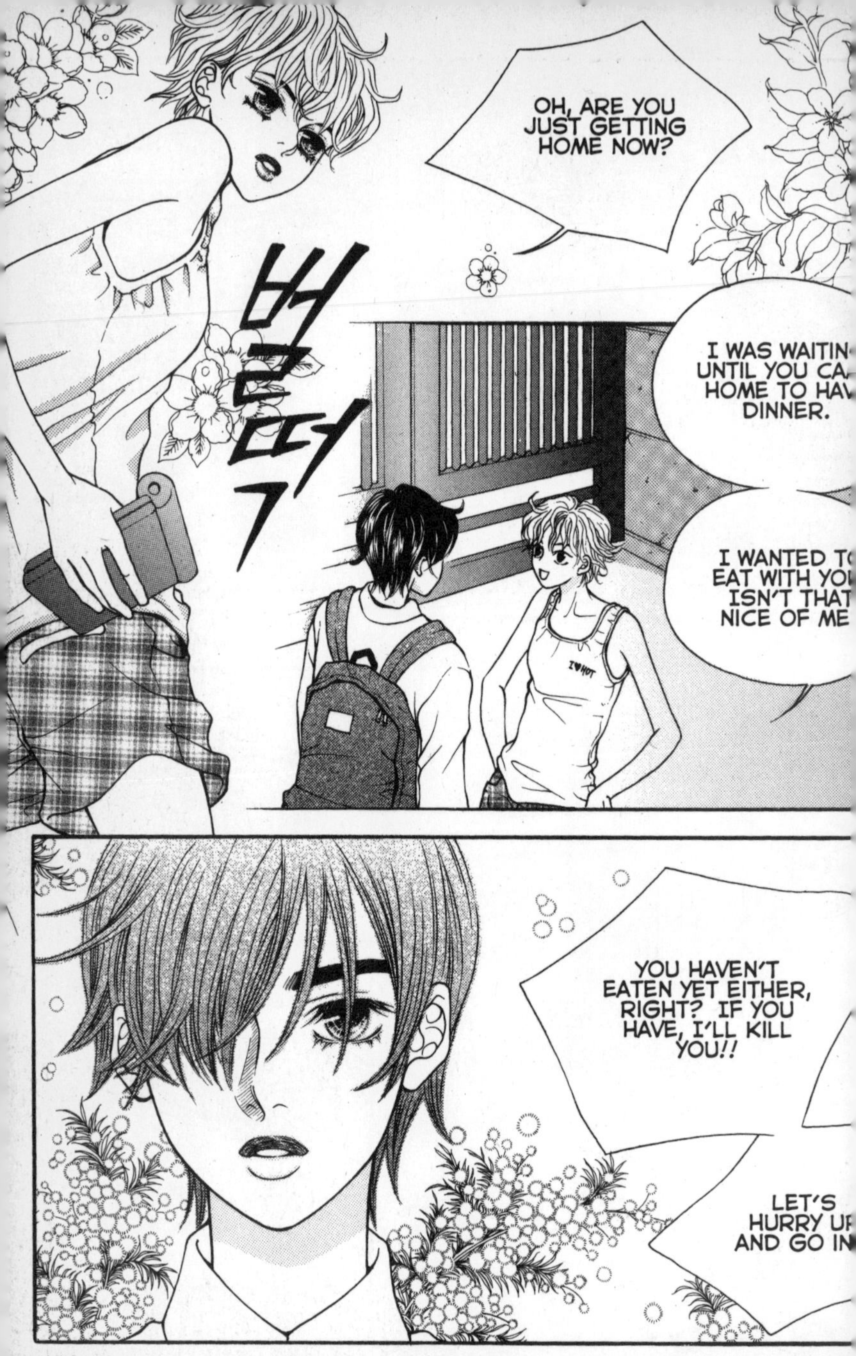
OH, ARE YOU JUST GETTING HOME NOW?
벌떡
I WAS WAITIN UNTIL YOU CA HOME TO HAV DINNER.
I WANTED T EAT WITH YO ISN'T THAT NICE OF ME
I♥HOT
YOU HAVEN'T EATEN YET EITHER, RIGHT? IF YOU HAVE, I'LL KILL YOU!!
LET'S HURRY U AND GO IN

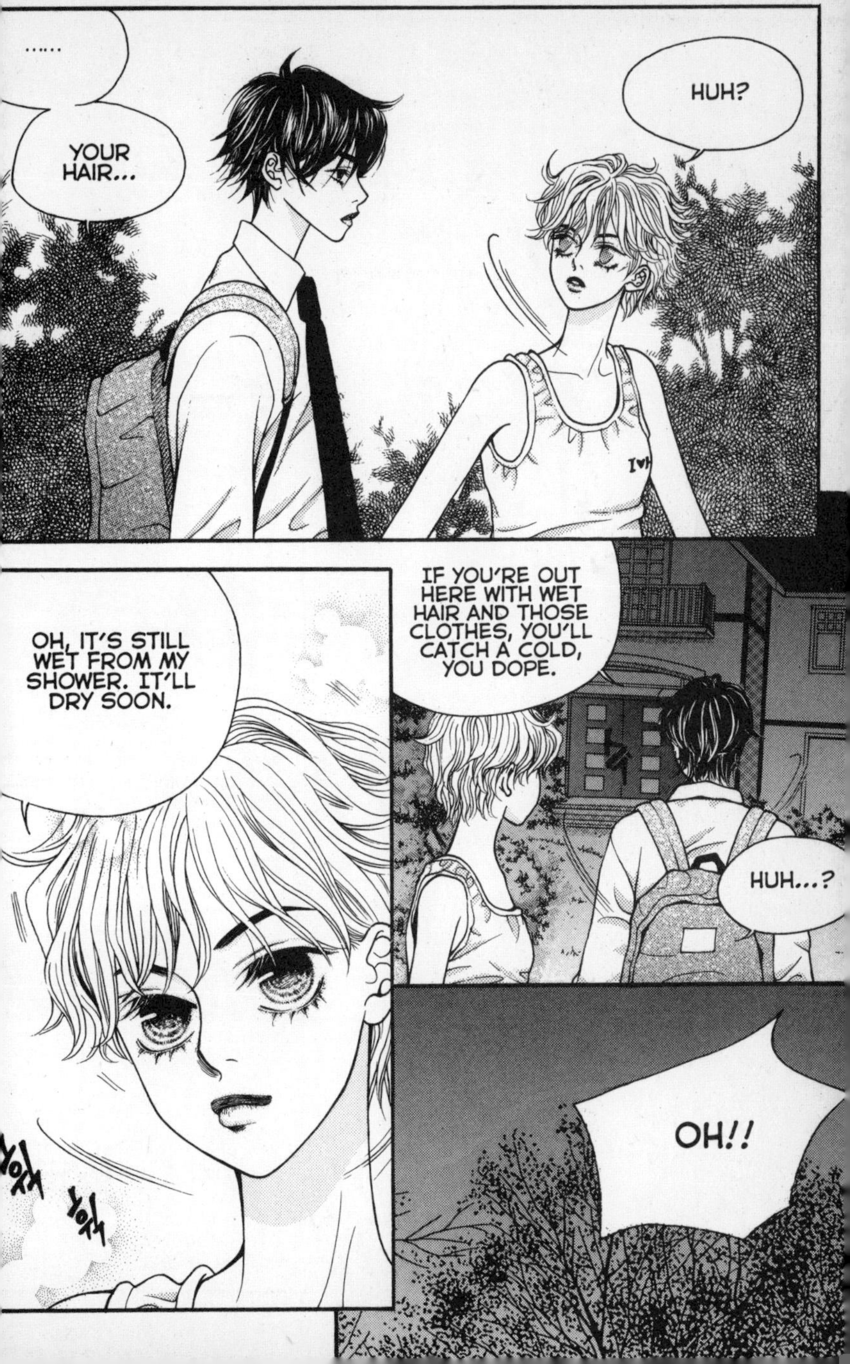
......
YOUR HAIR...
HUH?
OH, IT'S STILL WET FROM MY SHOWER. IT'LL DRY SOON.
IF YOU'RE OUT HERE WITH WET HAIR AND THOSE CLOTHES, YOU'LL CATCH A COLD, YOU DOPE.
HUH...?
OH!!

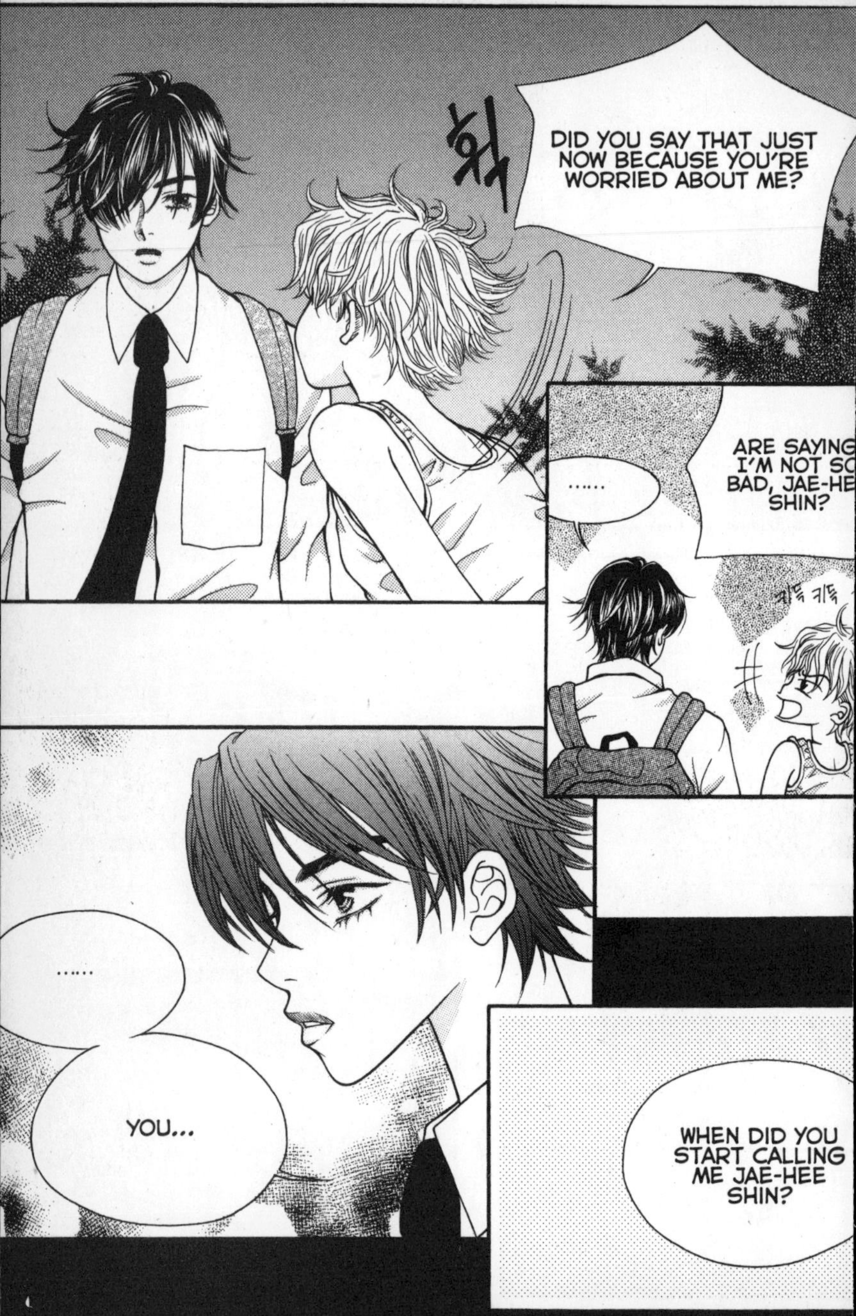
휙
DID YOU SAY THAT JUST NOW BECAUSE YOU'RE WORRIED ABOUT ME?
......
ARE SAYING I'M NOT SC BAD, JAE-HE SHIN?
키득 키득
......
YOU...
WHEN DID YOU START CALLING ME JAE-HEE SHIN?

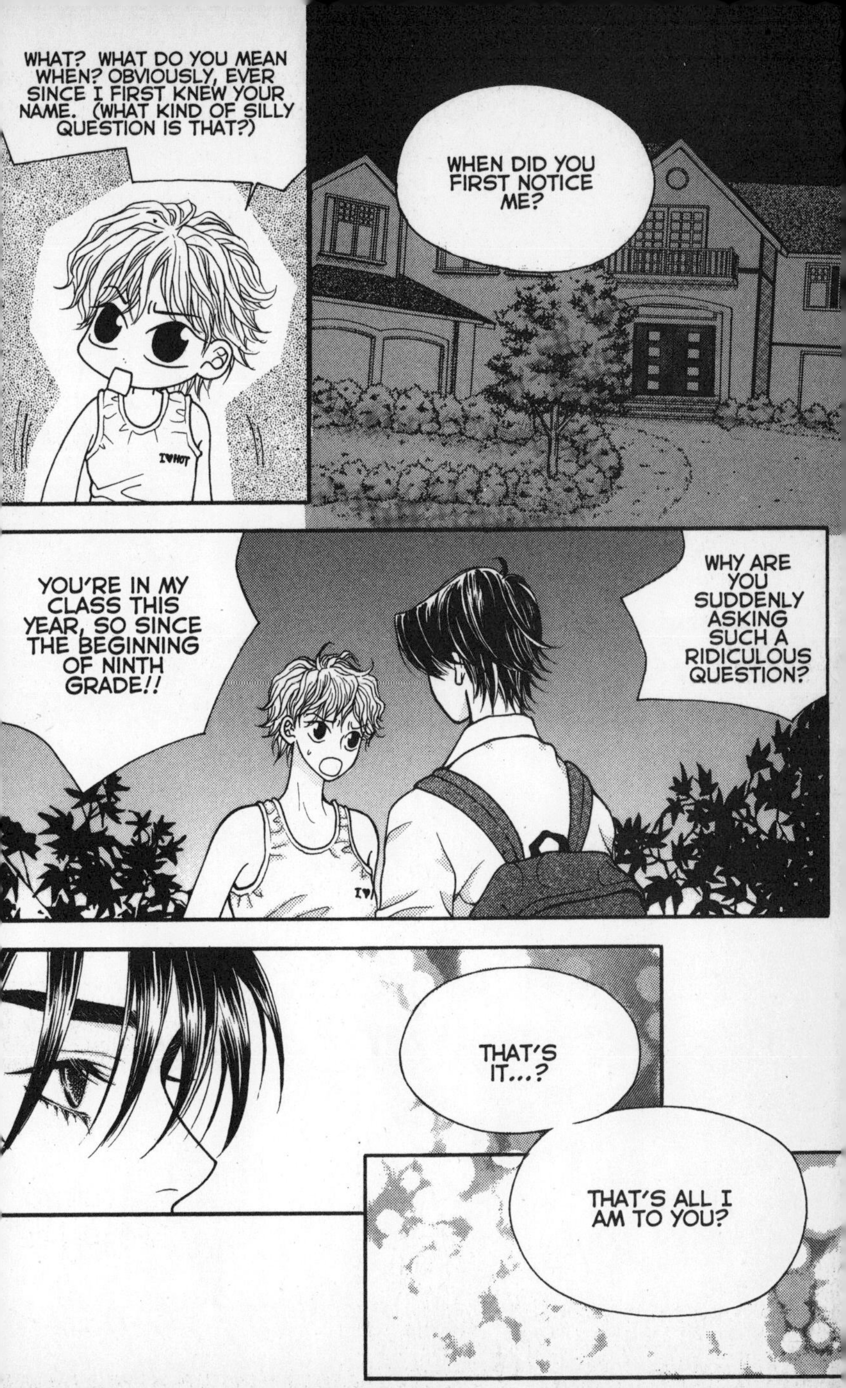
WHAT? WHAT DO YOU MEAN WHEN? OBVIOUSLY, EVER SINCE I FIRST KNEW YOUR NAME. (WHAT KIND OF SILLY QUESTION IS THAT?)
WHEN DID YOU FIRST NOTICE ME?
YOU'RE IN MY CLASS THIS YEAR, SO SINCE THE BEGINNING OF NINTH GRADE!!
WHY ARE YOU SUDDENLY ASKING SUCH A RIDICULOUS QUESTION?
THAT'S IT...?
THAT'S ALL I AM TO YOU?

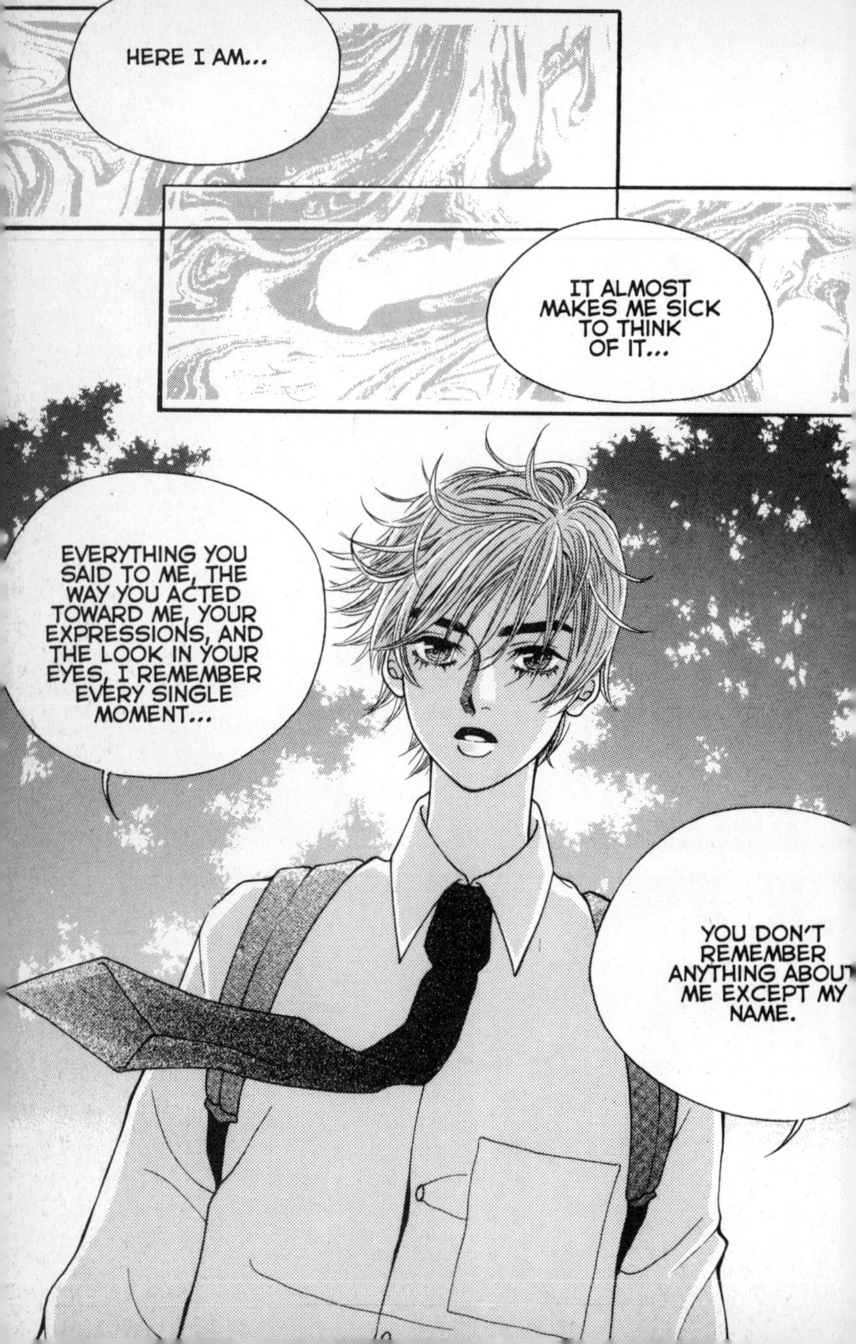
HERE I AM...
IT ALMOST MAKES ME SICK TO THINK OF IT...
EVERYTHING YOU SAID TO ME, THE WAY YOU ACTED TOWARD ME, YOUR EXPRESSIONS, AND THE LOOK IN YOUR EYES, I REMEMBER EVERY SINGLE MOMENT...
YOU DON'T REMEMBER ANYTHING ABOUT ME EXCEPT MY NAME.

IT EVEN SEEMS MEANINGLESS...
BUT I CAN'T BRING MYSELF TO HATE YOU...EVEN AFTER YOU HURT ME SO BADLY...
AND EVEN THOUGH I KNOW THAT YOU'LL HURT ME AGAIN.
IT'S FUNNY...
I FEEL STUPID!
IT MAKES ME MAD!

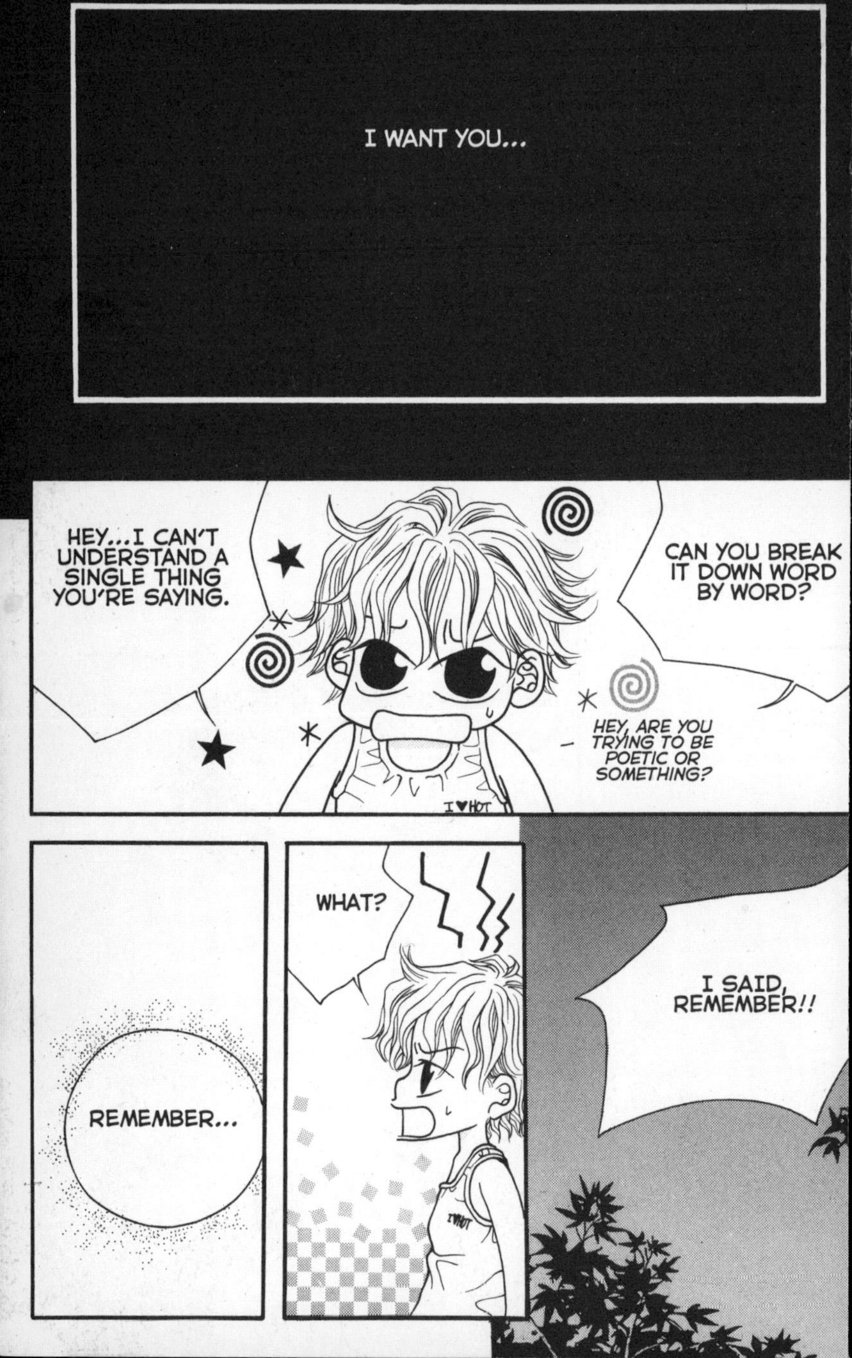
I WANT YOU...
HEY...I CAN'T UNDERSTAND A SINGLE THING YOU'RE SAYING.
CAN YOU BREAK IT DOWN WORD BY WORD?
HEY, ARE YOU TRYING TO BE POETIC OR SOMETHING?
I♥HOT
REMEMBER...
WHAT?
I SAID, REMEMBER!!

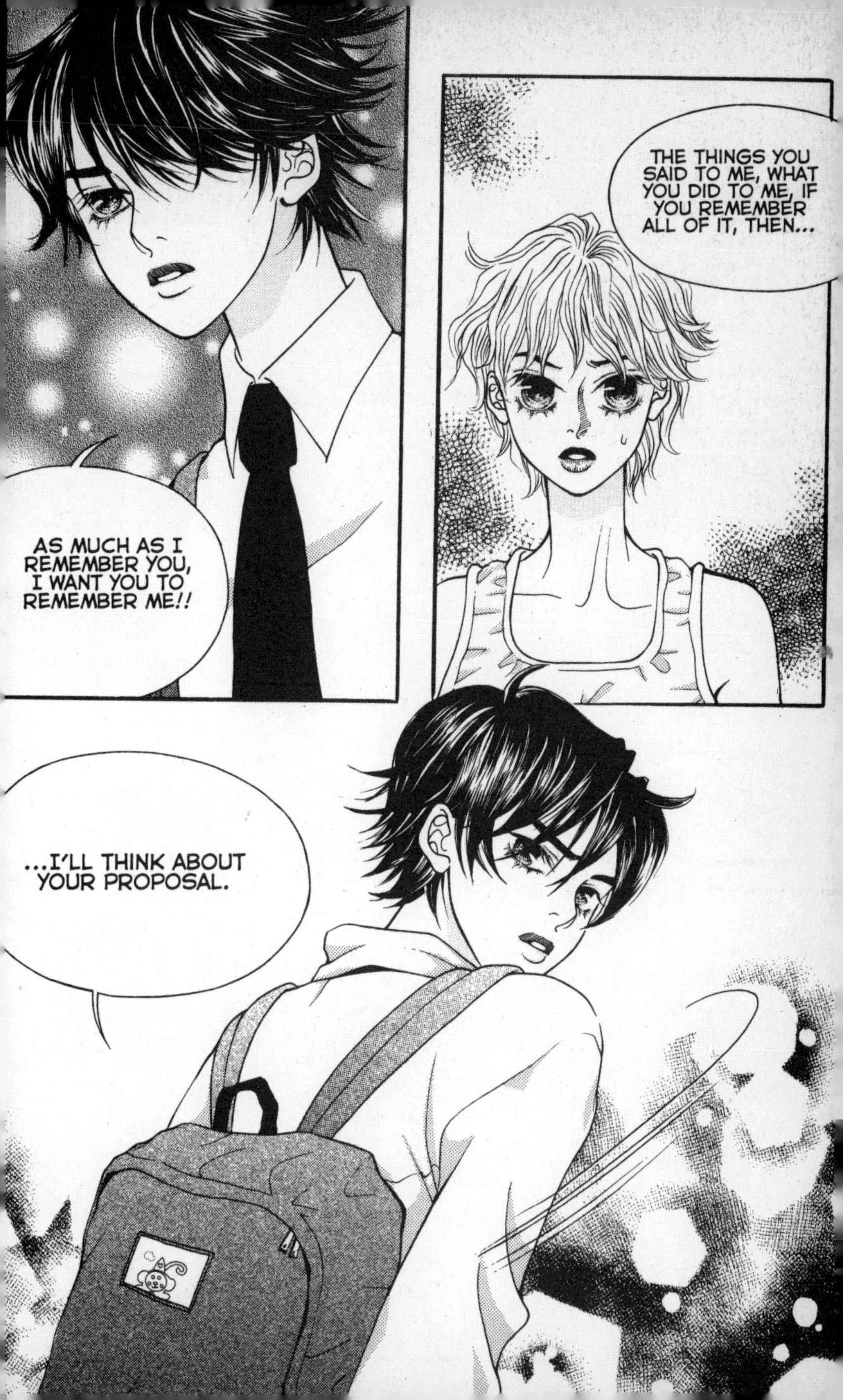
AS MUCH AS I REMEMBER YOU, I WANT YOU TO REMEMBER ME!!
THE THINGS YOU SAID TO ME, WHAT YOU DID TO ME, IF YOU REMEMBER ALL OF IT, THEN...
...I'LL THINK ABOUT YOUR PROPOSAL.

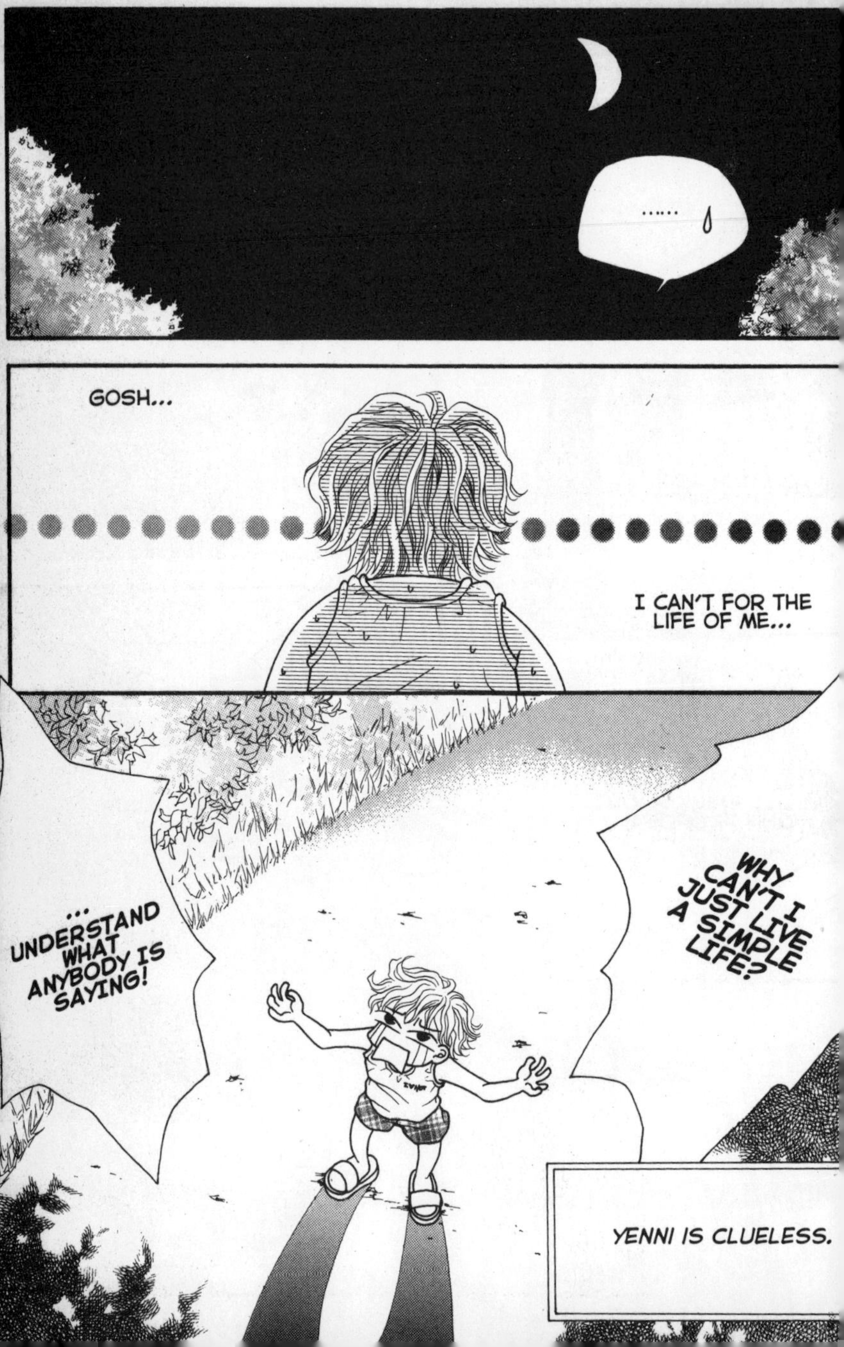
......
GOSH...
I CAN'T FOR THE LIFE OF ME...
... UNDERSTAND WHAT ANYBODY IS SAYING!
WHY CAN'T I JUST LIVE A SIMPLE LIFE?
YENNI IS CLUELESS.

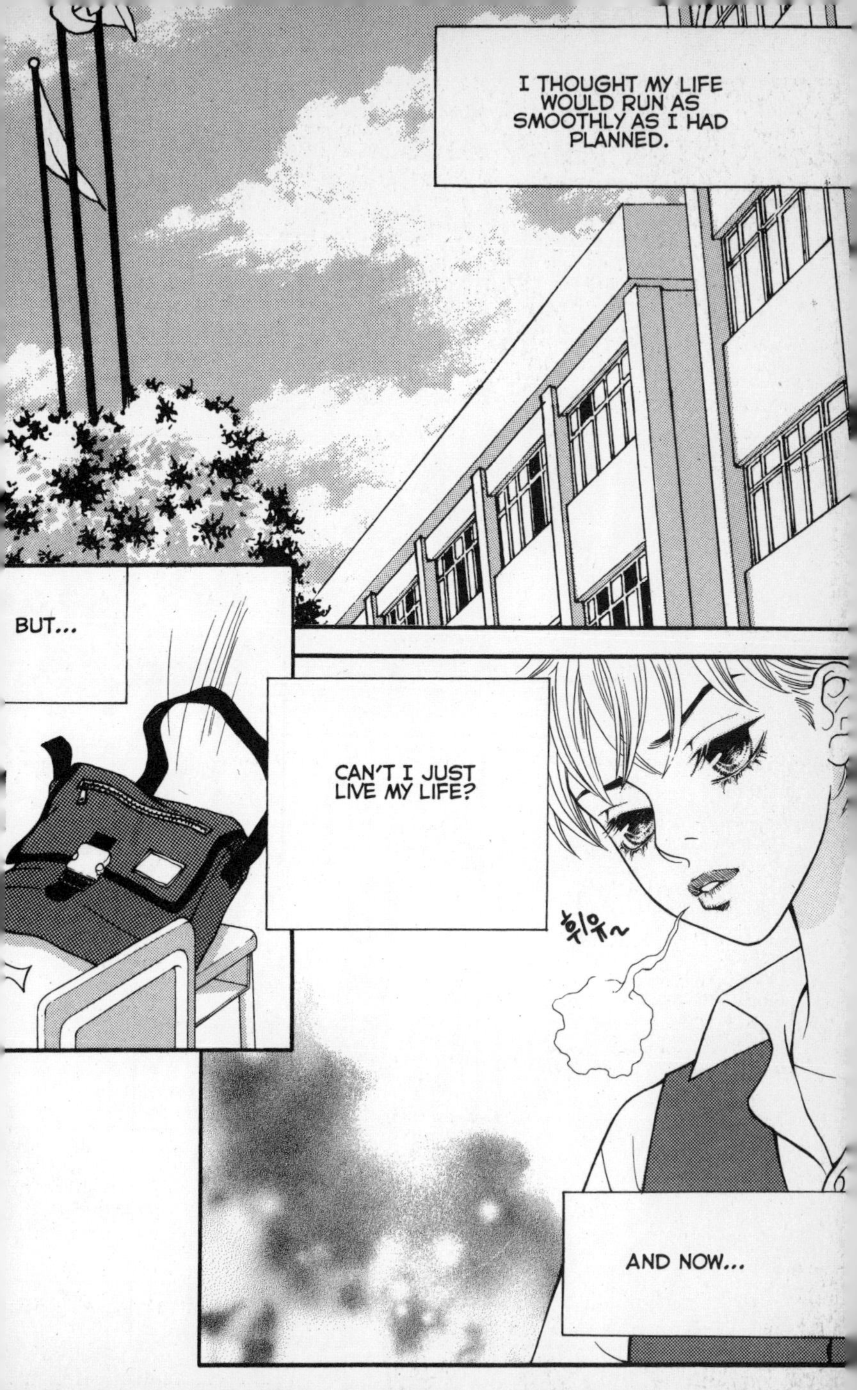
I THOUGHT MY LIFE WOULD RUN AS SMOOTHLY AS I HAD PLANNED.
BUT...
CAN'T I JUST LIVE MY LIFE?
후우~
AND NOW...

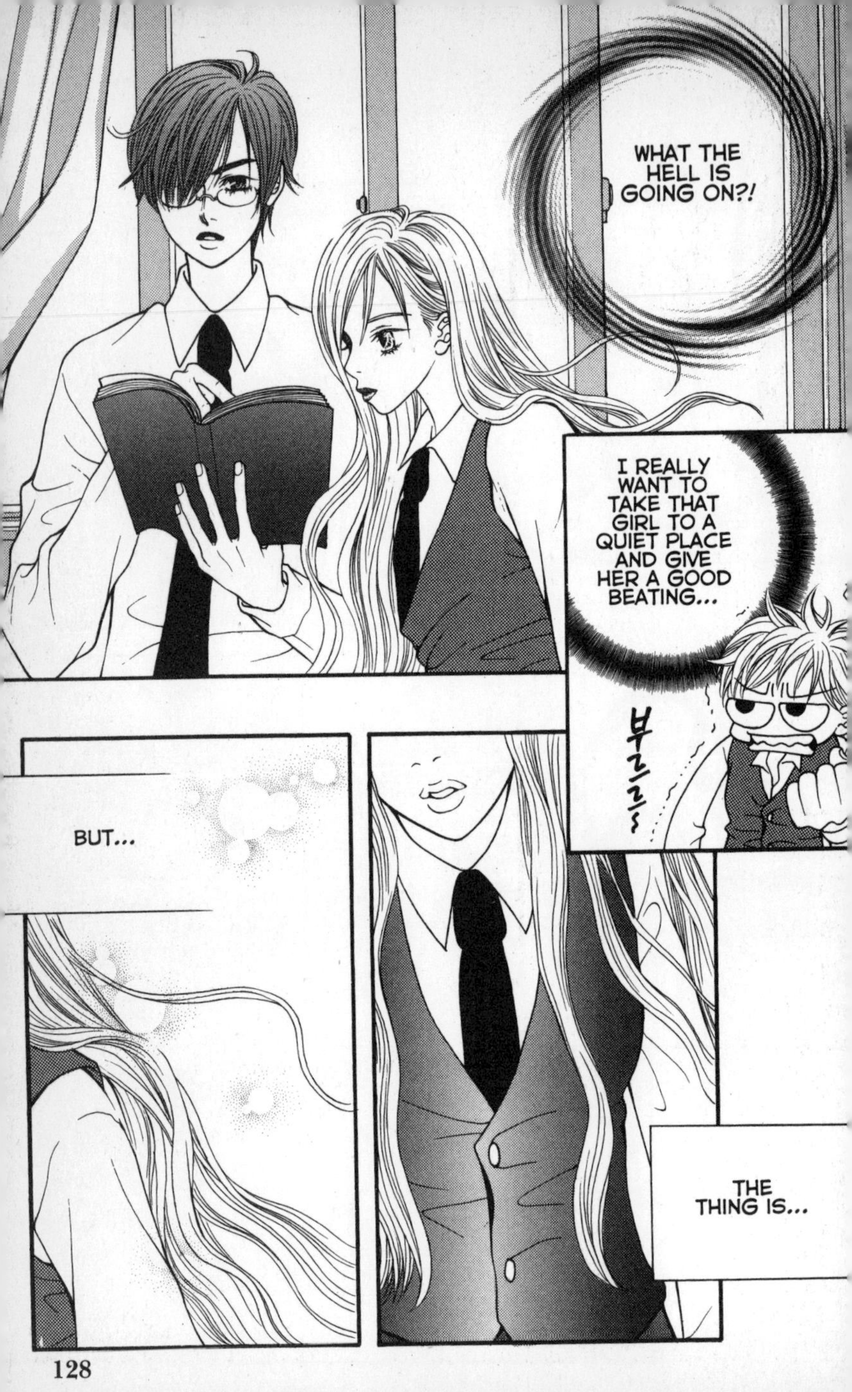
WHAT THE HELL IS GOING ON?!
I REALLY WANT TO TAKE THAT GIRL TO A QUIET PLACE AND GIVE HER A GOOD BEATING...
BUT...
THE THING IS...

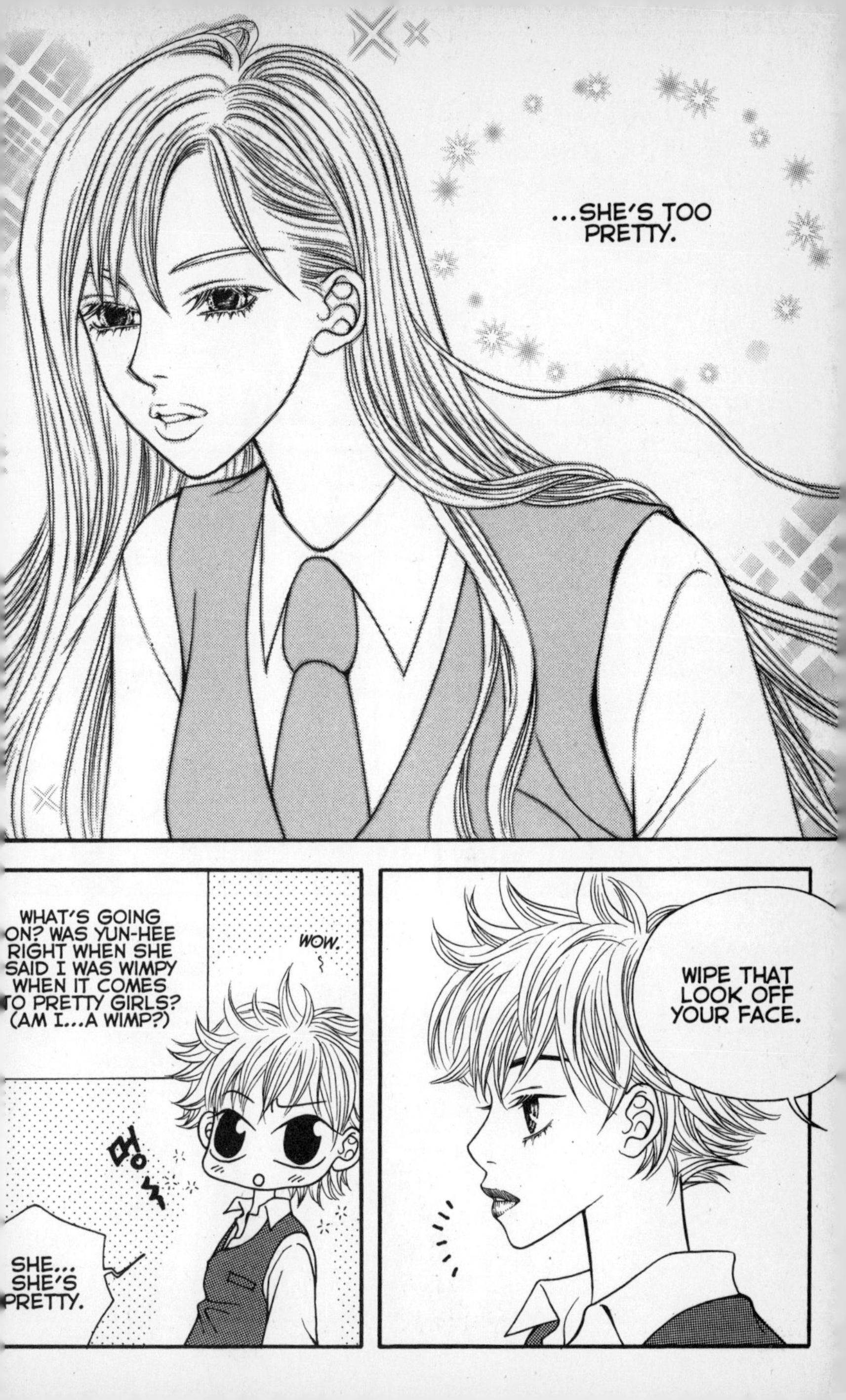
...SHE'S TOO PRETTY.
WHAT'S GOING ON? WAS YUN-HEE RIGHT WHEN SHE SAID I WAS WIMPY WHEN IT COMES TO PRETTY GIRLS? (AM I...A WIMP?)
WOW.
SHE... SHE'S PRETTY.
WIPE THAT LOOK OFF YOUR FACE.

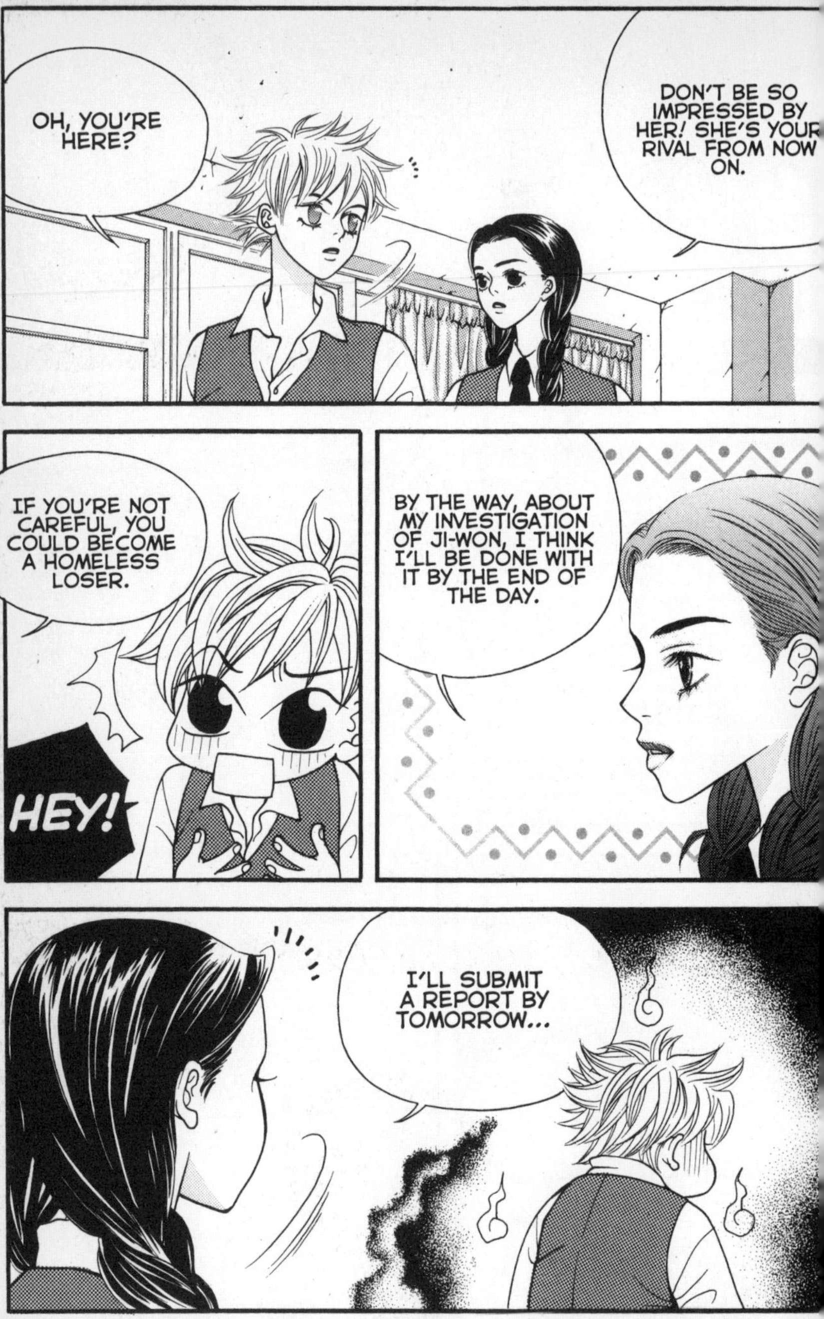
OH, YOU'RE HERE?
DON'T BE SO IMPRESSED BY HER! SHE'S YOUR RIVAL FROM NOW ON.
IF YOU'RE NOT CAREFUL, YOU COULD BECOME A HOMELESS LOSER.
HEY!
BY THE WAY, ABOUT MY INVESTIGATION OF JI-WON, I THINK I'LL BE DONE WITH IT BY THE END OF THE DAY.
I'LL SUBMIT A REPORT BY TOMORROW...

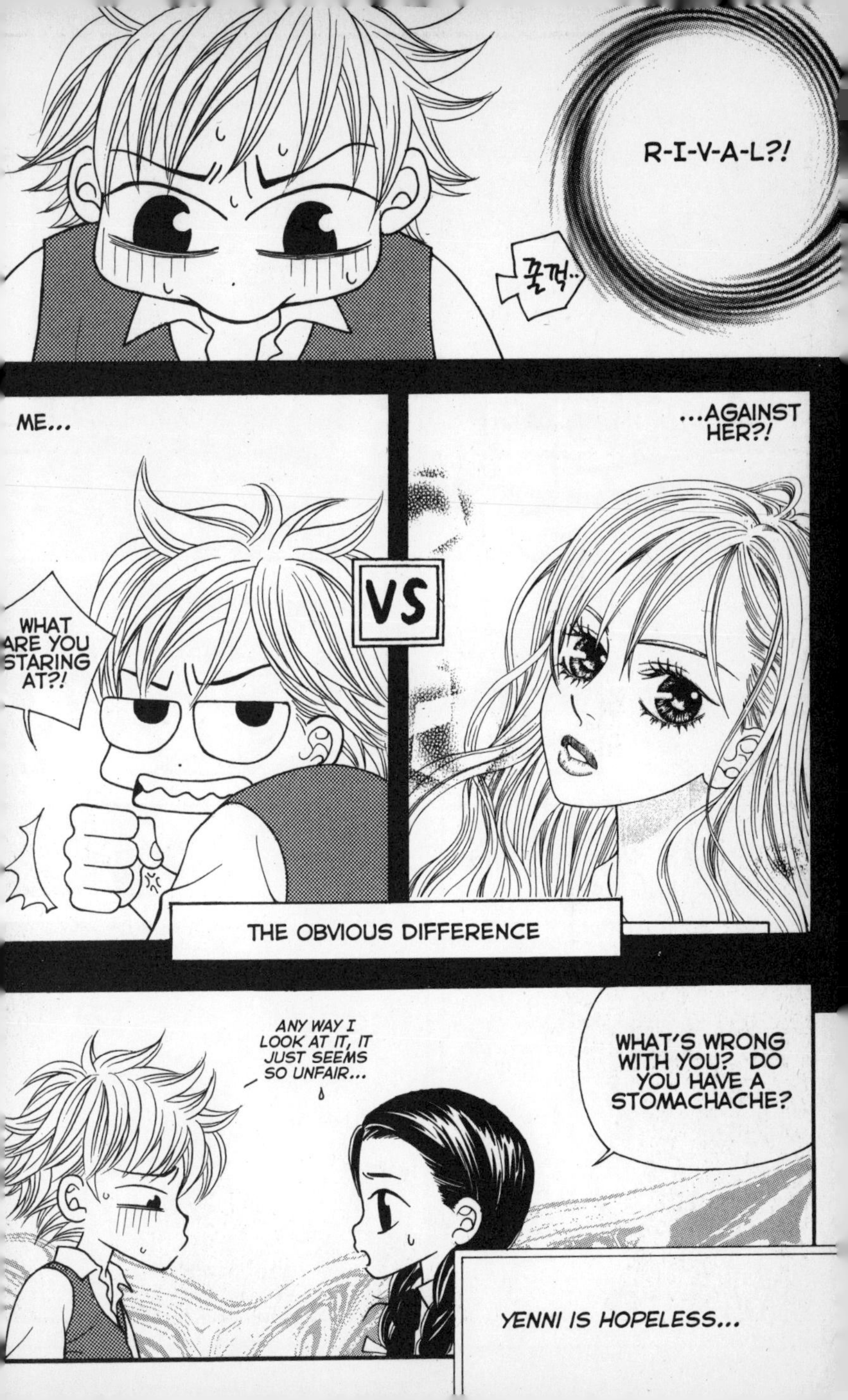
R-I-V-A-L?!
꿀꺽..
ME...
WHAT ARE YOU STARING AT?!
VS
...AGAINST HER?!
THE OBVIOUS DIFFERENCE
ANY WAY I LOOK AT IT, IT JUST SEEMS SO UNFAIR...
WHAT'S WRONG WITH YOU? DO YOU HAVE A STOMACHACHE?
YENNI IS HOPELESS...

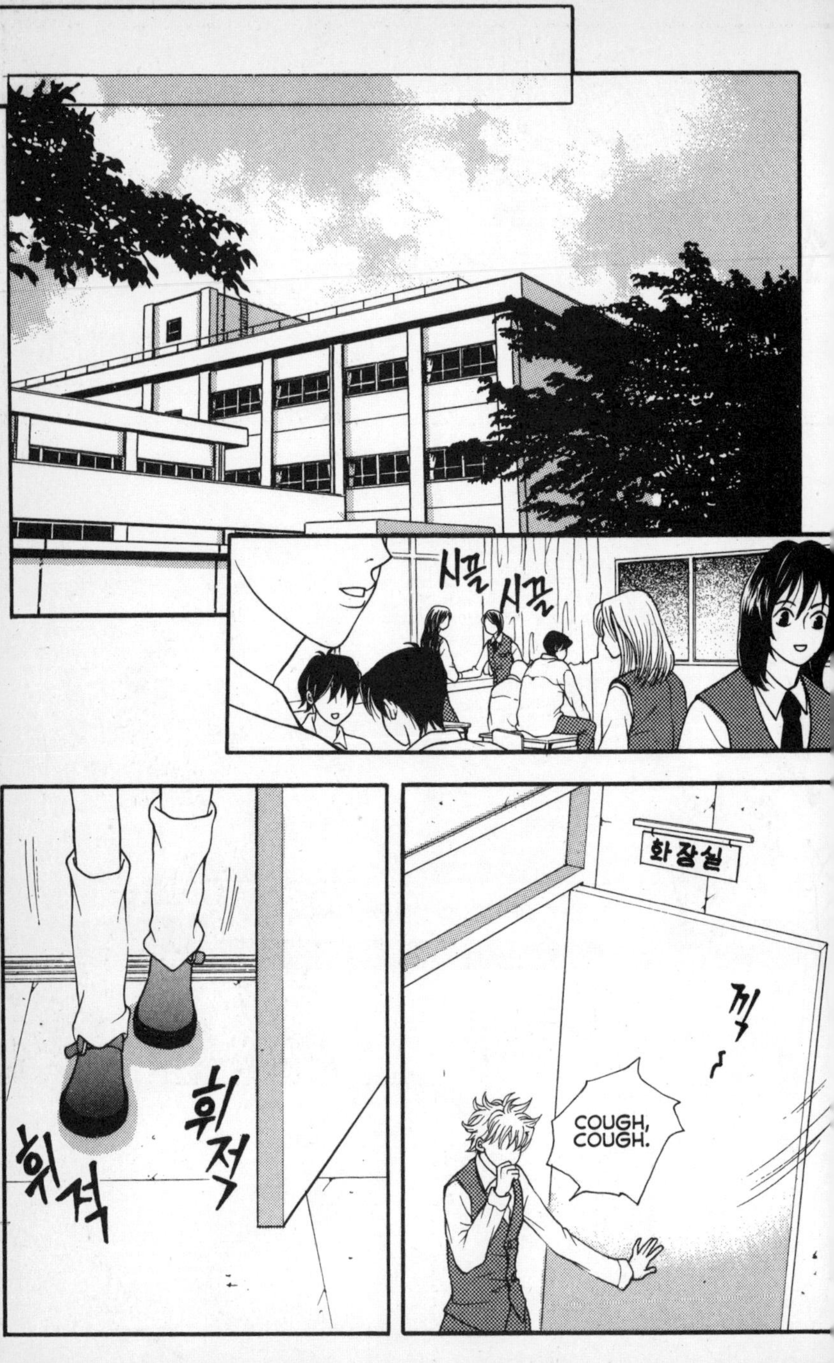
시끌 시끌
휘적 휘적
화장실
끽~
COUGH, COUGH.

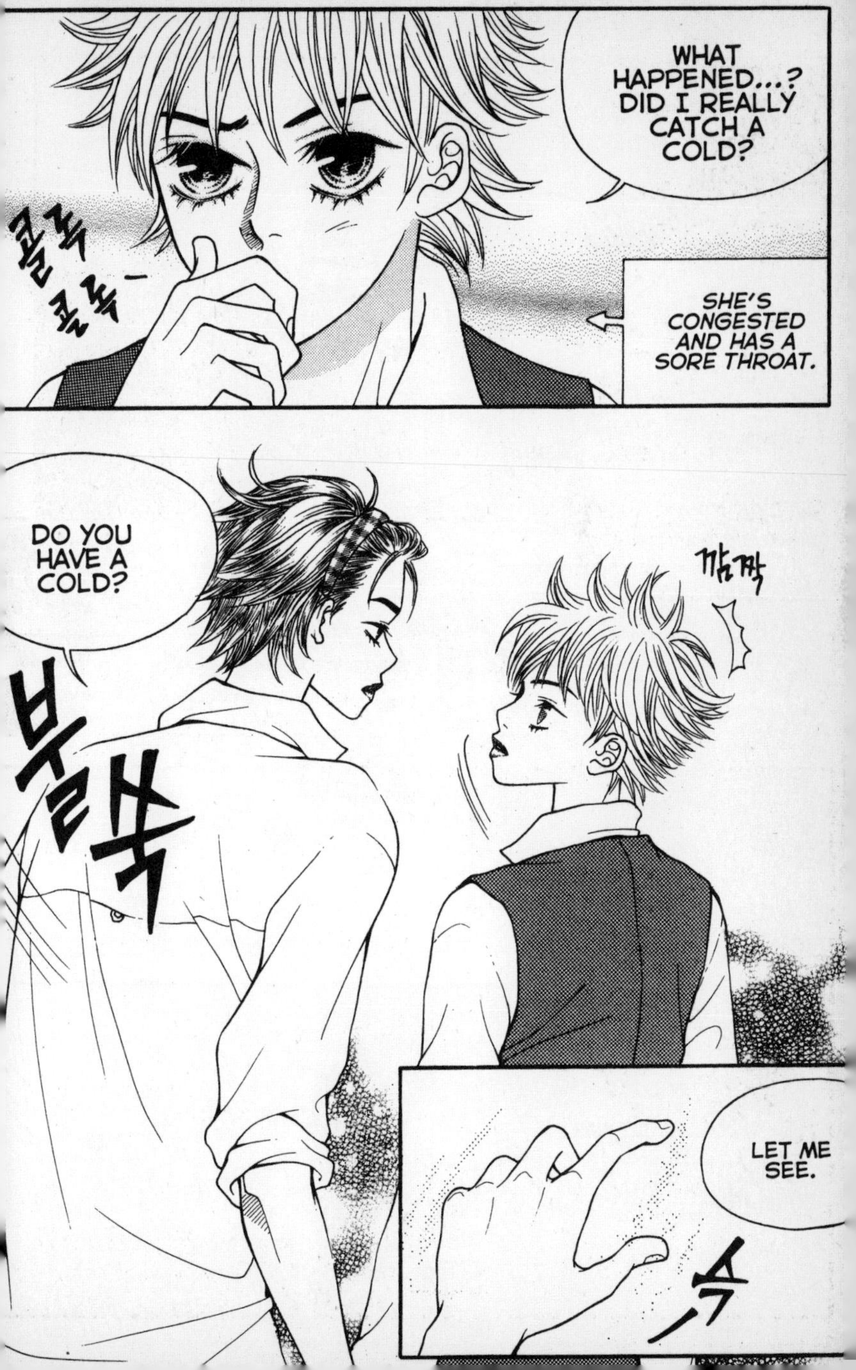
콜록 콜록
WHAT HAPPENED...? DID I REALLY CATCH A COLD?
SHE'S CONGESTED AND HAS A SORE THROAT.
DO YOU HAVE A COLD?
깜짝
불쑥
LET ME SEE.
슥

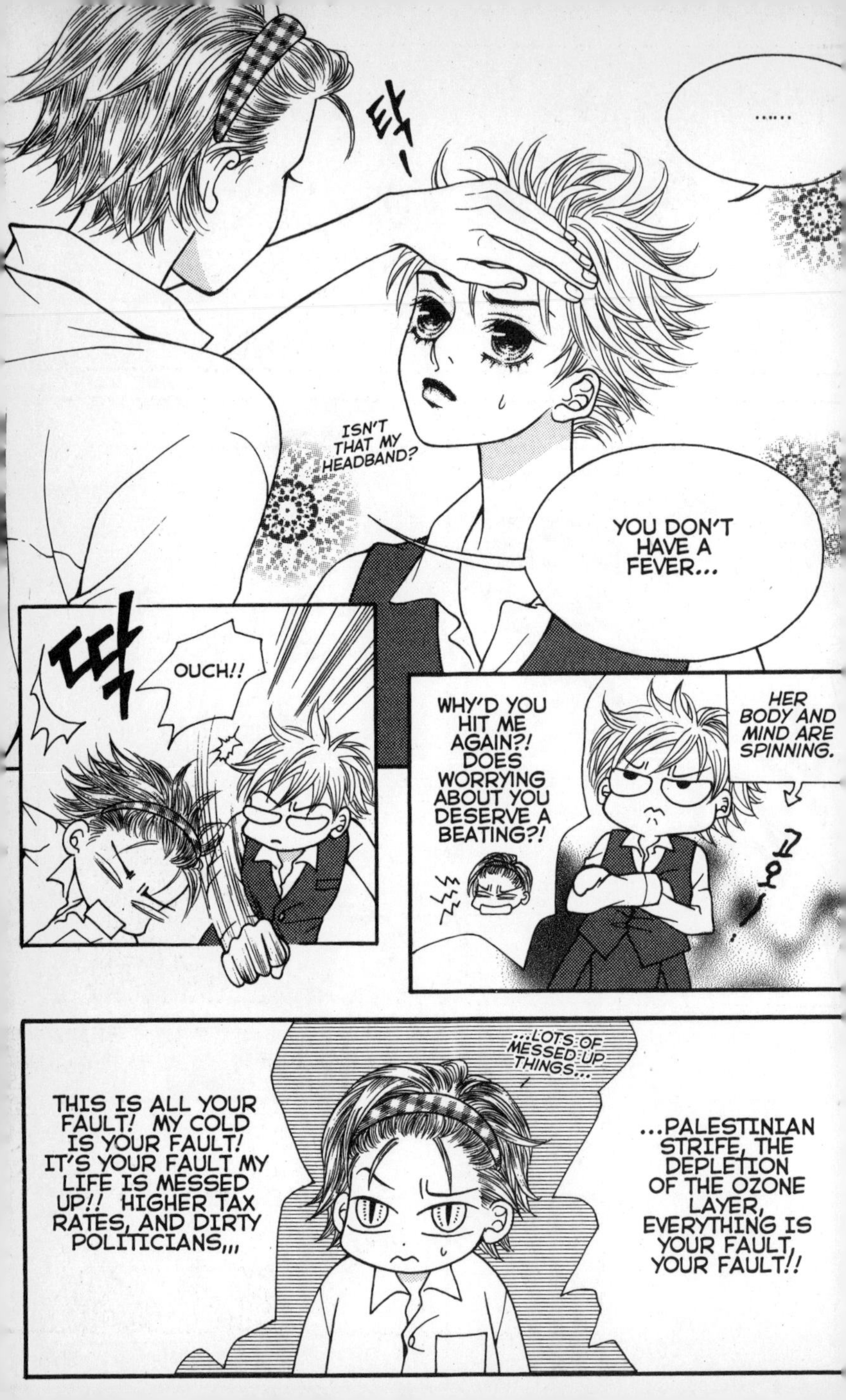
탁
......
ISN'T THAT MY HEADBAND?
YOU DON'T HAVE A FEVER...
딱
OUCH!!
WHY'D YOU HIT ME AGAIN?! DOES WORRYING ABOUT YOU DESERVE A BEATING?!
HER BODY AND MIND ARE SPINNING.
THIS IS ALL YOUR FAULT! MY COLD IS YOUR FAULT! IT'S YOUR FAULT MY LIFE IS MESSED UP!! HIGHER TAX RATES, AND DIRTY POLITICIANS,,,
...LOTS OF MESSED UP THINGS...
...PALESTINIAN STRIFE, THE DEPLETION OF THE OZONE LAYER, EVERYTHING IS YOUR FAULT, YOUR FAULT!!

ARE YOU DONE?

WITH EVERYTHING!!

AM I HER PUNCHING BAG?

YOU MUST BE IN A REALLY BAD MOOD...OR YOU WOULDN'T BE SAYING SUCH MEAN THINGS.

WELL...ANYWAY, I REALLY DON'T FEEL LIKE MESSING WITH YOU RIGHT NOW.

HMPH, YOUR WHOLE LIFE IS ABOUT MESSING WITH PEOPLE!!

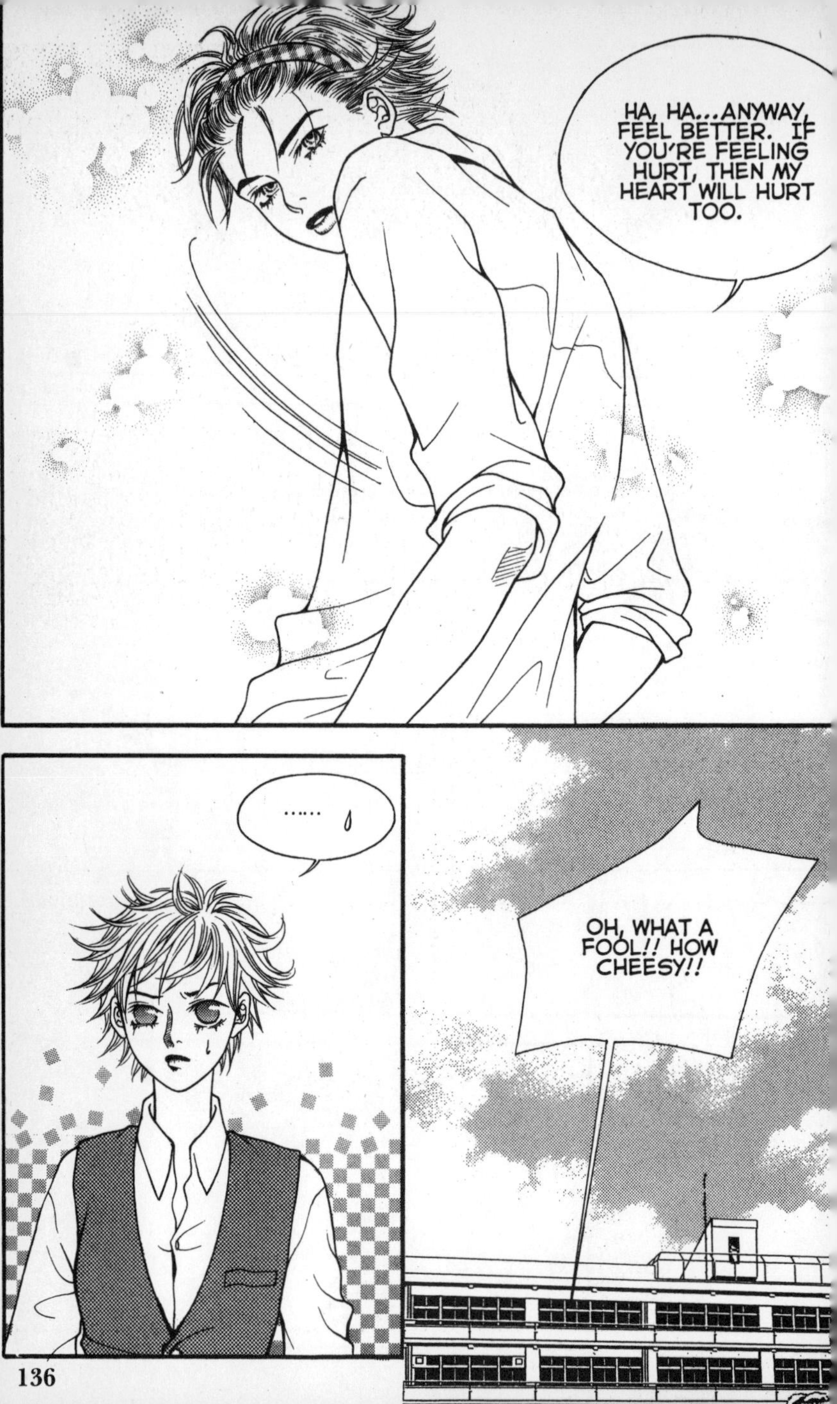
HA, HA...ANYWAY, FEEL BETTER. IF YOU'RE FEELING HURT, THEN MY HEART WILL HURT TOO.
......
OH, WHAT A FOOL!! HOW CHEESY!!

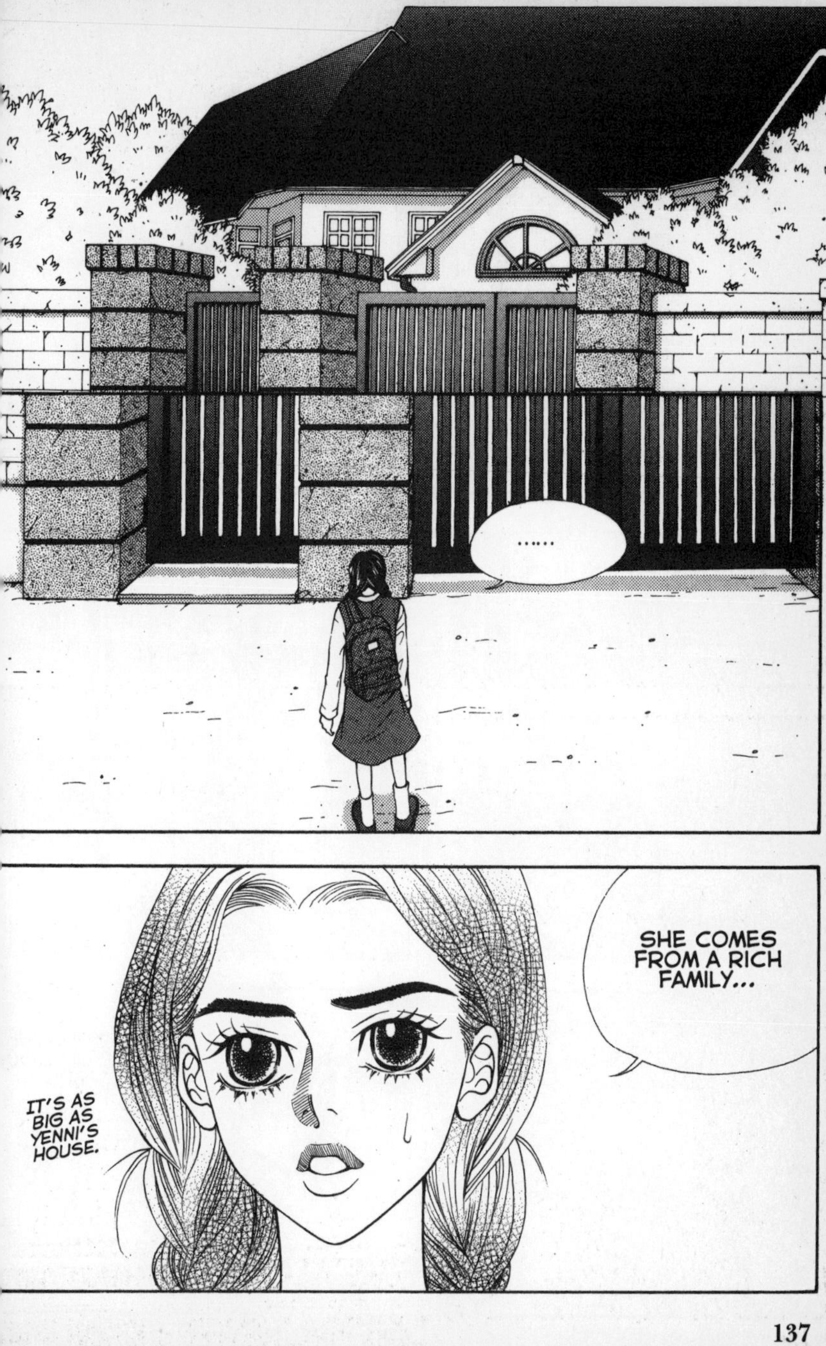
......
SHE COMES FROM A RICH FAMILY...
IT'S AS BIG AS YENNI'S HOUSE.

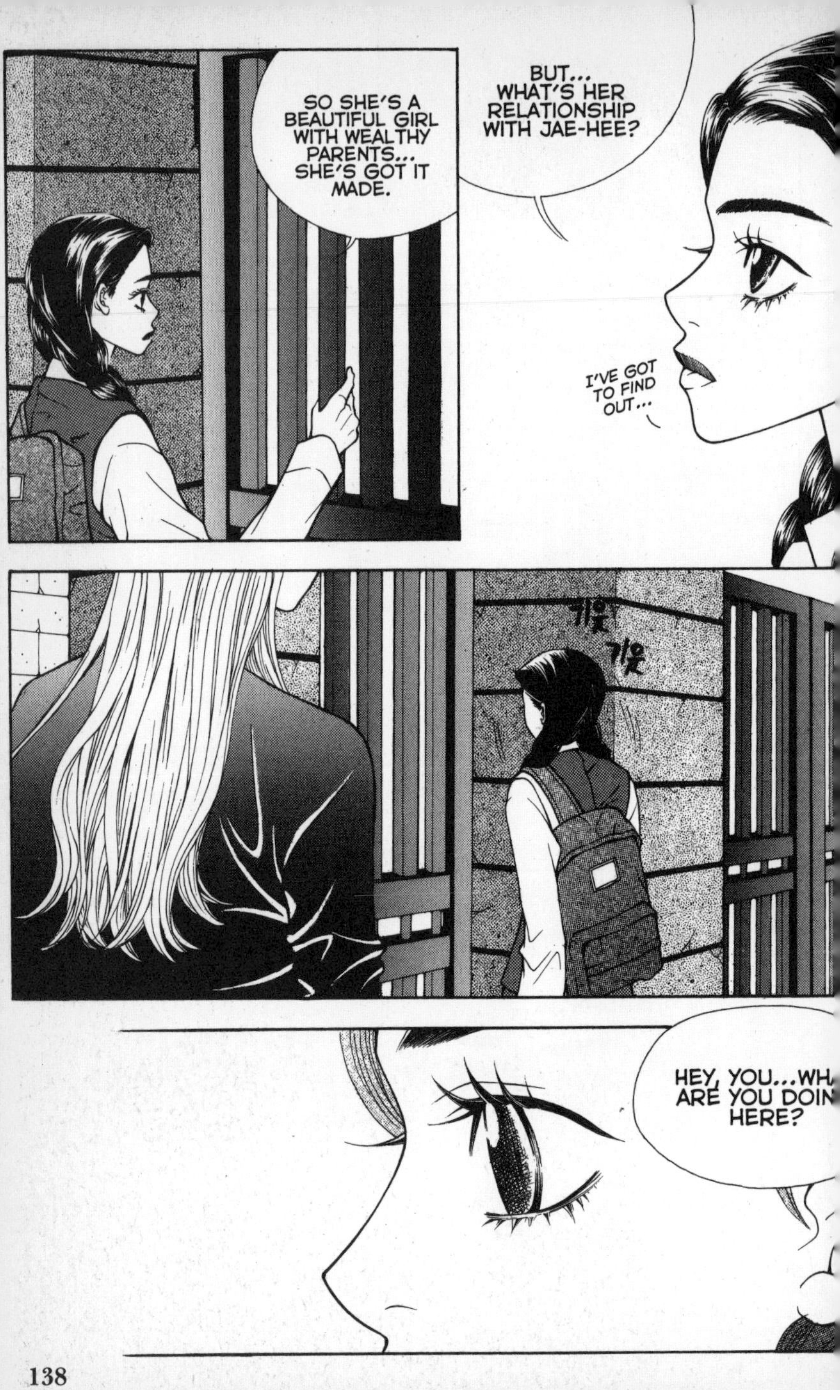
SO SHE'S A BEAUTIFUL GIRL WITH WEALTHY PARENTS... SHE'S GOT IT MADE.
BUT... WHAT'S HER RELATIONSHIP WITH JAE-HEE?
I'VE GOT TO FIND OUT...
기웃
기웃
HEY, YOU...WH ARE YOU DOIN HERE?

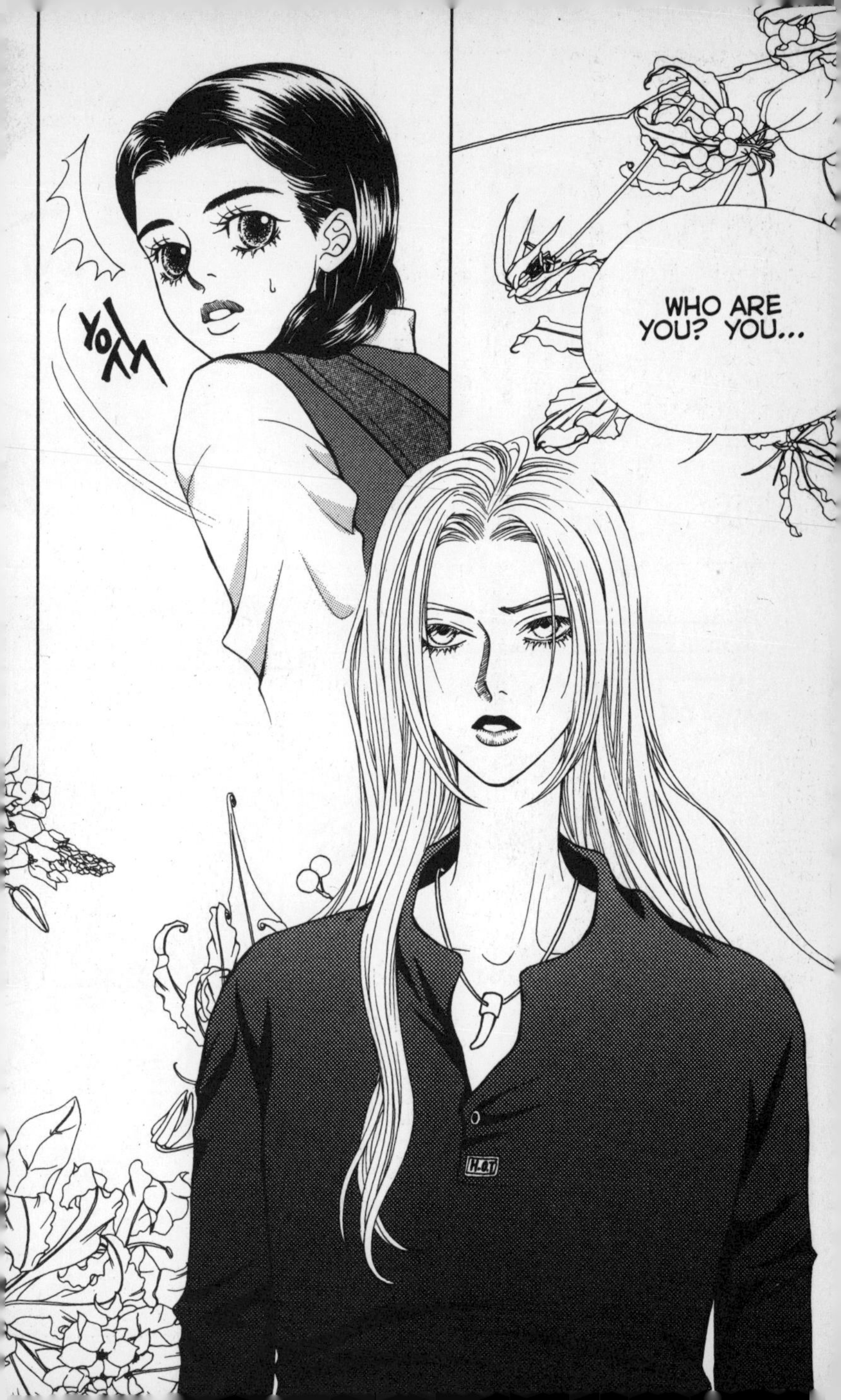
WHO ARE YOU? YOU...

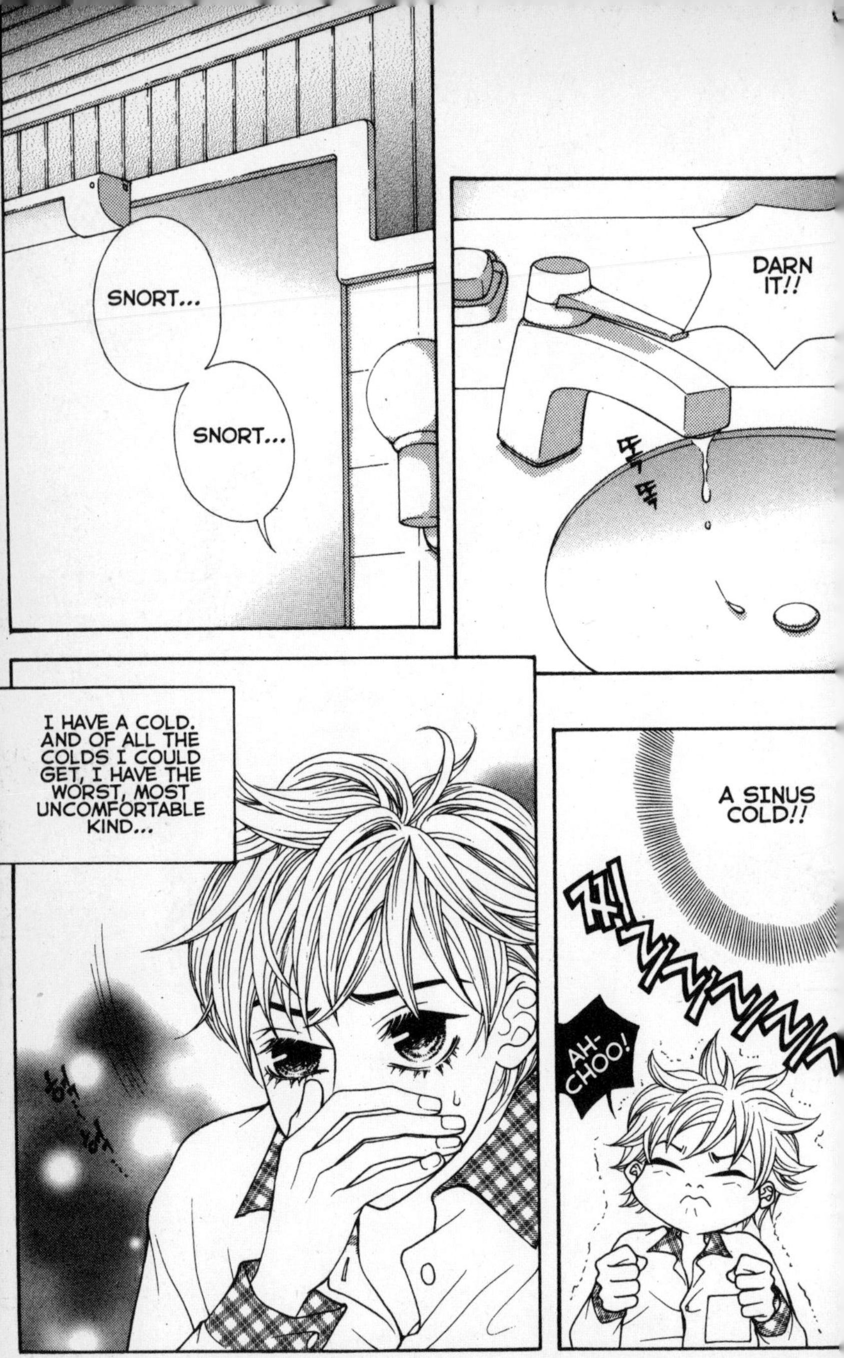
SNORT...
SNORT...
DARN IT!!
I HAVE A COLD. AND OF ALL THE COLDS I COULD GET, I HAVE THE WORST, MOST UNCOMFORTABLE KIND...
A SINUS COLD!!
AH-CHOO!

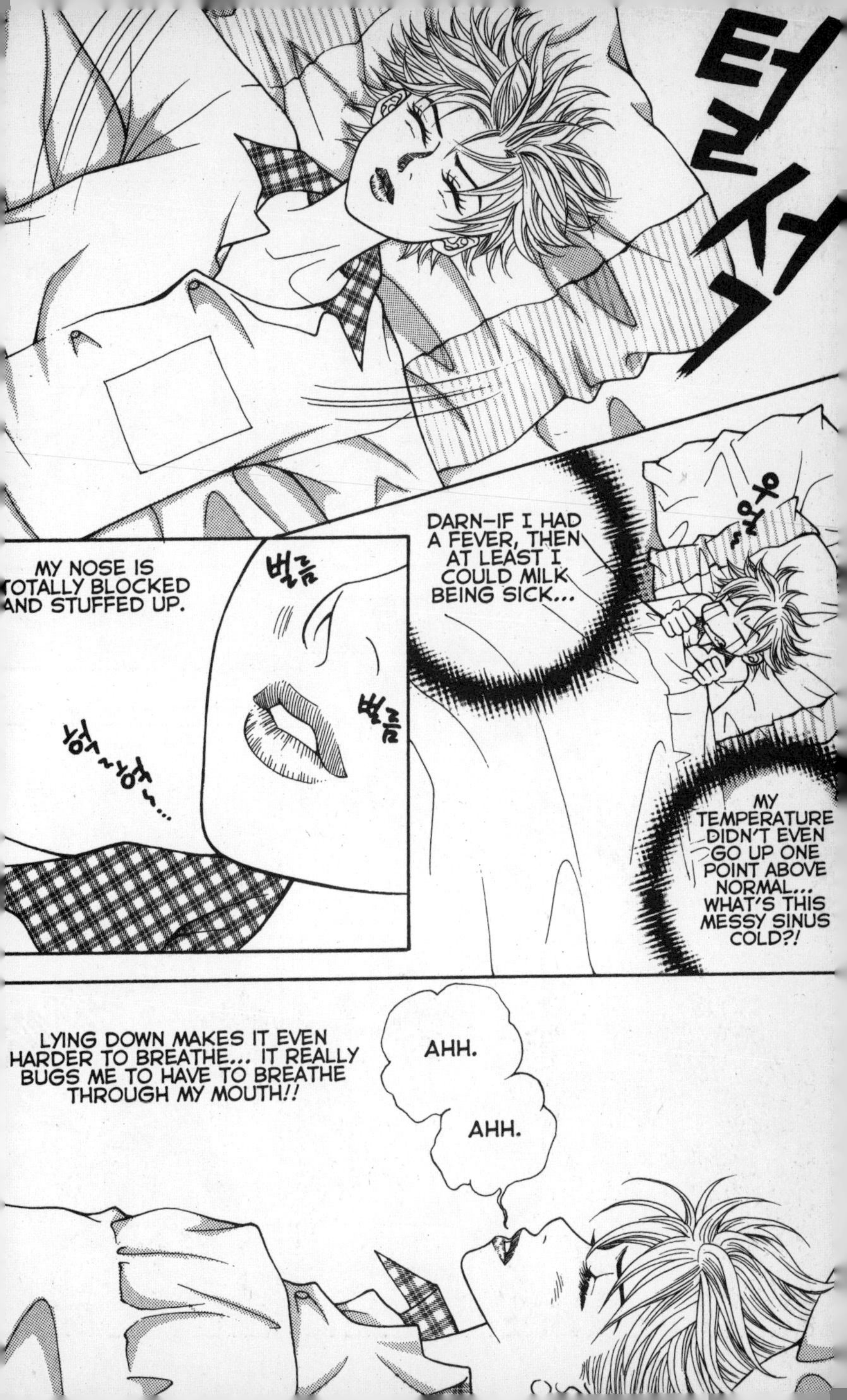
털석
MY NOSE IS TOTALLY BLOCKED AND STUFFED UP.
벌름
벌름
헝~헝~...
DARN—IF I HAD A FEVER, THEN AT LEAST I COULD MILK BEING SICK...
MY TEMPERATURE DIDN'T EVEN GO UP ONE POINT ABOVE NORMAL... WHAT'S THIS MESSY SINUS COLD?!
LYING DOWN MAKES IT EVEN HARDER TO BREATHE... IT REALLY BUGS ME TO HAVE TO BREATHE THROUGH MY MOUTH!!
AHH.
AHH.

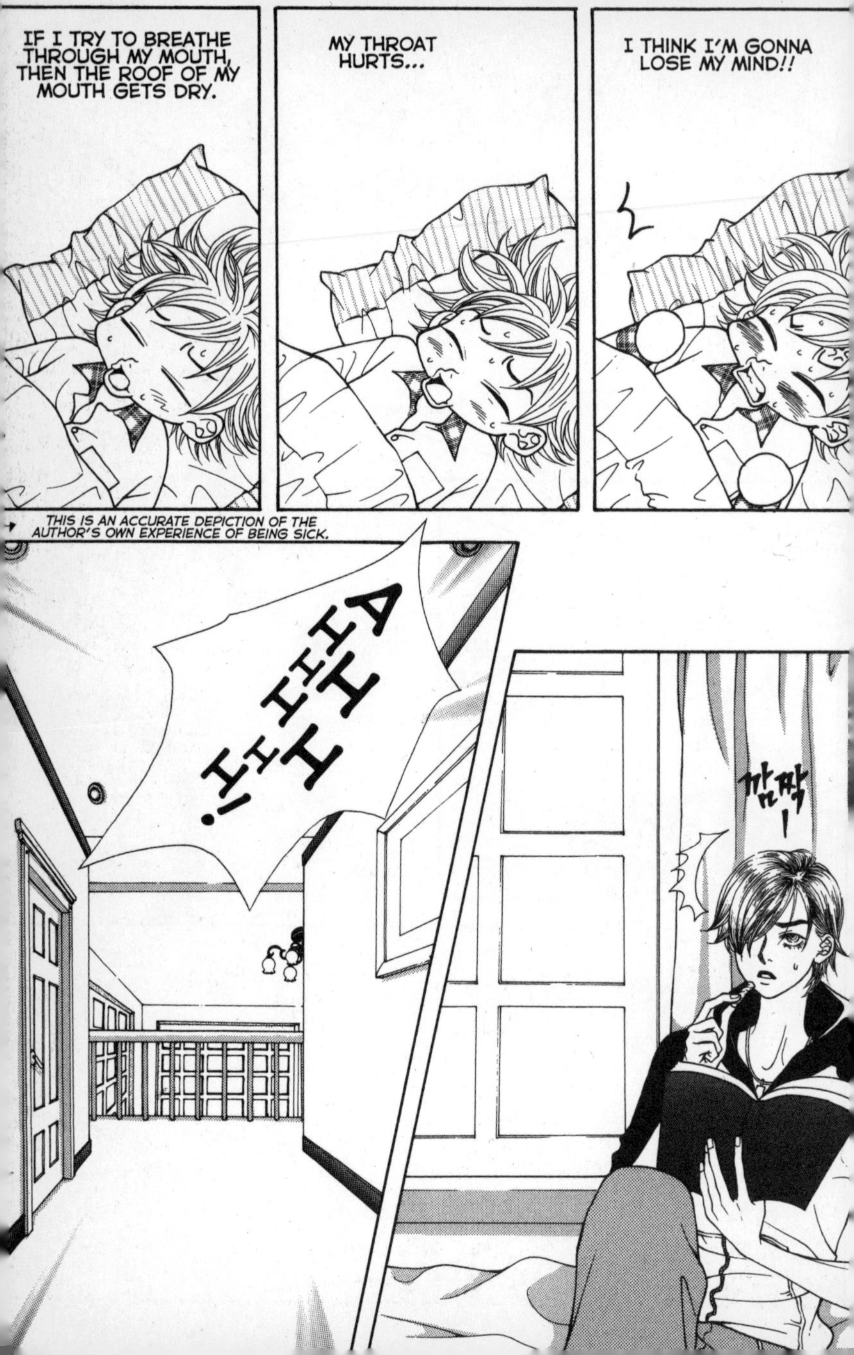
IF I TRY TO BREATHE THROUGH MY MOUTH, THEN THE ROOF OF MY MOUTH GETS DRY.
MY THROAT HURTS...
I THINK I'M GONNA LOSE MY MIND!!
THIS IS AN ACCURATE DEPICTION OF THE AUTHOR'S OWN EXPERIENCE OF BEING SICK.
AHHHHH!!
깜짝!

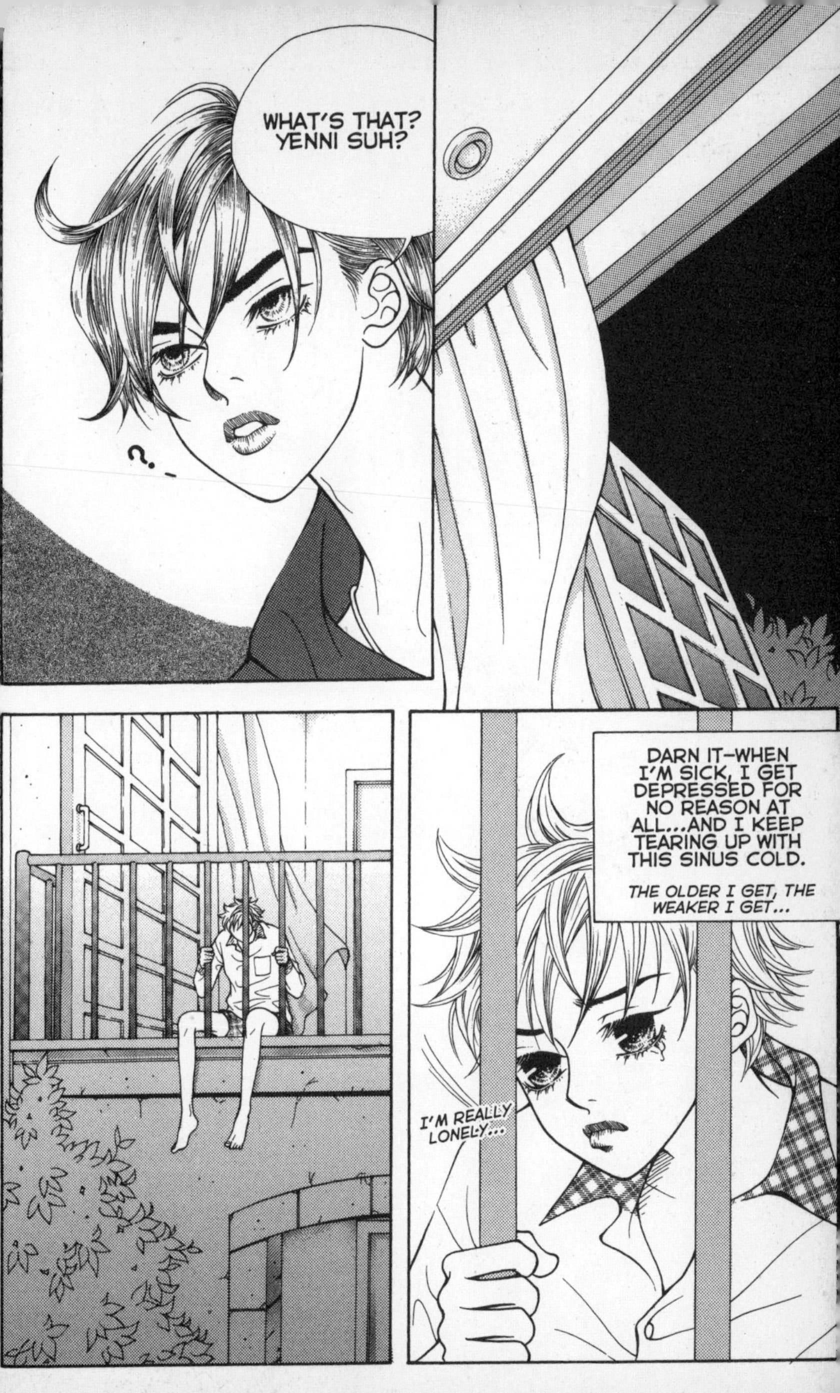
WHAT'S THAT? YENNI SUH?
?..
DARN IT—WHEN I'M SICK, I GET DEPRESSED FOR NO REASON AT ALL...AND I KEEP TEARING UP WITH THIS SINUS COLD.
THE OLDER I GET, THE WEAKER I GET...
I'M REALLY LONELY...

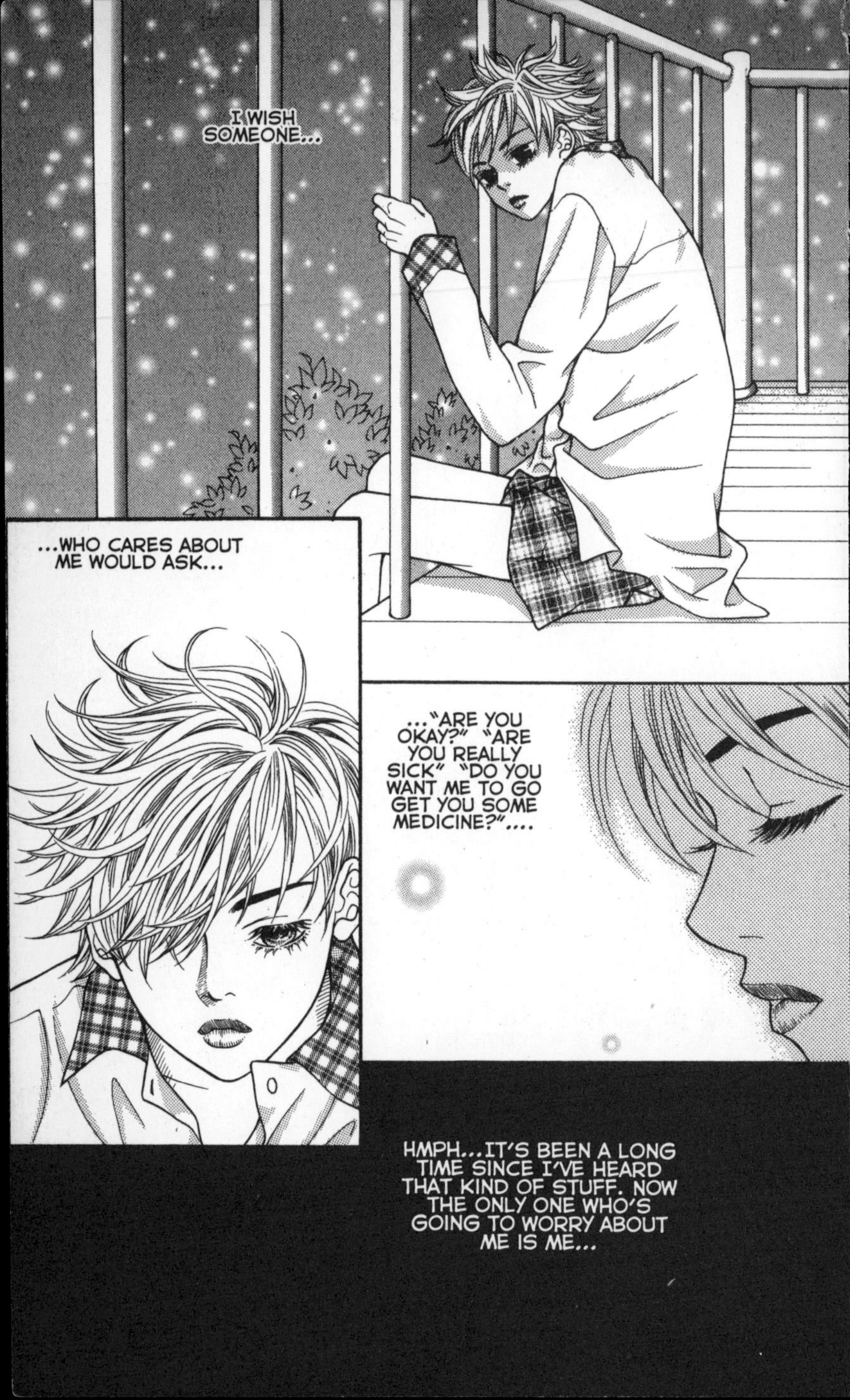
I WISH SOMEONE...
...WHO CARES ABOUT ME WOULD ASK...
..."ARE YOU OKAY?" "ARE YOU REALLY SICK" "DO YOU WANT ME TO GO GET YOU SOME MEDICINE?"....
HMPH...IT'S BEEN A LONG TIME SINCE I'VE HEARD THAT KIND OF STUFF. NOW THE ONLY ONE WHO'S GOING TO WORRY ABOUT ME IS ME...

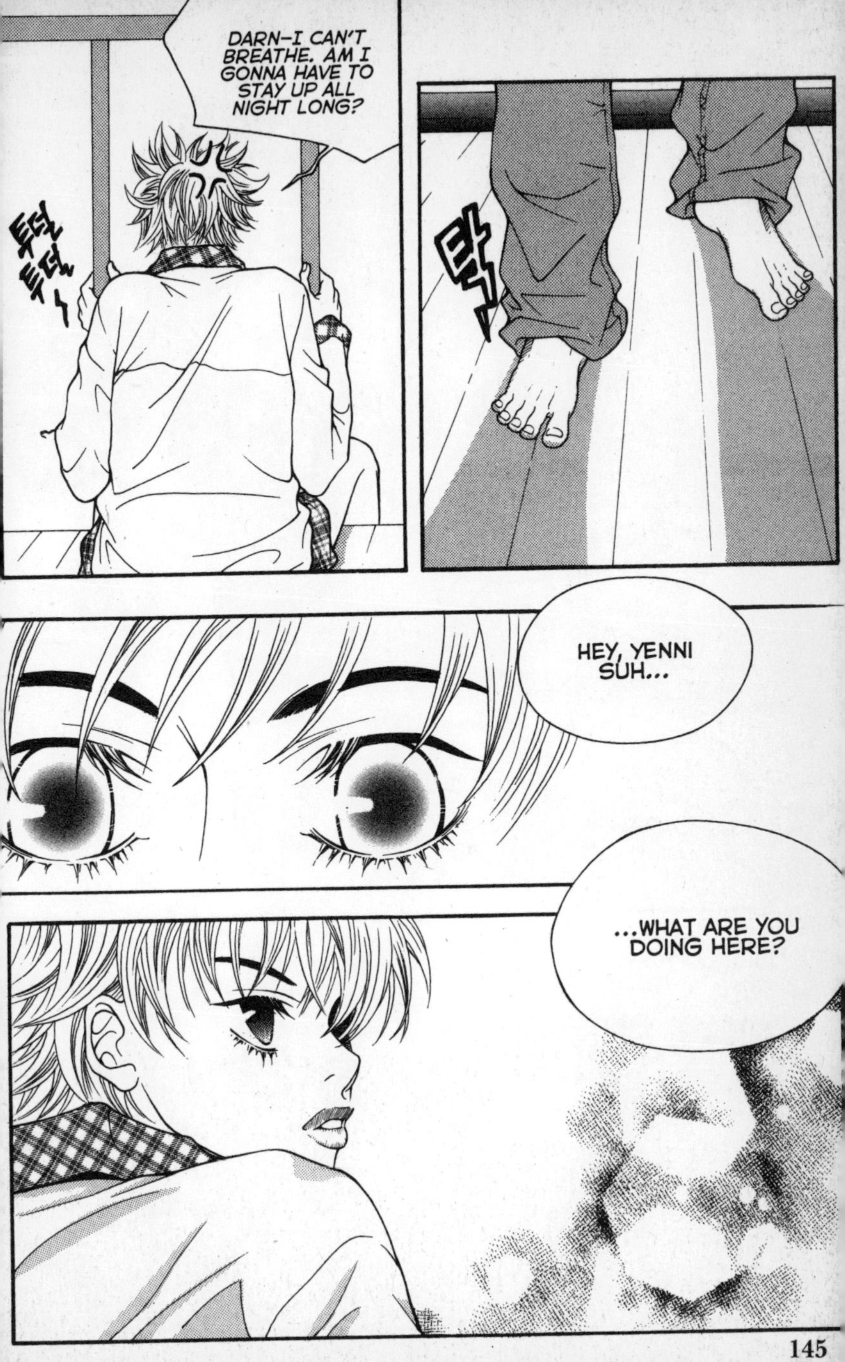
DARN–I CAN'T BREATHE. AM I GONNA HAVE TO STAY UP ALL NIGHT LONG?
투덕 투덕
탁
HEY, YENNI SUH...
...WHAT ARE YOU DOING HERE?

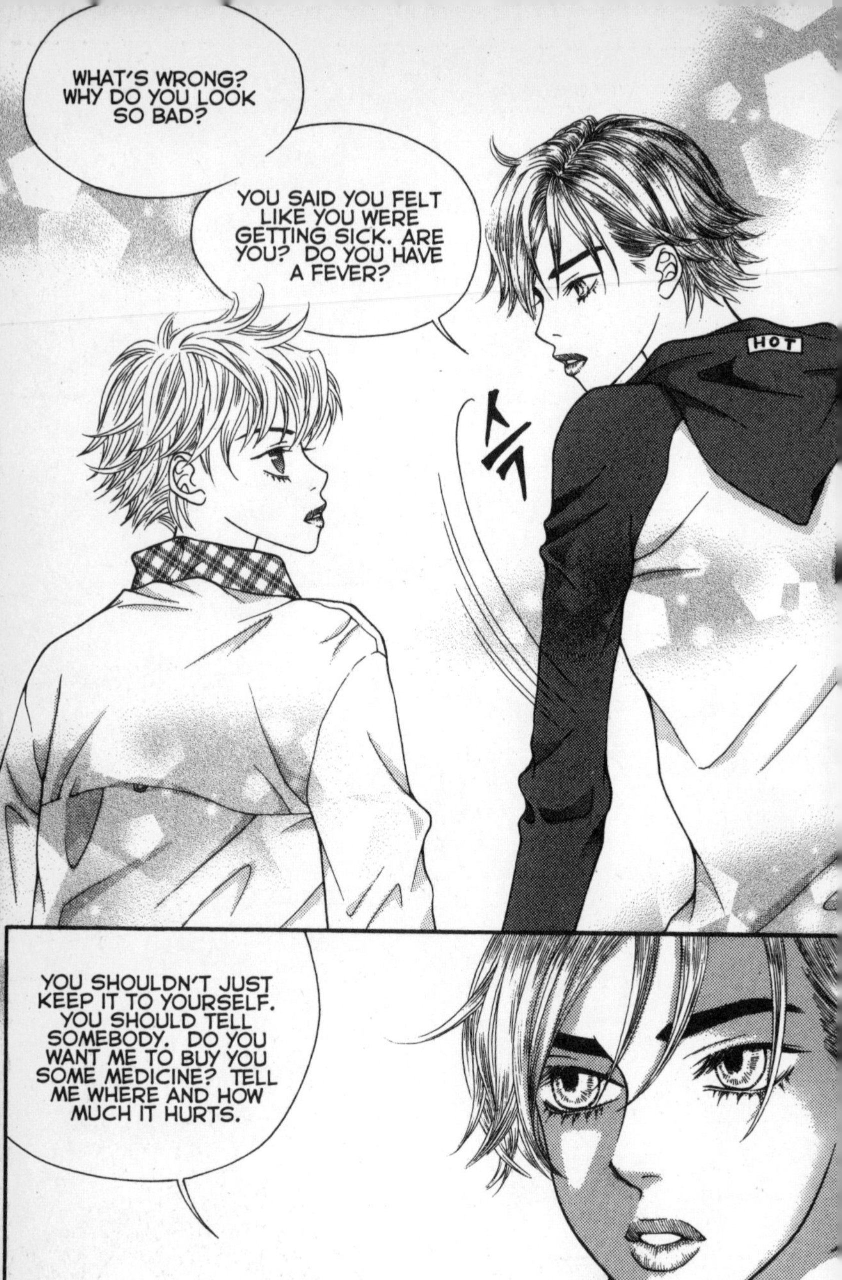
WHAT'S WRONG? WHY DO YOU LOOK SO BAD?
YOU SAID YOU FELT LIKE YOU WERE GETTING SICK. ARE YOU? DO YOU HAVE A FEVER?
HOT
YOU SHOULDN'T JUST KEEP IT TO YOURSELF. YOU SHOULD TELL SOMEBODY. DO YOU WANT ME TO BUY YOU SOME MEDICINE? TELL ME WHERE AND HOW MUCH IT HURTS.

HMM, IT'S NOT SO BAD TO HEAR THIS, EVEN IF IT IS FROM THIS GUY...

HEARING SOMEONE WORRY ABOUT ME...MAKES ME FEEL PRETTY GOOD...

I FEEL BETTER NOW.

I'M DOING MY BEST.

WHY ARE YOU LAUGHING?! AREN'T YOU SICK?

EVEN A JERK LIKE THIS CAN BE HELPFUL TO MY EMOTIONAL WELL-BEING.

I AM SICK. BUT I'M NOT GOING TO DIE OR ANYTHING, SO DON'T WORRY ABOUT ME. JUST DO YOUR OWN THING, DUDE.

147

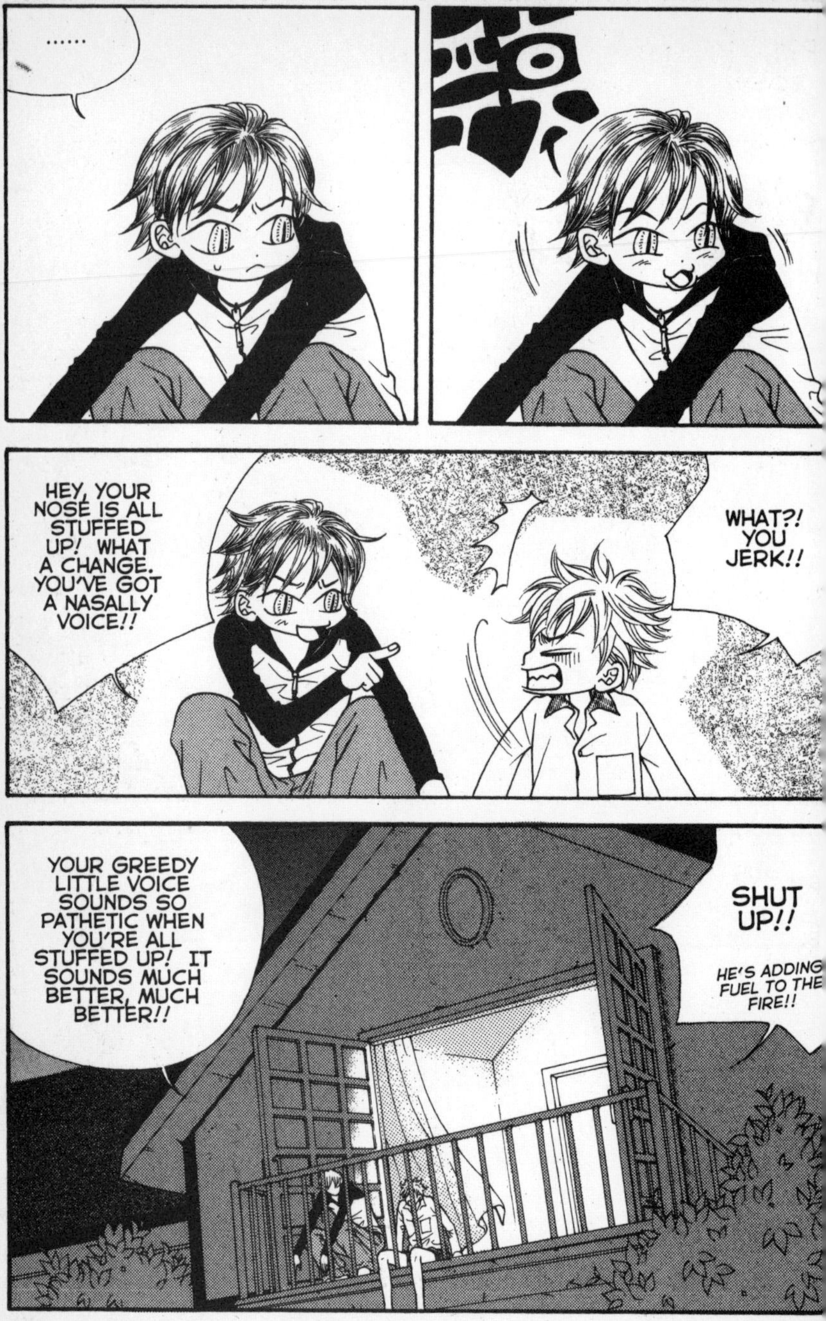
......
HEY, YOUR NOSE IS ALL STUFFED UP! WHAT A CHANGE. YOU'VE GOT A NASALLY VOICE!!
WHAT?! YOU JERK!!
YOUR GREEDY LITTLE VOICE SOUNDS SO PATHETIC WHEN YOU'RE ALL STUFFED UP! IT SOUNDS MUCH BETTER, MUCH BETTER!!
SHUT UP!!
HE'S ADDING FUEL TO THE FIRE!!

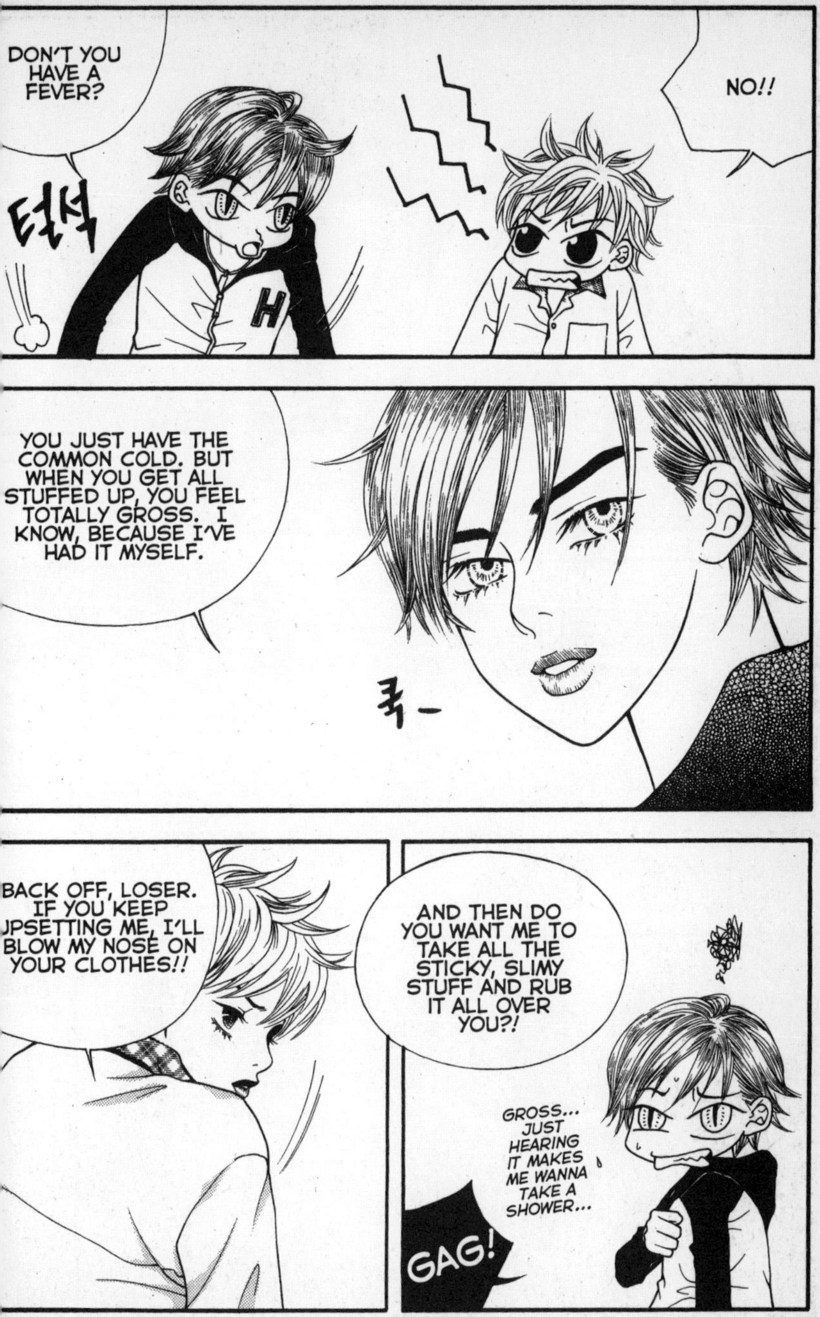
DON'T YOU HAVE A FEVER?
털석
NO!!
YOU JUST HAVE THE COMMON COLD. BUT WHEN YOU GET ALL STUFFED UP, YOU FEEL TOTALLY GROSS. I KNOW, BECAUSE I'VE HAD IT MYSELF.
커—
BACK OFF, LOSER. IF YOU KEEP UPSETTING ME, I'LL BLOW MY NOSE ON YOUR CLOTHES!!
AND THEN DO YOU WANT ME TO TAKE ALL THE STICKY, SLIMY STUFF AND RUB IT ALL OVER YOU?!
GROSS... JUST HEARING IT MAKES ME WANNA TAKE A SHOWER...
GAG!

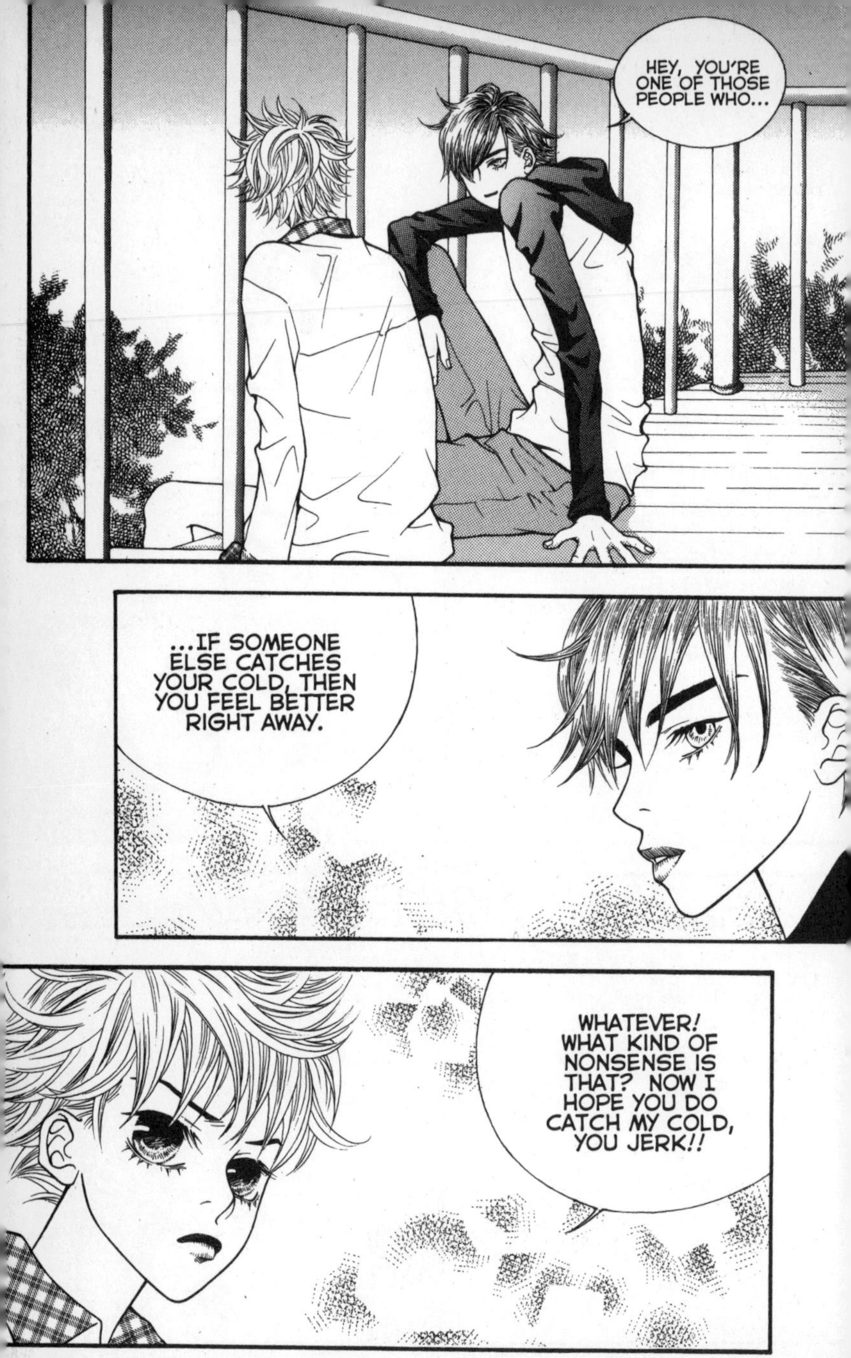
HEY, YOU'RE ONE OF THOSE PEOPLE WHO...
...IF SOMEONE ELSE CATCHES YOUR COLD, THEN YOU FEEL BETTER RIGHT AWAY.
WHATEVER! WHAT KIND OF NONSENSE IS THAT? NOW I HOPE YOU DO CATCH MY COLD, YOU JERK!!

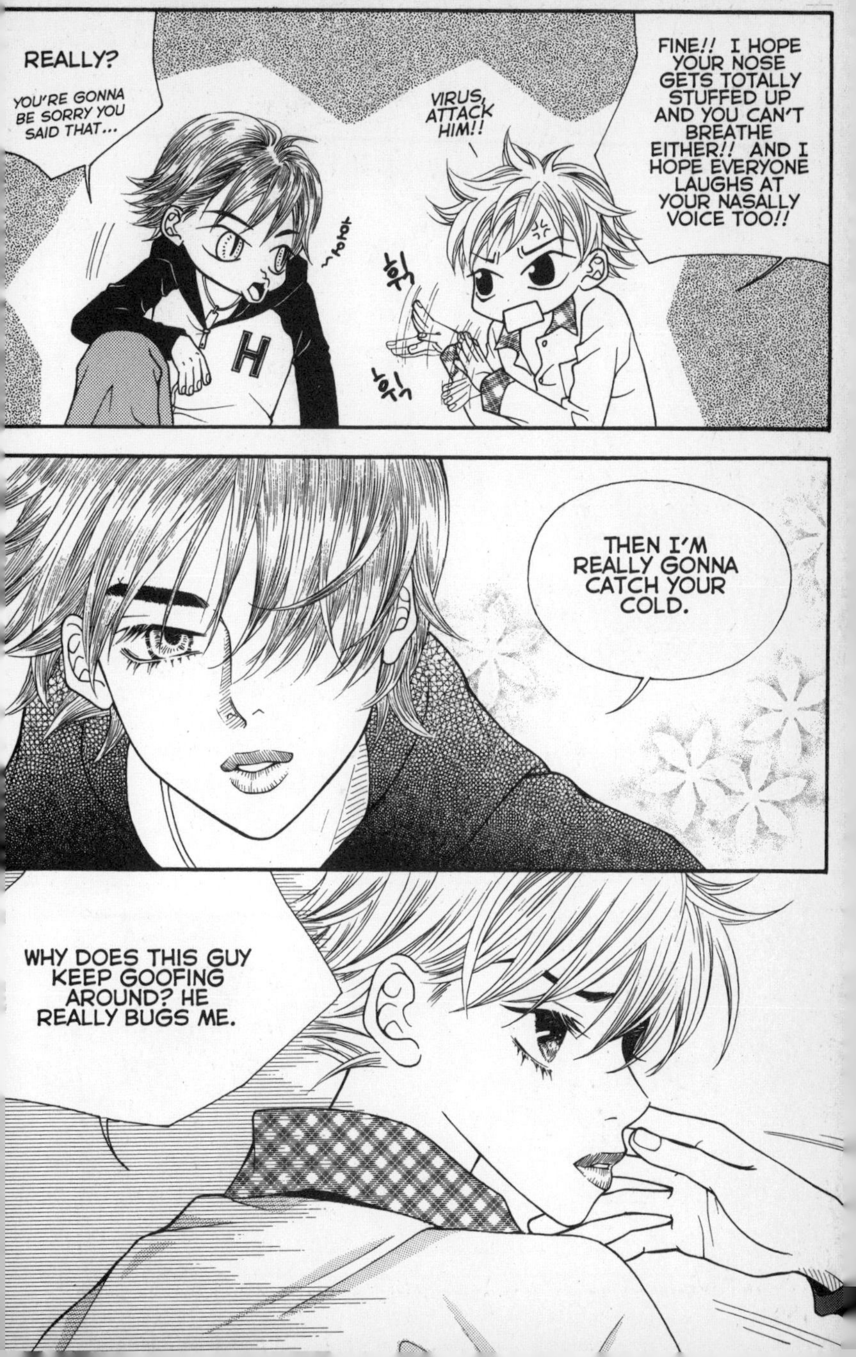
REALLY?
YOU'RE GONNA BE SORRY YOU SAID THAT...
VIRUS, ATTACK HIM!!
FINE!! I HOPE YOUR NOSE GETS TOTALLY STUFFED UP AND YOU CAN'T BREATHE EITHER!! AND I HOPE EVERYONE LAUGHS AT YOUR NASALLY VOICE TOO!!
THEN I'M REALLY GONNA CATCH YOUR COLD.
WHY DOES THIS GUY KEEP GOOFING AROUND? HE REALLY BUGS ME.

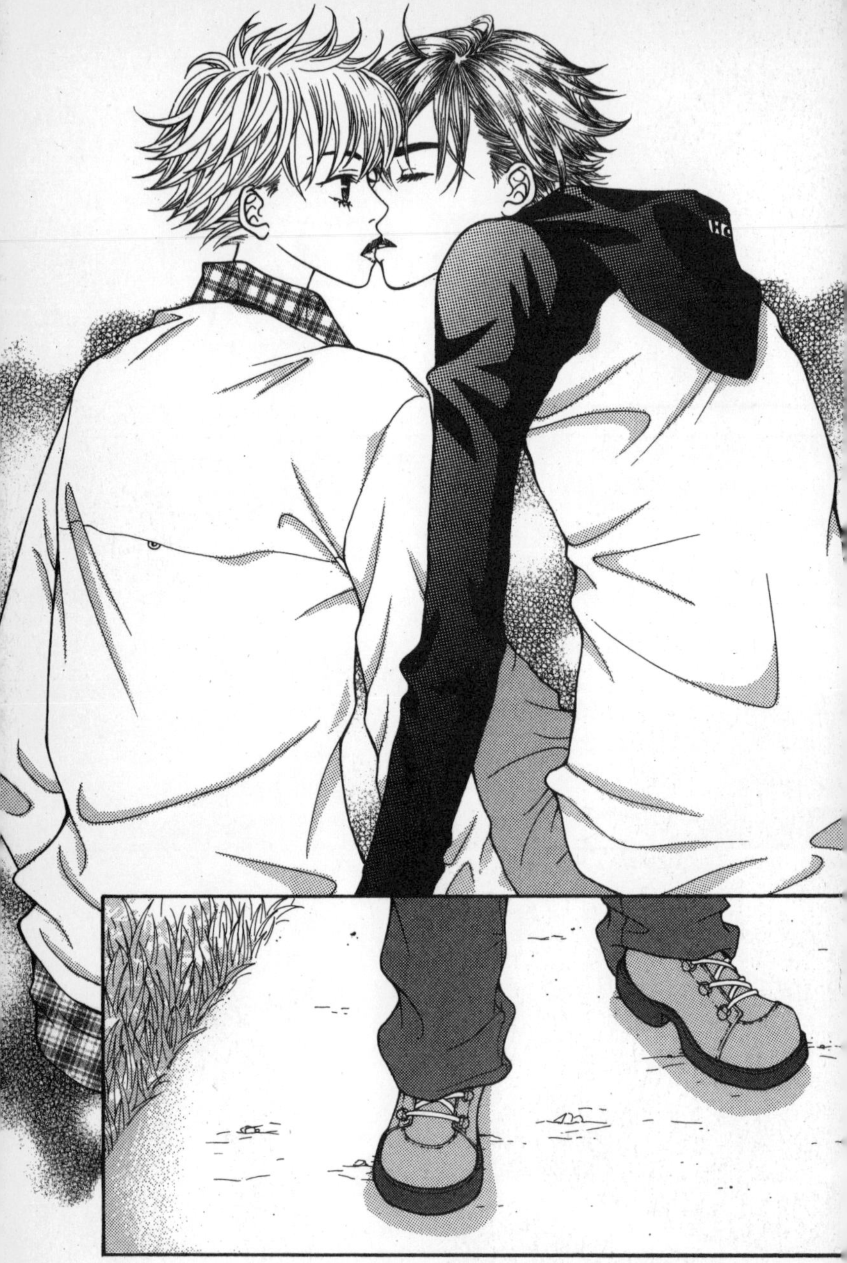

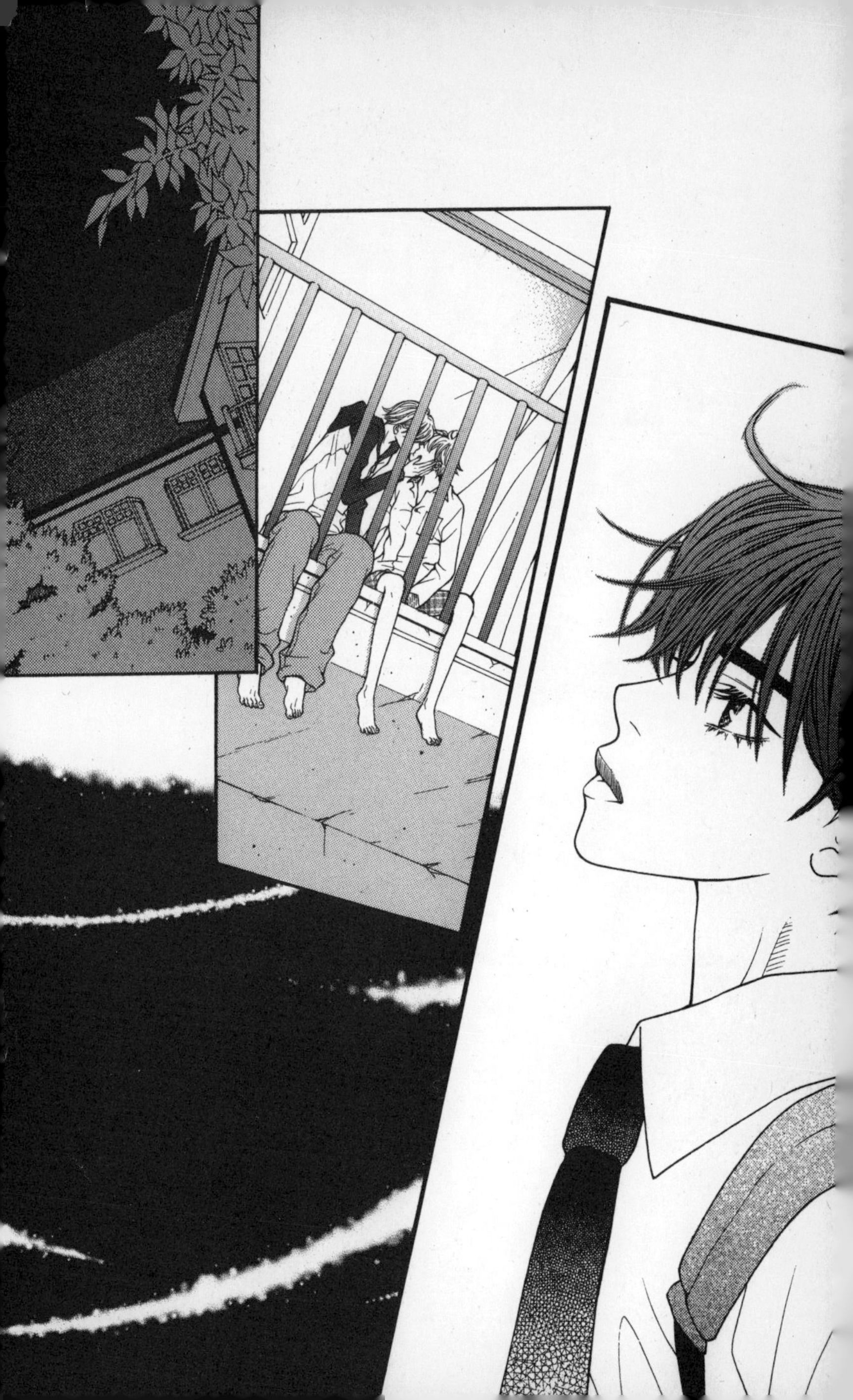

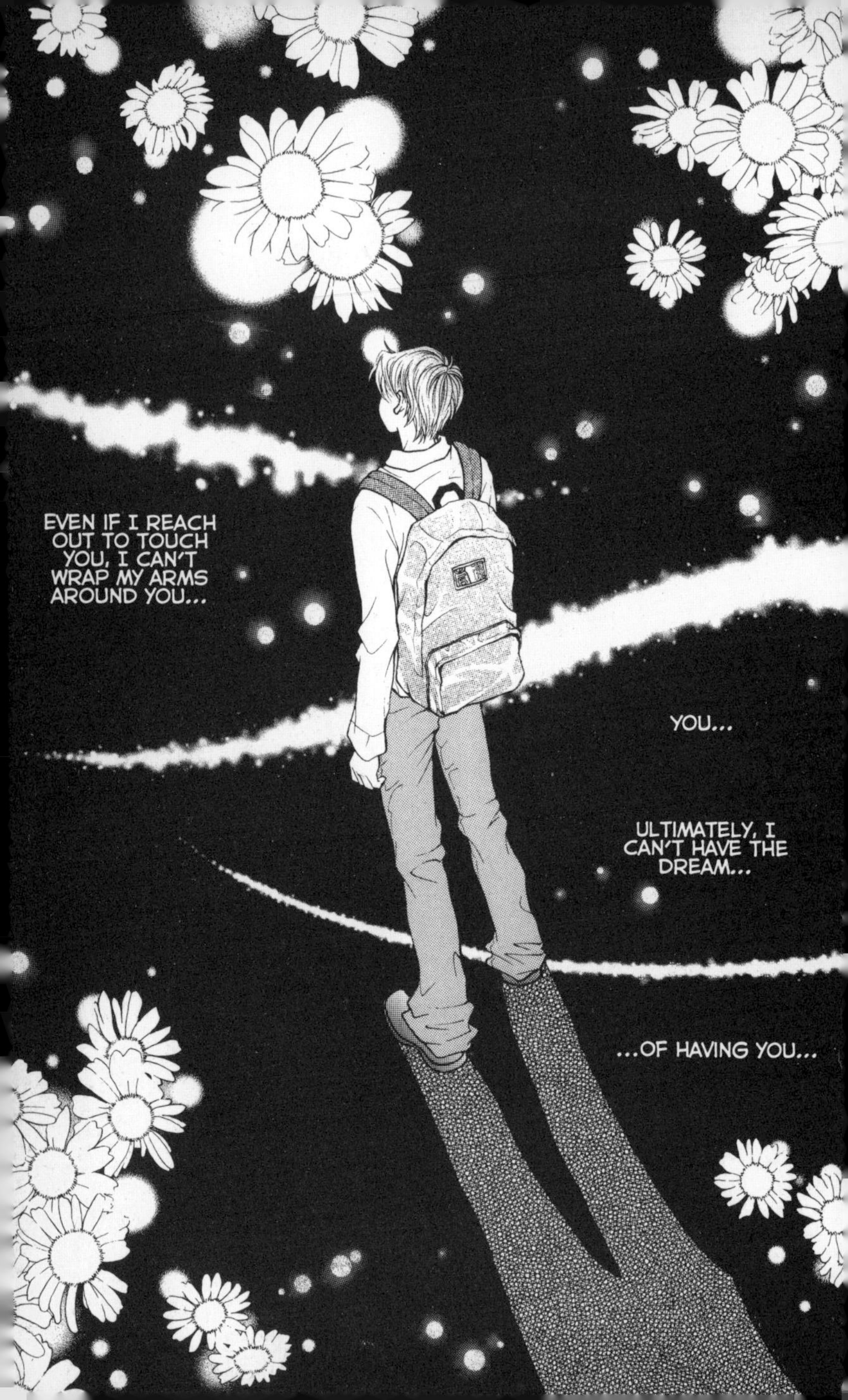
EVEN IF I REACH OUT TO TOUCH YOU, I CAN'T WRAP MY ARMS AROUND YOU...
YOU...
ULTIMATELY, I CAN'T HAVE THE DREAM...
...OF HAVING YOU...

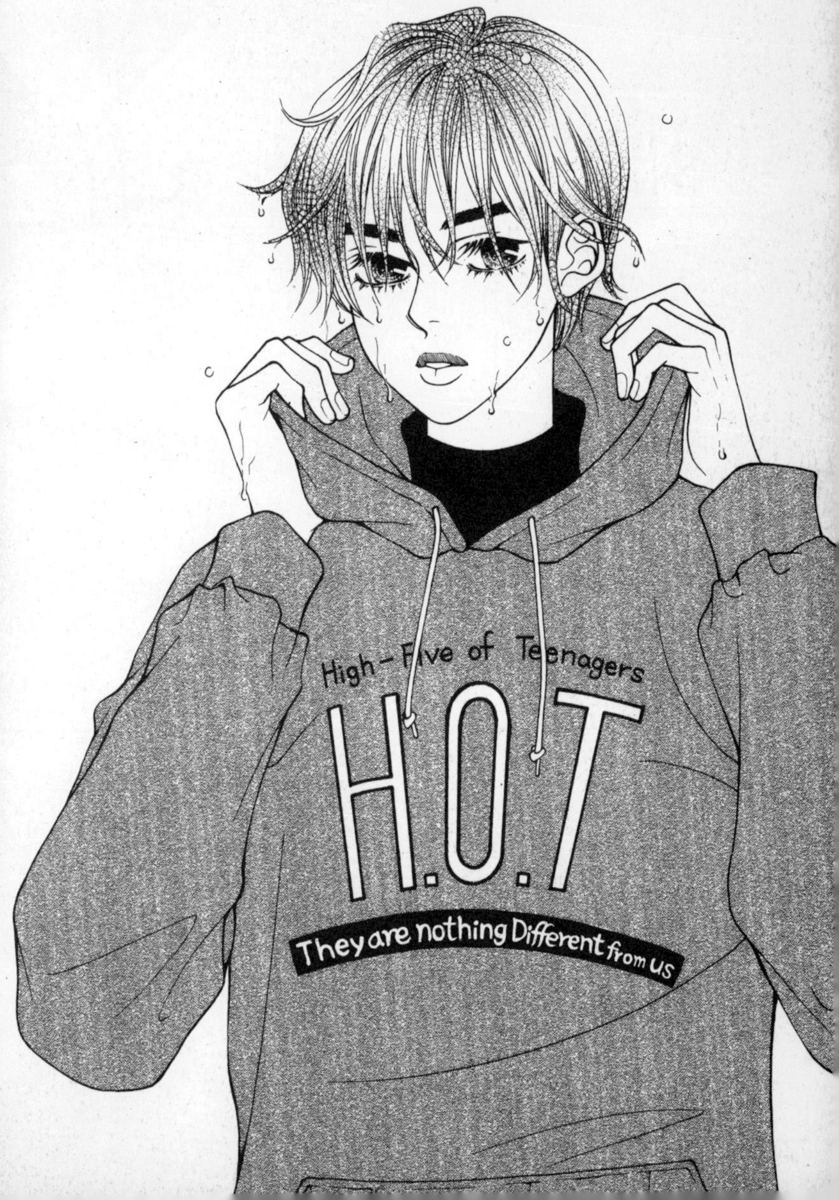
High-Five of Teenagers
H.O.T
They are nothing Different from us

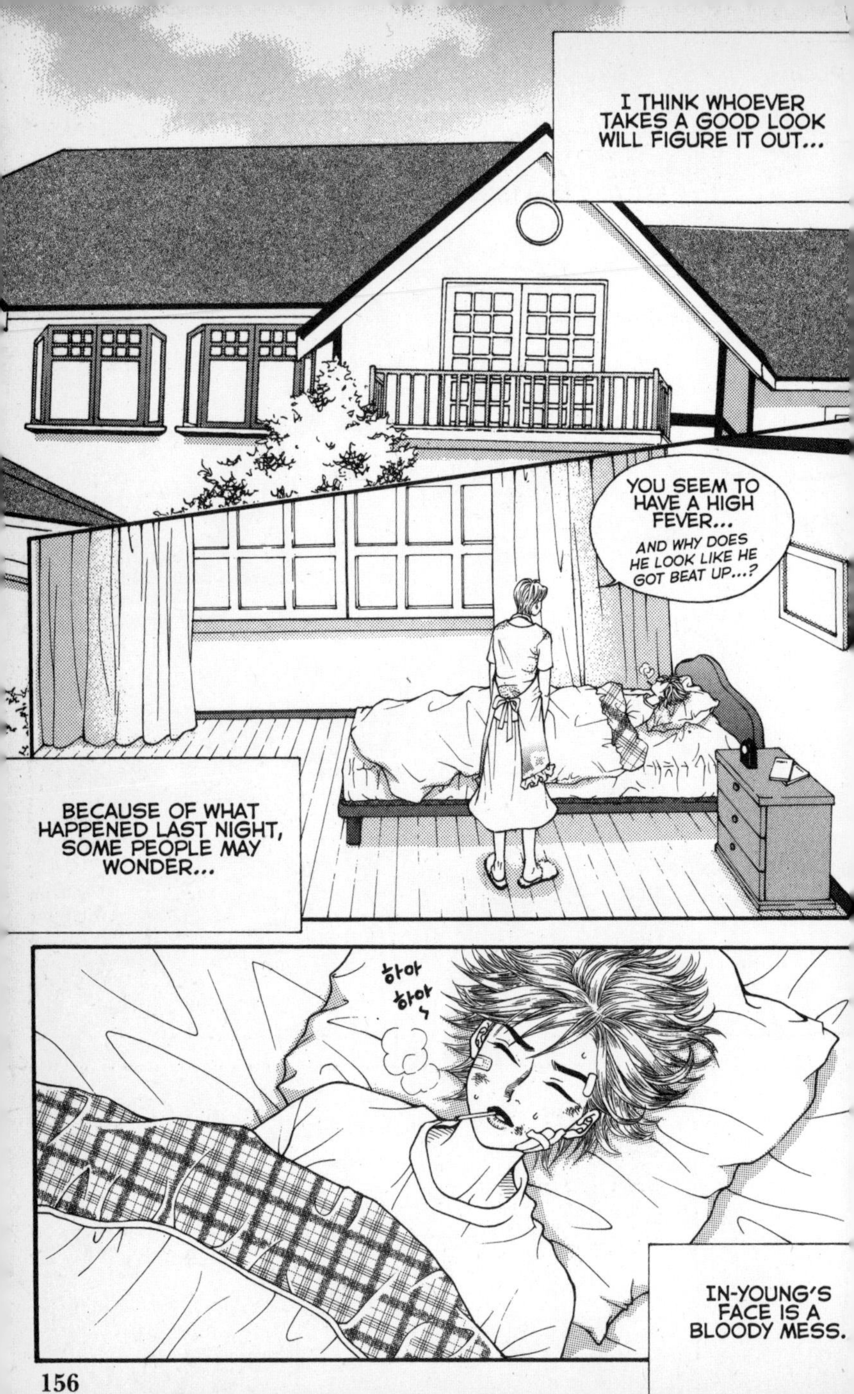
I THINK WHOEVER TAKES A GOOD LOOK WILL FIGURE IT OUT...
YOU SEEM TO HAVE A HIGH FEVER... AND WHY DOES HE LOOK LIKE HE GOT BEAT UP...?
BECAUSE OF WHAT HAPPENED LAST NIGHT, SOME PEOPLE MAY WONDER...
하아 하아
IN-YOUNG'S FACE IS A BLOODY MESS.

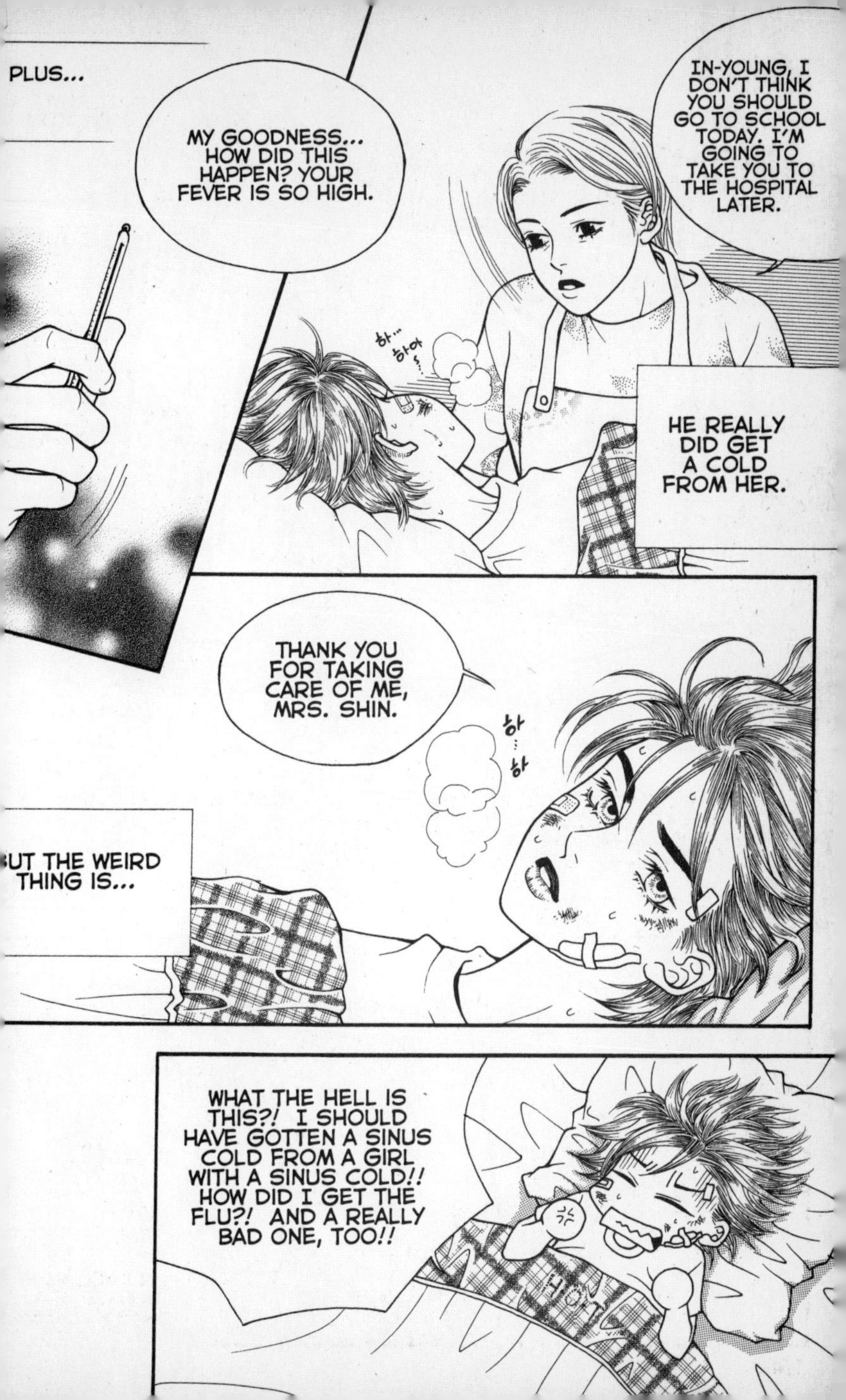
PLUS...
MY GOODNESS... HOW DID THIS HAPPEN? YOUR FEVER IS SO HIGH.
IN-YOUNG, I DON'T THINK YOU SHOULD GO TO SCHOOL TODAY. I'M GOING TO TAKE YOU TO THE HOSPITAL LATER.
하... 하아...
HE REALLY DID GET A COLD FROM HER.
THANK YOU FOR TAKING CARE OF ME, MRS. SHIN.
하... 하
UT THE WEIRD THING IS...
WHAT THE HELL IS THIS?! I SHOULD HAVE GOTTEN A SINUS COLD FROM A GIRL WITH A SINUS COLD!! HOW DID I GET THE FLU?! AND A REALLY BAD ONE, TOO!!

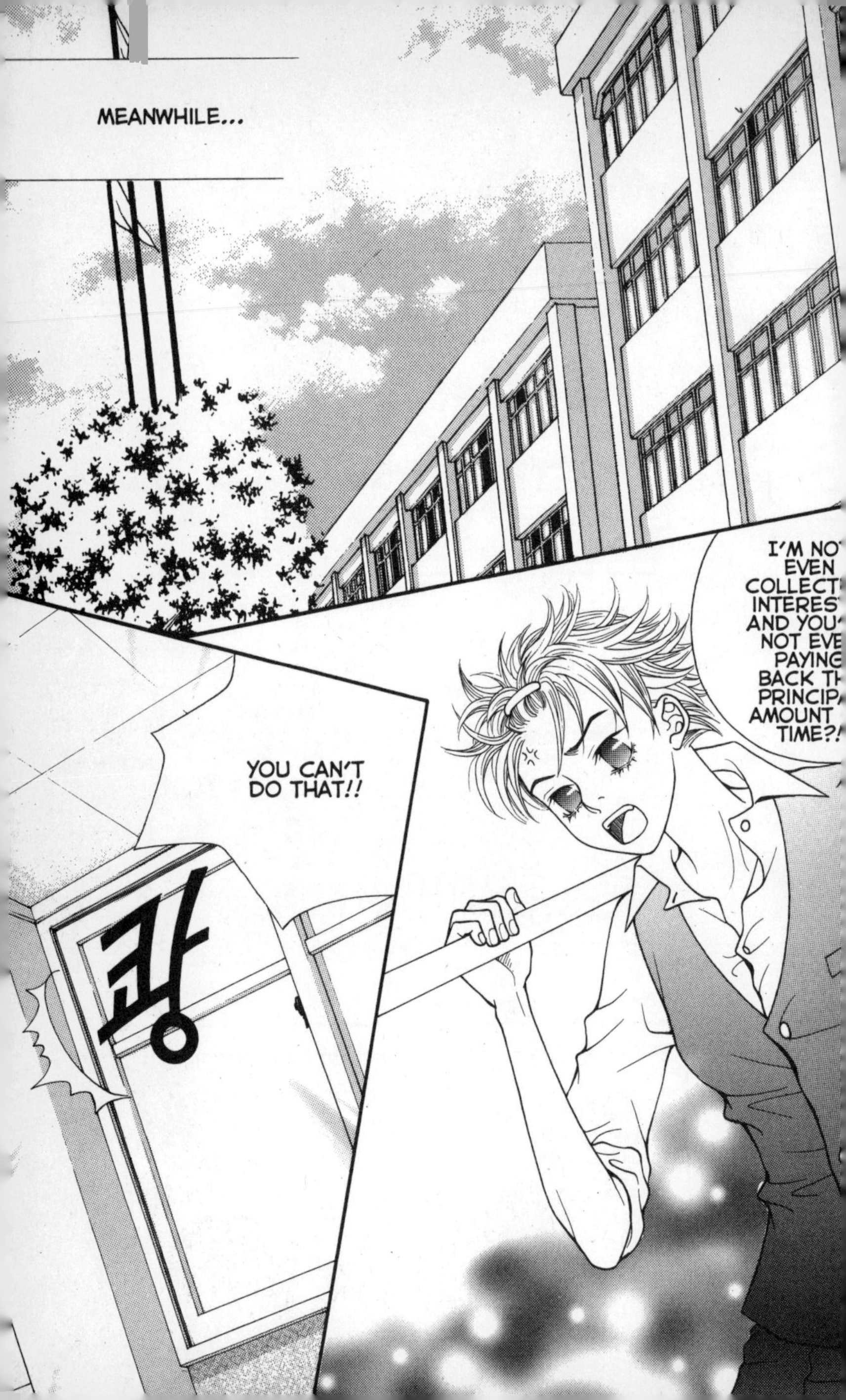
MEANWHILE...
YOU CAN'T DO THAT!!
I'M NO EVEN COLLECT INTERES AND YOU NOT EVE PAYING BACK TH PRINCIPA AMOUNT TIME?!

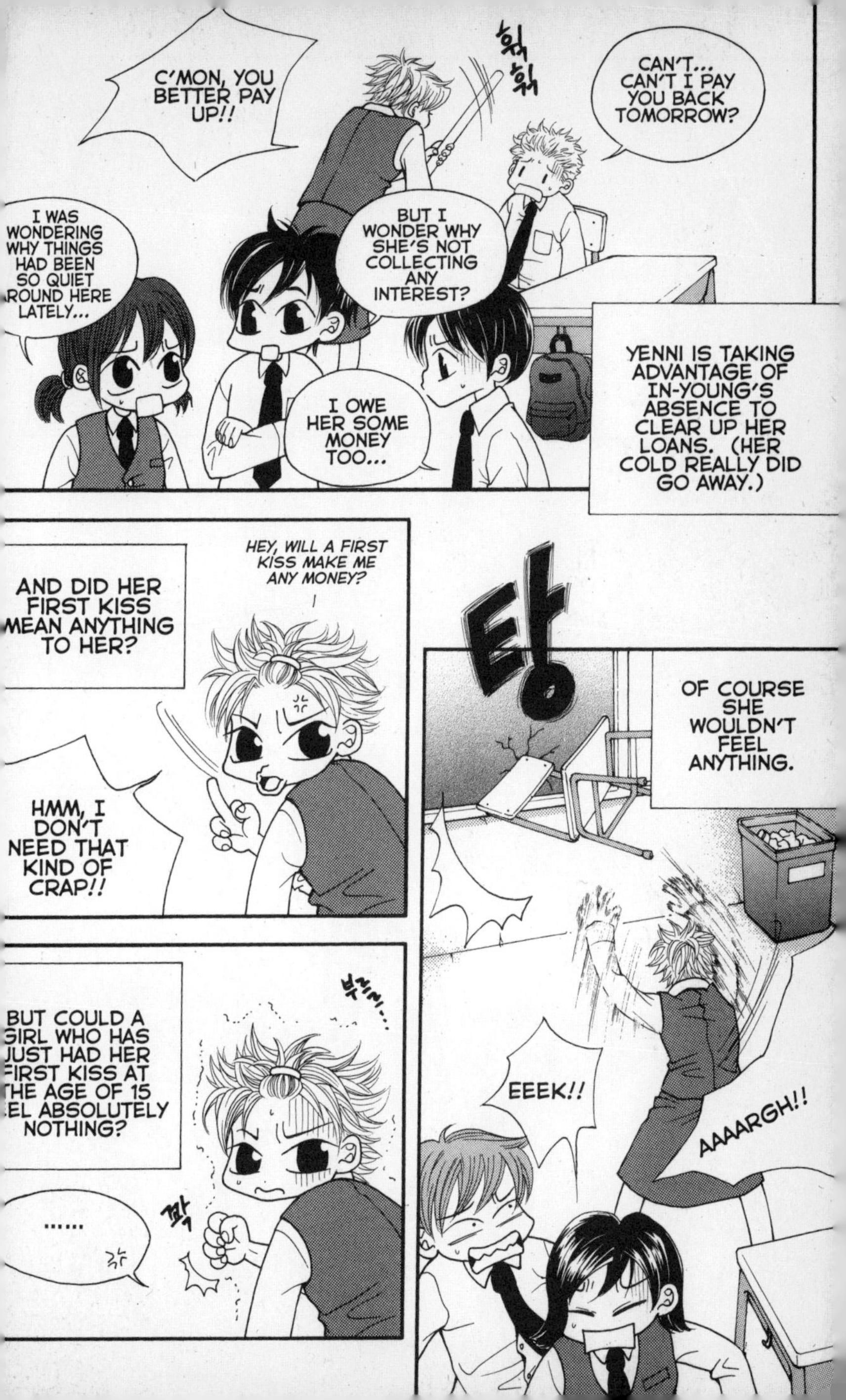
C'MON, YOU BETTER PAY UP!!
휙휙
CAN'T... CAN'T I PAY YOU BACK TOMORROW?
I WAS WONDERING WHY THINGS HAD BEEN SO QUIET ROUND HERE LATELY...
BUT I WONDER WHY SHE'S NOT COLLECTING ANY INTEREST?
I OWE HER SOME MONEY TOO...
YENNI IS TAKING ADVANTAGE OF IN-YOUNG'S ABSENCE TO CLEAR UP HER LOANS. (HER COLD REALLY DID GO AWAY.)
AND DID HER FIRST KISS MEAN ANYTHING TO HER?
HEY, WILL A FIRST KISS MAKE ME ANY MONEY?
HMM, I DON'T NEED THAT KIND OF CRAP!!
BUT COULD A GIRL WHO HAS JUST HAD HER FIRST KISS AT THE AGE OF 15 EL ABSOLUTELY NOTHING?
......
꽉
탕
OF COURSE SHE WOULDN'T FEEL ANYTHING.
EEEK!!
AAAARGH!!

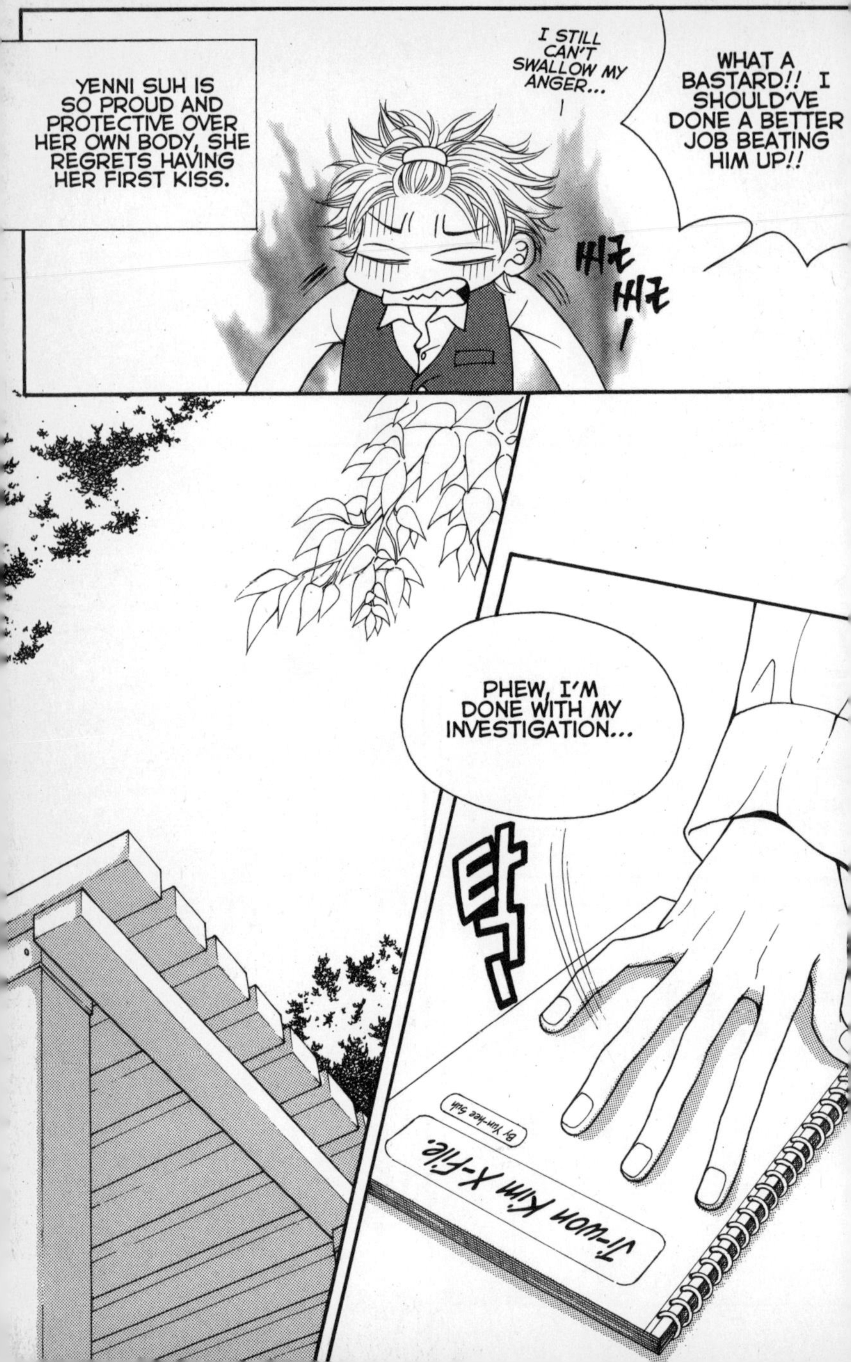
YENNI SUH IS SO PROUD AND PROTECTIVE OVER HER OWN BODY, SHE REGRETS HAVING HER FIRST KISS.
I STILL CAN'T SWALLOW MY ANGER...
WHAT A BASTARD!! I SHOULD'VE DONE A BETTER JOB BEATING HIM UP!!
PHEW, I'M DONE WITH MY INVESTIGATION...
탁
Ji-won Kim X-File.
By Yun-hee Suh

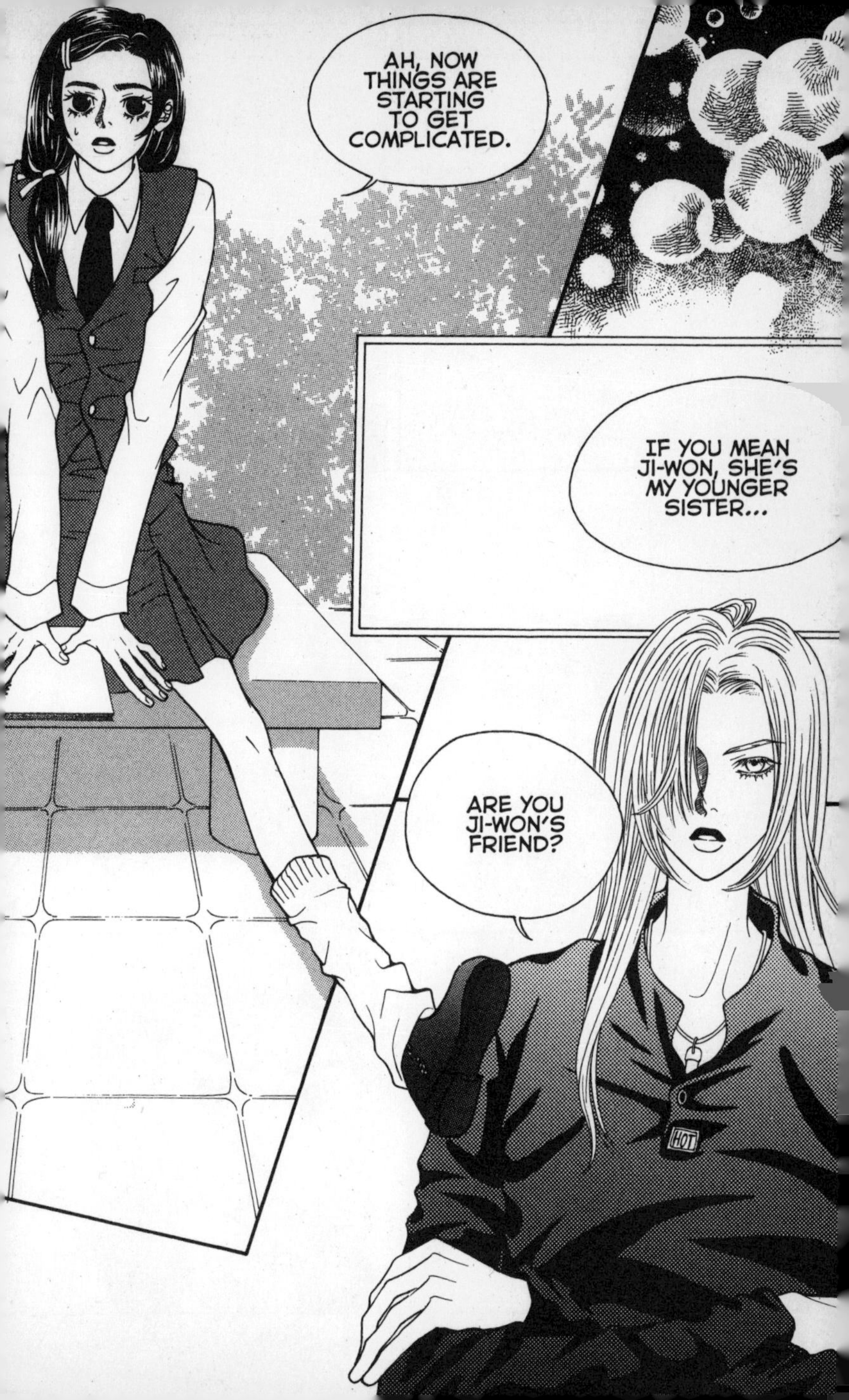
AH, NOW THINGS ARE STARTING TO GET COMPLICATED.
IF YOU MEAN JI-WON, SHE'S MY YOUNGER SISTER...
ARE YOU JI-WON'S FRIEND?
HOT

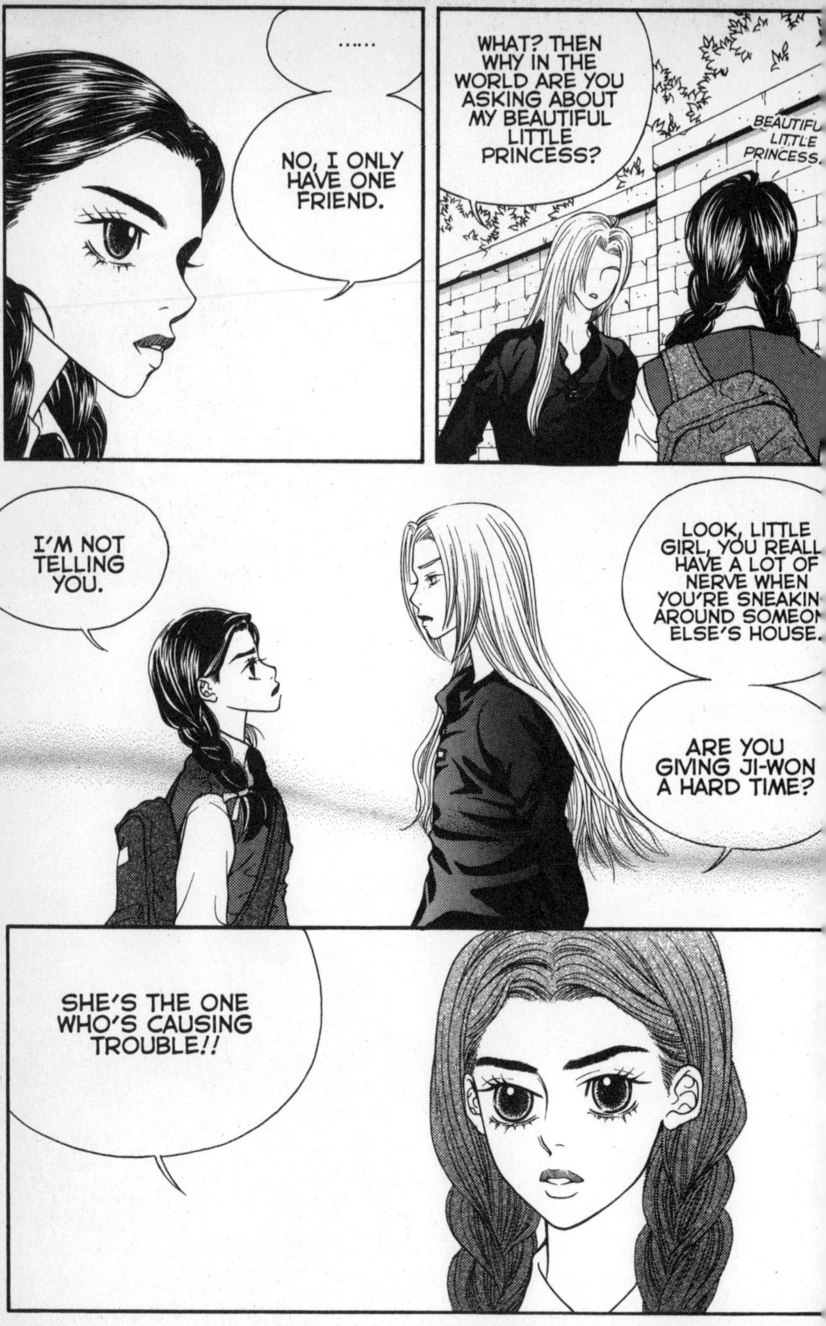

......
NO, I ONLY HAVE ONE FRIEND.
WHAT? THEN WHY IN THE WORLD ARE YOU ASKING ABOUT MY BEAUTIFUL LITTLE PRINCESS?
BEAUTIFU LITTLE PRINCESS.
I'M NOT TELLING YOU.
LOOK, LITTLE GIRL, YOU REALL HAVE A LOT OF NERVE WHEN YOU'RE SNEAKIN AROUND SOMEO ELSE'S HOUSE.
ARE YOU GIVING JI-WON A HARD TIME?
SHE'S THE ONE WHO'S CAUSING TROUBLE!!

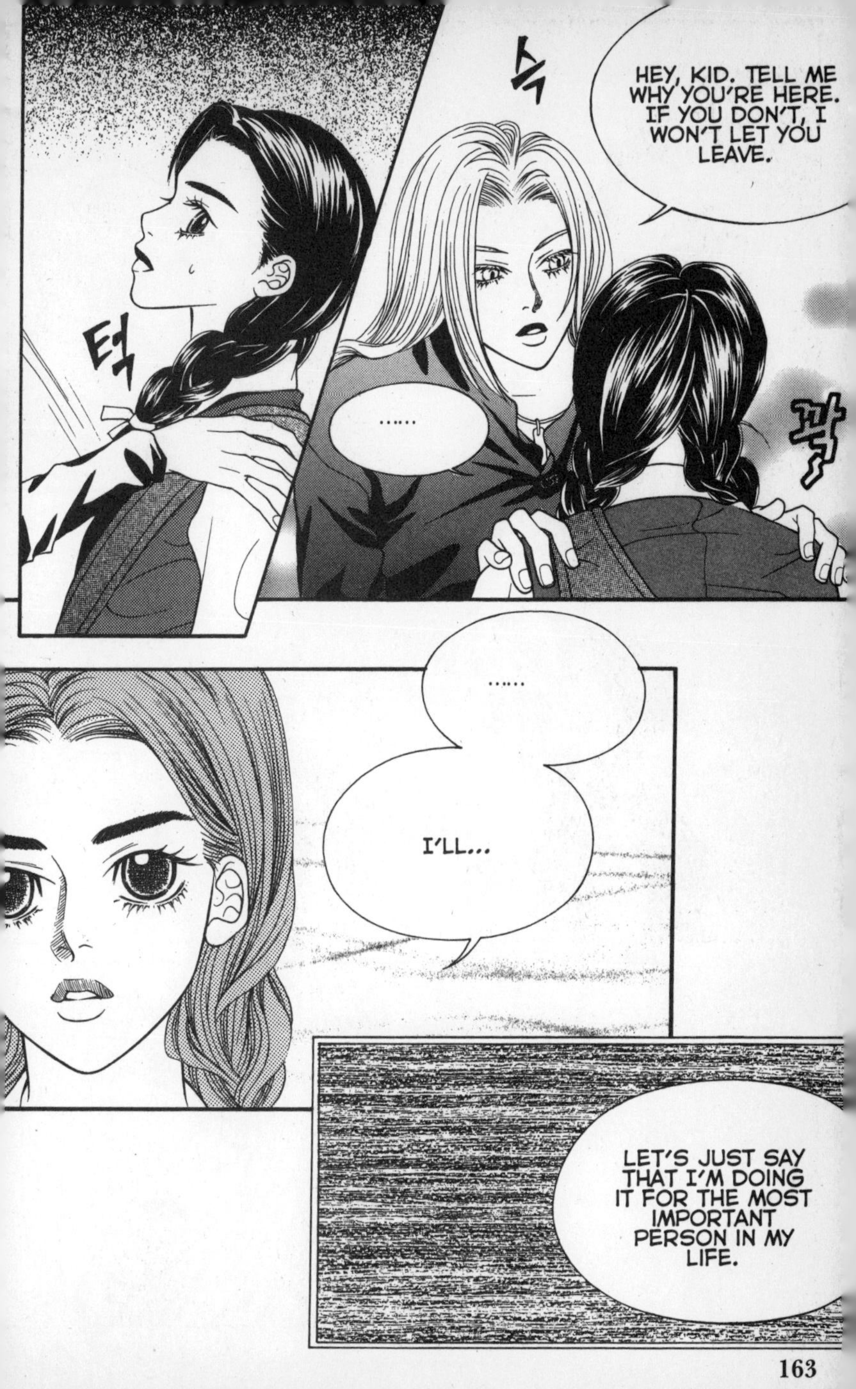
턱
슥
HEY, KID. TELL ME WHY YOU'RE HERE. IF YOU DON'T, I WON'T LET YOU LEAVE.
......
꽉
......
I'LL...
LET'S JUST SAY THAT I'M DOING IT FOR THE MOST IMPORTANT PERSON IN MY LIFE.

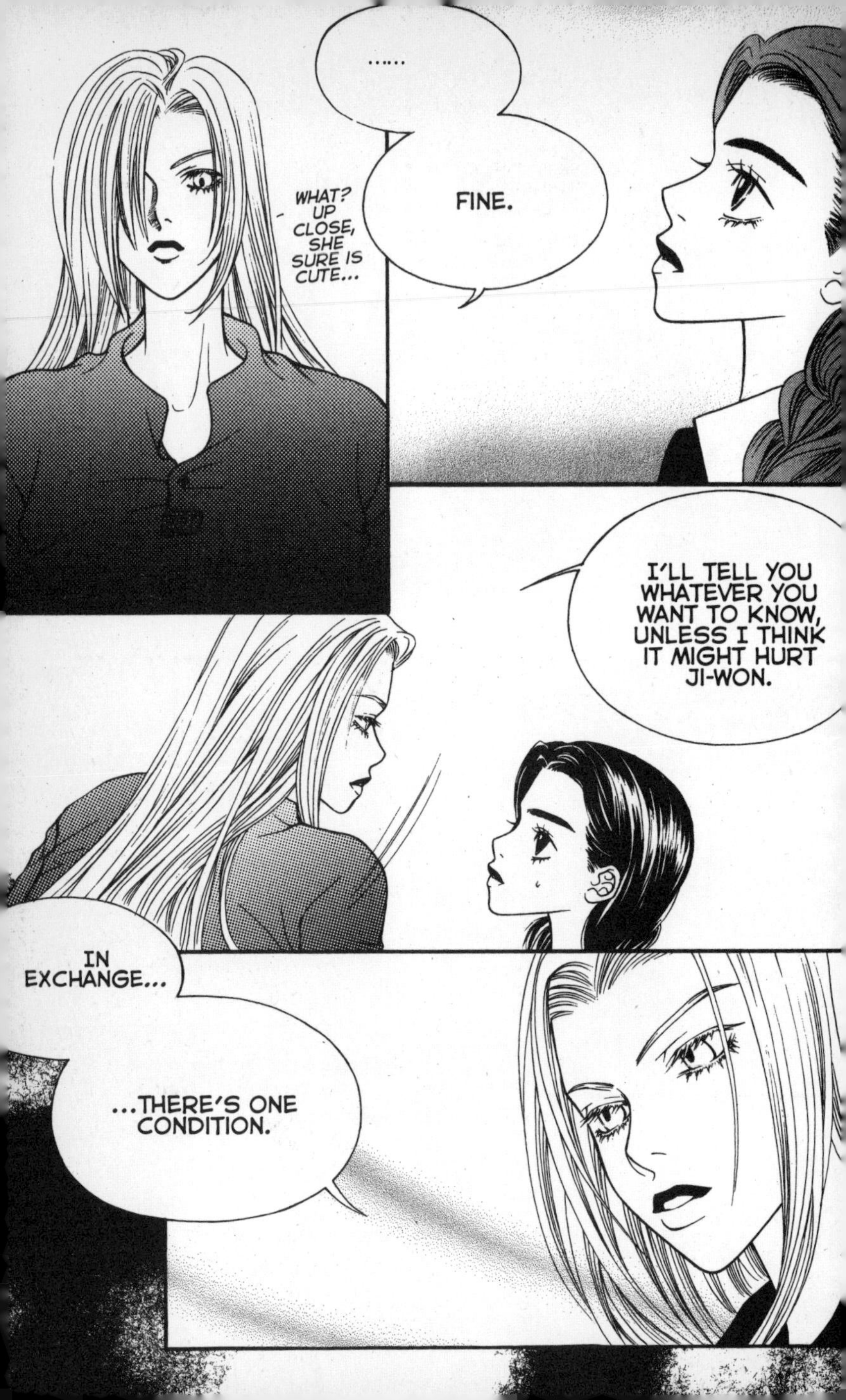
WHAT? UP CLOSE, SHE SURE IS CUTE...
......
FINE.
I'LL TELL YOU WHATEVER YOU WANT TO KNOW, UNLESS I THINK IT MIGHT HURT JI-WON.
IN EXCHANGE...
...THERE'S ONE CONDITION.

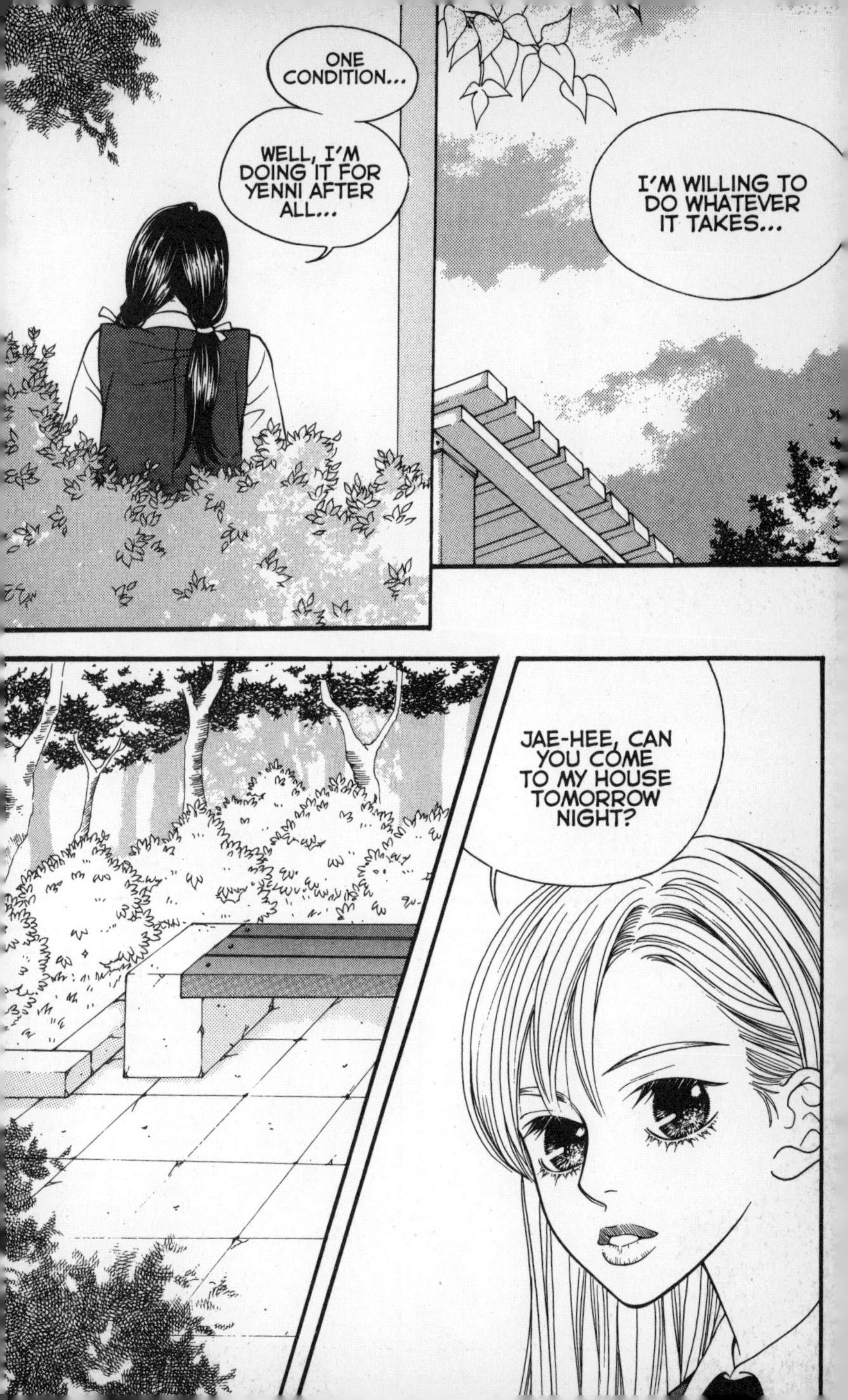
ONE CONDITION...
WELL, I'M DOING IT FOR YENNI AFTER ALL...
I'M WILLING TO DO WHATEVER IT TAKES...
JAE-HEE, CAN YOU COME TO MY HOUSE TOMORROW NIGHT?

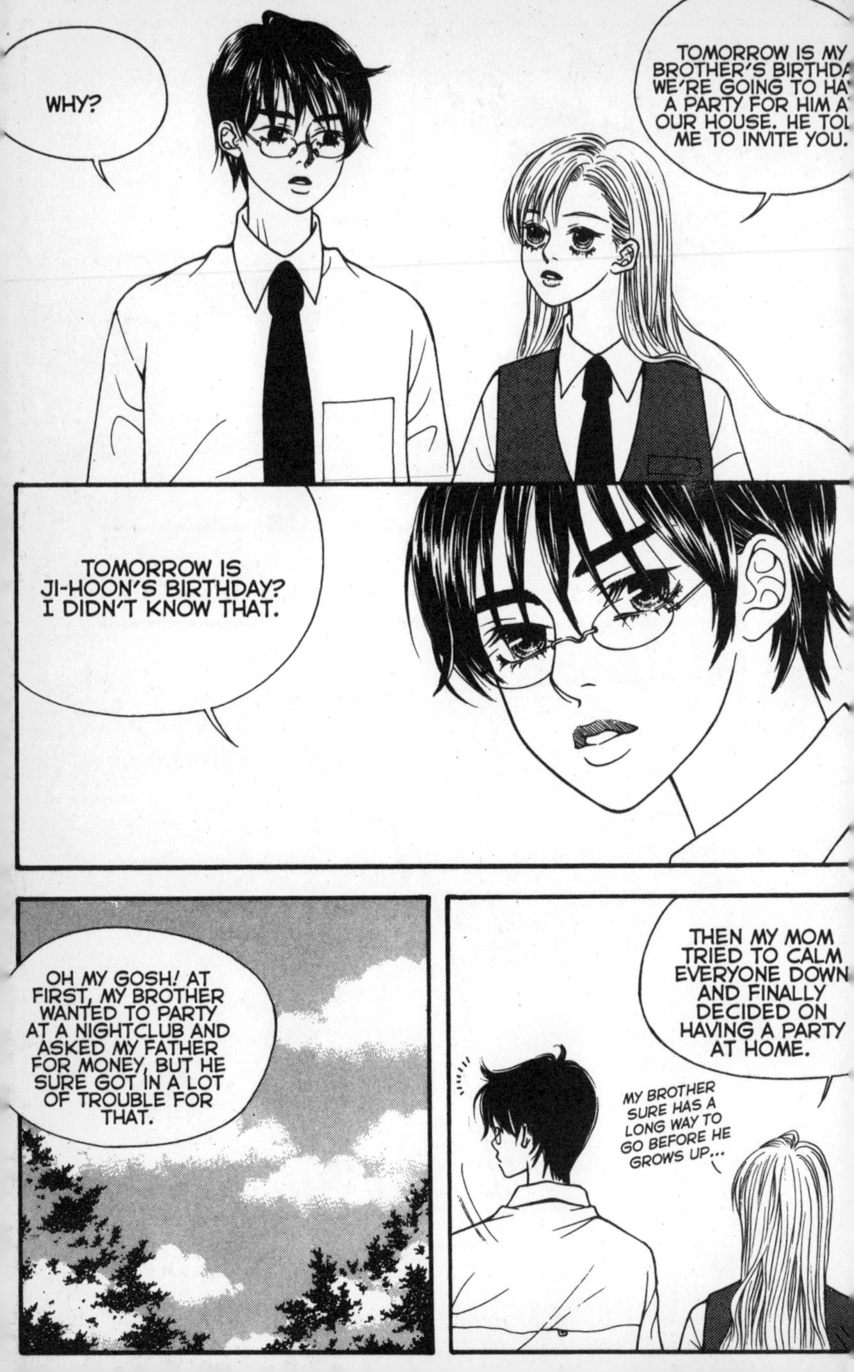
WHY?
TOMORROW IS MY BROTHER'S BIRTHDA WE'RE GOING TO HA A PARTY FOR HIM A OUR HOUSE. HE TOL ME TO INVITE YOU.
TOMORROW IS JI-HOON'S BIRTHDAY? I DIDN'T KNOW THAT.
OH MY GOSH! AT FIRST, MY BROTHER WANTED TO PARTY AT A NIGHTCLUB AND ASKED MY FATHER FOR MONEY, BUT HE SURE GOT IN A LOT OF TROUBLE FOR THAT.
THEN MY MOM TRIED TO CALM EVERYONE DOWN AND FINALLY DECIDED ON HAVING A PARTY AT HOME.
MY BROTHER SURE HAS A LONG WAY TO GO BEFORE HE GROWS UP...

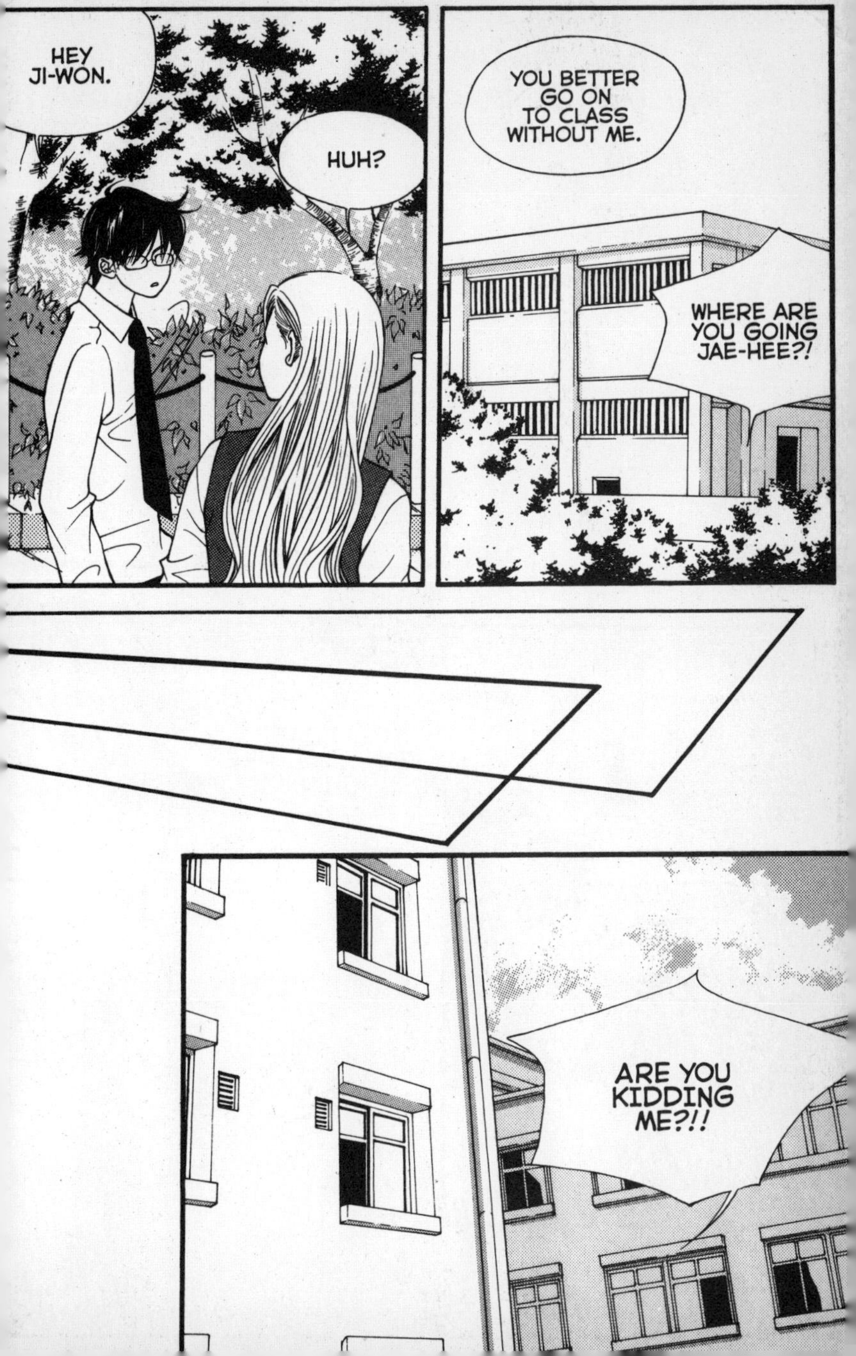
HEY JI-WON.
HUH?
YOU BETTER GO ON TO CLASS WITHOUT ME.
WHERE ARE YOU GOING JAE-HEE?!
ARE YOU KIDDING ME?!!

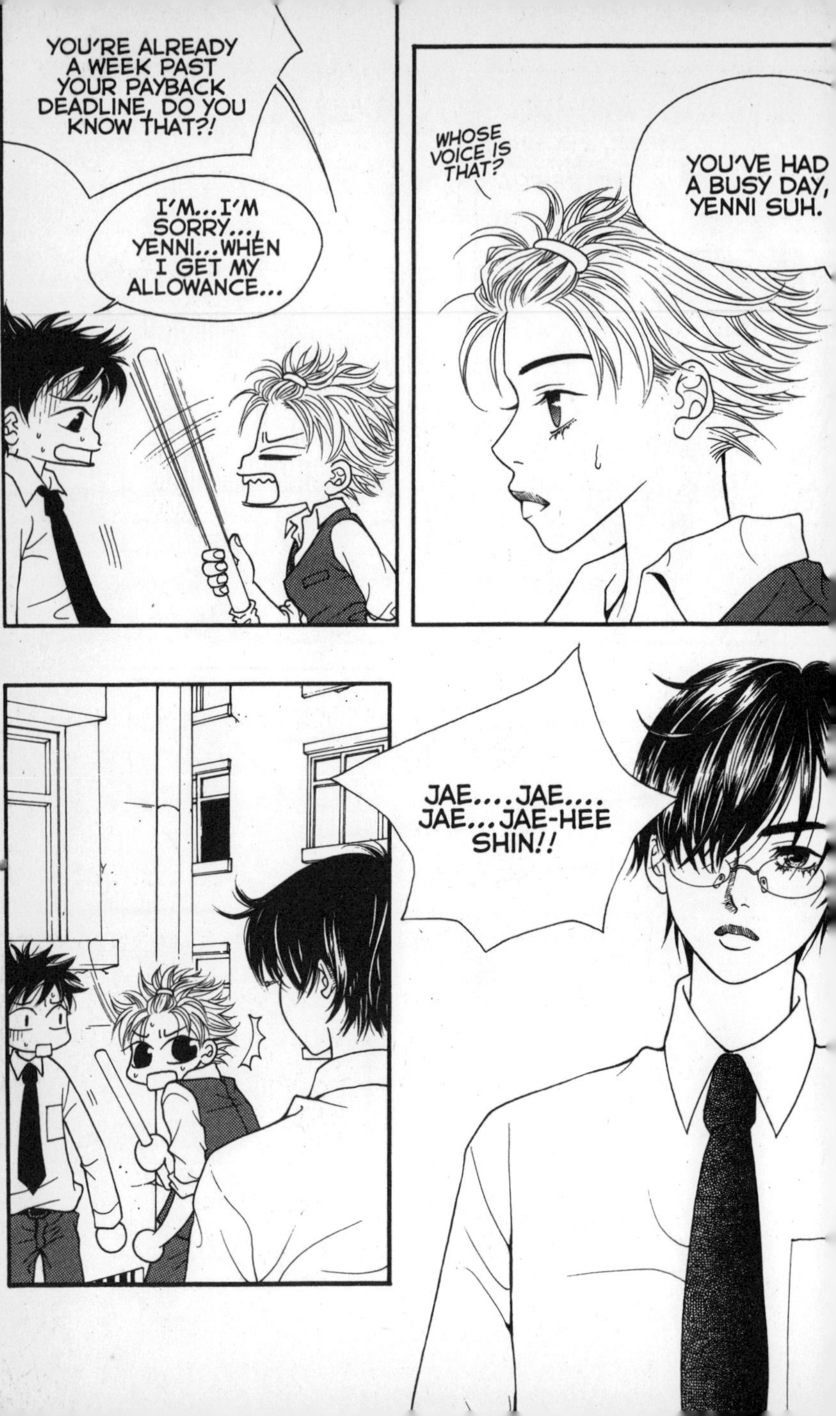
YOU'RE ALREADY A WEEK PAST YOUR PAYBACK DEADLINE, DO YOU KNOW THAT?!
I'M...I'M SORRY..., YENNI...WHEN I GET MY ALLOWANCE...
WHOSE VOICE IS THAT?
YOU'VE HAD A BUSY DAY, YENNI SUH.
JAE....JAE.... JAE...JAE-HEE SHIN!!

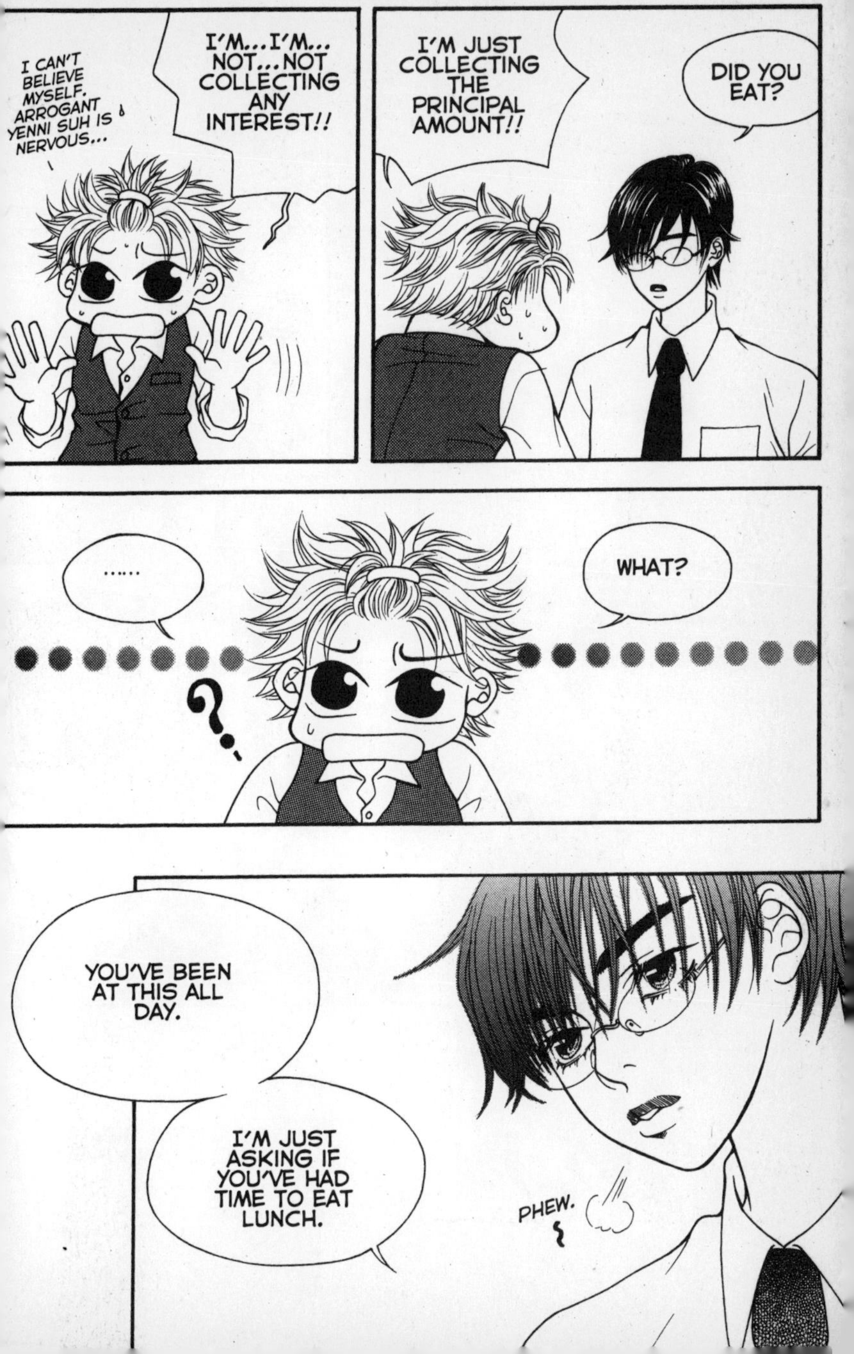
I CAN'T BELIEVE MYSELF. ARROGANT YENNI SUH IS NERVOUS...
I'M...I'M... NOT...NOT COLLECTING ANY INTEREST!!
I'M JUST COLLECTING THE PRINCIPAL AMOUNT!!
DID YOU EAT?
......
WHAT?
YOU'VE BEEN AT THIS ALL DAY.
I'M JUST ASKING IF YOU'VE HAD TIME TO EAT LUNCH.
PHEW.

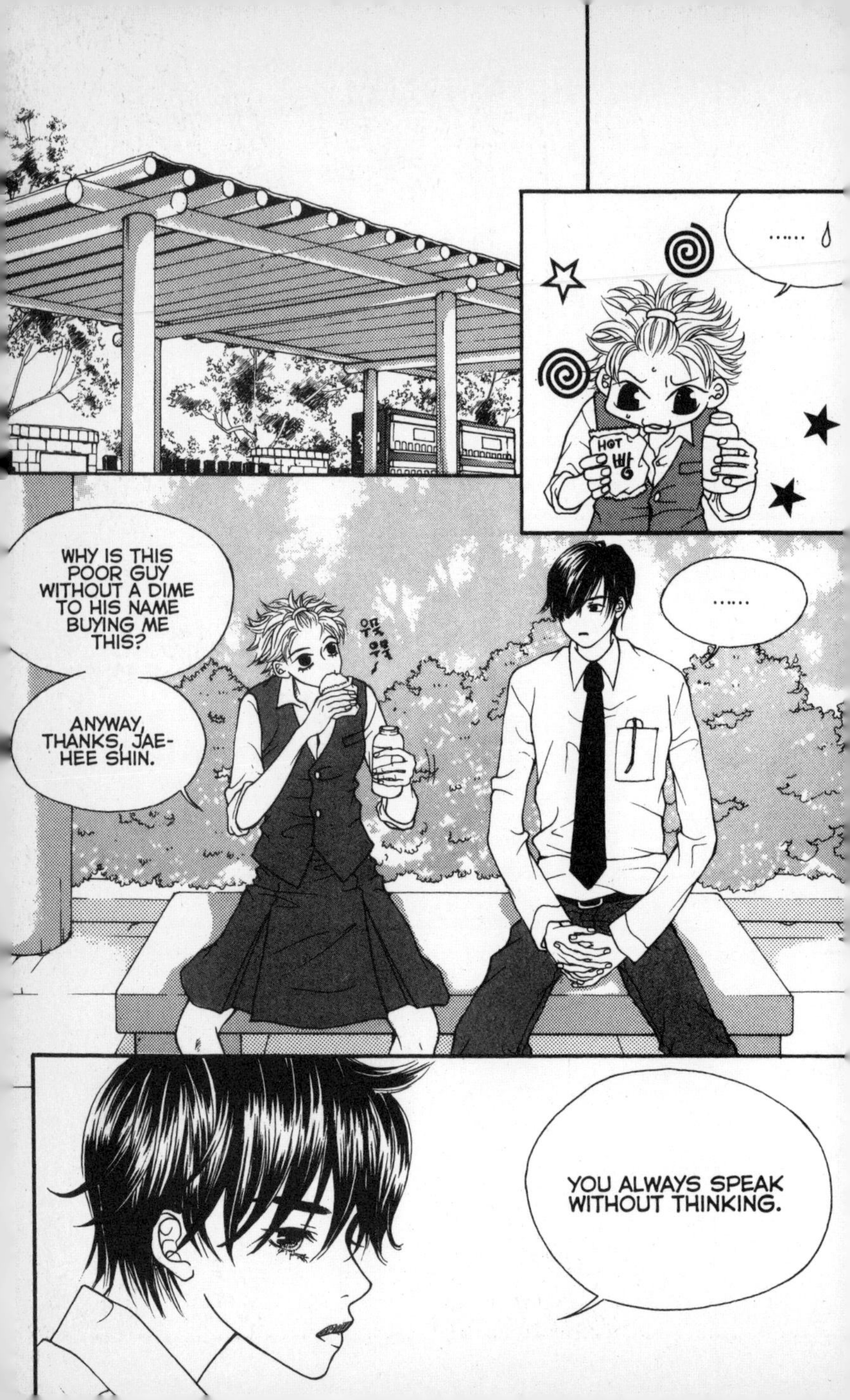
......
HOT
빵
WHY IS THIS POOR GUY WITHOUT A DIME TO HIS NAME BUYING ME THIS?
ANYWAY, THANKS, JAE-HEE SHIN.
......
YOU ALWAYS SPEAK WITHOUT THINKING.

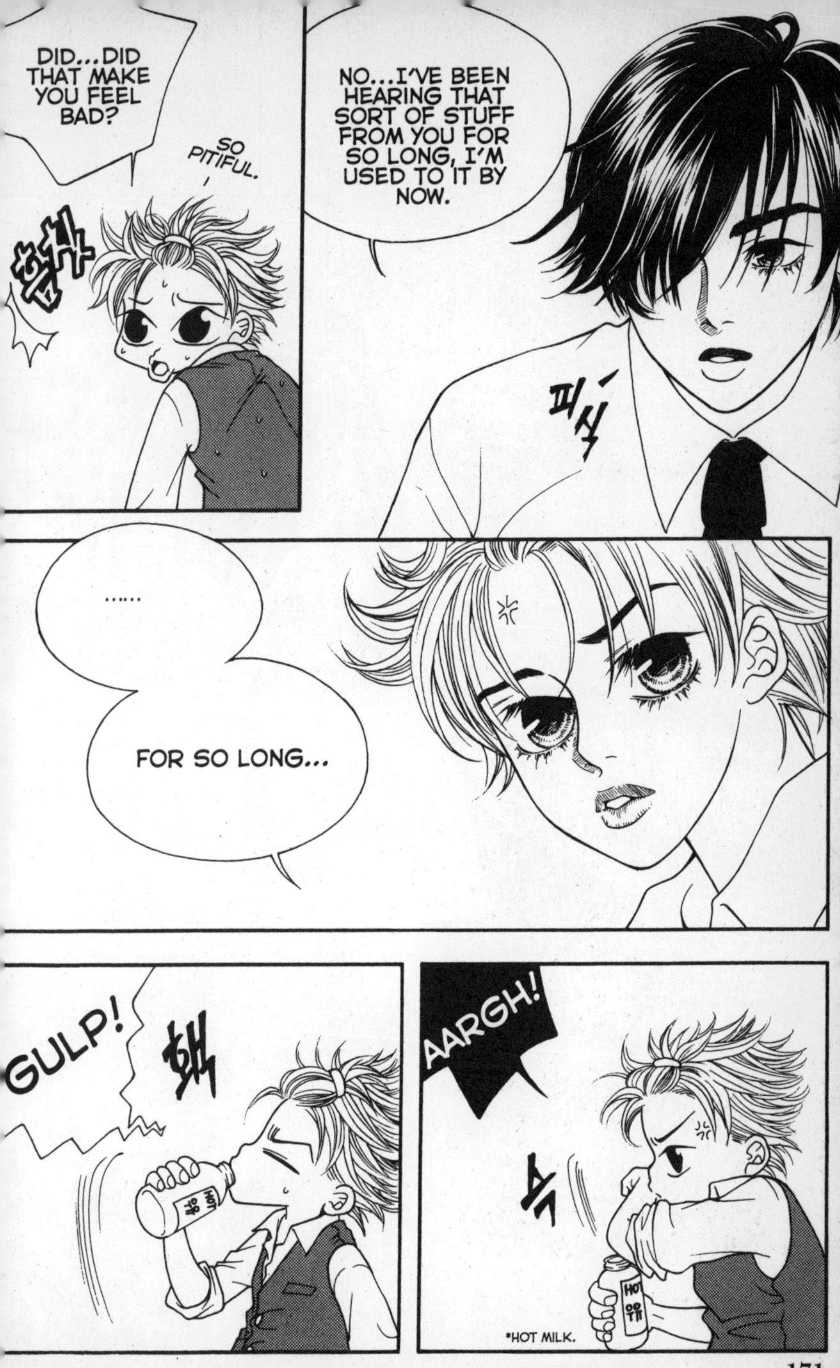
DID...DID THAT MAKE YOU FEEL BAD?
SO PITIFUL.
NO...I'VE BEEN HEARING THAT SORT OF STUFF FROM YOU FOR SO LONG, I'M USED TO IT BY NOW.
......
FOR SO LONG...
GULP!
AARGH!
*HOT MILK.

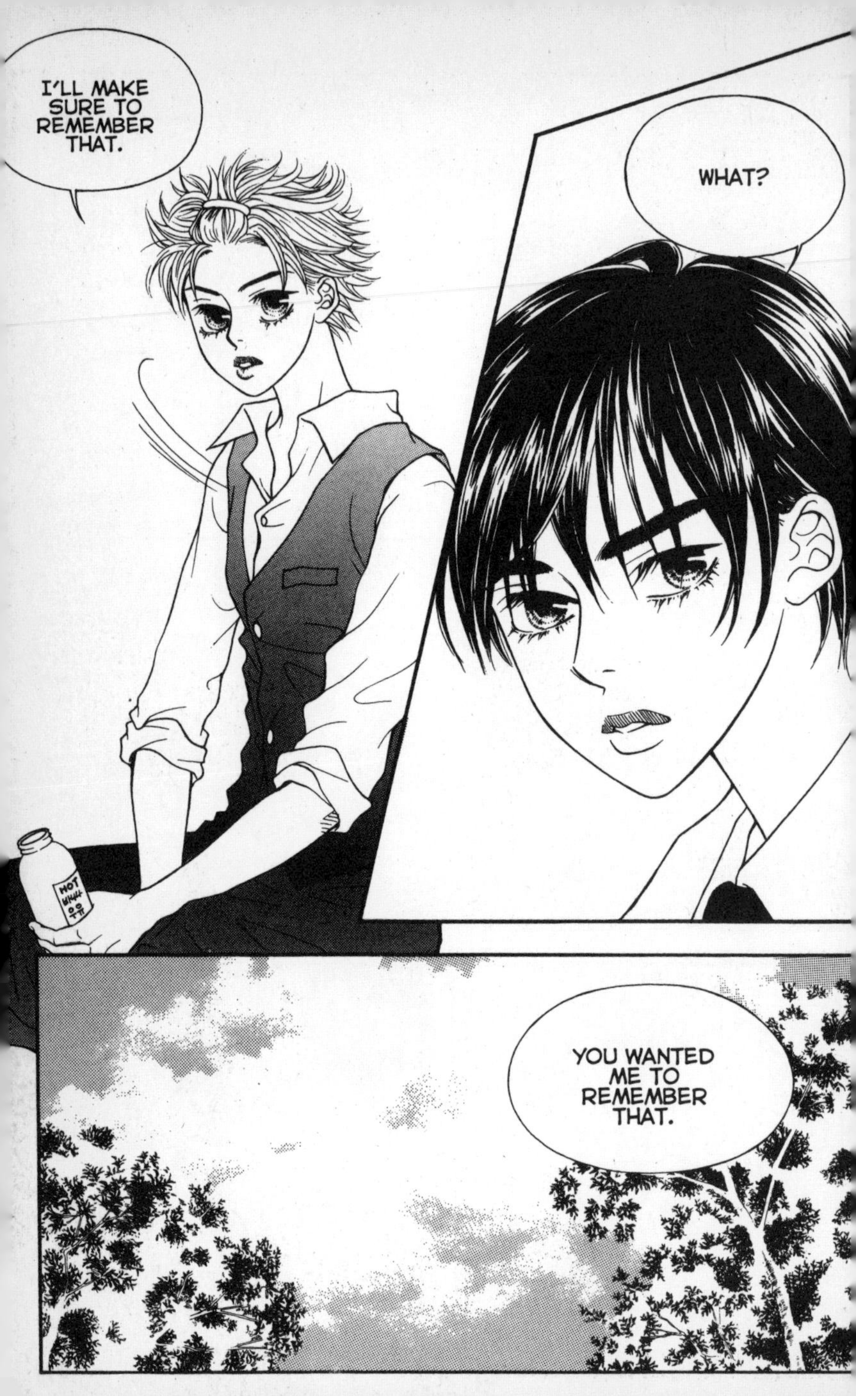
I'LL MAKE SURE TO REMEMBER THAT.
WHAT?
YOU WANTED ME TO REMEMBER THAT.

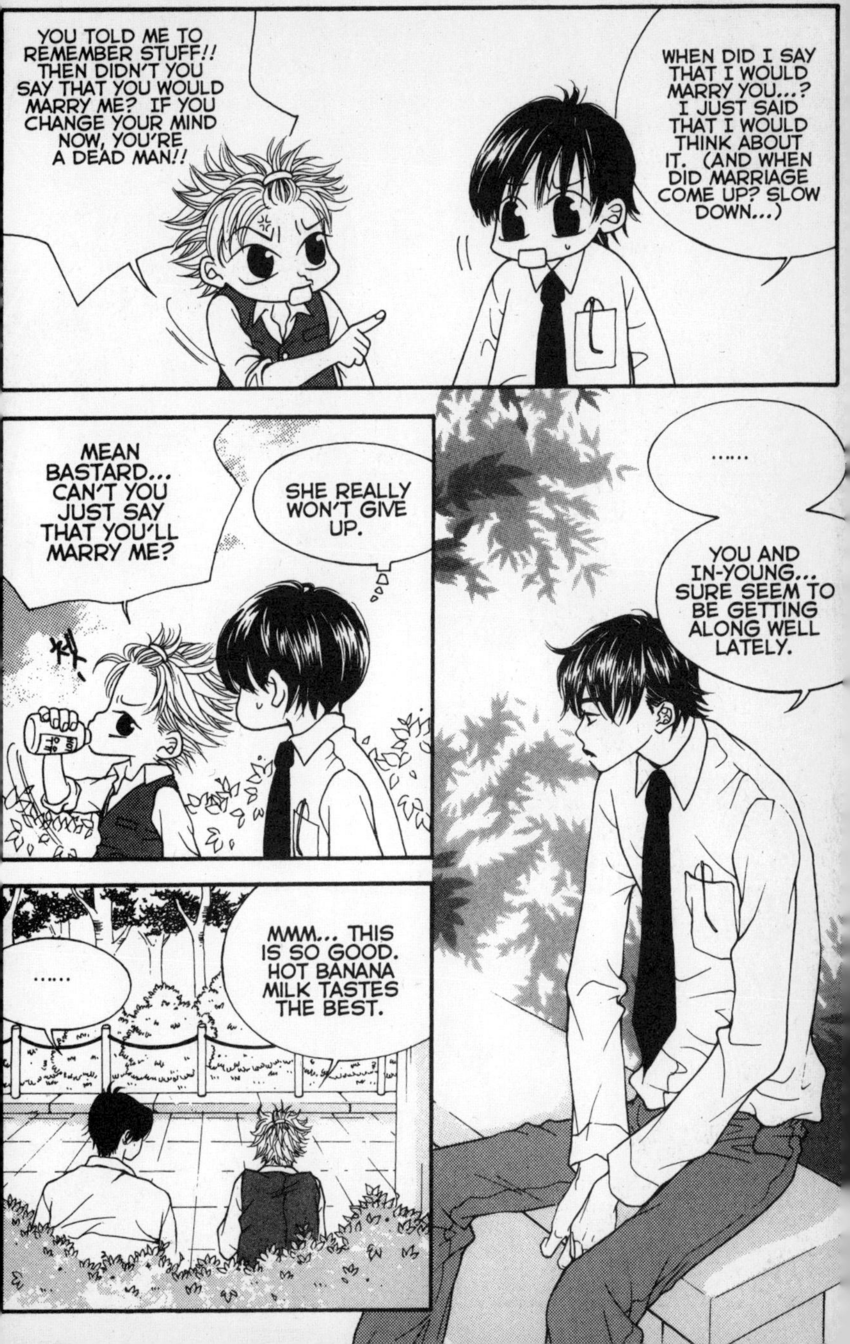
YOU TOLD ME TO REMEMBER STUFF!! THEN DIDN'T YOU SAY THAT YOU WOULD MARRY ME? IF YOU CHANGE YOUR MIND NOW, YOU'RE A DEAD MAN!!
WHEN DID I SAY THAT I WOULD MARRY YOU...? I JUST SAID THAT I WOULD THINK ABOUT IT. (AND WHEN DID MARRIAGE COME UP? SLOW DOWN...)
MEAN BASTARD... CAN'T YOU JUST SAY THAT YOU'LL MARRY ME?
SHE REALLY WON'T GIVE UP.
칫
......
MMM... THIS IS SO GOOD. HOT BANANA MILK TASTES THE BEST.
......
YOU AND IN-YOUNG... SURE SEEM TO BE GETTING ALONG WELL LATELY.

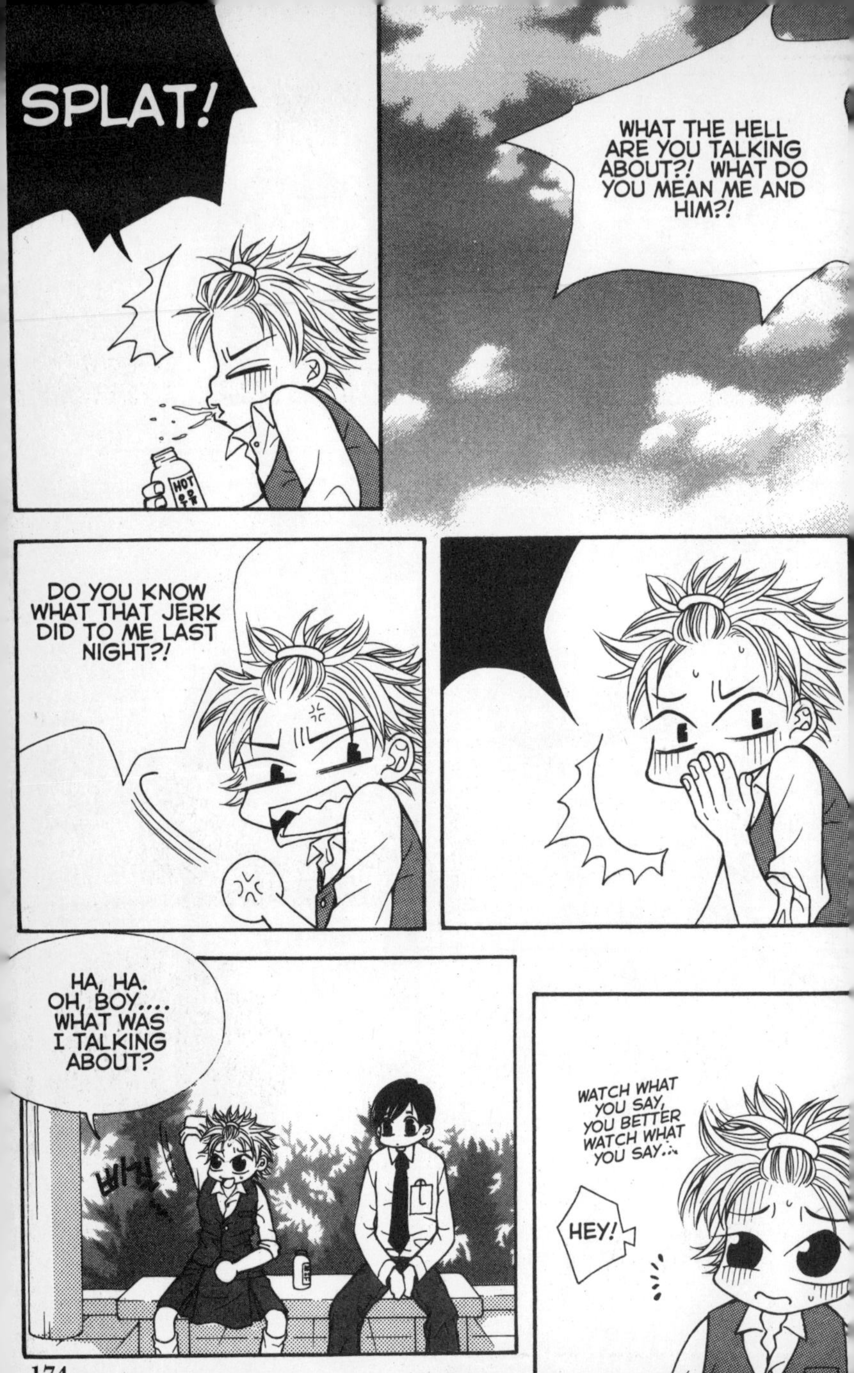
SPLAT!
HOT
WHAT THE HELL ARE YOU TALKING ABOUT?! WHAT DO YOU MEAN ME AND HIM?!
DO YOU KNOW WHAT THAT JERK DID TO ME LAST NIGHT?!
HA, HA. OH, BOY.... WHAT WAS I TALKING ABOUT?
WATCH WHAT YOU SAY, YOU BETTER WATCH WHAT YOU SAY...
HEY!

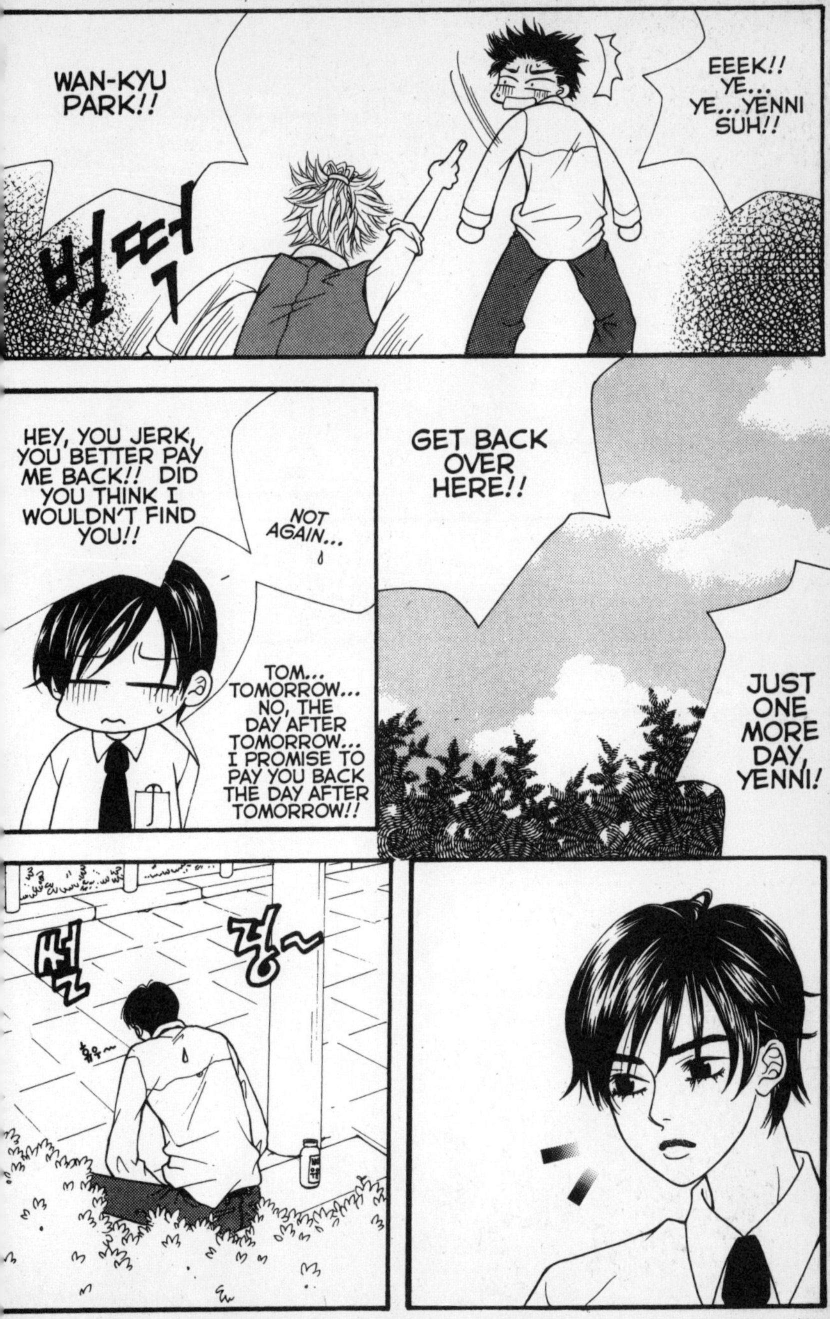
WAN-KYU PARK!!
벌떡
EEEK!! YE... YE...YENNI SUH!!
HEY, YOU JERK, YOU BETTER PAY ME BACK!! DID YOU THINK I WOULDN'T FIND YOU!!
NOT AGAIN...
TOM... TOMORROW... NO, THE DAY AFTER TOMORROW... I PROMISE TO PAY YOU BACK THE DAY AFTER TOMORROW!!
GET BACK OVER HERE!!
JUST ONE MORE DAY, YENNI!
벌 렁~
휴우~

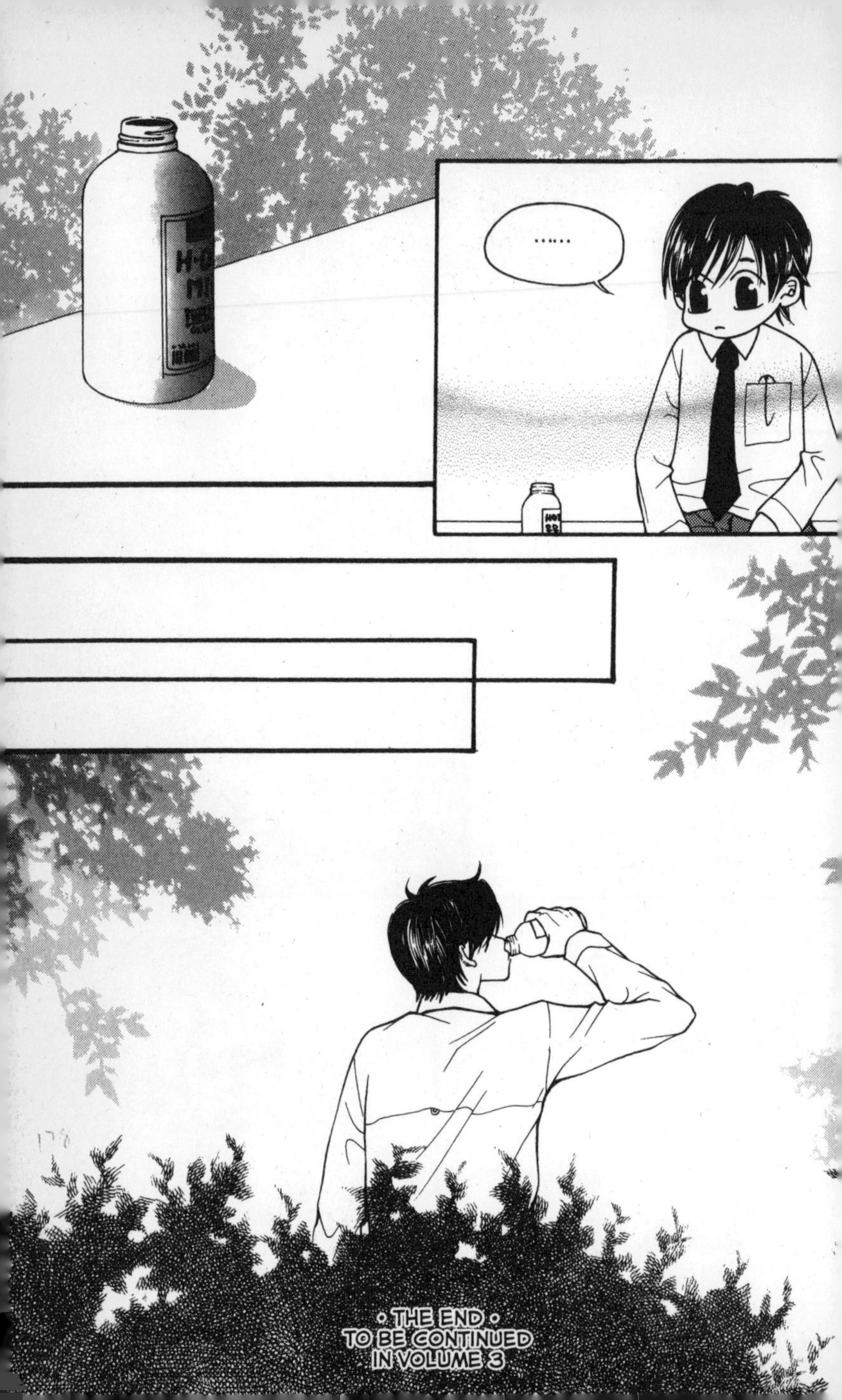
......
• THE END •
TO BE CONTINUED IN VOLUME 3

HELLO, AGAIN, EVERYONE. MANY BLESSINGS TO ALL OF YOU WHO HAVE BEEN READING MY BOOK, *LOVE OR MONEY* VOLUME TWO... FOR SOME REASON, VOLUME TWO HAS BEEN ALL ABOUT RELATIONSHIPS. IN VOLUME THREE, THE LAWYER/GRANDFATHER CHARACTER WILL AGAIN MAKE AN APPEARANCE. IT'S ALSO TIME FOR YENNI TO SLOWLY CHANGE HER AGGRESSIVE PERSONALITY... JAE-HEE NEEDS TO CHANGE HIS STUCK-UP MINDSET. IN-YOUNG NEEDS TO CEASE HIS RECKLESS AND CARELESS ACTS. HOW CAN THESE THINGS HAPPEN...? IF YOU'RE WONDERING...IT'S BECAUSE OF...THE POWER OF LOVE... WOOHAHAHAHA...

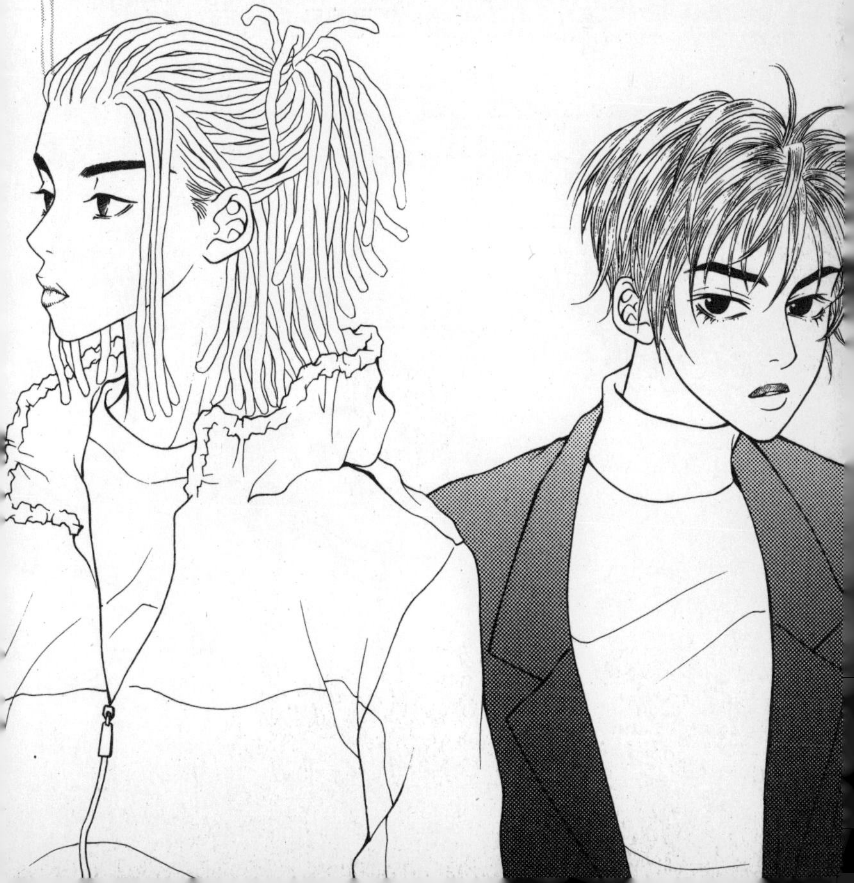

ANYWAY, TO ALL MY FRIENDS, I WANT TO THANK YOU AND GIVE YOU HONOR FOR HELPING ME TO MAKE *LOVE OR MONEY* VOLUME TWO POSSIBLE. THANKS TO MY SUPERVISOR, SAE JUNG, I HEARD THAT YOU'RE TAKING ENGLISH CLASSES. LET'S PRACTICE OUR CONVERSATIONAL ENGLISH SKILLS LATER. IN ADDITION, TO MY LOVELY, DEAR FRIEND YOUNG BOK AND HIS YOUNGER BROTHER, YOUNG GU; TO MY TEMPORARY ASSISTANTS JI-WON AND HYUN HEE; MY LOYAL AND LONG-SUFFERING ART CLUB MEMBERS, MU YOUNG'S CUTE DAUGHTER, JI-SOO; AND JI-WON, WHO WILL LEAVE FOR THE U.S. WITH BYUNG-HO; CUTIE PIE TAE WON; CHANG EUN YI, THE NUMBER-ONE MATHEMATICS TEACHER IN KOREA; EUN JOO; AND MY COMRADE, HAESUN, ANNA; TO EVERYBODY, THANK YOU! IN ADDITION, TO YOON JUNG, MY PASSIONATE COMRADE, WHO IS ON THE SAME JOURNEY WITH ME. I WISH MUCH SUCCESS WITH THE BOOK (*WING*)!! I LOVE ALL THE FANS IN THE WORLD WHO LOVE H.O.T. I LOVE H.O.T. AND I WORSHIP MOON HEE JOON. HMM...I'M INCLINED TO WRITE A TEENAGE STORY, BUT I HOPE MY FANS WILL RECOVER.

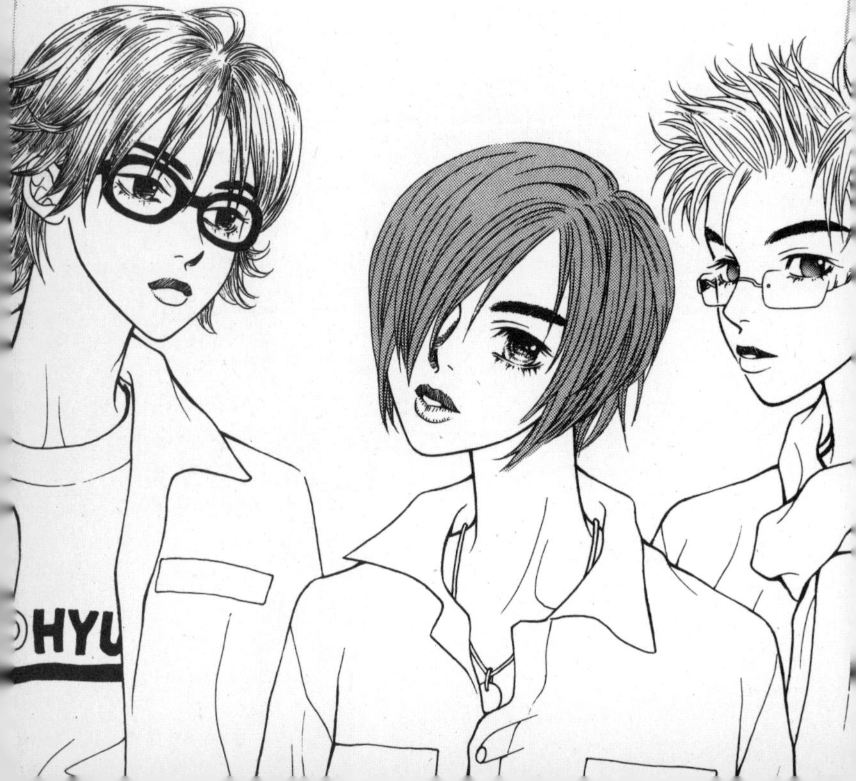

HYU

IN THE NEXT

LOVE OR MONEY

VOLUME 3

YENNI IS OBSESSED WITH TRYING TO GET JAE-HEE'S ATTENTION. BUT SHE'S GOT SOME COMPETITION: A PRETTY GIRL NAMED JI-WON WHO WANTS JAE-HEE ALL TO HERSELF! WHEN YENNI FINALLY CONFRONTS JI-WON AND TELLS HER TO BACK OFF, IT'S CAT FIGHT TIME! WILL THE TWO GIRLS MAKE NICE BEFORE SOMEONE GETS HURT? ADDING FUEL TO THE FIRE IS IN-YOUNG, WHO'S SUDDENLY DEVELOPING FEELINGS FOR YENNI--BUT SHE THINKS IT'S ALL A SCAM. IT'S A CLASSIC LOVE TRIANGLE WITH A 15-MILLION-DOLLAR TWIST.

TOKYOPOP SHOP

WWW.TOKYOPOP.COM/SHOP

HOT NEWS!

Check out the
TOKYOPOP SHOP!
The world's best
collection of manga in
English is now available
online in one place!

WARCRAFT

SLAYERS MANGA NOVEL

WWW.TOKYOPOP.COM/SHOP

THE TAROT CAFÉ

- LOOK FOR SPECIAL OFFERS
- PRE-ORDER UPCOMING RELEASES!
- COMPLETE YOUR COLLECTIONS

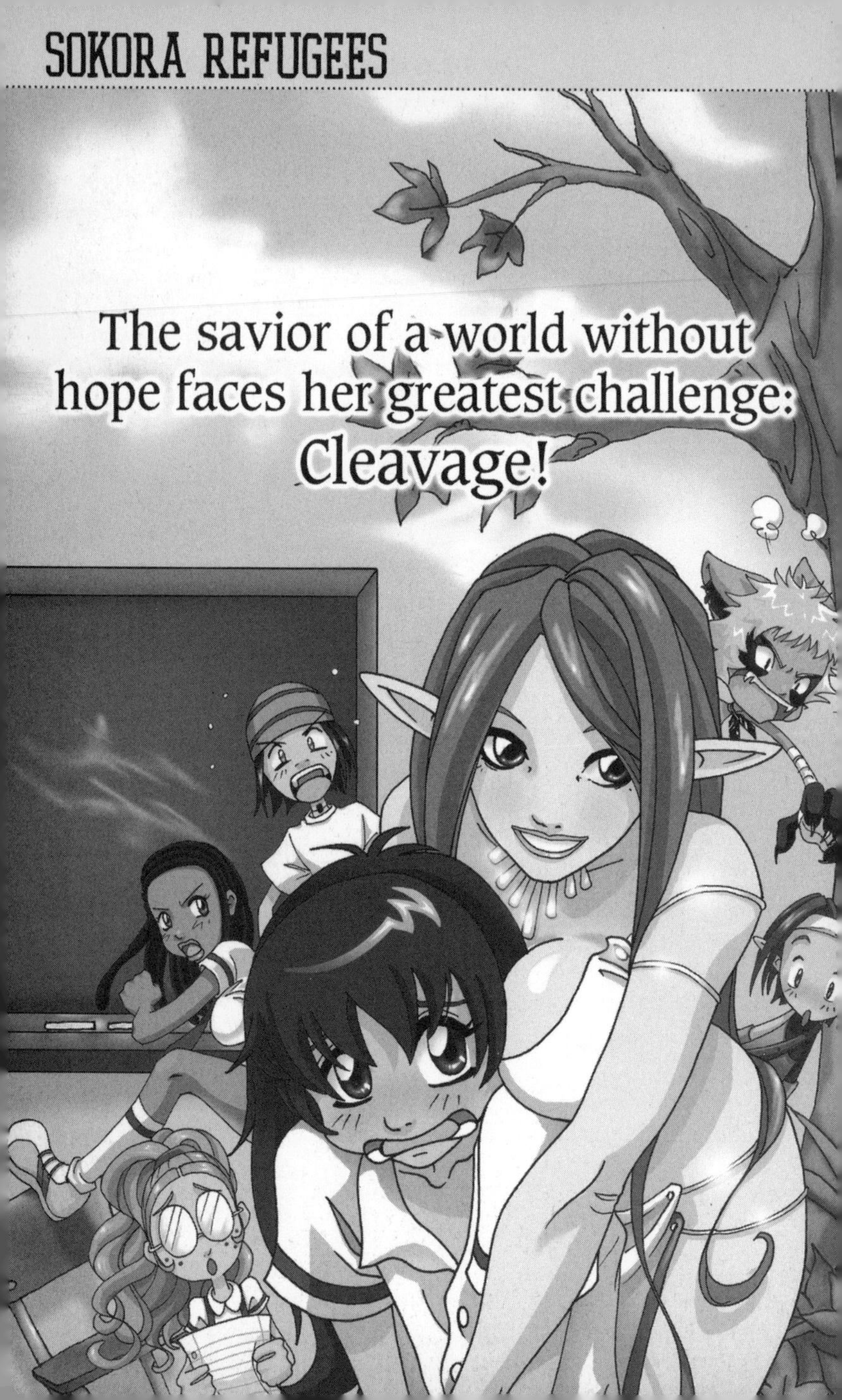

SOKORA REFUGEES
The savior of a world without hope faces her greatest challenge:
Cleavage!

SOKORA REFUGEES™

Kana thought life couldn't get any worse—behind on her schoolwork and out of luck with boys, she is also the only one of her friends who hasn't "blossomed." When she falls through a magical portal in the girls' shower, she's transported to the enchanted world of Sokora—wearing nothing but a small robe! Now, on top of landing in this mysterious setting, she finds that her body is beginning to go through some tremendous changes.

Preview the manga at:
www.TOKYOPOP.com/sokora

T
TEEN
AGE 13+

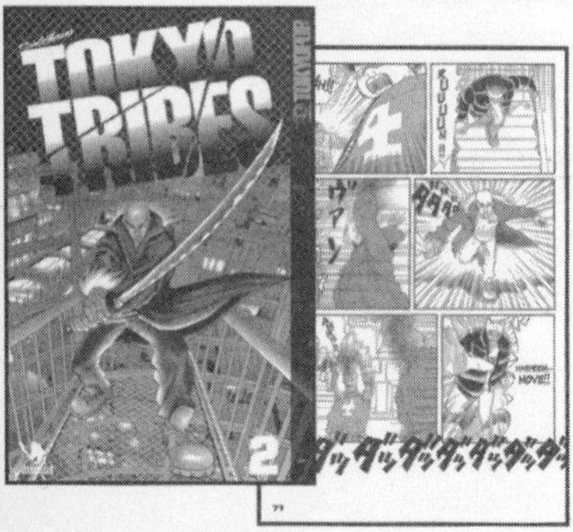
TOKYO TRIBES
2

BY SANTA INOUE

TOKYO TRIBES

Tokyo Tribes first hit Japanese audiences in the sleek pages of the ultra-hip skater fashion magazine *Boon*. Santa Inoue's hard-hitting tale of Tokyo street gangs battling it out in the concrete sprawl of Japan's capital raises the manga storytelling bar. Ornate with hip-hop trappings and packed with gangland grit, *Tokyo Tribes* paints a vivid, somewhat surreal vision of urban youth: rival gangs from various Tokyo barrios clash over turf, and when the heat between two of the tribes gets personal, a bitter rivalry explodes into all-out warfare.

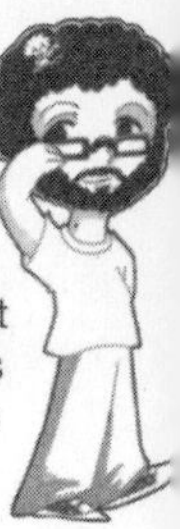

~Luis Reyes, Editor

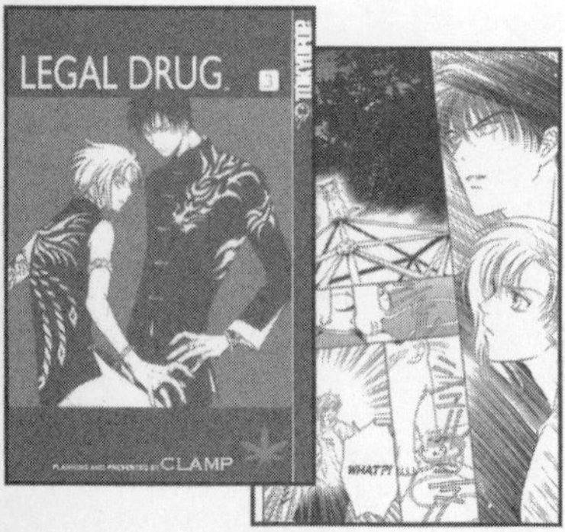
LEGAL DRUG
CLAMP
WHAT?!

BY CLAMP

LEGAL DRUG

CLAMP is the four-woman studio famous for creating much of the world's most popular manga. For the past 15 years they have produced such hits as the adorable *Cardcaptor Sakura,* the dark and brooding *Tokyo Babylon,* and the sci-fi romantic comedy *Chobits.* In *Legal Drug,* we meet Kazahaya and Rikuou, two ordinary pharmacists who moonlight as amateur sleuths for a mysterious boss. *Legal Drug* is a perfect dose of mystery, psychic powers and the kind of homoerotic tension for which CLAMP is renowned.

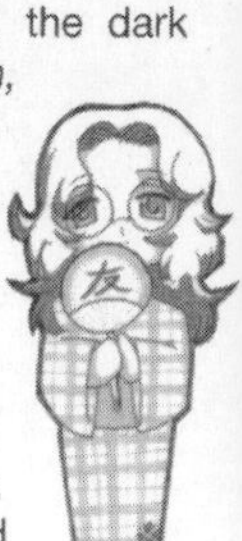

~Lillian Diaz-Przybyl, Jr. Editor

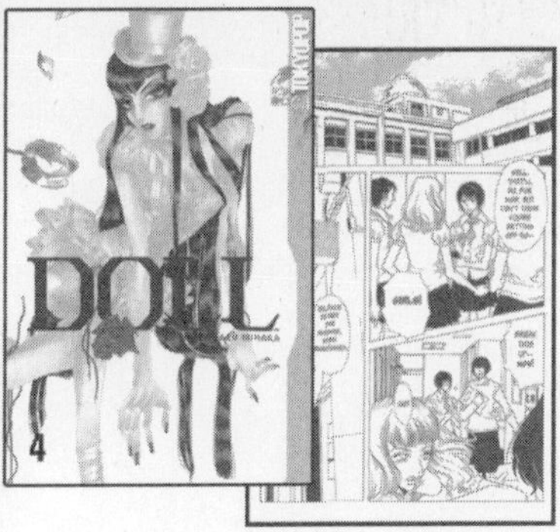
DOLL
4
TOKYOPOP

BY MITSUKAZU MIHARA

DOLL

Mitsukazu Mihara's haunting *Doll* uses beautiful androids to examine what it means to be truly human. While the characters in *Doll* are draped in the chic Gothic-Lolita fashions that made Mihara-sensei famous, the themes explored are more universal—all emotions and walks of life have their day in *Doll*. *Doll* begins as a series of 'one-shot' stories and gradually dovetails into an epic of emotion and intrigue. It's like the *Twilight Zone* meets *Blade Runner!*

~Rob Tokar, Senior Editor

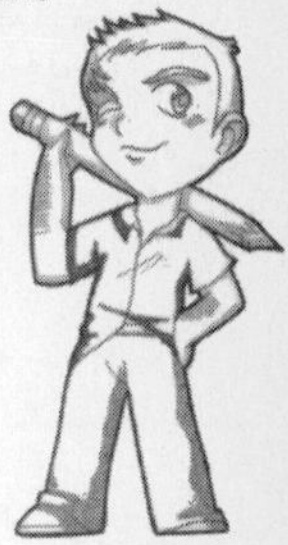

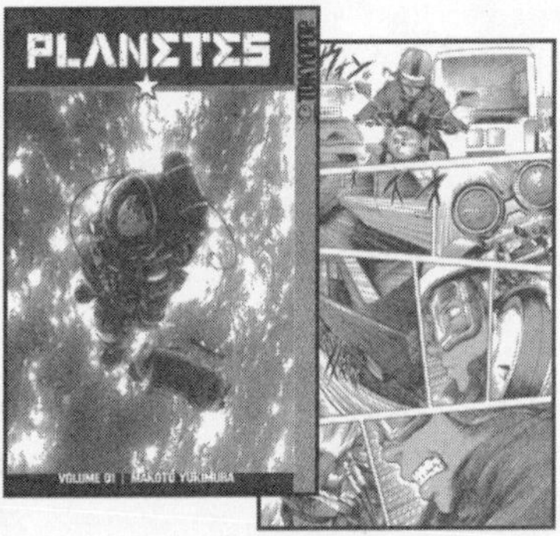
PLANETES
VOLUME 01 | MAKOTO YUKIMURA
TOKYOPOP

BY MAKOTO YUKIMURA

PLANETES

Makoto Yukimura's profoundly moving and graphically arresting *Planetes* posits a near future where mankind's colonization of space has begun. Young Hachimaki yearns to join this exciting new frontier. Instead, he cleans the glut of orbital junk mankind's initial foray into space produced. He works with Fee, a nicotine-addict beauty with an abrasive edge, and Yuri, a veteran spaceman with a tragic past in search of inner peace. *Planetes* combines the scope of Jules Verne (*Around the World in Eighty Days*) and Robert Heinlein (*Starship Troopers*) with the philosophical wonder of *2001: A Space Odyssey.*

~Luis Reyes, Editor

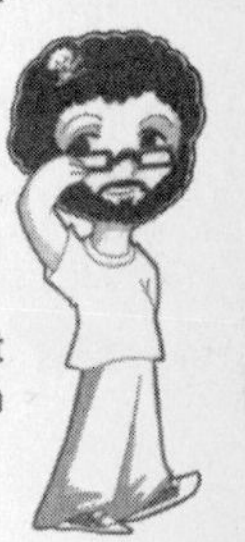

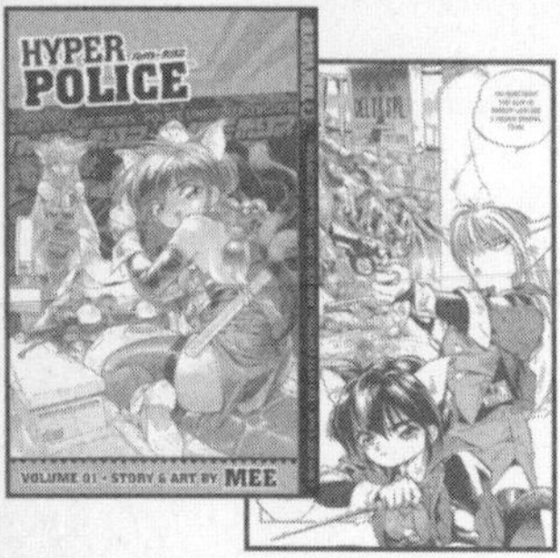
HYPER POLICE
VOLUME 01 • STORY & ART BY MEE

HYPER POLICE

BY MEE

In a future rife with crime, humans are an endangered species—and monsters have taken over! Natsuki is a cat girl who uses magical powers to enforce the law. However, her greatest threat doesn't come from the criminals. Her partner Sakura, a "nine-tailed" fox, plots to eat Natsuki and gobble up her magic! In this dog-eat-dog world, Natsuki fights to stay on top!

OT
OLDER TEEN
AGE 16+

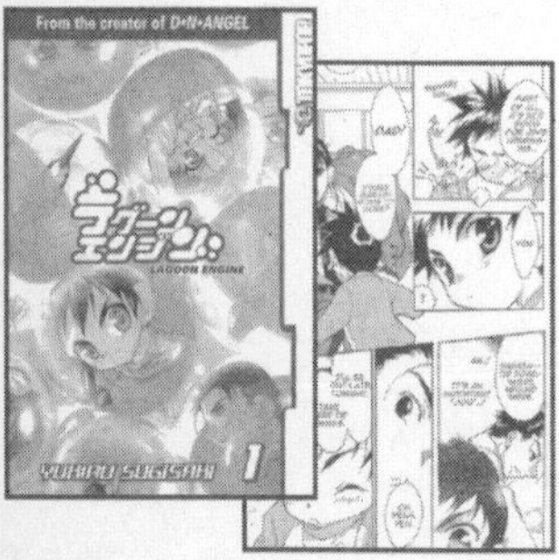
From the creator of D•N•ANGEL
LAGOON ENGINE
YUKIRU SUGISAKI 1

LAGOON ENGINE

BY YUKIRU SUGISAKI

From the best-selling creator of *D·N·Angel!*

Yen and Jin are brothers in elementary school—and successors in the Ragun family craft. They are Gakushi, those who battle ghosts and evil spirits known as "Maga" by guessing their true name. As Yen and Jin train to join the family business, the two boys must keep their identities a secret...or risk death!

T
TEEN
AGE 13+

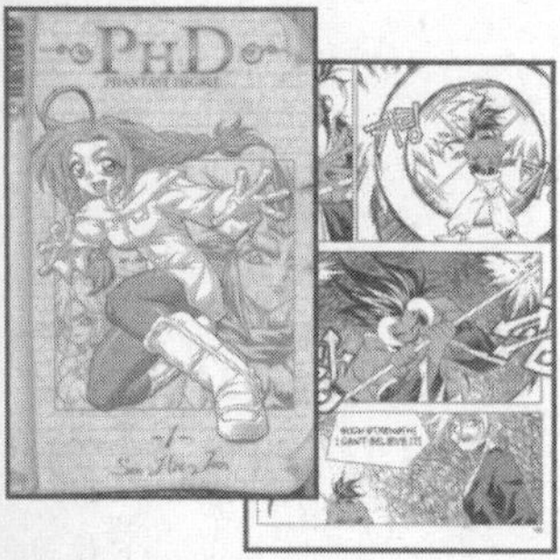
PHD

PHD: PHANTASY DEGREE

BY HEE-JOON SON

Sang is a fearlessly spunky young girl who is about to receive one hell of an education...at the Demon School Hades! She's on a mission to enroll into the monsters-only class. However, monster matriculation is not what is truly on her mind—she wants to acquire the fabled "King's Ring" from the fiancée of the chief commander of hell!

T
TEEN
AGE 13+

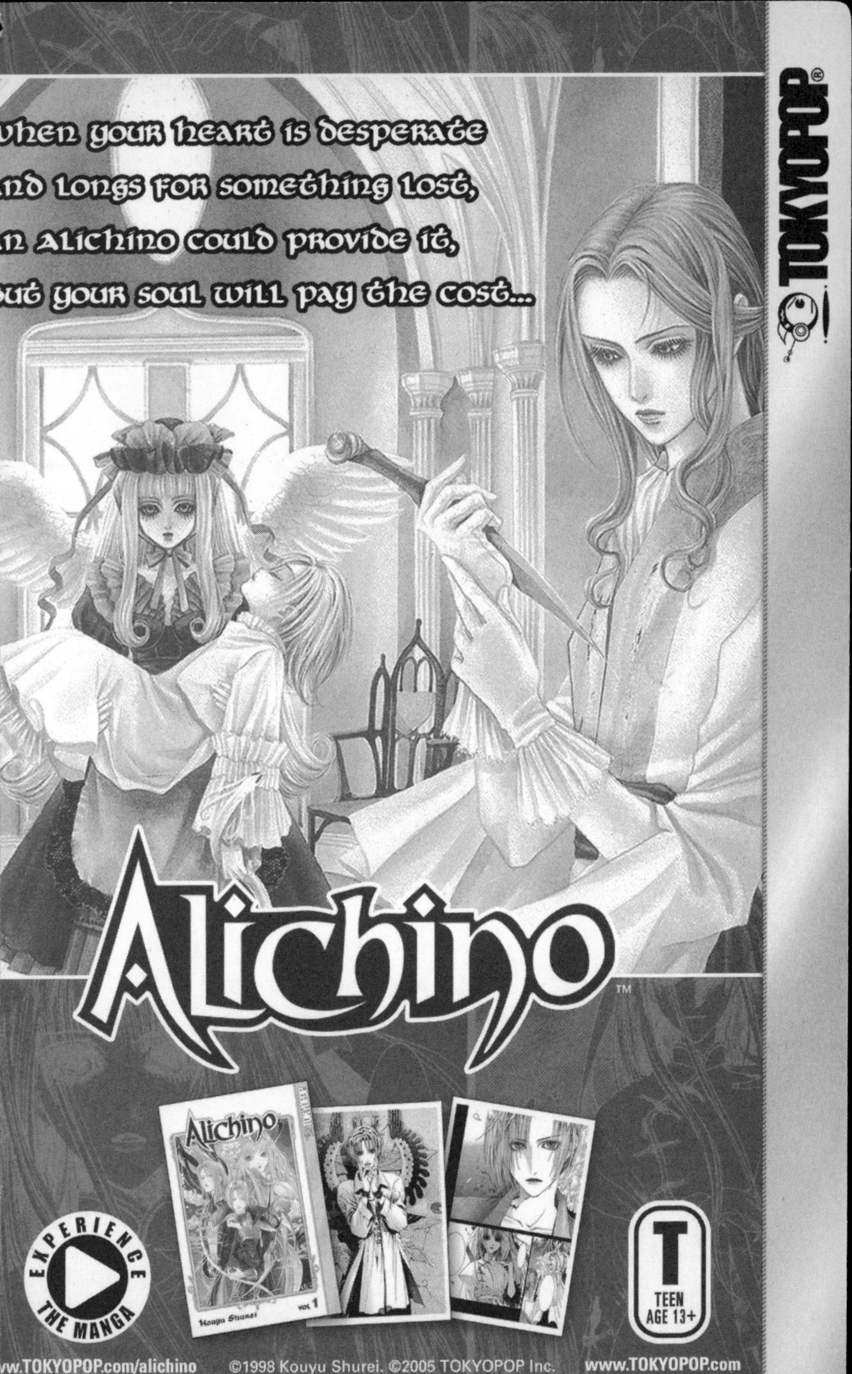
vhen your heart is desperate
nd longs for something lost,
n alichino could provide it,
ut your soul will pay the cost...
Alichino™
Alichino
VOL 1
Kouyu Shurei
EXPERIENCE THE MANGA
T
TEEN
AGE 13+
TOKYOPOP®

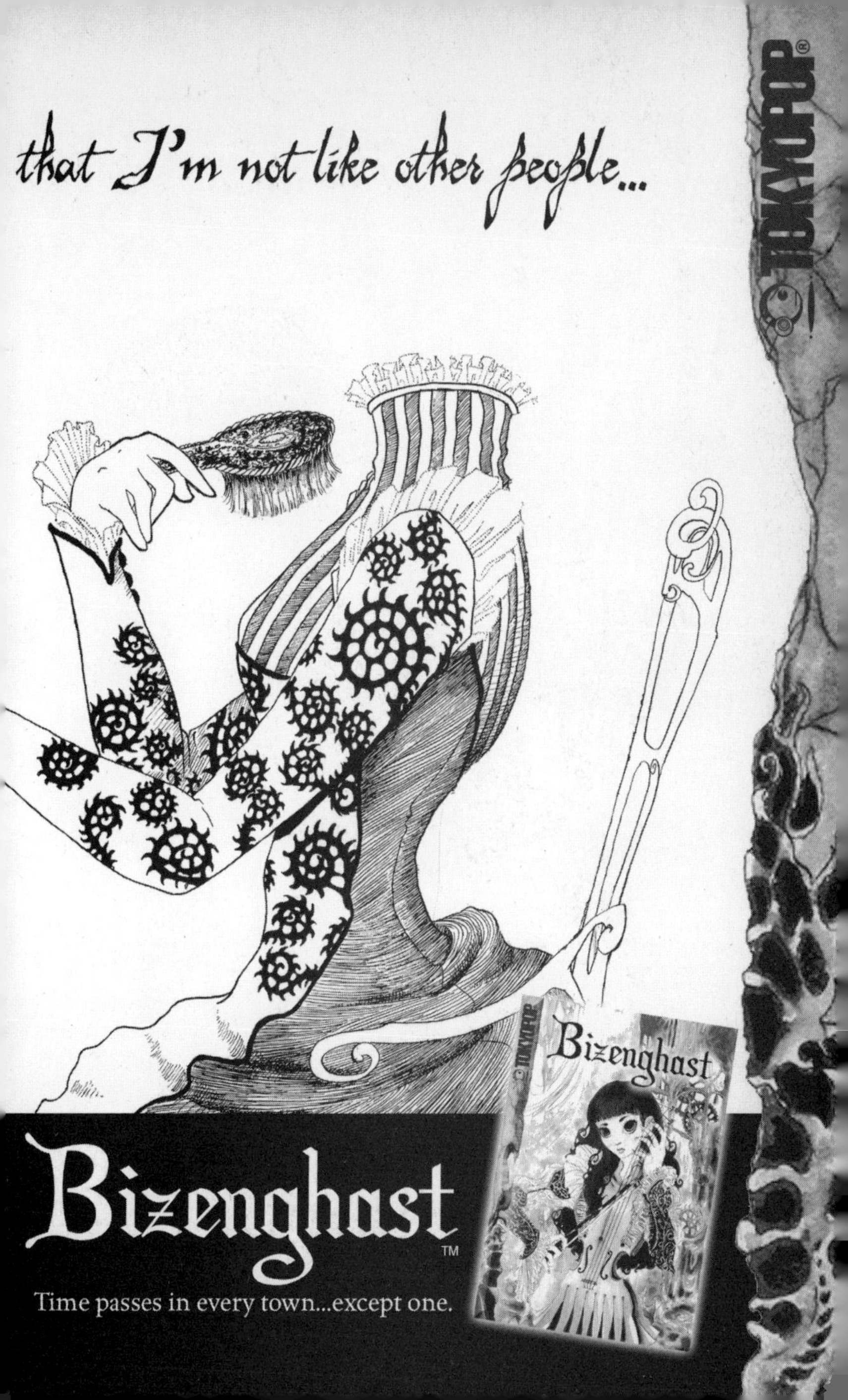
that I'm not like other people...
TOKYOPOP®
Bizenghast
Bizenghast™
Time passes in every town...except one.

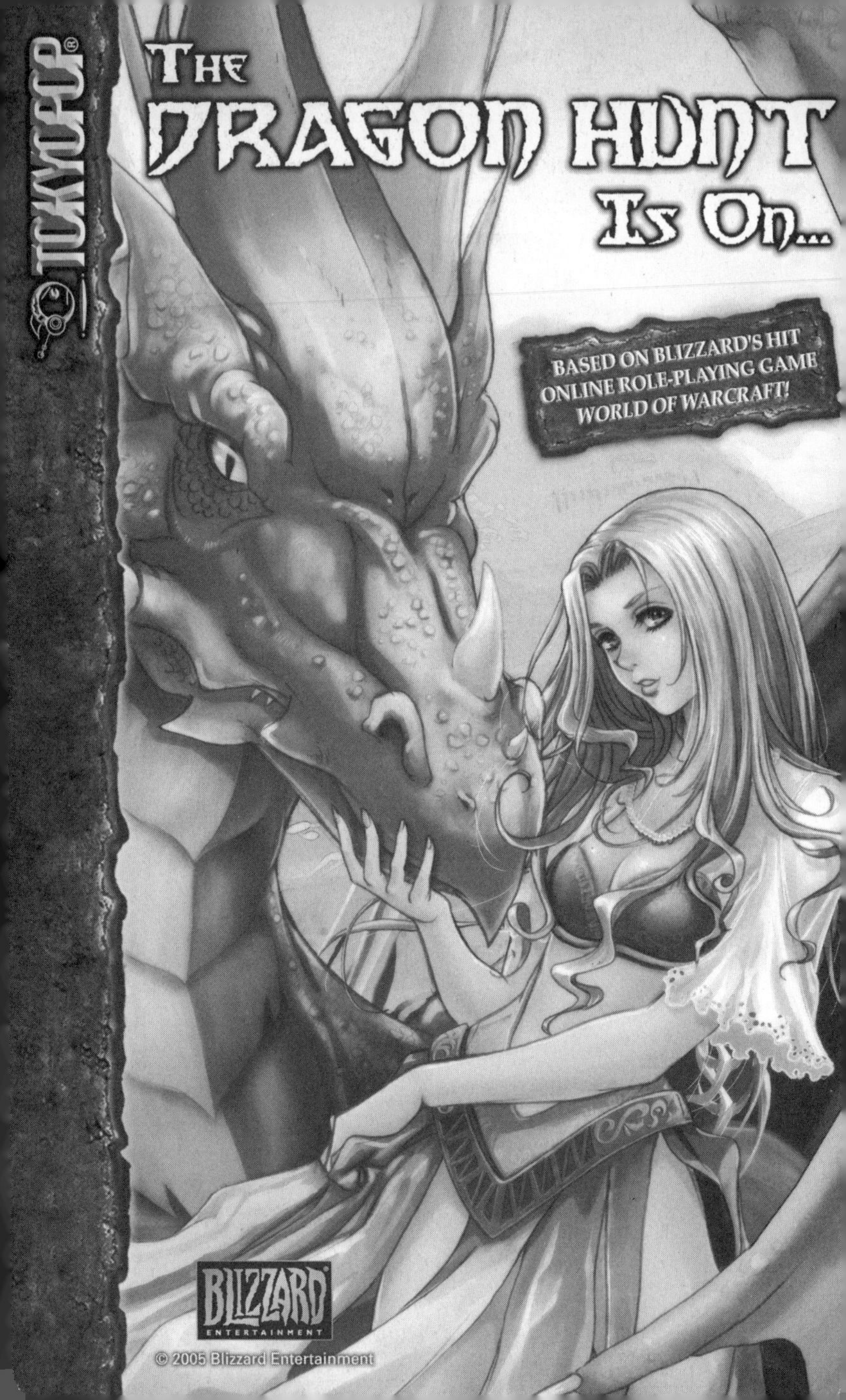
TOKYOPOP®
THE DRAGON HUNT IS ON...
BASED ON BLIZZARD'S HIT ONLINE ROLE-PLAYING GAME WORLD OF WARCRAFT!
BLIZZARD ENTERTAINMENT
© 2005 Blizzard Entertainment

WARCRAFT
THE SUNWELL TRILOGY

RICHARD A. KNAAK · KIM JAE-HWAN

From the artist of the
best-selling *King of Hell* series!

It's an epic quest to save the entire High Elven Kingdom from the forces of the Undead Scourge! Set in the mystical world of Azeroth, *Warcraft: The Sunwell Trilogy* chronicles the adventures of Kalec, a blue dragon who has taken human form to escape deadly forces, and Anveena, a beautiful young maiden with a mysterious power.

EXPERIENCE THE MANGA

T
TEEN
AGE 13+

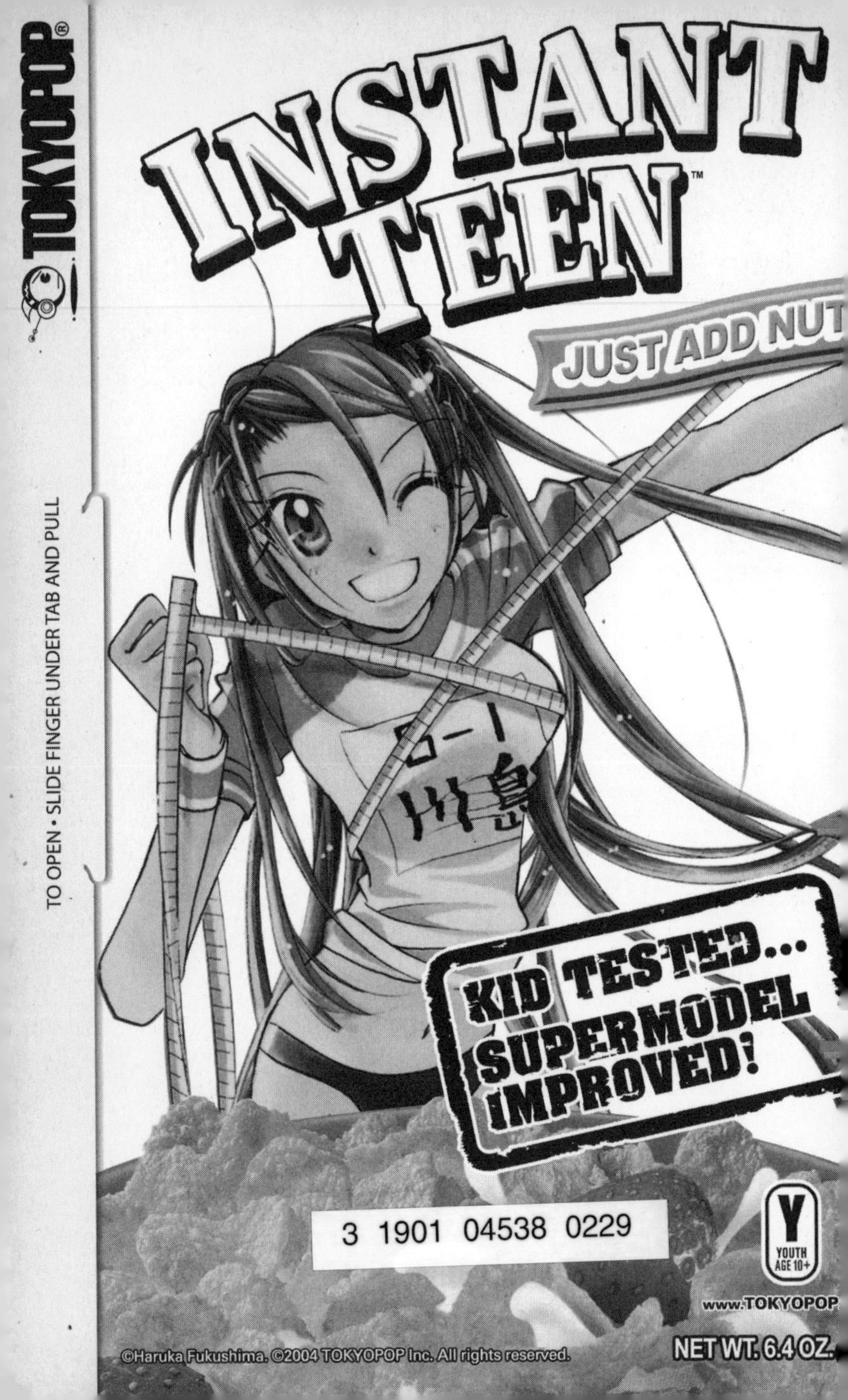

TOKYOPOP®
TO OPEN • SLIDE FINGER UNDER TAB AND PULL
INSTANT TEEN™
JUST ADD NUT
KID TESTED... SUPERMODEL IMPROVED!
Y
YOUTH AGE 10+
www.TOKYOPOP.
NET WT. 6.4 OZ.